Martin Heidegger and the Holocaust

MARTIN HEIDEGGER AND THE HOLOCAUST

Edited by
Alan Milchman and Alan Rosenberg

HUMANITIES PRESS
NEW JERSEY

First published 1996 by Humanities Press International, Inc.
165 First Avenue, Atlantic Highlands, New Jersey 07716

Library of Congress Cataloging-in-Publication Data
Martin Heidegger and the Holocaust / edited by Alan Milchman and Alan Rosenberg.
p. cm.
Includes index.
ISBN 0-391-03925-3 (cloth)
1. Heidegger, Martin, 1889–1976—Views on Jews. 2. Holocaust, Jewish (1939–1945) I. Milchman, Alan, 1940- . II. Rosenberg, Alan, 1939-
B3279.H49M2847 1996
193—dc20 95-21824
CIP

A catalog record for this book is available from the British Library.

Printed in the United States of America

CONTENTS

Acknowledgments

The appearance of this volume would not have been possible without the support of a number of individuals. We are indebted to Keith M. Ashfield of Humanities Press, who saw the value of this project at its very inception. We are fortunate in having a group of contributors and translators who not only fulfilled all deadlines, but from whom we have learned so much. The completion of this volume would not have been possible without the professionalism, and enthusiasm, of the secretarial staff of the Department of Philosophy of Queens College: Elsie Gerken, Joan Lesnoy, and Maria Migliaccio. A special debt is owed to Morris Rabinowitz, for his tireless efforts to assure a perfect copy. Finally, our gratitude and appreciation goes to Nancy Stutesman, our Production Editor at Humanities Press, who has done so much to turn a manuscript into a book.

Alan Milchman would like to especially thank his wife, Madelyn Simring Milchman, whose constant companionship and intellectual sustenance mean so much, and his aunt, Gertrude Rof, granddaughter, niece, and cousin of numerous Holocaust victims, who first showed him the human dimension of the Auschwitz-apocalypse.

Alan Rosenberg would like to especially thank the late R.W. Sleeper, who from the beginning of his work on the Holocaust was very supportive at a time when this kind of work was not yet being done by professional philosophers. He also owes a special debt of gratitude to James Jordan, and the Department of Philosophy of Queens College, for their support for a course on philosophy and the Holocaust, and to Morris Rabinowitz, whose intellectual companionship and dialogue has meant more than he realizes.

Introduction

The essays collected in this volume focus on a neglected aspect of the Heidegger controversy: the question of Martin Heidegger's relationship—as person and as thinker—to the industrialization of death, symbolized by the smokestacks of Auschwitz. While the ongoing Heidegger affair, sparked by the publication of books by Victor Farías and Hugo Ott,[1] has as its central concern Heidegger's relationship to National Socialism and the Hitler-state, his actions as Rector of Freiburg University in 1933–34, and as an internationally renowned figure in the German academic world under the Third Reich, as well as the philosophical question of possible links between Heidegger's decisionism, concept of the *Volk*, and Nazism,[2] the focus of this volume lies elsewhere—both chronologically and philosophically. Chronologically, our focus is the postwar epoch, when an open discussion of the Holocaust, and its meaning, became possible in Germany. Philosophically, our central concern is the significance of what the German-Jewish social theorist Dan Diner has designated as *das Ereignis Auschwitz*,[3] the techno-industrial mass murder through which millions of non-combatant human beings were exterminated on the basis of a deliberate plan.

The point of departure for *Martin Heidegger and the Holocaust* is the insistence of a number of thinkers, including several who have been profoundly influenced by Heidegger's thinking, that what is most shocking in the Heidegger affair is not the thinker's behavior, writings, and speeches, during the Nazi epoch, but his silence about the Holocaust in the thirty-one years that he lived, wrote, and spoke, after the destruction of the Hitler-state. For Emmanuel Levinas, it is this silence that implicates Heidegger in what he terms "Hitlerian thinking":

> But on the issue of Heidegger's participation in "Hitlerian thinking," I do not believe that any kind of historical research, archival data, or eyewitness accounts—even when they do not rest on pure misunderstandings—can equal the certainty that comes to us in the famous Testament in *Der Spiegel*, from his silence concerning the Final Solution, the Holocaust, the Shoah. . . . But doesn't this silence, in time of peace, on the gas chambers and death camps lie beyond the realm of feeble excuses and reveal a soul completely cut off from any sensitivity, in which can be perceived a kind of consent to the horror?[4]

For Maurice Blanchot too, "Heidegger's irreparable fault lies in his silence concerning the Final Solution,"[5] while Jacques Derrida has found Heidegger's silence in the face of the Holocaust "as monstrous as that about which he remained silent."[6]

The meaning of Heidegger's silence, as well as his few, enigmatic public statements concerning the Holocaust, is precisely what is at issue in many of the essays in this volume. Moreover, while the conclusions drawn by Levinas, Blanchot, and Derrida are by no means shared by all of our contributors, the impetus for this project can, indeed, be found in Levinas's conviction—if not in the precise ethical terms in which he formulates it—that "it is in the 'final solution,' in the pure extermination of the death camps that—beyond all the major injustices that stamp the thirteen years of the Hitlerian regime—National Socialism revealed the diabolical criminality, the absolute evil, of what cannot be called 'thought.'"[7] For us, *das Ereignis Auschwitz* is not only the culmination of the horror wrought by the Hitler-state, but a transformative event in human history. A transformative event is one which has the potential to radically alter the prevailing conditions in the historical world, which can reshape the human landscape in a decisive way. The systematic extermination of six million Jews and at least five million non-Jews (Gypsies, Slavs, etc.), all designated as *Untermenschen* (sub-humans) by the Nazis, under conditions in which the achievements of modern science and technology were devoted to the industrial production of death, constituted such a phenomenon. The Holocaust opened a door into a genocidal universe in which human-made mass death becomes constitutive of the socio-economic, political, and cultural matrix. And therein lies its awesome futurity.

The transformative character of *das Ereignis Auschwitz*, and its unprecedented union of technology and extermination, provides further impetus for this volume in that it would seem that a *Denken* such as Heidegger's, so preoccupied with the implications of the development of *Technik*, would, indeed, provide a meditation on the Holocaust, would at least have something to tell us about the factories of death and their historial basis. The absence of such a meditation—if that is the case—would be philosophically significant, telling us something profound about the *Denken* itself.

In soliciting contributions to *Martin Heidegger and the Holocaust*, we were guided by two concerns. We wanted to assure the participation of contributors who would reflect the whole spectrum of views that have arisen in the course of the Heidegger wars. Difficult as that may have been, given the often acrimonious character of the debate, we were determined to avoid both censorship and partisanship in our choice of contributors. Despite the fact that several potential contributors, who were seemingly well placed to make the case for the centrality of Heidegger's thinking to an understanding of technicized genocide, chose not to participate in this project, we feel that we did suceed in publishing a volume in which a lively debate, and open confrontation of views, takes place.

We also wanted to make sure that the different essays, however diverse their interpretations of Heidegger's thinking, had as their point of departure a concern with the Holocaust conceived as a central event in the history of the West, one which is revelatory with respect to salient features of the path to modernity or of the structuration of our techno-scientific civilization. To that end, we offered potential contributors the possibility of discussing one, or several, of four basic themes. First, the issue of Heidegger's almost total silence with respect to the Holocaust; a silence that has troubled so many whose own path of thinking has its point of departure in Heidegger. Second, the meaning, and significance, of the few references in the Heideggerian *oeuvre*—public and private—to the Holocaust. Third, the ways in which Heidegger's thinking might illuminate the Holocaust as a transformative event, despite the lack of explicit references to it in his writings. Thus, Heidegger's reflections on *Technik*, the reign of *das Ge-stell*, and the triumph of nihilism might yield important insights into the Auschwitz-apocalypse and the historial basis for it. Fourth, how the experience of the Holocaust itself might illuminate the later Heidegger's thinking, sharpening our understanding of the meaning of "the danger" (*die Gefahr*) or the "un-world" (*Unwelt*), which cast their dark shadow over his history of Being. Our own contributors added a fifth theme: whether or not a *Denken* such as Heideggers is capable of comprehending *das Ereignis Auschwitz* in all its horror, and of grappling with its profound implications for humankind.

Berel Lang argues that Heidegger's concept of the *Volk*, and the privileged position he accorded to the Germans, made him impervious to the existence of otherness. As a result, in Lang's view, "for Heidegger there was no 'Jewish question' . . . there was nothing to be thought or said about the Holocaust as such. . . ." By contrast, Robert Manning asserts that Heidegger's thinking is based on a concept of Being-with (*Mitsein*), and that he can, indeed, hear the cry and the pain of the other—provided it is the cry and pain of others "who are near and who are like us," who are part of our historical community; a limitation that Manning insists is unfortunately not confined to Heidegger but characterizes most humans. Wilhelm Wurzer, however, insists that Heidegger's philosophy "disregards human suffering itself." For Wurzer "Dasein's necessary turning to Being" is an "extremely perilous turning away from human beings"; and it is here that we find the source of Heidegger's silence about the Holocaust. George Leaman shows that Heidegger's silence was shared by virtually the whole of the postwar German philosophical establishment; indeed, the whole of German culture, of which Heidegger was, in this respect, an exemplar. Moreover, in Leaman's opinion, Heidegger's silence was part of a carefully crafted effort to insulate himself from criticism and reproach, an effort that also involved the "politically motivated editing of some of his manuscripts prior to their publication after the war."

In addition to finding that "Heidegger's silences are something more than a mere political strategy of denial," William Vaughan chooses to link Heidegger's *Denken* to the *Dichten* of Paul Celan, the Jewish poet who articulated his vision of the Holocaust in the German language, and who turned to Heidegger for a possible answer to the question of why. For Vaughan, Heidegger's silence in the face of Celan's question may itself be pregnant with meaning: "What was such a silence if not the attempt to move already beyond the horizon of the technological noon and the holocaustic eve, a movement which eludes us still?" Otto Pöggeler also reflects on the Heidegger/Celan relation. However, for Pöggeler, the belated encounter of poet and thinker may have been futile: "Could a philosopher who thought from the site of Greek tragedy and Heraclitus, meet a lyric poet who translated the poets of the Russian revolution, and who incorporated Jewish mysticism into his poetry? . . . Could a German who bore some responsibility for the events of 1933, and a Jew who only narrowly escaped the extermination operations, commonly strive for a 'word'?"

Ultimately, Pöggeler's is a meditation on the question of whether or not Heidegger could have thought Auschwitz. Tom Rockmore argues not merely that Heidegger "never addresses the topic directly," but that philosophically, "even when Heidegger's theory is read against Heidegger, there are simply no resources to come to grips with the Holocaust within the wider framework of the theory." For Rockmore, the source of the problem is the ontological difference itself, the distinction between the ontological and the ontic realms: "Heidegger is basically a dualistic thinker, but the historical specificity of the Holocaust cannot be captured within the dualistic Heideggerian framework." Rainer Alish also believes that Heidegger's *Denken* must be mute before the enormity of the Holocaust. However, for Alisch, Heidegger's silence stems from his denial of representational thinking and the critique of subjectivity: "The guiding thesis is the idea that it is the philosopheme of criticism of the subject which lies at the root of his silence. . . ." Where Alisch finds the basis for Heidegger's purported inability to confront the Holocaust, even in his later thinking, after the famous *Kehre*, Henri Crétella insists that, thanks to that *Kehre*, Heidegger could overcome his own momentary surrender to the lure of Nazism and bring himself "to the point of enabling *us* to think the Shoah." Thus, for Crétella, Heidegger's thinking is crucial if we are to confront Nazism, not viewed retrospectively, but rather prospectively, "as the true, unique danger which confronts humanity, especially in technologically advanced societies." James Watson shares Crétella's foreboding about the futurity of the Holocaust; indeed, he has elsewhere persuasively argued that today we all inhabit "planet Auschwitz."[8] However, Watson believes that while Heidegger's thinking cannot be ignored, "neither can we wounded ones afford to leave his texts in their fittings." Our posture toward Heidegger's texts must be an effort to "take them away from their 'belongingness' to that shameful choice," to which their author originally committed them.

For Joseph Margolis, the issue is not whether or not Heidegger's thinking was adequate to the task of confronting the Holocaust, but whether our fixation with those murdered by the Nazis, and on Heidegger's silence, does not blind us to new holocausts, new genocides, in Iraqi Kurdistan or Bosnia, for example. For Margolis, the very preoccupation with the Heidegger case may be linked to a kind of monumental history that by insisting on the singularity of the Holocaust fails "to sense the Holocaust's continuation in another guise. . . ." In a sense, for Margolis, we are perhaps always a holocaust too late!

Hans Seigfried provides us with a startlingly fresh reading of Heidegger's "Letter on Humanism," one which insists that this important postwar text must be understood as a contribution to the French debate sparked by Sartre's "Existentialism Is a Humanism," itself conceived as a response to Nazism and directly linked to the war crimes trials at Nuremberg. For Seigfried, this preoccupation with the Holocaust, and the reading of the "Letter on Humanism" that it makes possible, far from distracting us from the horrors that assail us in the contemporary world, can "provide some help today for dealing with one of the central issues of the Nuremberg Trials, namely, individual responsibility for crimes against humanity. . . ."

Alan Milchman and Alan Rosenberg show how the later Heidegger's meditation on planetary technics and the reign of *das Ge-stell* can illuminate the conditions that produced the Holocaust and its obscene reduction of millions of humans to *Bestand* (standing reserve), even as the resistance of those who would not simply perish may shed light on what the later Heidegger meant by the saving. Elisabeth de Fontenay focuses on Heidegger's famous (or infamous) statement that "Agriculture is now a mechanized food industry, in essence the same as the manufacture of corpses in the gas chambers and extermination camps," to show, by a series of close readings, the multiple meanings of the Heideggerian text, and the ambiguities contained within the thinker's confrontation with nihilism. Michael Zimmerman finds in Heidegger's thinking "an agonized response to a widely shared concern about the 'disenchantment' of the world in technological modernity." However, for Zimmerman, Heidegger's rejection of modernity was fraught with danger because in its celebration of mythic revolt it prepared the way for Nazism and the rule of "charismatic leaders who promise salvation, but deliver death and destruction."

We believe that a confrontation with the diverse viewpoints contained in these fifteen essays, and the opening up of a side of Heidegger's *Denken* that has been largely unexplored, will not only help us to think Auschwitz, but also to re-think the legacy of one of this century's most influential thinkers.

Alan Milchman and Alan Rosenberg

NOTES

1. Victor Farías, *Heidegger and Nazism* (Philadelphia: Temple University Press, 1989); Hugo Ott, *Martin Heidegger: A Political Life* (New York: Basic Books, 1993).
2. Among the voluminous, and growing, literature, see Richard Wolin (ed.), *The Heidegger Controversy: A Critical Reader* (New York: Columbia University Press, 1991); Tom Rockmore and Joseph Margolis (eds.), *The Heidegger Case: On Philosophy and Politics* (Philadelphia: Temple University Press, 1992); Günther Neske and Emil Kettering (eds.), *Martin Heidegger and National Socialism: Questions and Answers* (New York: Paragon House, 1990); Tom Rockmore, *On Heidegger's Nazism and Philosophy* (Berkeley: University of California Press, 1992); Jacques Derrida, *Of Spirit: Heidegger and the Question* (Chicago: The University of Chicago Press, 1989); and Philippe Lacoue-Labarthe, *Heidegger, Art and Politics: The Fiction of the Political* (Oxford: Basil Blackwell, 1990).
3. Dan Diner, "Vorwort des Herausgebers" in Dan Diner (ed.), *Zivilisationsbruch: Denken nach Auschwitz* (Frankfurt am Main: Fischer Taschenbuch Verlag, 1988), p. 7.
4. Emmanuel Levinas, "As If Consenting to Horror" in *Critical Inquiry* 15,2 (Winter 1989), p. 487.
5. Maurice Blanchot, "Thinking the Apocalypse: A Letter from Maurice Blanchot to Catherine David" in *Critical Inquiry*, 15,2 (Winter 1989), p. 479.
6. Jacques Derrida, "On Reading Heidegger: An Outline of Remarks to the Essex Colloquium" in *Research in Phenomenology* XVII (1987), p. 173.
7. Emmanuel Levinas, "As If Consenting to Horror," p. 487.
8. See James Watson, *Between Auschwitz and Tradition: Postmodern Reflections on the Task of Thinking* (Amsterdam and Atlanta, GA: Rodopi, 1994).

1

Heidegger's Silence and the Jewish Question

BEREL LANG

My title invites an immediate objection: Why, this late in the day, return to the archaic formula of the "Jewish Question"—a phrase which on the rare occasions that we now encounter it almost always comes framed by the quotation marks of obsolescence? Put quite simply, there *is* no Jewish Question today, at least as the phrase at one time immediately and unmistakably brought to mind a single question about the Jews, evidently the one that mattered. To recall the currency of the Jewish Question in the 19th and the first half of the 20th centuries is to establish the historical contrast, for during that time it appeared in a constant variety of linguistic and ideological appearances: as the "Judenfrage" that Marx and Herzl (agreeing on that one provocation) sought to answer; in the French of Bernard Lazare, the Hebrew of Ahad Ha'am, the English of Justice Brandeis—and by innumerable other writers in those or other languages—a common title or marker for both Jewish and non-Jewish writers, used without prejudice (at least *that* far) by philosemites and antisemites alike. The term or phrase was understood by anyone who thought about the Jews because there *was* a (that is, the) Jewish Question whose formulation was accepted by all sides, however they disagreed after that: the question, that is, of how the Jews were to live among the nations—or, conversely, from the perspective of "nations," how the nations were to live with the Jews.

But the phrase and the Question itself have now lost that currency, and there are two main reasons for this displacement. The first of these explains the disappearance of the Jewish Question by claiming its resolution: The Jewish Question ceased to exist—so the contention—because it was answered, in 1948, by the establishment of the State of Israel. With that event,

Jews, wherever they were and willingly or no, entered a relationship with a country that resembled other countries in political definition; thus, the most obvious source—or cause—of the Jewish Question disappeared, and so also the Question itself. There *was* a Jewish country; Jews living outside it would accordingly be addressed in similar terms to those characterizing other people who had historical or ethnic ties to a nation other than the one they happened to inhabit. No longer was it a question for European or Asian or American governments of how to classify this group of people, who until then, although insisting they were more than just a religion, had been unable to point to any other visible means of support. Governments understand governments; and so Jews around the world—Zionists, anti-Zionists, non-Zionists alike—benefitted from the fact of Israel's existence, if only to the extent that they could stop hearing references to the Jewish Question. Even the fact that most Jews chose not to "return" to Israel was incidental; Israel was the answer to the Jewish Question as a *question* even if, for many Jews individually, it did not answer the question of how or where they should live individually, indeed, even if the question itself had never occurred to them. (But then the Question had not been addressed to them as individuals either.)

Israel's existence, however, is only a partial (both incomplete and tendentious) explanation for the disappearance of the Jewish Question; it is one in any event that hardly touched Martin Heidegger one way or the other. Any scruples about the reaction, however, are slight when measured by Heidegger's response to the second reason for the obsolescence of the Jewish Question, which involved an event that occurred several years before the declaration of Israel's independence. Like the Jewish Question itself, this event was named by having the definite article attached to a common, not a proper noun. I refer, of course, to "the Holocaust" and the stop *it* put to the Jewish Question. For in the aftermath of the Nazi genocide, it became clear to almost everyone that *now* to ask the traditional question of how Jews might live (or not) among the nations must be at least an occasion for embarrassment, at most, a moral offense. And this for the obvious reason that the answer the Nazis had proposed for the Question—how *they* thought to resolve it—disabled the Question itself; this was the case even though their intention was realized only in part. It was, after all, the Jewish Question as a question for which the "Final Solution" was designed as a solution—*Frage* eliciting *Losung*. And if it is unfair to ascribe responsibility for the answer given a question to the question rather than to those who answer it, it is nonetheless evident that answers are not given unless questions make them possible; thus a necessary, if not a sufficient condition.

From this twofold perspective, furthermore, the genealogy of the Jewish Question, the sources of its history, appears no more mysterious than does the cause of its demise. It was the Enlightenment—or just as euphemistically from the viewpoint of Jewish history, the Emancipation—that made the Jewish Question a question; and it is the inheritors of the Enlightenment—us—who even at this distance, otherwise stirred by the inclusiveness of its fraternal principles, look back now with like measures of awe and disbelief at the conflicting answers that the Question evoked. To be sure, we are not obliged to decide exactly what we would have been willing to forego in the Enlightenment in order to avoid a question to which the "Final Solution" was an answer, but the very possibility of such a connection casts a shadow both backward and forward: backward to the origins of the Jewish Question, forward to its present discussion as that has now to be justified retrospectively, through the framework of quotation marks.

The justification for recalling the Jewish Question here, that is, as the "Jewish Question," begins in an expanded version of my title, which discloses itself as a thesis: For Martin Heidegger, there was no Jewish Question retrospectively in the post-Holocaust era (when it would be the "Jewish Question"); and the reason for that absence is that there had been no Jewish Question for Heidegger even when the Question existed, that is, before the Holocaust.

The possible confusion of the two appearances of the Jewish Question in this thesis (once as the "Jewish Question," once as the Jewish Question)[1] will, I hope, be soon cleared up. Certainly the first appearance—the Jewish Question seen retrospectively, framed by quotation marks—can be rephrased in terms that are well-known; these are the terms of Heidegger's post-Holocaust silence or, on the few occasions when he broke that silence, what was arguably still more evasive and in this sense no less "silent," the combination of what he omitted to say and of what, even in speaking, he formulated in unreachable abstraction—the refuge, in sum, that he found in obliqueness and avoidance. I shall elaborate on this representation mainly by reassembling here the now familiar evidence of those few overt expressions of Heidegger's post-Holocaust response to the Holocaust as they serve to underscore his *more* overt, louder, silence.[2] The conclusion at which this evidence points is, at any rate, clear and concise: Even after the Holocaust was over and its consequences known, fully in the public domain, Heidegger, who had met certain manifestations of the Holocaust at first-hand and was well aware of many others, remained silent. There was for him no "Jewish Question," no issue of what it was that had happened to the Jews among the nations (not even within or at the hands of *his* nation), of why what happened to them happened or how to assess that occurrence in moral terms or of what any of these implied for future conduct (including his own). In the thirty post-Holocaust and otherwise prolific years of his life, about these matters there was silence.

For many commentators, including some who find in Heidegger's writing during those thirty years the most valuable elements of his work, this silence is more troubling than anything Heidegger did or said while the Nazis (and for a year, he himself) were in power. Even the excuses sometimes made for this absence reflect the concession they more explicitly deny: lame and rhetorical, on the one hand ("What if he *had* spoken of Auschwitz? Would this change anything in our appreciation of other aspects of his work, except perhaps to make that work easier to ignore for those who wished to do so anyway?")—or, on the other hand, tendentious and unverifiable ("His writing and lecturing after 1934 were through and through oppositional, he was speaking out virtually *all the time*; to see this, one has only to read him subtly, supplely, correctly").

Well, for the latter claim, there is the test of reading itself; for the former, the more accessible measure of common sense. And prior to either of these, the challenge posed by Heidegger's *ostensive* silence and the few interruptions of it that he ventured. Together, it seems to me, these disclose the apologias that have been offered as specious, since in the end they are committed to denying that the silence was, indeed, silent notwithstanding the loud sound by which that silence announced itself. They are, moreover, also bound to ignore the evidence that provides an explanation of origins: If there was no silence, then there would be no reason why the silence occurred. And yet I should argue exactly the opposite: Heidegger's post-Holocaust silence mirrors—*follows* from—his silence before that. There was no "Jewish Question" after the Holocaust for Heidegger, in other words, not because of the Holocaust but because the Jewish Question had not existed for him before then either. Indeed, one might argue that it would have been factitious, in bad faith, for Heidegger to agree to a question in retrospect that he had earlier denied or ignored, at a time when it *was* real. And in fact, or so I would claim, he made no such pretense. Thus the fulcrum of my thesis overall is also the fulcrum of Heidegger's position: There was no Jewish Question for Heidegger even when the Jewish Question existed, and that is why there would also be no "Jewish Question" for him retrospectively, after the Holocaust marked a stopping point in the history of the Question.[3]

In this way, my second and conceptually more basic concern (to which the first, although later chronologically, serves as preface) reaches farther back historically, asking how it was that even when there was a Jewish Question, it did not exist for Heidegger. I provide a more detailed account of the latter point elsewhere,[4] but its general outline can be stated concisely. What precludes acknowledgment of the Jewish Question for Heidegger is the metaphysical status he ascribes to the concept of the *Volk*—and within that general concept, the privileged role he assigns specifically to the German *Volk*—in relation to Being (to both Sein and Dasein) and to Truth. As he construes the concept of the *Volk* in its history and destiny, there is, quite simply, no place for the Jews in Heidegger's thinking, not as a matter of prejudice (although also *that* was a part of his denial) but as a matter of categories. In establishing this, we also learn as much as we can about Heidegger's relation to the Jews (and by inversion, about Heidegger's relation to one central theme of Nazi Germany, its campaign against the Jews).

In this rejection of the Jewish Question and in the reconstruction that I present here of Heidegger's denial, retrospectively, of the "Jewish Question," I shall be attending to what Heidegger did not say and what he might have said as much as to what he in fact did say; considering, that is, the matters he would have had to address if indeed the Jewish Question, early or late, existed for him. The two topics of "Heidegger and the 'Jewish Question'" and "Heidegger and the Jewish Question" can, I believe, be represented quite impersonally and even, up to a point, non-judgmentally. Indeed, one might argue that this twofold formulation itself impedes any later assessment: Supposing that he *did* deny or ignore the "Jewish Question" and/or the Jewish Question: Well, what then? Surely there were many other questions (and "questions") that he (like any other writer) also failed to acknowledge; and surely no one can dictate to someone else the order of questions they "ought" to consider. Interests, to say nothing about caring or concern, cannot be commanded. Why then call attention to either a "Question" or a Question that Heidegger, as it happened, chose not to ask?

But Heidegger cannot leave the room so easily or impersonally, for there remains yet another issue that makes its presence known just at the point where accounts of his denial of the Jewish Question—whatever interpretations they give that denial—end; namely, the matter of his antisemitism. To be sure, the importance of this matter should not be exaggerated. It is no doubt possible that the main theses asserted here—that there was no "Jewish Question" for Heidegger, and that this was the case because there had been for him no Jewish Question—could be sustained even if antisemitism were not uncovered as a later factor in the causal chain. In this sense, antisemitism is not necessary as an element in Heidegger's rejection of both the "Jewish Question" and the Jewish Question. (I suggest in fact that there had been no Jewish Question for Heidegger *first* because of his attitude toward the Germans, not toward the Jews.) But if—on independent grounds—there is *also* evidence of antisemitism in any of its traditional kinds, a philosophical circle would have been completed: There would then be a concrete ground in experience itself that motivated the denial of those two questions. There is, I believe, sufficient evidence of this, too—that is, of Heidegger's antisemitism.[5] And in this sense, his not-thinking about the Jewish Question (or about the Holocaust) appears as a form of thinking from the ground up, absence as denial, omission as assertion. Thus, a connection between "merely" psychological or personal dispositions—the minimal grounds of antisemitism—and philosophical reflection also announces itself as a factor in Heidegger's own history. Exactly how the two considerations of personal predisposition and theoretical reflection are related systematically—the logic of their relationship—is a separate issue; whatever position one takes on that issue in general, however, the *specific* conjunction in Heidegger speaks for itself.

There was then—so the part of my general thesis that I address here—no post-Holocaust "Jewish Question" for Heidegger, certainly nothing in or around the "Question" that he found worth talking about. The few intimations he gives of admitting even the possibility of that Question are oblique, subordinated to other, larger (in his view) concerns, or concluding, even when provoked by direct challenge, in denial; thus, their effect is to intensify rather than to overcome the silence. This absence cannot be attributed to a lack of information in or after 1945 or to the speed with which events moved around him. The nature and extent of the Nazi genocide against the Jews were widely known (the Nuremberg Trials ensured the availability of this information if by unlikely chance other sources had failed), and Heidegger himself, with the leisure forced on him because of his (as it turned out, temporary) exclusion from the University of Freiburg as a result of the "denazification" hearings in 1945, if anything increased his already remarkable productivity during those and later years. Even aside from such specific evidence, moreover, it seems impossible on prima facie grounds to find explanations for Heidegger's silence in ignorance or inadvertence. Unaware he *could* not have been; preoccupied he is unlikely to have been. Is there evidence of any subject that Heidegger wished to write about but did not get around to? And since the act of "thinking" is a keystone in his own philosophical architectonic, there seems no alternative here to a conclusion of active rejection: Heidegger *refused* to think about the Holocaust, let alone to think it, with the refusal itself having been thought. (I echo here Hannah Arendt's tribute to Heidegger on his eightieth birthday: "Heidegger never thinks 'about' something; he thinks something."[6]) What this amounts to, one might say, is an act of "post-meditation" at least equal in moral weight to what pre-meditation adds to other evidence of agency. (We could speak here of weight added to weight: The most extreme Holocaust "revisionists"—Faurisson, Rassinier, Butz[7]—do not deny that *if* the Holocaust had occurred, it would have been a moral enormity warranting reflection and judgment; they only deny that it *did* occur. Heidegger does not deny that the Nazi genocide against the Jews took place—only that having occurred, it does not warrant thinking or talking about.)

Let me first summarize the evidence for claiming that for Heidegger there was no "Jewish Question"—his view, that is, that there was nothing to be thought or said about the Holocaust as such, let alone as he himself stood in relation to it. Since the argument here claims Heidegger's deliberate or thoughtful refusal to think about the Holocaust, the primary evidence for this ought to appear in his most "thoughtful" work, that is, from his writings that would ordinarily be classified as philosophical rather than popular or public or personal.[8] To be sure, there occurs here the same problem of ambiguity that any claim to interpret "silence" encounters—not only of deciding whether or not the silence at issue (once *that* is demonstrated) was calculated and deliberate (it might be no more than an expression of indifference or ignorance), but then also, assuming such calculation, of determining what its rationale was. For silence is at least as ambiguous, certainly no less open to interpretation, as the spoken word: the silence of horror—announcing the unspeakable—posed against the silence of consent; silent agreement or even pleasure as an alternative to suffering in silence; at times (and this, I believe, has a special relevance to Heidegger and the Jewish Question) silence may come from a decision not to say what one has in mind, in contrast to the silence that reflects indifference or the absence of opinion. And there might of course be still other unspoken reasons that have to do less with the occasion of a particular silence than with the state of the respondent. Psychic causality, after all, does not always mirror the connections of the external world. None of these possibilities can be ruled out a priori as explaining Heidegger's silence on the Holocaust, and although he himself would point us toward the last option mentioned (more of this below), I shall be claiming that it is the earlier and more substantive reasons that put their mark on his silence. Again, the problem of interpreting Heidegger's silence does not depend only on either the fact or content of what he did not say, since he did mention or allude to the Holocaust on a few occasions. But these references, too, in the context of the whole, only reinforce the louder impression of silence. That is, Heidegger's silence becomes more intense because of what he says on the few occasions when he breaks it. Admittedly, the passages in question are as slight as they are well-known (they are well-known in part *because* they are so slight). It is not even certain, in fact, that some of them do refer to the Nazi genocide against the Jews, and we have then to qualify even these statements with a caveat: They come as close as Heidegger ever does to referring to the Holocaust in his formal writings or teaching. There are in fact but two such statements, from the second and third of the so-called Bremen Lectures (1949) respectively:

> Agriculture is now a mechanized food industry, in essence the same as the manufacture of corpses in the gas chambers and extermination camps, the same as the blockade and starvation of the countryside, the same as the production of the hydrogen bombs.

And then:

> Hundreds of thousands die en masse. Do they die? They perish. They are cut down. They become items of material available for the manufacture of corpses. Do they die? Hardly noticed, they are liquidated in extermination camps. And even apart from that, in China millions now perish of hunger.

The lecture in which the first of these statements appeared was later revised and published as "Die Frage nach der Technik" ("The Question Concerning Technology"). In its later appearance the statement quoted here is radically emended;[9] the lecture in which the second statement appears ("Die Gefahr," "The Danger") has not been published at all.

Especially the former reference has drawn comment for the likeness it finds between the mechanization of agriculture and the "manufacturing" of corpses. To be sure, the fact of that likeness is part of the point that Heidegger is asserting *against* one likely outcome (and, in his view, abuse) of technology. But even making allowance for this purpose does not relieve Heidegger of the onus which that statement imposes; namely, the moral disproportion between the two forms that he asserts are essentially alike. It is Heidegger himself who is asserting about the consequences of an abusive technology that there is to be found in them no essential difference between the mechanized food industry and extermination camps: the likeness is what *he* is claiming.

Now of course, analogies are always possible; they can be drawn between *any* two objects or practices. But it is not this truism that is pertinent to Heidegger's words that have been cited but the fact that analogies are also open to evaluation. They are, after all, intended to make—to come to—a point, to establish continuity between two ostensibly and otherwise dissimilar things. Thus, any likeness proposed is meant to be a significant feature in each of the two things (or events or practices) compared—and that common feature is also required to warrant consideration in a larger context that finds the feature itself to be of consequence. And it is on both these points that Heidegger's comparison is open to challenge—as ignoring the overriding *difference* between the mechanization of farm labor (presumably for the purpose of raising food) and the mechanization of killing (in fact for the purpose of genocide)—as well as in the unmediated abstraction of the concept of technology that he both applies and finds in his analogy. A related objection applies to the second statement, which is even loftier than the first in its reach for abstraction. The focus here is on what Heidegger distinguishes as two varieties of dying—the one referring to an individual and authentic process (where dying virtually becomes an *act*), the other ("perishing") which is done en masse, mechanically, something that has been "manufactured." The latter qualities Heidegger assigns to death in the "extermination camps"—implying that death in those circumstances has less character, is less real or genuine than it would be under the other conditions referred to. The distinction, as Heidegger asserts it, is *meant* to be invidious—and thus what is at issue here is the forced abstraction that Heidegger imposes on the concepts of death and technology: the distance assumed in his distinction between them as ideas and in practice.

Even putting aside certain literal-minded questions that bear on the two statements (why, for example, does Heidegger speak of "hundreds of thousands" dead in the extermination camps and "millions" in the famine of China? Is this a challenge to the supposed number of victims in the extermination camps? And which Chinese famine is he speaking of, or is the reference only a figure of speech?), we return to the issue of their substance: what they leave out and what is left out around them as well as what they assert. Let us assume for the moment that these are indeed references to the genocide against the Jews (perhaps not only to that, but to that as well as to other instances of victimization; the vagueness is itself part of what is being asserted). Is it that all the groups of victims are alike? Is it that in respect to what is being asserted the groups of victims are "in essence" alike? But what does it mean to claim this and then not to consider the question of how those victims came to be victims, of who they were, and still more incisively, who *made* victims of them? Even in the unlikely event that all the victims indeed were "in essence" alike, these questions would not yet have been answered or even articulated. A reader of the two passages who did not know that Heidegger had written them after living through, in, the twelve years of Nazi rule, might reasonably imagine their author as inhabiting a distant land, perhaps in another age, as having at most second- or third-hand knowledge of the events he refers to, and caring (at most) academically about their histories (including the question of responsibility, of *whose* extermination camps they were; for all we know—and revisionist historians would later make just this claim[10]—there would be little or nothing to distinguish the Nazi death-camps from Stalin's *gulag*, with the latter even serving as a provocation and model for the former.)

This is indeed as close as Heidegger comes to the "Jewish Question" in his formal writings from 1945 on. And few references can be added to this brief list even if one moves beyond the "Jewish Question" to the Nazi regime as a whole, whose crimes extended, after all, to millions of non-Jews, including tens of thousands of German non-Jews. There is, of course, the widely cited passage in the *Introduction to Metaphysics* (first presented as lectures in 1935, published in 1953) in which Heidegger speaks of "the inner truth and greatness of this movement [i.e., National Socialism]." The dispute over whether the parenthetical comment that in the 1953 text immediately qualifies the claim of Nazism's "inner truth and greatness" ("namely, the encounter between planetary technology and modern man") was or was not present in the original version[11] hardly seems to matter. Indeed, it could be argued that the parenthetical phrase underscores the willful and malicious abstraction that the other phrase would represent if it appeared by itself. Certainly the two, taken together, have the effect of articulating the *specific* memory that Heidegger would transmit of National Socialism, bring into the post-Holocaust present; the feature of Nazism it approvingly recalls—Nazism's solution to the "technology question"—is sufficient, evidently, not only to outweigh but to justify omitting reference to everything else that occurred in the course of National Socialism. Those other events or acts are by implication reduced to accidents or mistakes, the merely "external." Thus, National Socialism is to be remembered for its potential "greatness" on the overriding issue of technology—and then also, regretfully, for its failure to realize that potential, to make external its "inner" truth. Once again, then, silence about the "Jewish Question."

But there remain the putatively non-philosophical writings or statements as well, those which are more informal, whether they were initially conceived with an eye to publication (as in the ase of the *Spiegel* interview) or not (as in Heidegger's letter to Herbert Marcuse). These too, after all, are statements in which Heidegger has a specific opportunity to address the "Jewish Question" and once again declines to, or comes so close to declining to as only, once again, to underscore that impression. I add this last, qualifying clause specifically in reference to his response to Herbert Marcuse, who in the opening letter of his postwar correspondence with Heidegger (August 28, 1947) challenged the latter's silence about Nazism in general and about the "Jewish Question" in particular ("You are still identified with the Nazi regime [that . . . killed millions of Jews—merely because they were Jews]. Many of us have long awaited a statement from you . . . that would clearly and finally free you from such identification. . . .").[12] To this formulation of the "Jewish Question" Heidegger then responds (January 20, 1948):

> To the serious legitimate charges that you express "about a regime that murdered millions of Jews . . ." I can merely add that if instead of "Jews" you had written "East Germans", then the same holds true for one of the allies, with the difference that everything that has occurred since 1945 has become public knowledge, while the bloody terror of the Nazis in point of fact had been kept a secret from the German people.

Heidegger's reference here to the "bloody terror of the Nazis" is, I believe, the strongest expression of condemnation to appear in his writings, public or private; this, together with his acknowledgment of the "legitimate" charges Marcuse had made in respect to the millions of Jews murdered, accounts for the qualification in my own comment above, about the "virtual" (not complete) silence he maintained even in the face of Marcuse's direct challenge.

It may be objected that the words of Heidegger thus cited deserve more than I grant them, that they *do* break the silence. And had they appeared by themselves and without qualification, I would agree. But the context in which they are set makes a crucial difference to the force of the words. In his own subsequent response to Heidegger, Marcuse contends that to equate what the Nazis had done to the Jews with the fate of the East Germans after the war's end (presumably on the responsibility of the Russians) raises the question of how "a conversation between men is even possible"—and to assess that equation more than forty-five years later can hardly lead to any other response. Should we say rather that in conceding the "Jewish Question" Heidegger was only adding to it an "East German" Question? But then, we would still have to ask what the "Jewish Question" amounts to if Heidegger is instructing us to view it in the same terms as the expulsion of Germans from the East (the issue, obviously, is not about justifying the latter, but about its *equation* to genocide). One way to attempt to make something disappear is to place it—like a grain of sand in the desert—in the midst of a mass of supposed likeness; this is how Heidegger makes the "Jewish Question" invisible for himself and so sustains the silence.

Two other documents add significantly to our assessment of Heidegger's post-Holocaust stance. Unlike his letter to Marcuse, Heidegger formulated these with the understanding that they would eventually be published, and this fact, together with the issues they address, places them on the boundary between Heidegger's personal or informal discourse and his more professional writings. The first of these—a memorandum written in 1945 and then given to his son, Hermann Heidegger, for use as he saw fit—was not published until 1983; the second—the *Spiegel* interview—was recorded in 1966 and then published, in accordance with Heidegger's stipulation, after his death, in 1976.[13] The two statements are autobiographical in character; they are evidently intended to represent Heidegger's own view of his Nazi associations, partly in response to the charges made against him about those associations, partly as a more general reflection on that period of his life which began, formally, at least, with his assumption of the Rectorship of the University of Freiburg in April 1933.

Here again, our interest in the two statements, which speak also of other matters, is with the "Jewish Question." Both are "post-Holocaust," written after the Jewish Question had encountered the "Final Solution." And also on these two occasions, which are intended specifically to reflect on and even to judge the past, Heidegger meets the "Jewish Question" with silence. This does not mean that he does not utter the words "Jewish" or "Jew": he does—six times in more than forty pages of printed text, four of these times in citing by its informal title the "Judenplakat" or "Jewish Notice" (whose message was "Juden nicht erwunscht"); the other two occasions as the terms pertain to single events or persons, not to the Jewish Question. So, in the *Spiegel* interview, he mentions the "so-called Jewish Notice" which his predecessor as Rector had refused to post and to which, he emphasizes, he added his own refusal (although not, as he leaves unmentioned, his refusal to enforce what it proclaimed: It is as if he is here concerned with what is *posted* on university walls more than on the policy advocated by the notice itself).[14] He denies the charge that had been made against him of having removed books by Jewish authors from the Philosophy Library. In response to a question asked by his interviewers about his Jewish students, he speaks of one (Helene Weiss) who when she later received her doctorate from Basel ("this was no longer possible at Freiburg") included an acknowledgment to Heidegger. He avoids a direct answer to the question of how the breach between him and Jaspers developed although denying that it occurred (only?) because of Jaspers' Jewish wife. He offers an explanation on philosophical grounds for the end of his relationship with his one-time teacher Husserl and a confession of "human failing" in having ignored him and the Husserl household at the time of Husserl's last illness and death (1938), for which, he says, he subsequently apologized to Husserl's wife.

Heidegger makes other references to National Socialism in general, but the allusions mentioned are the only ones to the terms "Jew" or "Jewish"—and in neither the former *nor* the latter references, as they constitute Heidegger's Last Will and Testament concerning the "Jewish Question," his last words (or silence) on the subject, is there the glimmering of a general reflection on the consequences of the policies of National Socialism for the Jewish Question or of his own relation to those policies. Admittedly, his interlocuters do not force that issue, although they question at some length Heidegger's general views on other topics, including the "condition of the world." Even after they remind Heidegger of his extraordinary assertion in 1933 that "the Fuhrer and he alone *is* the present and future German reality and its law" (does any statement ever made by a serious philosopher—whether off-duty or on-duty—approach this usurpation of metaphysics by ideology?),[15] they do not question his rejoinder that these words appeared in a "local Freiburg student paper," that as Rector he knew he would have to make certain "compromises," that he "would not write those words today [1966!]," and that already in 1934 he "did not say them."

In "The Rectorate 1933/34: Facts and Thoughts," the document that he entrusted to his son, Hermann, Heidegger also alludes to his resistance to posting the "Jewish Notice" and mentions the spontaneous silence with which a group of which he was part responded to a lecture on race by a Nazi official.[16] He mentions at some length the Rectoral Address and other more professional writings from the same period and after his resignation, emphasizing what he alleges was the hostile reaction to them by Nazi orthodoxy. (That alleged reaction bears a considerable weight here and elsewhere in his apologia, putatively demonstrating the *difference* between him and other Nazis, a difference that Nazi officialdom itself thus supposedly recognized). But once again, about the "Jewish Question," either during the 1933/34 period he is specifically considering or in its subsequent outcome, nothing more than what has been indicated.

One last document that has quasi-official standing should be cited here, a letter, dated November 4, 1945, in which Heidegger requested of the then Rector of the University of Freiburg his own reinstatement to the faculty. This personal formulation has a more specific purpose than the other two cited above in the second category I have distinguished, and perhaps this makes the absence of any general reference in it to the "Jewish Question" less egregious. In fact, he calls attention here as he does not in the others to his early (and presumably continuing) dissent from the orthodox version of Nazi biological racism. Glossing a passage in the Rectoral Address which asserts that "The greatness of a Volk is guaranteed by its spiritual world values," he contends that "For those who know and think, these sentences express my opposition to Rosenberg's conception, according to which, conversely, spirit and the world of spirit are merely an 'expression' . . . of racial facts and of the physical constitution of man." In a later passage of this same letter, he reiterates his (then) opposition to "the dogmatism and primitivism of Rosenberg's biologism."[17] As I argue elsewhere, and contrary to what has often been held (including by Heidegger himself), this passage or others in the same spirit does not by itself defuse the charge of antisemitism against Heidegger, since even for Nazi antisemitism, and certainly for its older traditions, the biological ground was at most one of its elements. Moreover (and this too requires more elaboration than can be given it here), Heidegger's endorsement in these passages of the principle of the *Volk* on spiritual grounds reflects a basic and consistent line in his thinking, one which is in the end responsible, as I would argue, for his denial of the Jewish Question, also at a time when the Question itself was quite real. Even in this context, moreover, his emphasis is on the alleged reaction of the Nazi hierarchy to his views, not to the consequences that followed historically from the Nazi concept of the *Volk*, of which the biological ground was but one, albeit an important, element and to whose *other* grounds, the evidence shows, Heidegger himself was fully committed.

There may be other documents in the second category of evidence (i.e., of "public" versus professional writings or personal letters written by Heidegger himself) that I have missed or that will yet become known (almost certainly the still-closed Heidegger archives at Marbach include material in this category). But, both in what they say and what they omit, the documents mentioned seem sufficient, when added to the more strictly "philosophical" statements, to justify the claim that for Heidegger, the "Jewish Question"—that is, the Jewish Question seen through the lens of the Holocaust—did not exist.

An objection might be raised to this summary of the evidence concerning "Heidegger and the 'Jewish Question'" that combines two points of his previously cited defense or apologia. The first point echoes Heidegger himself, contending that much of his philosophical writing was oppositional, posed against Nazi doctrine, even if it did not say *that* explicitly. This is, again, his own explication of his (implied) rejection in the Rectoral Address of Rosenberg's biological racism. In the same letter (1945) in which he asks for reinstatement at the university, he recalls his writing and lecturing on Nietzsche also as a gesture of dissent:

> It is unjust to assimilate Nietzsche to National Socialism, an assimilation which—apart from what is essential—ignores his hostility to anti-Semitism and his positive attitude with respect to Russia. But on a higher plane, the debate with Nietzsche's metaphysics is a debate with nihilism as it manifests itself with increased clarity under the political form of fascism.[18]

Again, the detail of this passage raises questions about what constitutes a defense (Heidegger never, early *or* late, disguised his antagonism to communism and Russia; thus his work on Nietzsche represented no retraction on *that* count. Why then should we believe that Nietzsche's attacks on antisemitism were an aspect of Nietzsche's writing that Heidegger demonstrated approval of by emphasizing Nietzsche's more general significance?). But more importantly, even if one accepts Heidegger's construal of his own writings as tacitly oppositional, the evidence he adduces for this comes from the period of Nazi rule itself. If, however, he understandably felt obliged at *that* time to write obliquely—in effect joining the philosophical tradition that Leo Strauss characterizes under his title of "Persecution and the Art of Writing"[19]—he faced no similar danger after the war's end, when he openly called his audience's attention to his earlier opposition. Why, one might ask in this connection, if he had earlier lectured tacitly in opposition, did he not speak out explicitly in the new present, during the thirty years of productive writing when he faced no such threat of punishment or censure? (And this, of course, leaves out the question of how much weight to attach to Heidegger's reading of his own texts; in fact, his glosses on his own writing seem at times no less contestable than certain of his glosses on other writers.)

The second point joining this first one is in its own terms imponderable; this is (again) the question of how silence is to be interpreted. For even if we provisionally accept the thesis I have been asserting—that after taking into account everything Heidegger says explicitly about the "Jewish Question," we find that this amounts to a denial, in effect to silence—there remains the fact that silence is itself ambiguous, that it may represent a variety of motives or principles. What, in other words, do we know even if we agree that for Heidegger there *was* no "Jewish Question?" The finding that he does not confront the "Question" does not mean by itself that he denied or chose to exclude it: The issue might more simply not have occurred to him, or he might have avoided it not because of what *it* entailed but because, in addressing it, he would have been obliged to speak on other matters that he preferred to avoid.

I have already suggested that we can usefully advance on these issues by considering those moments, public or private, when intimations of the "Jewish Question" do in fact arise for him. A number of these moments we have considered, and I have argued that they too affirm the predominant silence. An important additional source is to look at what Heidegger *was* thinking and writing about *other* questions (or even "questions"). He was not, after all, silent through and through; he spoke and wrote largely and widely—and surely the absence of some one matter or question can often be understood by seeing what else *was* present. We might find in these other words, for example, a basis for his exclusion of what is excluded—or we might find there a clue which forces us to revise our sense of that exclusion. In any event, silence by itself, here as elsewhere, is inconclusive.

Well, perhaps. And indeed, in explaining elsewhere how Heidegger's silence on the Jewish Question is a source for his silence on the "Jewish Question," I make broader reference to what Heidegger *was* saying at the same time that he was not speaking about these topics. It is certainly arguable, in any event, that the more crucial test of Heidegger's views will be there, in the pre-Holocaust texts, without the pressure that his knowledge of history (of both Nazi history and his own history) then inevitably exerted on what he was saying by indirection. Putting those earlier references aside, however, one might grant all the possibilities mentioned and yet insist that the nature of what is absent must weigh heavily *no matter what* else is or may yet be said—that is, no matter how the silence is framed or hedged. When Heidegger writes in his letter to Marcuse that "a confession after 1945 was impossible for me, because the Nazi partisans announced their change of allegiance in the most loathesome way; and I, however, had nothing in common with them," we have some idea of what he saw as his own motives for silence. Presumably, if he had spoken against the genocide against the Jews (as against any other Nazi crime), he might have been misunderstood as identifying himself with those other "partisans" who had none of the solid basis for a commitment to "true" Nazism that he had; they could much more easily deny their earlier allegiance because for them the allegiance itself had been easier, more superficial. Yet even if we accept Heidegger's contention here as credible, a question forces itself forward that is at least as obvious as the ground that Heidegger claims for himself. Is it not true that about *some* matters the risk of silence outweighs the risk of being misunderstood or misrepresented? But also about the latter question, Heidegger is silent. He is evidently willing to run the risk of silence, whatever the consequences—and since he implies also this claim in silence, we can only speculate about whether he recognized the risk of silence as a risk at all. It is at least possible—*probable*, I would contend—that for him the loss would be entirely on the other side. That is, only if he were to break the silence; that is, to speak.

NOTES

1. The issues raised here seem to have evoked a "rhetoric of quotation marks": so, for example, Lyotard's *Heidegger and "the jews,"* trans. Andreas Michel and Mark S. Roberts (Minneapolis: University of Minnesota Press, 1990), and Derrida's *Of Spirit: Heidegger and the Question*, trans. Geoffrey Bennington and Rachel Bowlby (Chicago: The University of Chicago Press, 1989), in which the analysis revolves around the difference between Heidegger's references to 'Geist' and to "Geist," respectively, are obvious precedents. To be sure, the issues at stake in these several accounts (and in mine) differ significantly—also on the question of what conclusions follow from the several uses of quotation marks.
2. At least at the most obvious and explicit level of that silence, there is little disagreement about the fact itself which has been the focus of numerous discussions. See, e.g., Jacques Derrida, *Of Spirit*; Victor Farías, *Heidegger and Nazism* (Philadelphia: Temple University Press, 1989); Luc Ferry and Alain Renaut, *Heidegger et les Modernes* (Paris: Grasset, 1988); "Symposium on Heidegger and Nazism," Arnold Davidson (ed.), *Critical Inquiry*, XV (1989), pp. 407–488; Günther Neske and Emil Kettering (eds.), *Martin Heidegger and National Socialism*, trans. Lisa Harries (New York: Paragon House, 1990). What subsequently divides the accounts of Heidegger's silence, of course, is the question of what elements constitute that silence and how they are to be interpreted.
3. For purposes of the account given here, I set the date of the dividing line—between pre- and post-Holocaust—at 1945. Obviously, the Holocaust had been going on during the four years before that; I use the 1945 date because after Germany's formal surrender not only did the systematic extermination cease but there can also be no doubt of Heidegger's awareness of the occurrence and extent of the genocide against the Jews.
4. In "Heidegger and the Jewish Question," forthcoming in *Remembering for the Future: II.*
5. This evidence has a positive form—in statements made by Heidegger himself, e.g., his denunciation in *1929* of the *Verjudung* [Jewification] of German culture; cf. Ulrich Sieg, "Die Verjudung des deutschen Geistes," in *Die Zeit*, December 22, 1989, p. 50; and in statements reported by others, such as his reference,

according to Karl Jaspers, to the "dangerous international fraternity of Jews; cf. Karl Jaspers, "Philosophical Autobiography," in P. A. Schilpp, (ed.), *The Philosophy of Karl Jaspers* (LaSalle, IL: Open Court, 1981, second edition), p. 75. And it has a negative form—in Heidegger's denials; for example, in his own variation on the cliche that "some of my best friends [for him, students] are [i.e., were] Jews." A more significant (because less persuasive) version of his denial of antisemitism is the emphasis he puts on his rejection of biological racism, as though by this rejection the charge of antisemitism would be conclusively refuted. (So, for example, his own reading of his Rectoral Address.) That the pre-Darwinian history of antisemitism *and* Nazi antisemitism reflected numerous sources and themes quite independent of genetic theory was something that he evidently was unwilling to consider.

6. Hannah Arendt, "For Martin Heidegger's Eightieth Birthday," in Neske and Kettering, *Martin Heidegger*, p. 210.
7. See Robert Faurisson, *Mémoire en défense* (Paris: La Vieille Taupe, 1980); Paul Rassinier, *Le Drame des Juifs européens* (Paris: Les Sept Couleurs, 1964); Arthur Butz, *The Hoax of the Twentieth Century* (Torrance, CA: Noontide Press, 1977).
8. I introduce this distinction provisionally and for the sake of argument, mainly because it would be easier (if the evidence warranted this) to take it back or overrule it later than to introduce it for the first time retroactively. The distinction represents in itself a substantive issue: What *is* the relation between Heidegger's "public" or exoteric statements and his more deliberately and technically philosophical texts? That the two were (at least at times) intended for different audiences (and thus, presumably, for different "implied readers") suggests an obvious point of difference, but neither this nor other stylistic factors entails incongruity or a sharp discontinuity between the two forms (although this position has been proposed, most radically by Richard Rorty). I believe, to the contrary, that the stylistic and substantive evidence argues for continuity and, indeed, often identity between the two forms; but since that is rather a separate issue from the central one raised here, I treat the evidence in the two categories separately (although the distinction is very sharp even when one *tries* to sustain it).
9. "Agriculture is now the mechanized food industry. Air is now set upon to yield nitrogen, the earth to yield ore, ore to yield uranium, for example; uranium is set upon to yield atomic energy, which can be released either for destruction or for peaceful use" ("The Question Concerning Technology" in Martin Heidegger, *The Question Concerning Technology and Other Essays*, trans. William Lovitt [New York: Harper & Row, 1977], p. 15).
10. See Ernst Nolte, *Das Vergehen der Vergangenheit: Antwort an meine Kritiker im sogenannten Historikerstreit* (Frankfurt/M: Ullstein, 1987).
11. If it was not—and the balance of evidence seems to point in that direction (see Rainer Marten, "Ein rassistisches Konzept von Humanität" in *Badische Zeitung*, December 19–20, 1987; see also Fred Dallmayr, "Heidegger and Politics," in Tom Rockmore and Joseph Margolis, *The Heidegger Case* [Philadelphia: Temple University Press, 1992], p. 292), then there seems no alternative to assessing Heidegger's claims to the contrary (in the *Spiegel* interview) at least as mistaken and at most as a lie. For the present discussion, at any rate, the parenthetical expression is no less significant in respect to Heidegger's silence than the assertion about National Socialism would be if it appeared *without* the parentheses
12. Reprinted in Richard Wolin (ed.), *The Heidegger Controversy* (Cambridge, MA: The MIT Press, 1992), p. 161.

13. Heidegger gave a television interview after the *Spiegel* interview, on the occasion of his eightieth birthday (broadcast on September 24, 1969), but in the preparatory discussion for that interview, he made clear to Richard Wisser, the interviewer, that he would not address questions concerning his own political past or, by implication, about the Nazi period more generally. (He mentions to Wisser that these are taken up in the *Spiegel* interview.) See Richard Wisser, "Afterthoughts and Gratitude," in Neske and Kettering, *Martin Heidegger*, pp. 89–124.
14. The "Law for the Restoration of the Professional Civil Service," which called for the expulsion of Jewish faculty, had been issued before Heidegger took office; thus he knew what he would be obliged to implement. This task was made easier because a number of Jewish faculty had been forced out of the university before he became Rector (see Hugo Ott, *Martin Heidegger: Unterwegs zu seiner Biographie* [Frankfurt/M: Athenaum, 1988], p. 171).
15. The statement appeared in the *Freiburger Studentenzeitung*, November 3, 1933, as part of an appeal by Heidegger as Rector for student support of Hitler's withdrawal of Germany from the League of Nations in the November 12 plebiscite on that matter. It is perhaps about these lines that Heidegger, in his January 20, 1948, letter to Herbert Marcuse, writes: "A few sentences in [the statement] I regard today as a slip [*Entgleisung*]. That is all."
16. Farías gives a conflicting account of that meeting. See Farías, *Heidegger and Nazism* p. 131.
17. Cited in Wolin, *The Heidegger Controversy* pp. 62, 64.
18. Letter to the Rector of the University of Freiburg, November 4, 1945, cited in Wolin, *The Heidegger Controversy* p. 64.
19. In Leo Strauss, *Persecution and the Art of Writing* (Glencoe, IL: The Free Press, 1952). Heidegger himself does not make this association, either with the tradition or with Strauss.

2

The Cries of Others and Heidegger's Ear: Remarks on the Agriculture Remark

ROBERT JOHN SHEFFLER MANNING

There are many very troubling issues and questions wrapped up in what has come to be known as the "Heidegger controversy" or the "Heidegger case," the philosopher's association with National Socialism. To what extent was Heidegger a believer in National Socialism? Which National Socialist policies did he believe in and which did he oppose? Is there any relation or continuity between his philosophy and his conservative politics? For how long was he associated with National Socialism? Was it an eleven-month blunder, or did he remain a loyal National Socialist throughout the war? What was his view of National Socialism after the war? What was his view of the Holocaust after the war when its full horror was revealed to all?

These are all very difficult questions to answer, and they have all rendered Heidegger at this point a very controversial and, indeed, a widely indicted figure. Of all these very contentious issues, perhaps the most contentious of all is the last mentioned, the question of Heidegger's attitude toward the Holocaust. In point of fact, there is not much ground upon which to build an answer to this question, because Heidegger maintained a determined silence on the Nazi extermination of the Jews. This silence has brought upon him severe condemnation. As Arnold Davidson correctly says, "for Lacoue-Labarthe, as for Blanchot and Levinas, Heidegger's silence concerning the Final Solution, his failure to pronounce the name of the Jews, is what remains beyond pardon."[1] Even so, it probably would have been better for Heidegger had he kept complete silence on the Holocaust, because as John Caputo has pointed out,[2] the few times he did mention the Holocaust have not helped his case but rather have severely damaged it.

Probably the most damaging and infamous remark in which Heidegger referred to the Holocaust occurred in a 1949 lecture on technology. Here Heidegger was not talking about the Holocaust directly but about the invasion of technology into agriculture:

> Agriculture is now a mechanized food industry. As for its essence, it is the same thing as the manufacture of corpses in the gas chambers and the death camps, the same thing as the blockades and reduction of countries to famine, the same thing as the manufacture of hydrogen bombs.[3]

Nearly everyone who has written on the Heidegger controversy has condemned this statement in the harshest terms. Thomas Sheehan refers to it as "damning beyond commentary."[4] Lacoue-Labarthe describes it as "scandalously insufficient."[5] Maurice Blanchot calls it a "terrible remark."[6] Richard Wolin states that the remark "suggests a fundamental incapacity for both moral and theoretical discernment."[7] Davidson says that when one considers this remark, "one cannot but be staggered by his [Heidegger's] inability—call it metaphysical inability—to acknowledge the everyday fate of bodies and souls. . . ."[8] The technology remark stunned Emmanuel Levinas, at once one of Heidegger's most important students and critics, into silence: "This stylistic turn of phrase, this analogy, this progression, are beyond commentary."[9] The remark has prompted John Caputo to write of the possible and the impossible. It is possible, he says, to understand the remark, "but I do not believe it is possible to remove the scandal" that the remark brings upon philosophy.[10]

It is possible to understand the remark. True, but have we yet done so? This is precisely the question I wish to raise. Have we yet understood this remark? But what would it mean to understand this remark? This, of course, would mean more than to merely understand what Heidegger meant by this remark. More importantly, to understand this remark would be to understand what this remark says about Heidegger, about his philosophy, and about the place of ethics, and correspondingly of human beings, in his philosophy. If to understand this remark means to understand all of these things, then I would argue that we have not yet understood this remark completely. We have understood it only superficially, only to the extent that it has provided us the occasion to criticize Heidegger and his insensitivity, his lack of ethics. We have not yet understood the remark in such a way that it challenges and criticizes not merely Heidegger but us, challenges and criticizes our own conception of ethics. In other words, we have only understood this remark in such a way that it renders Heidegger very separate from us, very different from us, and leaves us safe and secure and reaffirmed in our own morality. To understand this remark in a deeper sense, however, is, I believe, to become disturbed by the awareness that expressed within Heidegger's remark is a morality that is not nearly so far away from us and our own morality as we would like to think.

In order to clarify how Heidegger's agriculture remark has thus far been understood, I would like to present John Caputo's treatment of the remark in his essay "Heidegger's Scandal: Thinking and the Essence of the Victim." I choose Caputo's essay for several reasons. First, it is Caputo who treats this notorious remark most at length, and, secondly, his interpretation of it may be considered representative in that, in his more extended treatment of the remark, he comes to more or less the same conclusion as those who criticize the remark more summarily. In short, Caputo concludes that the remark reveals a certain lack of ethics in Heidegger's thought, and more specifically a lack of concern for actual, existing human beings. Finally, I choose Caputo's essay because he situates the interpretation of the remark within the same problematic that I wish to. He argues that the ethical deficiency of Heidegger's philosophy boils down to a certain deafness on Heidegger's part, a certain inability to hear.[11] Although I do not agree with the way Caputo resolves this auditory problematic, I too think that what most needs to be thought in and through the agriculture remark is the question of hearing. What or who is Heidegger able to hear? To what or to whom does he turn a deaf ear? This is why in my title I have suggested that the interpretation of the agriculture remark concerns Heidegger's ear.

Caputo begins his treatment by explaining what Heidegger is trying to say, that all the things Heidegger mentions—the mechanization of the food industry, the gas chambers and death-camps, the blockading of nations, the manufacture of hydrogen bombs—are manifestations of the essence of technology. He confesses that he is still troubled, still scandalized by this remark. Quickly, Caputo makes the interpretation of this remark a matter of hearing, of hearing correctly, and of what is not heard: "Have we failed to hear the thinker? Or has the thinker failed to hear everything that calls, failed to respond to everything that addresses him, failed in his responsibility?"[12]

Caputo's unsettling question raises another question. Though Heidegger's remark makes a certain sense and may be quite logical, still there is something monstrously insensitive to it. In making this remark, what did Heidegger not hear? What was he deaf to, a deafness which enabled him to articulate this monstrous equation? Caputo first answers this in the form of a question: "Is there not something deeply unsettling in a thinking that is anaesthetized before unspeakable suffering, deaf to the cries of the victim?"[13]

First, Caputo asks a question, but very soon he proffers an answer. This answer comes repeatedly, incessantly, in the most direct and severe tone. This answer answers the question not merely of what Heidegger meant by the statement, but more importantly, answers the question of what this remark means for Heidegger's philosophy and for the place of ethics and of people in his philosophy. It answers the question of what Heidegger could and could not hear, of Heidegger's ear: "Nowhere in the call of Being is the cry of the victim to be heard, nowhere the plea for mercy, the summons for help. The silent peal of Being is deaf to the appeal of suffering."[14] Again, Caputo will level the accusation that Heidegger may hear and respond to the Call of Being, but in Heidegger's world "a wholly other kind of responsiveness and responsibility has been silenced, a responsibility to those who live and die, to those who are embodied, who suffer or are in pain, who grow old and infirm—above all, to innocent victims. The thinker leaves no room at all for the victim in the history of Being's self-showing."[15] Again, even more directly, louder: "That is why the gas chamber is the same as the tractor, as motorized farm equipment. The victim is invisible in the history of Being, is not a matter of concern, is not what is at issue. The victim does not come toward us and concern us (*an-wesen, angehen*) in the history of Being, does not call to us. The victim has no voice in the call of Being, cannot speak, cannot be heard."[16]

Caputo's answer is clear and unmistakable: The problem revealed within and by the agriculture remark is a problem of Heidegger's ear, of his hearing, of what he is unable to hear. Heidegger can hear the call of Being, but he cannot hear the call of people, especially the victim, the suffering, the Other. This is why Heidegger could never have an adequate ethics within his philosophy. And this inability to actually hear other human beings goes far in explaining why and how Heidegger—for eleven months or eleven years or even longer—could willingly associate himself with National Socialism. Now it all makes sense.

And after all, didn't Levinas tell us all this? Sure, he tried to tell us this a long time ago, before we knew him, when he was too Other to us to actually be heard by us. Now, however, things are different. Now we hear him. Now, in fact, we would be embarrassed to say that we didn't hear him, or at least hear of him. And we are comforted by the fact that Levinas says of Heidegger what Caputo says of Heidegger: that Heidegger heard the call of Being, but he did not, could not hear the call of people.[17] We are comforted by the fact that we are not like Heidegger, but like Levinas. We hear the call of people. We are comforted by proving our differences with Heidegger by testifying to our own hearing abilities, to our own ability to hear other people. And what better way to do this than to hear Levinas and to echo Levinas? This is exactly what Caputo does in his essay when he writes of that "wholly other kind of responsiveness and responsibility,"[18] and when he asks if the matter for thought "be more profoundly disrupted by an otherness to which it has systematically made itself deaf,"[19] and when he asks "What if, rather, thinking would become thoughtful concern for the Other, responsiveness to the call of the Other?"[20]

With this, the case is closed. What the agriculture remark reveals about Heidegger's philosophy and its lack of ethics and its absence of people is fully explicated. Heidegger is pronounced deaf to other people and, hence, unethical and unlike Caputo, Levinas, and all who are capable of hearing the voices of other people.[21] Now the battle is over. Heidegger has lost and Levinas, Caputo, and we have won. Our victory consists in the increased security of our good conscience that we obtain from passing a very well-reasoned judgment upon the peculiar and unethical deafness of Heidegger's ear.

As well reasoned and reasonable as this judgment on Heidegger's agriculture remark is, complications arise. The unavoidable fact is that Heidegger was at least not always deaf to all others. At least in some texts, the voices of other people do speak and are heard by Heidegger.

This is nowhere more evident than in *Being and Time*, with its extended discussion of Being-with (*Mitsein*) and Dasein-with (*Mitdasein*). It is true that Heidegger in *Being and Time* presents the crowd, the "They" (*Das Mann*), as a negative influence upon Dasein, and that Dasein must get away from the crowd's pressures to conform through the process of individuation in order to achieve authenticity. This fact is very often stated by those who wish to argue that there is a deficient depiction of sociality in Heidegger's philosophy.[22] However, what is heard less often in *Being and Time* is Heidegger's constant insistence that even the Dasein who flees from the crowd and individuates does not do so as a separate individual away from all other persons. This is because Being-with others is for Heidegger "equiprimordial with Being-in-the-world."[23] In other words, one could no more flee from Being-with than one could flee from Being-in-the-World, because Being-with others is as basic a component or aspect of the structure of Dasein as Being-in-the-World.[24] We are in our very being Being-with others, and the World I am always already immersed in "is always the one that I share with Others. The World of *Dasein* is a with-world. Being-in is Being-with."[25] We are Being-with others always already, and we cease being this only when our Being-toward-death becomes Being-at-an-end, or in other words, only when we die.

But what does Heidegger say about the Others with whom I always am as Being-with? Who are these others? Heidegger wishes to make clear that he is not talking about an isolated subject, identifying others who are separate and stand apart: "By 'Others' we do not mean everyone else but me—those over against whom the 'I' stands out. They are rather those from whom one does not distinguish oneself—those among whom one is too."[26]

For Heidegger, Being-with means "Being-there-too" among others, and "the 'too' means a sameness of Being as circumspectively concernful Being-in-the-world."[27]

And what is for Heidegger the nature of the relationship one has with those others from whom one does not distinguish oneself, those others among whom one is too? Heidegger is quick to point out that other Dasein are not the objects of mere concern, like one has concern for things, but rather of a much more penetrating and embracing concern which Heidegger calls "solicitude" (*Fursorge*). Of course, for Heidegger, as always, there are deficient and positive modes of solicitude. "Being for, against, or without one another, passing one another by, not 'mattering' to one another—these are possible ways of solicitude." Heidegger insists, however, that these are deficient modes of solicitude, and he contrasts them with two positive modes.[28] Positive solicitude can "leap in for the Other" or "leap ahead of him." Leaping in for entails taking the other's concerns away from her and upon oneself. Leaping ahead entails not taking the other's care away, but rather giving the Other's care back to him authentically for the first time.[29] These positive modes of solicitude reveal the truth of Dasein as Being-with, that Dasein exists not only with others, but also for others: "As Being-with, *Dasein* 'is' essentially for the sake of others."[30]

As we can see, in *Being and Time* Heidegger makes clear his contention that to live authentically, we must understand ourselves correctly, and part of our correct understanding of ourselves is the fact that we exist always already with and for others. The question then presses upon us: If Caputo is correct in his explication of the meaning of the agriculture remark, then what happened to Heidegger's own solicitude toward others? Where did it go? When did it go? When did he lose his ability to hear the voices of others? For, if Caputo's interpretation of the agriculture remark is on track, and in light of Heidegger's emphasis in *Being and Time* on Being-with and on the positive modes of solicitude, it cannot be that Heidegger was always deaf to others. Rather, the issue then becomes a matter of Heidegger's losing his hearing. And the question then becomes: When and how did he become deaf to others. When and how did he lose his hearing? This raises the ugly possibility that Heidegger didn't just lose his hearing, but that he had it stolen away. But by whom? By the war and its atrocities? By the Nazis?

But this assumes too much. This assumes that Caputo is correct in his interpretation of the meaning of the agriculture remark, and this is exactly what we wish to throw into question, to continually question. The way to do this, the way to determine where or whether Heidegger ever lost his hearing, is to read some of Heidegger's texts between 1927 and the agriculture remark of 1949, to see if in these texts Heidegger exhibits solicitude toward others, to see if in these texts Heidegger's ear is capable of hearing others.

Let us begin with a text from early 1934, a notorious text from the period of Heidegger's rectorate. The Nazi administration of the city of Freiburg had found employment for six hundred unemployed laborers. In February of 1934, the workers marched to the largest lecture hall of the University of Freiburg for the official beginning of their National Socialist education. The workers were greeted warmly in a speech by the Rector of the University, Martin Heidegger.[31]

Heidegger begins by remarking on the uniqueness of this occasion, this heretofore "unheard of event," the encounter between the workers and the students and professors of the university. Heidegger then asks: "What does this event mean?" Heidegger makes clear his belief that the great significance of this event lies in the greater awareness of the true bond that exists between the workers and the educated classes. The workers will be taught by the students of the university, who are ready to help, but who look at themselves not as scholars, but as comrades. The students, says Heidegger,

> will not come to you as "educated" people condescending to a class, or even a "lower class," of uneducated men, but as comrades. They will listen to your questions, your needs, your difficulties and your doubts, talk these through with you, and by your common work bring you to clarity, freedom and decision."[32]

Heidegger then asks again: "What does it mean that we are met here in this hall of the university?" It is he says, a sign of a new common resolve "to throw up a bridge between those who labor with their hands and those who perform brain work." He goes on to celebrate the unity that exists between scholars and workers, because "every worker is a learned man in his own way." Heidegger insists that the knowledge a farmer or a miner or a lumberjack possesses is not fundamentally different from the knowledge of an educated scholar. This National Socialism understands, that knowledge and its possession do not "divide the classes, but rather bind and unite the people in the one great will of the State."[33] This can happen only if scholars and everyone else realize that "the production of the miner is not fundamentally less spiritual than the action of the scholar."[34]

If we analyze this speech from the perspective of both the loss of concern for people in Caputo's reading of the agriculture remark and the discussion of Being-with and solicitude in *Being and Time*, what must we say? As notorious and as politically objectionable as this text is, aren't we forced to admit that this text is also a celebration of Being-with? Far from not being concerned with others, Heidegger here in this text is not only welcoming others but also showing that the Dasein of scholars is actually Being-with the Dasein of workers, that the workers are those others from whom one is not distinct, those others "among whom one is too." Heidegger's entire speech, his attitude toward the workers assembled before him, could very easily be defended and interpreted as the unfolding of positive solicitude, authentic Being-with. In fact, what Heidegger says about the students' comportment toward the workers and about what the students will do and will help the workers do could well be seen as a precise example of the positive mode of solicitude that Heidegger in *Being and Time* calls "leaping ahead."

Clearly, if Caputo is correct in saying that the agriculture remark reveals that in Heidegger's thought there is no room for people, this speech reveals that, at least in early 1934, near the end of Heidegger's rectorate, Heidegger's thought still exhibited solicitude for others. This speech shows that Heidegger's ear was not deaf to the voices of others, at least not yet.

Let us look at another text from 1934, this one written after he had resigned the rectorate. He was offered, for a second time, a position at the University of Berlin. He turned it down, and in March of 1934 in a newspaper article explained why, in what may be the most self-revealing text Heidegger ever wrote, "Why Do I Stay in the Provinces?"[35] Here again, Heidegger celebrates Being-with, his own sense of his own Being-with the peasants in the Black Forest, among whom he is too. His philosophical work, he says, is not aloof and removed, but rather

> belongs right in the midst of the peasants' work. When the young farmboy drags his heavy sled up the slope and guides it, piled high with beech logs, down the dangerous descent to his house, when the herdsman, lost in thought and slow of step, drives his calf up the slope, when the farmer in his shed gets the countless shingles ready for his roof, my work is of the same sort. It is intimately rooted in and related to the life of the peasants.[36]

He explains that the inner-relatedness of his work to the Black Forest and its people "comes from a centuries-long and irreplaceable rootedness in the Alemmannian-Swabian Soil."[37]

Again, this text clearly reveals Heidegger's own sense of Being-with others. Indeed, Heidegger is unusually unabashed about testifying to his sense of connectedness with others, even to the point of being overly sentimental and romantic.[38] Certainly, it would be a strange prejudice to accuse Heidegger, at least at this time, of living in a world without others, of living without connection to and concern for others. Quite the contrary, Heidegger's connection to and concern for others seems to be a very big part of who Heidegger is, of his own Dasein. These two texts of 1934 go far to show that Heidegger himself lived the existence of authentic Dasein, which, as Being-with, "'is' essentially for the sake of Others."[39]

Let us move beyond the 1930s to a text much nearer in time to the agriculture remark of 1949, to the very important text Heidegger wrote in 1947 in the form of a letter to Jean Beaufret, the "Letter on Humanism."[40] Surely here, in this letter where Heidegger insists that his philosophy is not a humanism, we will see evidence of the same lack of concern for others and of the same deafness to human beings that Caputo says are expressed in the agriculture remark.

A very superficial reading of "Letter on Humanism" may very well support this suspicion. After all, Heidegger not only denies that his philosophy is a humanism, but he also states that it opposes humanism: "The thinking of *Being and Time* is against humanism."[41] However, the reasons Heidegger gives for opposing humanism may surprise us. He says that the problem with humanism is that even its "highest determinations of the essence of man . . . still do not realize the proper dignity of man."[42] Humanism is opposed not because it values humanity so highly, but because it "does not set the *humanitas* of man high enough."[43]

If this is not enough to convince us that even in 1947 Heidegger had not yet become deaf to and unconcerned about other human beings, Heidegger in this text directly raises the question of whether his thinking entails a concern for humanity. When Heidegger writes that man must prepare himself to be claimed by Being, he asks: "But in the claim upon man, in the attempt to make man ready for this claim, is there not implied a concern about man?"[44] Heidegger not only affirms this but expresses that this is obvious when he then asks: "Where else does 'care' [the Being of Dasein] tend but in the direction of bringing man back to his essence? What else does that in turn betoken but that man become human?"[45] Heidegger then clearly answers the question he has just posed: "Thus *humanitas* really does remain the concern of such thinking."

Heidegger goes on to give his own definition of humanism. This definition he will not eschew but will take upon himself and his philosophy, a definition he will employ in maintaining that his own thinking is "humanism in the extreme sense":[46] "For this is humanism: meditating and caring, that man be human and not inhumane, 'inhuman,' that is, outside his essence." This prompts Heidegger to raise another question: "But in what does the humanity of man consist? It lies in his essence."[47]

Our humanity lies in our essence. And what has Heidegger said about the essence of Dasein in *Being and Time*? And what has Heidegger not only said about the essence of human beings in the world, but shown about it in a personal way in the two texts of 1934? Clearly, Heidegger has said and shown that the essence of Dasein is Being-with others.

In light of these three Heideggerian texts leading up to the text on technology in 1949 and its agriculture remark, what can we say? Are we not left with two possibilities: Either Caputo is correct in his reading of the Heidegger remark, which would entail that Heidegger's profound concern for others, which seems to be as much a part of his own being as Being-with, somehow evaporated or fell by the wayside sometime between 1947, the time of the "Letter on Humanism," and 1949, or Caputo is in some way off the mark in his interpretation of the agriculture remark. This would mean that we need a new way to think the meaning of the agriculture remark, of what it means for Heidegger's philosophy and for the role of ethics and of other people in Heidegger's philosophy.

Obviously, I don't think it very likely that Heidegger dropped his concern for others, stopped being Being-with in 1949, stopped being what was obviously so important a part of his own Being-in-the-World. I would propose instead that we think and hear the agriculture remark differently. Instead of hearing in the remark the absence of Being-with, I propose that we hear the remark just as it is possible to hear the "Letter on Humanism" and "Why Do I Stay in the Provinces?" and the speech Heidegger gave to the workers who came to the university in 1934, as a concernful saying of Being-with, as an act of positive solicitude for and with those others among whom Heidegger always was too.

I believe we can hear this remark in this way if we listen closely to what Heidegger is actually saying, and to the concerns which drove him to make this remark. What is Heidegger talking about in this remark? Certainly, he is not talking about the Holocaust. That is not the subject of his remark, but something he mentions in passing to make a point about something else. Did Heidegger really break his silence on the Holocaust with this remark? He certainly didn't mean to, certainly didn't make the Holocaust the subject of his remarks. Clearly, here he was talking about something else. About what?

About agriculture. Listen closely to the remark: "Agriculture is now a mechanized food industry. As to its essence, it is the same as. . . ." And then Heidegger mentions the analogous phenomena: gas chambers, death-camps, blockades, reduction of countries to famine, hydrogen bombs. What does Heidegger mean by "its essence" and by "it"? Agriculture, or more specifically, the mechanization of agriculture—that is what Heidegger is talking about.

But what does philosophy have to do with agriculture? Why is Heidegger, a philosopher, talking as a philosopher about agriculture? Doesn't this seem odd? How many times do philosophers talk about agriculture? Even though I myself grew up in rural Pennsylvania and spent some time on a farm, and even though I teach in the Middle West and have as students many farmers and daughters and sons of farmers, I don't believe I have ever made a philosophical reference to agriculture either in my writing or in my teaching. Why is Heidegger the philosopher talking about agriculture?

We can come to an answer to this question if we consider what Heidegger is saying about agriculture. He is saying that agriculture is now a mechanized industry. What does this mean? It means in one sense simply that tractors and combines and other large equipment have replaced the plough and other primitive tools, saving people hours of monotonous, back-breaking labor and producing more food in the process. So what is to be decried here? In another sense, however, the fact that farming has been turned into a mechanized industry means that the days of smaller farms, where people work by hand the same lands that their relatives before them worked in the same way for hundreds of years, are gone. In the first sense, looking at the issue simply in terms of efficiency of production, there is no problem. However, one can think, one can hear a very serious problem if one thinks of the situation in the other way, from the viewpoint of the small farmers, the peasants, meaning the people of the country, if one hears the sound of the tractors in the same way that the peasants may hear them, and so interprets the mechanization of the food industry with the ear of a peasant, with an ear attuned to the life of the peasantry.

Heidegger heard in the mechanization of the food industry a very ominous sound. He listened to it with the ear of a peasant, with an ear attuned to the voices of and the concerns of the peasants. This is the startling thing we must think about the agriculture remark. As insensitive as the remark is, it is not a remark that reveals Heidegger's total insensitivity, his inability to hear everyone, his lack of concern for all others. Rather, and quite to the contrary, Heidegger's agriculture remark exists only because of Heidegger's ability to hear some others. His remark is not the denial of Being-with others but a genuine expression of Heidegger's own sense of Being-with. The remark expresses Heidegger's positive solicitude with and toward his fellow German peasants, those others among whom he was too, those others whom he always heard, those others to whom he always turned (can it be?) a very acute, sensitive ear. Heidegger's ability to hear others led him to make the remark. His Being-with others was the reason why he was talking about agriculture in the first place.

If the remark is an expression of Heidegger's Being-with and concern for others, rather than the absolute absence of this, then what can we say about the agriculture remark, about its meaning, about what it means for Heidegger's philosophy and the place of ethics in Heidegger's philosophy? We can learn from the agriculture remark what we can learn from *Being and Time*, and from the two texts of 1934, and from the "Letter on Humanism," and from most if not all of Heidegger's texts: that Heidegger was not asocial monster living absolutely solipsistically in the isolated stratosphere of philosophy, totally shorn from any involvement with or concern for other human beings. And it is also not true that in all his philosophizing, his "thinking" as he arrogantly put it, he only cared for Being, and not a whit for humanity, as if for Heidegger Being and humanity were so distinct from one another that one could somehow separate them and prefer one to the other. Heidegger's texts, including the agriculture remark as we have understood it, testify against this notion.

What the agriculture remark and all the texts we have examined testify to is that Heidegger did hear the voices of some others, that he did have genuine solicitude for some others. Yet the scandal within the agriculture remark remains. It still stands as a towering testament to insensitivity. How could he compare the regrettable fact that because of technology there will be fewer peasants, slow of step,[48] thoughtfully planting seeds in the ground with the monstrous, intolerable fact of the willful and planned extermination of six million innocent people? This dumbfounded question expresses the shock and the scandal that Heidegger's remark causes, a shock and a scandal that momentarily stops thinking in its tracks.

Yet, when thinking begins again, we see that the answer to our question lies within the remark itself, and within the "Letter on Humanism," and within the two texts from 1934, and within *Being and Time*, and perhaps within everything Heidegger ever wrote and said, and perhaps within everything he maintained silence about.[49] Heidegger did have concern for others, and this concern speaks itself in the agriculture remark. But what also speaks itself here is that Heidegger had concern only for some others, for his others, for those with whom he was, for those among whom he was too, for those who were near, for those whose destiny it was to dwell with him in their particular neighborhood of Being.

This should not surprise us if we read *Being and Time* closely. When he discusses Being-with others, he says that by "Others" he does not mean everyone else but me, but only certain others, only "those from whom, for the most part, one does not distinguish oneself—those among whom one is too." But what does this mean? "The 'too' means a sameness of Being as circumspectively concernful Being in the World." What has Heidegger said? It is a basic constitutive aspect of our Dasein that we are thrown into a certain world at a certain place and at a certain time with certain others whose destiny it is to also be thrown into this same world at this same place and in this same time. Because of this destiny, we are Being-with others, but not with all others, but only with those others with whom we share "a sameness of Being." Hence, it is a basic, constitutive aspect of our Being that we exist within solicitude not toward all others, but toward certain others, toward those others with whom we share "a sameness of Being," meaning toward those others with whom we were thrown into Being at the same time and place.[50]

What Heidegger says very clearly here is that we are Being-with. We exist within and out of a concern for others, for the others who share our destiny, for the others who are like us, for the others who are near. In *Being and Time*, Heidegger is at great pains to explicate the simple fact that we are most concerned with those other human beings who are like us and near us. Or, in Heideggerian terms, it is part of our *Geworfenheit*, our thrownness into the world, that we are thrown together with certain other human beings and that we exist within and out of a certain concern for those who are near and with whom we share a sameness of Being.

Heidegger insists that it is out of this original concern for the near ones, this solidarity that he calls solicitude, that all ethics and all values systems are developed. This is why Heidegger maintained that he was not interested in ethics, while also insisting that this did not make him unethical. He was not interested in ethics because it was, as he said, secondary, derivative.[51] Ethics comes to pass only after the more originary, basic constitutive state of Being-with, of solicitude toward those others with whom we are, those others who are near. We develop ethics out of our natural connection to and bond with our neighbors. Here "neighbors" means exactly what it does in German, *Nachbar*, near dwellers, those who dwell near.

The fact of the matter is that Heidegger spoke the agriculture remark out of his very real and genuine concern for his neighbors, for those who dwelled near him, for those with whom he shared a sameness of Being: the German peasants he smoked with, and conversed with, and kept silence with, and dressed like,[52] and wrote so romantically about, and belonged to, and, in his own eyes at least, was. And it is also a fact that, for Heidegger, it is perfectly natural to be most concerned with his neighbors, with those who dwell near and are like him. Perfectly natural, or in Heideggerian terms, part of the destiny of Being, or in the language of the "Letter of Humanism," inside our essence.

Heideggerian thought is a celebration, a glorification, perhaps even a worshipping, a hallowing of what is perfectly natural, of what is, of what is given in Being. Heideggerian thought baptizes the natural with the grand vocabulary (what Adorno called the jargon) of Being. This is why, from a certain perspective, say a uniquely Jewish perspective (which is not to say that there are not Jewish perspectives), Heideggerian thought is not post-Christian nearly as much as it is pre-Christian and pre-Jewish, in other words, pagan. This is the perspective that came very early and very clearly from Heidegger's sharpest critics: Theodor Adorno, Emmanuel Levinas, and Hans Jonas.[53] From a Roman Catholic perspective, Heidegger's hallowing of what is may be a reaffirmation of Grace operating in nature, and from a Protestant perspective it may be an authentic encounter with the power of the divine within our own existential condition. Or it may be the denial and the ultimate sacrifice of that prophetically inspired critical capacity that Tillich referred to as the Protestant Principle. This possibility Christian theology, especially Protestant theology, still so influenced by Heidegger and Tillich, still needs to think.

However one feels about Heidegger's glorification of the natural, the fact is that as humans we do feel closer to, more connected with, more concerned about those who are near and who are like us. This is natural. To live like this is to live inside our essence. What most concerns us is what is near, what is similar, what is ours: our family, our friends, our race, our gender, our class, our city, our neighborhood within the city, our country, our fellow Americans. This is our natural orientation in the world. Very few of us live in the world in the way that John Berryman's novelist does:

> —It takes me so long to read the paper,
> Said to me one day a novelist hot as a firecracker,
> because I have to identify myself with everyone in it,
> including the corpses, pal.[54]

Most of us, instead, read the newspapers and watch CNN, and remain unmoved as long as it doesn't involve us or someone we care about, someone among whom we are too, someone we know. We may feel sorry and think it terrible, but we do not feel it in the same way we would feel it if the murder we read about in the morning paper or see on the news is the murder of our own child or friend.

Heidegger knew about the Holocaust. There is no evidence to think that he approved of it.[55] He probably thought it regrettable. He mentioned it in passing. But he did not feel it, did not feel it in the way he certainly would have felt it if the victims, rather than some of the perpetrators,[56] had been his neighbors, German peasants near and like him. If this had happened to his people, Heidegger would have been very affected, very moved, and he would have made it the matter for his thinking. What happened to his people is what he felt, what he heard, what he made the matter for thinking. This is why this remark is not about the Holocaust, but about how technology will affect the lives of the German peasants.

The remark remains, of course, monstrous, and we rightly marvel at Heidegger's insensitivity, his inability to feel the pain of others who aren't his others. Yet, in the baldness of the remark is an honesty. Most of us don't really feel the pain of others we don't know and aren't concerned with. The difference between how little Heidegger felt for the victims of the Holocaust compared to how much he would have felt if the victims had been Germans like him is analogous to the difference between the way we feel about the Kurds or the Bosnians compared to the way we would feel if someone were trying to practice "ethnic cleansing" on us and on our families and on our neighbors.[57]

This analogy does not remove the scandal from Heidegger's remark. It makes it more scandalous. It makes it our scandal in that it shows that Heidegger may not be as different from us as we would like to think. Like us, Heidegger had others who were his, his neighbors, those he was concerned about and heard, and he had other others who were strangers, who were not his concern, who never moved into his neighborhood of Being and so were never heard. And he accepted this as natural, as part of the essence of our humanity, and he lived as much as he could in positive modes of solicitude toward his others and in good conscience.

Are we really so different? Are we entitled to the moral outrage we can in such good conscience vent at Heidegger's agriculture remark? Or would it be better to use the agriculture remark to examine ourselves and the difference between the way we think of and hear the others who are near and like us and the others whose cries for the most part go unheard by us? But that would involve venturing into the risk of thinking that the good conscience we obtain from living with genuine concern for some others may not be in truth good conscience, but may actually be too easy conscience. And this experience of having other others continually trouble our good conscience by revealing it as too easy conscience may actually be, not the ethical life, but the life of ethics.[58]

This continual troubling of our good conscience by other others is always ethically and politically urgent, as we are always in danger of remaining within the good conscience of Heidegger, of always hearing and caring for the others who are near and similar while turning a deaf ear toward other others. Have we not seen recently within our society a diabolical manifestation of this tendency? When Saddam Hussein began to practice "ethnic cleansing" on the Kurds, did America and other countries and peoples not turn the same deaf ear that Heidegger turned toward the victims of the Holocaust? And are we not turning the same deaf ear now to the hundreds of thousands of Bosnian victims of another campaign of "ethnic cleansing"? But we responded very differently when Saddam Hussein invaded a country friendly to us, with whom we were bonded in the firm solicitude of many very important and lucrative financial dealings, and where our own vital, material interests were at stake. How did we respond as a nation? We resolved to learn from our mistakes in Vietnam and to stand united behind the mission of our country and our men and women in uniform over there. And we rightly stood in genuine Being-with with every casualty we suffered. Meanwhile, quietly, with great stealth and precision, and away from the carefully manipulated media, we inflicted what? What must it be? Seven thousand? Eight thousand? Ten thousand casualties for every one we suffered? Were these victims heard? Did these other others trouble our conscience?[59] How did the war make us feel about ourselves? We felt better, prouder of our soldiers and of ourselves. This time, we had not let ourselves become divided but stood together with our soldiers, took the proper care of our people in the Armed Forces, and got the job done right. Through this recent experience, have we turned toward ourselves as a nation and toward the enemy victims of that war a fundamentally different ear than the one Heidegger in the agriculture remark turned toward German peasants and toward the victims of the Holocaust?

The agriculture remark does speak out to us its monstrous insensitivity. It is a scandal. Within it, evil speaks. But the remark is not as easily understood as it appears. Then again, as Levinas warns, neither is evil, which is not limited to the wickedness easily heard and recognized by all. Evil, says Levinas, is sneaky. "It enters where it will" and it is often very difficult to discern. This is why "intellectual effort is needed to recognize it."[60] It is almost as if Levinas were warning us that in order to fully hear evil we must develop a different ear.

NOTES

1. See Davidson's essay "Opening the Debate," in *Critical Inquiry*, 15.2 (Winter 1989), p. 424. Habermas could well be added to the list. He writes in a rather odd passage that "Heidegger's entanglement with National Socialism is one thing, which we can leave to the morally sober judgment of later generations. But his conduct after the war is quite another. That affects us." See Jürgen Habermas, "Work and Weltanschauung: The Heidegger Controversy from a German Perspective" in the number of *Critical Inquiry* cited above.
2. In his essay "Heidegger's Scandal: Thinking and the Essence of the Victim," in Tom Rockmore and Joseph Margolis (eds.), *The Heidegger Case* (Philadelphia: Temple University Press, 1992), Caputo says "when the silence is broken, the scandal worsens" (p. 265).
3. Thomas Sheehan rendered this translation of the remark in his "Heidegger and the Nazis," in *The New York Review of Books*, June 16, 1988, pp. 41–43.
4. Ibid., p. 41.
5. Quoted by Davidson, "Opening the Debate," p. 423.
6. See Blanchot's "Thinking the Apocalypse: A letter from Maurice Blanchot to Catherine David," in the above cited number of *Critical Inquiry*, pp. 475–480.
7. Richard Wolin, *The Politics of Being: The Political Thought of Martin Heidegger* (New York: Columbia University Press, 1990), p. 167.
8. Davidson, "Opening the Debate," p. 424.
9. Emmanuel Levinas, "As if Consenting to Horror," in the above cited number of *Critical Inquiry*, p. 487.
10. Caputo, "Heidegger's Scandal," p. 276.
11. It was actually Theodor W. Adorno, in his very harsh attack on Heidegger's philosophy throughout *The Jargon of Authenticity* (Evanston: Northwestern University Press, 1973), who first raised the issue of Heidegger's deafness. Although it takes so much advantage of its ability to listen, charges Adorno,

Heidegger's philosophy actually "renders itself deaf to words. The emphatic nature of this philosophy arouses the belief that it fits itself into words, while it is only a cover for arbitrariness" (p. 58).

12. Caputo, "Heidegger's Scandal," p. 269.
13. Ibid., p. 275.
14. Ibid., p. 277.
15. Ibid., p. 277.
16. Ibid., p. 278.
17. Edith Wyschogrod, in her fine book *Spirit in Ashes: Hegel, Heidegger, and Man-Made Mass Death* (New Haven: Yale University Press, 1985), has a similar view of Heidegger's thinking, which she says is concerned with Being and with rivers and dams, but not with persons.
18. Caputo, "Heidegger's Scandal," p. 277.
19. Ibid., p. 279.
20. Ibid., p. 272.
21. By saying this, I am not trying to further what I regard as an erroneous interpretation of Levinas's reading of Heidegger, which one can find clearly in Farías' "Foreword to the Spanish Edition of *Heidegger and Nazism*," included in *The Heidegger Case*. Here (p. 337) Farías says that Levinas accuses Heidegger of constructing a philosophy incapable of founding an ethics. In my *Interpreting Otherwise Than Heidegger: Emmanuel Levinas's Ethics as First Philosophy* (Pittsburgh: Duquesne University Press, 1993), I have tried to show that Levinas does recognize what might be considered the ethical aspects of Heidegger's thought in constructing his own radical conception of ethics in his own philosophy.
22. Representative of this would be Richard Wolin, who, in *The Politics of Being* (p. 49), says that in *Being and Time* "the ontic sphere in general—worldliness in its entirety—has been colonized by the They. Here, we can see that Heidegger's pessimistic philosophical anthropology and his joyless social ontology join forces. The result is a rare devaluation of the life-world, that delicate substratum of everyday sociation which existential phenomenology claims to redeem."
23. Heidegger, *Being and Time*, trans. John Macquarrie and Edward Robinson (New York: Harper & Row, Publishers, 1962), p. 149. Despite Heidegger's insistence upon this point in *Being and Time*, Habermas, in his essay "Work and Weltanschauung" (p. 439), says of Heidegger: "Attributing a merely derivative status to *Mitsein*, he also misses the dimension of sociality and intersubjectivity."
24. Thus, I cannot agree with Edith Wyschogrod when she writes in *Spirit in Ashes* (p. 203) that Heidegger's concept of Dasein "suggests man's relation to world and things instead of to other persons," as if for Heidegger Dasein's relation to the world could somehow not include Dasein's relation to other people.
25. Heidegger, *Being and Time*, p. 155.
26. Ibid., p. 154.
27. Ibid.
28. Habermas in "Work and Weltanschauung" dismisses the positive modes of solicitude when he says (p. 439) that the "social contexts of life remained for him a dimension of the inauthentic." Similarly, Wolin in *The Politics of Being* states (p. 50) that "the category of Being-with others seems relegated a priori to the sphere of inauthentic dealings."
29. Heidegger, *Being and Time*, pp. 158–159.
30. Ibid., p. 160. Wyschogrod, in *Spirit in Ashes* (p. 166), gives these passages on Being-with in *Being and Time* a very different interpretation than the one that

I am attempting to render. Solicitude, for Heidegger, according to her, means that "I help the other with some matter, with work or in seeing his or her ownmost task. . . . But such relations as love, sexuality, and friendship, which occur primordially as relations between persons, circumvent the world, and represent a sphere of limited freedom, play no part in Heidegger's analysis." In contrast, my reading will argue that such primordial relationships with those who are near play a very significant role in Heidegger's analysis of Being and of Dasein.

31. One can find an English translation of this speech in Dagobert Runes, *German Existentialism* (New York: Philosophical Library, Inc., 1965), pp. 37–42.
32. Ibid., p. 39.
33. Ibid., p. 41.
34. Ibid., p. 42.
35. Translated by Thomas Sheehan and included in his *Heidegger: The Man and the Thinker* (Chicago: Precedent, 1981), pp. 27–30.
36. Heidegger, "Provinces," p. 28. This may sound very pastoral and bucolic, but when we see how close this is to the speech given by Burte, a high Nazi official, in 1940, wherein he declares that "intellectuals belong to the people or they are nothing," this beautiful and romantic little piece by Heidegger rightly becomes ominous and far from innocent. See Burte's text in George Mosse, *Nazi Culture* (New York: Schocken Books, 1983).
37. This is only one of many Heideggerian references to the concept of rootedness, of being rooted in the soil, in the *Volk*, in the blood, in the life of the peasantry, and in Being. Although here I am trying to make the point that Heidegger must be understood not as a solitary thinker unconcerned with others but as a thinker very much with and rooted in certain others, I am far from declaring Heidegger's notions of Being-with and rootedness innocent and unproblematic. George Mosse, in his lifetime of work dedicated to explicating the pre-Nazi and Nazi ideology, has made very clear the central and infamous role played by the mystical belief in being rooted in Germany's soil and in the blood of her peasantry. See especially *The Crisis of German Ideology* (New York: Schocken Books, 1976). These ideas were important steps on the way to Auschwitz, and the fact that they play a central role in Heidegger's philosophy, and not just merely in the political texts of 1933–34, indicates just how much has to be thought in thinking about Heidegger's Nazism, and just what the stakes are. Of course, Adorno long ago warned us of the dangers involved in Heidegger's employment of the concept of rootedness. See Adorno's discussion in *The Jargon of Authenticity* (pp. 54ff), where he declares that "rootedness" in Heidegger's jargon "puffs itself up" and serves as the cover for something dark.
38. Wyschogrod, in *Spirit in Ashes* (pp. 188–189), cites Heidegger's references to the life of peasants as a good example of how he "often resorts uncritically to pretechnological romantic models." Interestingly, Wyschogrod says that as a philosopher, Heidegger didn't really have the life of a peasant, but lived among peasants in the manner of a person on vacation. She perhaps exhibits a peculiar prejudice when she states that the philosophical life "demands hearers, a thinking with (Mitdenken), and is not, in its essence, a life comparable to that of a peasant."
39. Heidegger, *Being and Time*, p. 160.
40. See the "Letter on Humanism" in David Krell (ed.), *Martin Heidegger: Basic Writings* (Harper & Row, 1977), pp. 189–242.
41. Heidegger, "Humanism," p. 210.

42. Ibid.
43. Ibid.
44. Ibid., p. 199.
45. Ibid., pp. 199–200.
46. Ibid., p. 222.
47. Ibid., p. 200.
48. Here I have tried to echo the romantic, poetic way in which Heidegger always presented the life of the peasants. We have already encountered the herdsman in "Why Do I Stay in the Provinces?" who, "lost in thought and slow of step, drives his calf up the slope." See note 36 above. Also, in the famous last line of the "Letter on Humanism" (p. 242), Heidegger writes romantically of the furrows "that the farmer, slow of step, draws through the field."
49. It is possible to hear in Heidegger's silence on the Holocaust "a kind of consent to the horror," as Levinas says. I think it is also possible to believe that in keeping silent Heidegger kept the silence of his generation, that his silence was yet another expression of his Being-with the people whose destiny he shared, his fellow Germans. Either way, and both may certainly be possible, Heidegger's guilt is not diminished.
50. Note that for Heidegger the gift of Being to rare thinkers involves a certain loyalty to what is. In his lectures on Nietzsche during the war, Heidegger stated: "The historicity of a thinker, which is not a matter of him but of Being, has its measure in the original loyalty of the thinker to his inner limitation. Not to know this inner limitation, not to know it thanks to the nearness of what is unsaid and unsayable, is the hidden gift of Being to the rare thinkers who are called to the path of thought." The English version of these lectures has been published as *The End of Philosophy*, trans. Joan Stambaugh (New York: Harper & Row, 1973), p. 78.
51. See Heidegger's treatment of ethics in the "Letter on Humanism" (pp. 231–237). Here he appeals to Heraclitus and to an etymology of the word "Ethos" to get to a thinking which is more primordial than the way we usually think of ethics, as a system of value judgments. "Ethos," he says, originally meant "abode, dwelling place . . . the open region in which man dwells," and thus "original ethics" is not thinking in terms of right and wrong, but "thinking which thinks the truth of Being."
52. Several who personally knew Heidegger in the 1930s and later, including Gadamer, Habermas, and Löwith, remember that during this time Heidegger attended conferences and gave papers sometimes dressed not in usual academic attire but in the breeches and other attire of the Alemmannian-Swabian peasants.
53. See Jonas's "Heidegger and Theology," in *The Phenomenon of Life* (New York: Harper & Row, Publishers, 1966), pp. 235–261. This paper was originally read to a conference of Christian theologians, many of whom were very influenced by Heidegger. Jonas addressed them directly: "My theological friends, my Christian friends—don't you see what you are dealing with? Don't you sense, if not see, the profoundly pagan character of Heidegger's thought?" The gods appear often in Heidegger's thought, said Jonas, "but where the gods are, God cannot be" (p. 248). It might be interesting to compare this accusation and Heidegger's glorification of the natural with what Hitler said about Christianity, Judaism, and an earlier, more primitive, native Germanic religion. The German people, thought Hitler, once freed of the nefarious and weakening influence of Christianity, would revert to their natural religion, based on instincts and on all that

is natural. "What is natural," said Hitler, "is what is God willed." See some quotations by Hitler, and John Dewey's comments on them, in Dewey's *German Philosophy and Politics* (New York: Putnam, 1942).

54. Quoted in Wyschogrod, *Spirit in Ashes* p. 211.
55. This is not to excuse Heidegger for anything. Indeed, Heidegger did not have to wait until after the war to have more than enough ethical grounds to condemn Hitler. He must have known from the pages of *Mein Kampf* and from the activities of Hitler's thugs and ruffians, the Brownshirts, that certain people would suffer severely if he came to power. This could not have come as a surprise, even to the most unaware and uneducated citizen, let alone to someone of Heidegger's great intelligence and knowledge, and so Heidegger deserves the most severe condemnation even if he only supported National Socialism for eleven months; and who can still maintain faith in this comforting illusion? This of course assumes that Heidegger felt concern for people among whom he was not, for other others and not just for his others, for Jews and not just "pure" Germans like himself, and that is what we are forced to question.
56. I say "some of the perpetrators" out of the obligation to remember that it was not just Germans who were trying to exterminate the Jews and so bring about the "Final Solution." Many people in the occupied countries of Eastern Europe not only kept silent but did some of the killing themselves.
57. I must confess that even though I teach and write about the Holocaust and try to think and live out of solidarity for its victims, I had not thought very much about these other victims of other campaigns of genocide until I met a student at our university who is a Bosnian refugee and who brought this situation near to me, and who became one of my others.
58. I take this as the essential thrust of Levinas's quasi-phenomenology of ethics. Similarly, Richard Cohen, in his introduction to *Time and the Other* (Pittsburgh: Duquesne University Press, 1987), p. 27, says that "thought can no longer think in good conscience. Good conscience is not good enough." Cohen also states quite rightly that "Levinas insists that we take bad conscience seriously."
59. As the war was coming to a close, I drew up a list of questions to see how much my students knew about what had been going on in the Persian Gulf. I found that the eighty or so students I talked to were reasonably well informed. Nearly all knew the stated reasons for going there and the arguments involved, knew who the leaders and the generals were, knew how the war was being fought, even knew the names of some of the weapons used by both sides. Nearly all had been watching CNN or the major networks regularly during the war. When asked how many casualties our side had suffered, nearly all were able to answer the question quite accurately. The only question the majority of students missed—everyone missed, in fact—was how many casualties our side inflicted on the Iraqis. All said a lot more than we suffered. When asked how many more, most said ten or twenty times as many. Only a couple suggested that the figure could be as high as one hundred times as many. The astounding way information was manipulated and packaged during that war severely violated basic constitutional rights of the citizenry. Intellectuals, however, have for the most part remained silent.
60. Levinas, "As If Consenting to Horror," p. 488.

3

Heidegger's Silent Inhumanity: "To Think the Nobility of Being. . . ."[1]

WILHELM S. WURZER

Heidegger's failure to address the question of the Holocaust after 1945 illustrates his unbroken belief in a philosophy of decisionism articulated in *Beiträge zur Philosophie* (1936–38).[2] This text reflects the kind of conservative politics existing in Germany at the time. In particular, the analysis of decision (*die Entscheidung*), a name for Heidegger's turn,[3] manifests certain ideas explored by the prominent Third Reich theorist Carl Schmitt in *The Concept of the Political* (1927).[4] Indeed, Heidegger, who appeals to *Entscheidung* beyond the "moral-anthropological" dimension (*B*, 87), agrees essentially with Schmitt's specifically political distinction between friend and foe. Traces of this distinction can be found throughout the *Beiträge*. Here, Heidegger announces that the few who are eminent and futural are to resist the many who are unable to see the passing of the last god. This strife of the few and the many penetrates the very history of Being. Quite plainly, it determines the political implications of the ontic-ontological difference inasmuch as the ontological is secured under the rubric of friendship and the ontic is deployed as the specter of the enemy. Nonetheless, the enemy—a constellation of the ontic, the many, the everyday—belongs to the spiritual mission of Being. The Holocaust too is "a consequence of the *coordination* of evil and good in the clearing of Being."[5] This infamous ontological alliance, however, does not annul the strife of world and earth. Nor does it negate the historical difference of friend and foe, marked by the imprint of the few who recognize the dangers of nihilism and the many who are unable to ascend to the peaks of another beginning. The difficulties of differentiating Heidegger's thought from that of the National Socialists consists precisely in how the relation between friend (earth) and foe (world) unfolds. The National Socialists institute concentration camps in order to destroy the enemy from within. Heidegger displaces the political foe of nihilism by inscribing it into the history of Being as *Ereignis*. Thus he is able to wash his hands. Others do the work which he regards as necessary in order to bring to light a certain "turning away" (*Abdrängung*) from the preeminence of the mediocre. Nazi jurisprudence demands such turning away. That Heidegger imputes this turning away to Being is what makes his philosophy arguably just as problematic as the Nazi jurists' desire to demand specific political decisions based upon the distinction between friend and foe.

For Heidegger, the concept of friend marks the privilege of *Geist* shared by Greek and German alike. The concept of foe marks those who do not regard the *Volk* in relation to ontological trajectories, in short, those without *Seinszugehörigkeit*.[6] This "Freiburg National Socialism" is certainly not the kind that calls for the principle of extermination. Heidegger's will to decision does not fall into concrete attempts to destroy the enemy. To the contrary, *Streitigkeit* (dispute) protects the enemy from within. Paradoxically, this onto-historical sheltering appears to be quite the opposite of an extermination policy. Ironically, however, in its devastating abstractness it is the very condition for a Final Solution. For the latter too belongs to a historical *decision* which supposes the history of Being.

Carl Schmitt elucidates the concrete face of such a decision which marks "the most extreme degree of intensity in a connection or separation."[7] For Schmitt, a political decision is based upon the intensity of connection with the Movement or the intensity of separation from it. Separation corresponds to a political foe, "precisely that other, that alien being, and it suffices to identify his nature to say that he is existentially an other, an alien in a particularly intensive sense, so that in extreme cases conflicts with him are possible which can be decided neither by a previously determined general norm nor by the verdict of a third party who is not involved and therefore impartial" (*HJ*, 11). If the intensity of difference is such that it cannot be decided by norm or by law, there exists "the real possibility of physical killing." Indeed, this happened. After a few minutes, silence became an historical *Ereignis*.[8]

Yet, Heidegger dares to write: "But why the decision? Because only out of the deepest ground of Being is it possible to save beings. This salvation is a legitimate preservation of law and a mandate of the West" (*B*, 100). Thus he underscores the force of "*an either-or*"—friend or foe (*B*, 102). The essence of this force lies in a decisionism which challenges the collapse of the German spirit. The effects of this decisionism are immaterial since they, together with their cause, belong to Being. This makes it possible for Heidegger not to engage in self-criticism.

More clearly, decisionism belongs to *Ereignis*. The individual subject is historically insignificant. What matters is Dasein's necessary turning to Being, initially, *das Volk*. This extremely perilous turning away from human beings also reveals Heidegger's withdrawal from Kant's moral-critical philosophy. Radically transforming the latter's aesthetic project, Heidegger offers a post-aesthetic *Entscheidung*. This involves an immense fictioning of Kant's "free play of imagination." It is not surprising, then, that Pöggeler wonders whether Heidegger's thinking is able to make connections with reality.[9] As for the language, it is one of utter disinterestedness. *Die Sprache spricht*. Not a word about the Holocaust. Here too, silence signifies a certain violence, an equal partner in *Ereignis*. Silence belongs to the strategy of decisionism, the ironic operation of making a judgment for a higher connection: the friendship of *Seyn* (Being) and *Seiendes* (beings). This friendship survives all historical catastrophes. The question of friendship clearly belongs to Dasein's ceaseless questioning of Being. Yet, can one justify regarding the numerous horrors in concentration camps as constituents of a certain historicality within Being's open play?

Does not turning to *Seyn* in order to confront nihilism bring to light the darkest nihilism? If the consequences of National Socialism belong to *Ereignis*, what kind of fellowship emerges between Dasein and Being? Here it is no longer possible to distinguish between rift and jointure (*Fug*). The strife lingers. There is no resolution. The enemy prevails within. There can be no negation of beings. The dialectic does not work. And what happens in the camps is merely part of the ontological entanglement of truth with errancy. Moreover, some friends get rid of a lot of enemies. The friends lose and other enemies reappear. In part, Heidegger's silence signifies a distinct *Verdüsterung* (darkening): not just an obscuring of world but, more importantly, an obscuring of Being and beings. This darkening of the philosophical imagination marks a play ever so free and perilous as that of the Nazi epoch. After Heidegger, imagination may no longer protect itself in poetic beauty. Beyond his adventures, imagination will be free to forget Being but not beings, nor the coming of children's faces taking one last look at parents on the way to destruction. The ontological supplement is no longer necessary. It is time to let Being go. Too much can be placed into that openness, too much enmity, too many equal partners, too much error and sham.

Heidegger never renounces the higher philosophical privilege of *Entscheidung*. He regards his decisionist operation as a necessary struggle (*Kampf*) against the massification of Being. This is clearly a Nietzschean strategy, which can only be realized in an imaginary world. He wanted it to be realized in Freiburg, Germany, that is, in the real world as well. Such a turn to Being, however, leads to a dynamic exaltation of the earth, the ultimate beauty of peasantry. The question here bears upon the decision for the constellation of silence, earth, and strife. Yet, there is not much silence in the Movement. So, how is it possible for Heidegger to affirm a *Volk* that makes so much noise? No doubt, it is merely regarded as a condition for constructing the spiritual strength of the West. As Heidegger writes, quoting Plato, "All that is great stands in the storm" (*HC*, 39). What is sacrificed in the process of belonging to this community of struggle is precisely *Urteilskraft*—power-in-judgment. Specifically, it is the sacrifice of spirit's relation to judgment. This tells us the story of the new constellation of *Führer/ Volk/ Geist.* Paradoxically, Heidegger's strategy lets the will be in the service of *Sturm/ Geist*, "a truly *spiritual* world," "a world of the innermost and most extreme danger" (*HC*, 33).

Arguably, this turn to an authorial, knowing resolve on the part of *Denken* (thinking) reveals Heidegger's inability to come to terms with some of the crucial issues in Kant's *Critique of Judgment.* This derives, in fact, from his deconstruction of representation in general. Bound to a subversive reading of Kant's notion of "the free play of imagination," Heidegger frees the idea of judgment not only from the power of understanding (*Verstand*) but also from that of *Verstehen.* The turn to the poetic word would not be as perilous if it were a genuine opening to Hölderlin's world. Clearly, Heidegger gets lost in figurabilities that become entirely problematic. A dangerous supplement, the constellation of *Volk/ Geist/ Sturm* is not a responsible guide on the way to language. The open inscription marks a will to power. In extending this power, Heidegger abdicates any form of critique beyond ontological friendship. Thus, there appears a closure with regard to judgment which does not exclude "judging" the enemy but does exclude judging the consequences of the new constellation of subjectlessness, secrecy, and silence.

Heidegger's silence regarding the Holocaust, rooted in his decisionism, is also linked to letting presence be. And always already "presence" marks "a truly *spiritual* world"—beyond Christianity, beyond anything the West has to offer except for a philological fictioning of the Greek-German connection. On Heidegger's view, it is, of course, this connection that the Nazi movement might eventually enact. Preference for this connection belongs to the complex and strange friendship between thinker and Being, poet and earth, *Führer* and spirit. There is ample reason to suppose that Heidegger never sacrifices this complex friendship. His silence about the death camps, therefore, exhibits an indifference to the millions of victims. On a personal level, certainly, he felt very guilty. His thinking, however, does not yield to this level but only to the task of affirming a certain partnership with spirit beyond democracy, capitalism, and communism. "One must always ask oneself whether Heidegger doesn't speak a language which has become impossible" (*HC*, 233).

Additionally, one must also ask why he takes judgment out of ontological friendship and reserves it solely for the opposition. This, it seems to me, is the antinomy Heidegger never resolves. To the very end, he persists in renouncing democracy, in disregarding the legal and social accomplishments of our century, not to mention earlier revolutions in America and France. His philosophy, which radically doubts the significance of 1789, marks a restricted economy of poetic freedom. While it considers the question of the essence of pain, it disregards human suffering itself. This intolerable difference belongs to the necessary strife in *Ereignis*. Thus, there is no subject who takes direct responsibility for any actions. The decision to join in the struggle against the machinations (*Machenshaften*) of the West is not based on individual judgment. Instead, it is based upon the "judgment" in Being which determines a post-aesthetic play without critique. This play marks a decisive interlacing of spirit and imagination, of *Volk* and soil, of poetry and freedom.

Heidegger discerns the National Revolution as the New Germany in a poetic terrain. It is here that he finds true German essence. It is here that he sharpens his critique of everydayness. In this peculiar site, called spacing, thinker and *Führer* meet, far from Berlin, yet never far from an imaginal Third Reich. No doubt his politics is rooted in a poetic transcendentalism. While he resists the moral implications of Kant's philosophy, he transforms the transcendental dimensions of this philosophy into a "national post-aestheticism."[10] This makes the transcendental political in an exclusively poetic manner. Holding on to a precarious transcendental decisionism signifies Heidegger's dangerous supplement.

Such a decisionism is doubly dangerous, expressly because *Gelassenheit* permeates the open region. Thus, judgment becomes irrelevant inasmuch as Being "judges." The inconsistency arises when Heidegger begins to judge the nihilism of the West. While this particular judging belongs to *Ereignis*, it appears that it can do things for Being by taking a stand, making a decision, participating in the struggle. In consequence, this very doing, this historical *decisioning*, marks *Ereignis*. Decidedly, Being is *Ereignis*—the inexhaustible strife of decisioning. Heidegger's philosophy, then, demands resistance. It needs the German Revolution to challenge the absence of a resolve to assign greatness to one's time.

Beiträge points to the joint privilege of *Entsheidung* and *Ereignis*. Decisioning, therefore, turns into a primordial judging (*ur-teilen*). This means resisting nihilism, Americanism, and other modes of drifting from presence (*Seyn*). On the other hand, Being allows for such drifting, and *Ereignis* privileges separation and connection, enmity and friendship. Does it also grant extermination and generation, being and non-being? Here too, one might say with Derrida, "the violence of the dissymmetry should not come as a surprise."[11] Especially, if one regards Heidegger's thought as another beginning (*Aufbruch*) for metaphysics. This other beginning, however, unfolds a certain inhumanity, that is, a refusal to name the deed that becomes the utter darkness of Dachau.

HEIDEGGER'S PSEUDO-SCHELLING

Heidegger's refusal to name the Holocaust is undoubtedly related to his subversive reading of Schelling's philosophy of freedom. The latter's philosophy is quite different from the strategies of poetic dwelling. Schelling concedes that spirit opens itself to evil in a radical withdrawal from the absolute. But since spirit unfolds "presentation with complete indifference such that the universal is completely the particular,"[12] there is no possibility of actualizing evil in a philosophy rendered as work of art. Heidegger clouds this difference. He proceeds as if there were no distinction between Schelling's "sublime indifference" and the indifferent sublimity of poetic spacing. In short, Heidegger yields to the diabolical in a philosophy that steps out of the absolute. This turning away from the ideality of spirit is for Schelling the beginning of evil in philosophy. For him, there is no disjunction between spirit and nature. Modern philosophy, however, proceeds toward a subjective willfulness (*Eigenwille*), paradoxically, "an improper will" which withdraws from the principle of ground. This tendency, which can be traced to the absolute, remains invariably a mere possibility since spirit is not about to lose itself in particularity. For the human subject, however, the transition of evil from the possible to the actual begins with a desire to be the absolute. Thus, evil belongs to the horizon of the infinite, indeed, makes up the complexity of spirit-in-nature. However, insofar as it marks spirit's resolve to step out of itself in order to manifest itself, there is no reality of evil within this horizon. On Schelling's view, thinking is terrifyingly modern when it breaks the alliance with spirit residing in nature as language.[13]

A brief glance at Schelling's *Of Human Freedom* reveals that spirit is not an abstract necessity but the dynamic unity of ground and existence. More concretely, spirit "is not a system but a life, and this alone constitutes the answer to the question as to the possibility of evil in relation to God."[14] From a formal point of view, spirit contains a depth of darkness which never attains actuality. This chaos makes possible the transition of spirit to nature. It is a proper willfulness on the part of the absolute that makes possible its expression within the realm of particularity. This ability to turn away from itself is what Schelling calls spirit's possibility of evil. But since spirit cannot undo its being, evil lingers merely formally. Hence Schelling writes: "The Leibnizian concept of evil as a *conditio sine qua non*, can only refer to the basis, inasmuch as this aroused creature-will (the possible principle of evil) is the condition upon which alone the will of love could be realized" (*HF*, 83). Clearly, evil belongs to the very ground of absolute personality. Here

Schelling regards the phenomenon of evil from the perspective of a necessary awakening that moves spirit beyond itself into the natural. In the human Dasein, too, such an intensity of life is necessary in order to have creative goodness.[15]

Paradoxically, the good is haunted by evil—a wondrous interweaving. If both are one, evil does not become real. Hence, evil necessarily belongs to *Geist*. Indeed, Heidegger names the law of evil—*Geist*. Nonetheless, he disregards Schelling's thought that evil is shallow without the infinite triumph of the good and that "spirit is essentially love and goodness" (*HF*, 77). While the strife of good and evil persists, for Schelling, there is no evil beyond the good. Modernity, however, tends to split this bond. And Heidegger's thinking is hemmed into a nihilism fascinated by the possibility of evil. He avoids Schelling's thesis that evil does not exist (and ought not to be affirmed) unless it supplements spirit's diverse artistic strategies. There is a dissymmetry between the self-willing of spirit and that of modern philosophy. For Schelling, spirit is pure self-willing, even in willing to be nature and world. Within sociability, spirit expresses an absolute identity of light and darkness, of good and evil. That identity, needless to say, is entirely absent in Heidegger's recognition of the Nazi myth of pure willing, in which darkness lingers and the light of spirit fades.

Something disturbing comes to mind. The turn in Heidegger's philosophy belongs in part to an intriguing displacement of Schelling's understanding of evil.[16] Under the name of "poetic dwelling" (no doubt originally derived from Hölderlin) Heidegger marks the limits of his fictioning of *Of Human Freedom*. In a nutshell, he renders Schelling's text as one in which an ontology of evil signifies philosophy's *other* beginning. It is plain that he is fascinated by the metaphysical inflammation of the concept of evil. This inflammation, however, for Schelling is only important because of evil's unique tracing to the terrain of spirit. Indeed, evil is only possible as spirit.[17] To say that evil is only possible as spirit is, of course, not the same as to say that spirit is evil. Nonetheless, on Heidegger's account, Schelling believes that the very expression of evil is spiritual and that evil is the very essence of being human.[18] This (mis)interpretation reflects Heidegger's desire to disavow the absolute metaphysically, while retaining *spiritus* politically. In the end, Heidegger shows that evil is the privilege of a sublime poetics.

Reserving a poetic space for violence, Heidegger draws spirit into the silent itineraries of the finite. In this poetics of simple univocity, the exchange between the infinite and the finite disappears. Indeed, the infinite is entirely silenced. What lingers is the silent reign of the finite. As spirit becomes a stranger on earth, philosophy begins to address the question of alienation. Yet, the flame that kindles in the Trakl essay is no longer spirit in Schelling's sense but a spirit of dissension (*Entzweiung*). Beyond sociability, Heidegger provides poetic possibilities without historical necessities. We encounter, thereby, the loss of "the wondrous interweaving" of freedom and necessity. This poetic disenfranchisement of spirit is precisely what is at stake in Heidegger's later texts. "So much so," Derrida writes, "that we should now have to say of spirit what one says of the world for the animal: the animal is poor in spirit, it has spirit but does not have spirit and this not-having is a mode of its being-able-to-have spirit."[19] In brief, the abandonment of spirit suddenly becomes *Geist*. Here evil merges into a "new" and higher spiritual elevation. Indeed, it belongs to the "elevated practice" of thinking. It is no accident, then, that spirit turns out to be merely the soul of a stranger, a foreign philosopher. Beyond sociability, it plunges into the night of apartness. Suddenly, the intimacy between Heidegger and Schelling (as well as Hölderlin) fades. Heidegger's grand maneuver merely gives the appearance of kinship with German Idealism.

Clearly, then, for Heidegger the flaming wind of *Geist* turns out to be poor in world (*weltarm*). Ironically, he himself becomes a *weltarmes* "animal." This is compellingly thematized in Derrida's articulation of the "unquestioned possibility of the question" (*OS*, 10). Heidegger is eventually more concerned with questioning the privilege of the question in the history of philosophy than posing the question of spirit historically. What follows from this seductive turn to the un-thought questioning of the question is the anxiety of abandoning a necessary matter of *Denken*, namely, un-thought infrastructures. Consequently, the main difference between the open legacy of Kantian thought in Fichte, Hölderlin, and Schelling *and* Heideggerian deconstruction is that for the former philosophy matters insofar as it questions spirit's apartness and for the latter thinking matters solely insofar as it questions philosophy's desire to question (*Fragekraft*).

The danger here is not the grip of technicity but a heedless listening to a discourse poor in necessary infrastructures. What remains of spirit in *Denken* is an "onto-poetic sentimentality," a transgression of Kantian ethics by means of a transcendental detour, a fictioning of Schelling's presentation of evil. Such poetic exiting leads, no doubt, to the simultaneous loss of world, nature, and history. Poetic resources, displaced transcendentally, magnified politically, do not suffice to free philosophy from the preeminence of nihilism. The ec-static site of language, which bespeaks the stillness of the fourfold, becomes entirely problematic expressly because of a certain dispropriation of historical necessity. In short, Heidegger's onto-poetic thematics consists in disfiguration of language, violent intensifications of a distinctive site—an exclusive *Ort*, an excluding topos. In effect, the reader encounters an economy beyond exchange. This ontological destabilization of "what needs to be said" opens the way for saying the unsayable. Such an extraordinary *Aufbruch* does not occur in the texts of Schelling and Hölderlin. Heidegger, therefore, engages in a rigorous dissimulation (*Verstellung*) of their thinking. He (mis)reads both Schelling's concept of human freedom and Hölderlin's Hyperion motif. This (mis)reading spins off from his decision to abandon infrastructural concerns, notably the French Revolution. The soil of common life is too unclean for thinking to tread upon. Temporality is dehistoricized, and the French Revolution is merely a momentary event in the turpitude of Being's more encompassing, more authentic history.

Accordingly, for Heidegger, spirit is the flame that consumes experience. It is a kind of setting on fire of metaphysics, devouring tirelessly the bodies of language while retaining the shadows. Without the bodies, pain follows quickly. And the silence of Dachau lingers. Quite plainly, such thinking is still possible. Is it necessary?

From Freiburg to Terezin

Heidegger knew that many poets were also murdered. And more than a million Jewish children were killed on behalf of the *Führer*. Some of these children wrote poetry:

The Butterfly

The last, the very last,
So richly, brightly, dazzlingly yellow.
Perhaps if the sun's tears would sing
  against a white stone. . . .

Such, such a yellow
Is carried lightly 'way up high.
It went away I'm sure because it wished to
  kiss the world good-bye.

For seven weeks I've lived in here,
Penned up inside this ghetto.
But I have found what I love here.
The dandelions call to me
And the white chestnut branches in the court.
Only I never saw another butterfly.

That butterfly was the last one.
Butterflies don't live in here,
  in the ghetto.[20]

The young poet, Pavel Friedmann, who wrote this poem, was deported to the Terezin Concentration Camp in April 1942 and died in Auschwitz in the fall of 1944.[21] We are able to think this child's poetry more adequately if we heed Heidegger's words: "In the world's history we have first to learn that the making of poetry, too, is a matter of thinking."[22] Nonetheless, how much did Heidegger learn from poetic self-reflection? Did he listen to these "Lights Out" poems? Drawn into the ghetto, Pavel is not closed off from the Open. "I have found what I love here." Still, a distinct ambiguity emerges. Fused with the boundless, this child ventures into nothingness, voicing a powerful absence. "That butterfly was the last one." The colors fade in the ghetto. And hopes are carried away . . . "kiss(ing) the world good-bye."

About fifteen thousand children passed through Terezin—the arrival of *das Unheimliche*, total homelessness, the improper. Less than one hundred survived. "Where word breaks off no thing may be."[23] So, Heidegger renounces speaking (writing) about the wide, distant world of those children who looked daily toward their home.

> I look toward my home,
> the city where I was born.
> City, my city,
> I will gladly return to you.[24]

Is Heidegger's renunciation a refusal to see the inhuman? As Miroslav Kosek put it: "It all depends on how you look at it":

> Terezin is full of beauty.
> It's in your eyes now clear
> And through the street the tramp
> Of many marching feet I hear.
>
> In the ghetto at Terezin,
> It looks that way to me,
> Is a square kilometer of earth
> Cut off from the world that's free.
>
> Death, after all, claims everyone,
> You find it everywhere.
> It catches up with even those
> Who wear their noses in the air.
>
> The whole, wide world is ruled
> With a certain justice, so
> That helps perhaps to sweeten
> The poor man's pain and woe.[25]

For Heidegger, renunciation is keeping silent (*Schweigen*). It is a commitment to a precarious partnership with *das Unheimliche*.[26] His refusal to speak out marks a "transformed self-denial." "From now on may the word be" (*PLT*, 152). This commitment to the poetic word, however, does not speak to the daily misery of Terezin's victims. The word does not give reasons for what happened in numerous concentration camps. The word to which Heidegger appeals is no longer in the service of the principle of sufficient reason. It merely grants the theme of presence. Still, did Heidegger learn renunciation? He writes: "To learn means: to become knowing. In Latin, knowing is *qui vidit*, one who has seen, has caught sight of something, and who never again loses sight of what he has caught sight of" (*WL*, 143). Sadly, Heidegger does not attain such seeing.

> Something else, something very disturbing happens.
> The rivers flow another way,
> Another way,
> Not letting you die, not letting you live.
>
> And the canons don't scream and the guns don't bark
> And you don't see blood here.
> Nothing, only silent hunger.
> Children steal the bread here and ask and ask
>   and ask
> And all would wish to sleep, keep silent, and
>   just to go to sleep again. . . .
>
> The heaviest wheel rolls across our foreheads
> To bury itself deep somewhere inside our memories.[27]

The word is Terezin. And in Heidegger's own words: "What is disturbing is the fact that *with* the absence of the word, the treasure disappears" (*WL*, 146). Here, the treasure is the higher rule of poetic saying. The word, Terezin, remains absent in his texts. Not only this word is missing, but other words like Auschwitz, Buchenwald, Dachau, Flossenburg, Stutthof, Sachsenburg and many, many others. "Hence the treasure slips away" (*WL*, 146). For Heidegger, however, it does not disintegrate into nothingness. The names of these sites of inhumanities need only be awakened by a necessary regarding, re-writing of the improper. Lacoue-Labarthe writes: "In the face of the *Unheimliche*—the improper—mastery becomes possible only by taking it still further, by outdoing it with the *Unheimliche* . . . It makes the decision possible."[28]

Heidegger's decisionism is rooted in desistance of, Terezin, first of all. This means renouncing the priority of historical infrastructures. Such a denial belongs to the unique intimacy of Being and the word—a different experience with language. Indeed, this intimacy makes it possible to keep silent since the word no longer serves history. Instead, history yields to the higher rule of language, to the precarious friendship of Being and poetry. "This different rule of the word glances abruptly at the poet" (*WL*, 146). In effect, "beings no longer make a claim on us."[29] From this point of view, the thinker gives himself over to the mystery of a poetic economy. An economy of silence, *das Geläut der Stille*, guides all language. This enigmatic quality of language is deeply historical for Heidegger. Yet, the kind of history that is introduced here is undoubtedly that of the unspoken. In the face of the improper, everything is silenced. Such radical silencing disturbs. Regardless, for Heidegger, it marks the questionless constellation of sadness and joy. "The deeper the sadness, the more summoning the joy resting within it. Sadness and joy play into each other" (*WL*, 153).

What is proper to this thinking is the ontic-ontological difference which remains sovereign throughout the texts. Without this difference, the poetic economy, confirming the friendship between Being and language, would not be possible. While Heidegger insists that poetic renunciation is not negative, he forgets the history of human beings. In short, renunciation, friendship, *Ereignis*, belong to the "higher rule" of silence, the sovereignty of Being, *die Macht des Seyns*: "Every word and consequently all of logic stands under the power of Being" (*B*, 79). The West takes on a new beginning with the revolution of poetic renunciation. The improper is appropriated without granting the word concrete historical significance. While a certain presence is bestowed by the word, namely Being, there is no sign that marks the presence of a thing such as Terezin. As Heidegger claims: "The word does not give reasons for the thing" (*WL*, 151).

In essence, then, the word forgets Terezin. The play is bigger than the games played in the death camps. And, for one whose matter is *Denken*, it is the play that matters and nothing else. Without the least hesitation, Heidegger writes: "The play itself which attunes the two (sadness and joy) by letting the remote be near and the near be remote is pain" (*WL*, 153). Inscribed into poetic inflation, pain remains purely speculative. So, when Heidegger listens to the poem, he ponders poetry and not *die Sache selbst* (the thing itself). He sees the spirit attuned by pain but not the children suffering in Terezin.

For the Nazis, Terezin signifies a poetic concentration camp. Heinrich Himmler calls it a "model ghetto." It is regarded as a pleasant way to deal with the Final Solution.

The ghetto—starved, sick, redolent with dread—throbbed with culture: lectures, concerts, theatres. Theresienstadt was saturated with Jewish scholars, doctors, engineers, singers, diplomats, actors, composers, artists; it was a hothouse of European intellectuals. And there were sixty thousand books in the library. Culture was a collective means of resisting the deceptions practiced by the Nazis as well as a weapon against despair, a way of warding off the fearful pink slip—the deportation order to the darkness in the East.[30]

When the International Red Cross arrived to inspect the camp, the Nazis made sure that Terezin took on the appearance of a country resort. They tried to restore it to its former Theresienstadt, "a fortress town set in a serene world of meadows and low rolling hills and summer butterflies against a distant background of bluish Bohemian mountains" (*AB*, xi). Restoration, here, of course, means renunciation of what really happened. No one believed that of any of the Jews of Terezin would ever be set free. So, why the show and utter absence of *phainesthai*? Why the silence about Terezin? A child speaks about the site concealed by his oppressors:

> That bit of filth in dirty walls,
> And all around barbed wire,
> And 30,000 souls who sleep
> Who once will wake
> And once will see
> Their own spilled blood.
> In the flame of candles by my bed, I sleep
> And once perhaps I'll understand
> That I was such a little thing,
> As little as this song.
>
> These 30,000 souls who sleep
> Among the trees will wake,
> Open an eye
> And because they see
> A lot
>
> They'll fall asleep again. . . .[31]

The pain of Terezin does not strike sparks on Heidegger. He listens to Poetry but abandons the poems. There is a difference between Poetry and poems, between Theresienstadt and Terezin. Theresienstadt is a poetic site built by Joseph II for his mother, Maria Theresa. It is a place in a dream. Terezin, however, became a nightmare precisely in the dream of a higher rule—the sovereignty of strife between Being and beings. Suddenly, *Geist* becomes a ghost. It is silenced, it is set on fire. Only the ashes in the crematoria remain. Heidegger writes: "We listen to the poem. We abandon everything which we have now said to oblivion" (*WL*, 156).[32]

Little Eva Schulzova, a quiet child who died in Auschwitz, pens "An Evening in Terezin":

The sun goes down
and everything is silent,
only at the guard's post
are heavy footfalls heard.

That's the guard who watches his Jews
to make sure they don't run away from the ghetto.[33]

An anonymous child adds:

I'd like to live
And go back home again.[34]

The images remain; their faces tell the stories. There is no Being. *Ereignis* is mere emptiness after Auschwitz. It is the silence that comes with the forgetting of beings. It is utter disinterestedness without the *other* silence, that stillness of words which may still be heard in the stream flowing through the outskirts of Dachau's camp. Heidegger does not venture to read the poems of the children who died. These poems, and their distinctive poetic spacing, have their origin and essence in a necessary stillness.[35] Neglecting this stillness, Heidegger writes: "*Ereignis* 'is' the highest sovereignty" (*B*, 408). A catastrophic economy, the turn (*die Kehre*) becomes history thought in light of "solitude of sacrifices" and "singularity of decision" (*B*, 408). Suddenly, understanding too is silent. As one survivor notes:

> For the time being mankind does not understand what we have gone through and what we have experienced. We fear we will not be understood in the future. We unlearned to laugh, we cannot cry any more, we do not understand our freedom yet, all this because we are still with our dead comrades. We belong in the mass-graves of those shot in Kharkov, Lublin and Kovno. We belong to the millions gassed and burned in Auschwitz and Birkenau. We belong to those tens of thousands tormented by milliards of lice, living in mud on a starvation diet, with coldness and despair as companions. We are not alive. We are dead!"[36]

Thinking the inhuman means, first and foremost, letting presence (*Dasein*) show itself, in itself, for itself. It will find itself at home in what is, close up to its history, near the sending—the dates, places, numbers of documents, what is clearly a writing of exterminations. After Auschwitz, thinking gathers together expressly what has happened and what is still happening in philosophy's silence. After Heidegger, it demands a reading of an entirely different textuality—the deportations, the massacres, the destruction, in short, the tables, charts, and inscriptions of the Holocaust. And "then in place of burning all, one begins to love the flowers."[37] Each name, a subject taken from play, freely given over to a place without judgment, is granted a gift belatedly. Writing may now set on fire the Holocaust itself. Derrida writes: "Without the holocaust the dialectical movement and the history of Being could not open themselves, engage themselves in the annulus of their anniversary, could not annul themselves . . ." (*C*, 46). "Thus giving can no longer be thought starting from Being" (*C*, 48). Indeed, reading the atlas of the Holocaust and burning this very burning marks a possible return for philosophy to the human. Philosophy may then emerge as the Holocaust's holocaust, the blaze that burns the texts of ontological silence. Sacrificing itself, philosophy will burn out its inhumanities. Perhaps, then, philosophers will mourn the absence of exchange between a child's poeticizing and a thinker's authorial decisioning.

PHILOSOPHY'S OWN HOLOCAUST

Philosophy today continues to inflame the kind of discourse which ignores reality. Hence, the urgent need for resisting philosophemes foreign to opening up the meaning of what is. It is no longer tolerable to hide in the comfort of singular poetic spacings. It is time to set metaphysical discourse on fire. Heidegger remarks, "Spirit is what inflames."[38] What inflames sets fire to Heidegger's own textual unconcern with the Holocaust. Up to a certain point, philosophy proceeds singularly within a certain poetic spacing. However, this does not destroy its "essentially plurivocal language" (*OS*, 86). In fact, this allows us to think beyond inhumanities by attending vigilantly to a philosophy of resistance. Guided by the spirit that springs from writing the Holocaust's atlas, philosophy will move out of the violence of pure textuality.

Such writing will be rare and difficult. For what we are attempting to write about has no future presence. In Lacoue-Labarthe's words, it is "undermined by an unassignable gap, a kind of hiatus or gaping hole that nothing can ever close or fill up since it is anterior to any opening, any virtuality, any potency and any energy" (*T*, 173). Nonetheless, he believes that writing *works* (*T*, 136). It works because it "phenomenally installs under the aspect of the mere trace, the trace that is visible, perceptible, present to the eye, unerased" (*t*, 137). It also works in writing beyond the order of visibility, in Derrida's sense of the general text, in which textuality exceeds natural presence. In this double sense, however, writing points desperately to cinders. It offers itself up to the flame, the spirit-in-play, burning the purely speculative.

Derrida marks the limits of such play—a holocaust of the Holocaust in the genealogy of philosophy. When *Denken* is itself set on fire, philosophy may begin to be. The very act of burning opens its language for *the* Holocaust.[39] Unfolding a new mood within language, one which sacrifices restrictive spacings, philosophy is ready to focus on inhumanities. No longer deprived of mourning, it is equipped to "tell of the all-burning, otherwise called holocaust and the crematory oven, in German, in all the Jewish languages of the world" (*C*, 57).

The question, in the end, is not only Heidegger and the Holocaust but philosophers and the holocausts.[40] Philosophy cannot repeat the undecidability of responding to the many burnings, the prevailing progression of blazes, the sight of needless sacrifices. After necessary counter-fires, perhaps, after Auschwitz *and* Heidegger, philosophy may once and for all face "the first desired holocaust" (*C*, 64), the erotic journey to the beauty of *Geist* setting its Self on fire.

NOTES

1. Für die Seltenen, die den höchsten Mut zur Einsamkeit mitbringen, um den Adel des Seyns zu denken und zu sagen von seiner Einzigkeit," in Martin Heidegger, *Beiträge zur Philosophie* (Frankfurt am Main: Vittorio Klostermann, 1989), 11 [hereafter *B*]. This and other brief translations pertaining to *Beiträge* are mine: "For the exceptional, who bring with them the highest spirit of solitude, in order to think the nobility of Being and to speak of its singularity" (*B*, 11).
2. "Dann rückt, das was hier Ent-scheidung genannt ist, in die innerste Wesensmitte des Seyns selbst . . ." (*B*, 88).
3. "Der *Kehre*, die im Seyn selbst west und ein Licht wirft auf das, was hier mit Entscheidung genannt sein möchte" (*B*, 95). "What is here named de-cision is drawn into the innermost center of Being itself. . ." (*B*, 88). "Of the *turn*, which abides in Being itself and illuminates what might be meant here by decision" (*B*, 95).
4. Carl Schmitt, *Der Begriff des Politischen* (Duncker and Humblot, 1963).
5. Werner Marx, *Heidegger and the Tradition* (Evanston, IL: Northwestern University Press, 1971), 250.
6. "The belonging-to-Being" referred to in the *Beiträge*.
7. See Ingo Müller's, *Hitler's Justice*, trans. D. Lucas Schneider (Cambridge: Harvard University Press, 1991), 11 [Hereafter *HJ*].
8. "Das Erschrecken im Jubel der Seinszugehörigkeit" (*B*, 99): "The terror in the jubilation of Belonging-to-Being."
9. Richard Wolin, ed. *The Heidegger Controversy* (Cambridge: The MIT Press, 1993), 243 [hereafter *HC*].
10. This phrase is not dissimilar from Philippe Lacoue-Labarthe's "national aestheticism" in *Heidegger, Art and Politics* trans. C. Turner (Oxford: Basil Blackwell, 1990). However, my argument with regard to Heidegger's "post-aestheticism" differs from Lacoue-Labarthe's insofar as I make a necessary connection between Heidegger's political deficiency and the *Beiträge* theory of decisionism.
11. Jacques Derrida, *Of Spirit: Heidegger and the Question*, trans. G. Bennington and R. Bowlby (Chicago and London: The University of Chicago Press, 1989), 71 [hereafter *OS*].

12. See F. W. J. Schelling, *The Philosophy of Art*, trans. D. W. Stott (Minneapolis: University of Minnesota Press, 1989), 45.
13. And, "Language as the infinite affirmation that expresses itself in a *living* fashion is the ultimate symbol of chaos eternally residing in absolute knowledge," *Philosophy of Art*, 101. "Ohne Kunst ist Philosophie undenkbar," *Schellings Werke*, III, ed. Schroeter (Munich: Becksche Verlagsbuchhandlung, 1927), 403: "Philosophy is unthinkable without art."
14. Schelling, *Of Human Freedom*, trans. J. Gutmann (Chicago: The Open Court Publishing Co., 1936), 78 [hereafter *HF*].
15. In this respect, Schelling argues, "it is quite correct to say dialectically: Good and evil are the same, only regarded from different aspects; or evil in itself, that is regarded at the root of its identity, is goodness; just as goodness, on the other hand, regarded in its division of nonidentity, is evil. For this reason the statement is also quite correct whoever has no material or force for evil is himself also powerless for good" (*HF*, 80–81).
16. More than Nietzsche or Hölderlin, it is Schelling's thinking that marks the radical point of departure in Heidegger's philosophy since 1936.
17. "Das Böse ist Geist und daher nur als Geist wirklich" Martin Heidegger, *Shellings Abhandlung Über das Wesen der menschlichen Freiheit (1809)* (Tübingon: Max Niemeyer Verlag, 1971), 178: "The evil is spirit and thereby only real as spirit."
18. "*Das Wesen des Menschseins* . . . (*SA*, 176): "The essence of being human. . . ."
19. Jacques Derrida, *Of Spirit*, trans. G. Bennington and R. Bowlby (Chicago: The University of Chicago Press, 1989), 55 [Hereafter *OS*].
20. Pavel Friedmann, 4.6.1942, in . . . *I never saw another Butterfly* . . ., ed. Hana Volankova (New York: Schocken Books, Inc., 1993), 39 [hereafter *AB*].
21. See *AB*, 39. This poem was donated to the State Jewish Museum in Prague. Its archive number is 101516.
22. Martin Heidegger, *Poetry, Language, Thought*, trans. A. Hofstadter (New York: Harper & Row Publishers, 1975), 99–100 [hereafter *PLT*].
23. Martin Heidegger, *On the Way to Language*, trans. P. D. Hertz (New York: Harper and Row Publishers, 1982), 152 [hereafter *WL*].
24. *AB*, 11.
25. *AB*, 13.
26. "In such commitment, he who renounces denies himself to the claim which he formerly willed. . . . The 'self' is no longer in the dative but the accusative case, and the claim is no longer in the accusative but the dative case" (*WL*, 151).
27. *AB*, 17.
28. Philippe Lacoue-Labarthe *Typography*, trans. C. Fynsk (Cambridge: Harvard University Press, 1989), 94 [hereafter *T*].
29. "Das Seiende spricht nicht mehr an" (*Wegmarken, Gesamtausgabe*, Vol. 9 [Frankfurt/M: Vittorio Klostermann, 19], 111a).
30. (*AB*, xviii).
31. *AB*, 20–21.
32. I have reversed these two statements.
33. *AB*, 42.
34. *AB*, 28.
35. "Von hier nimmt alle Sprache des Da-seins ihren Ursprung und ist deshalb im Wesen das Schweigen" (*B*, 408): "From here all language of *Da-sein* takes its origin and its therefore essentially silence."

36. Martin Gilbert, *Atlas of the Holocaust* (New York: William Morrow and Co., Inc., 1993), 238.
37. Jacques Derrida, *Cinders*, trans. N. Lukacher (London: University of Nebraska Press, 1991), 46 [hereafter *C*].
38. *WL*, 179. "Der Geist ist das Flammende": "Spirit is what inflames."
39. See Derrida, *Cinders*, 48.
40. Philosophy's own holocaust exceeds the matter of Heidegger.

4

Strategies of Deception: The Composition of Heidegger's Silence

GEORGE LEAMAN

There *is* a dangerous international network of Jews.
—Martin Heidegger[1]

From the time of Germany's liberation from Nazism in 1945 until his death in 1976, Martin Heidegger had virtually nothing to say about the crimes of the Nazi regime. This fact has been at the center of much of the recent discussion of Heidegger's political engagement. Although some commentators have found this silence to be the most damnable aspect of Heidegger's relationship to Nazism,[2] others have argued that his silence is profoundly instructive. For example, George Kovacs believes that Heidegger's silence reveals our failure "to think the enormity of suffering and evil, of the power and anxiety in human responsibility."[3] William Vaughan has described Heidegger's silence as a kind of "restitution" and as a recognition of "the failure of language to grasp an event."[4] Still other commentators find this silence incomprehensible and doubt that it will be explained in the near future. For example, Theodore Kisiel has argued that Heidegger's silence cannot now be understood by philosophers, who will have to leave the pursuit of an answer "to the psychoanalysts, social analysts, and ideology critics of twentieth-century German history."[5] Philippe Lacoue-Labarthe finds Heidegger's silence "perplexing" and argues that the only hope of finding an answer "lies in our facing up to a rigorous reading of the texts."[6] Such arguments assume that there is some hidden meaning to be found in Heidegger's silence, some ciphered message that can only be decoded and correctly interpreted with the help of his texts. Such arguments also assume that Heidegger's silence was qualitatively different from that of the many other Nazis and Nazi sympathizers who had nothing to say after being directly confronted with the horrible legacy of their system of government.[7] In this paper I want to provide an explanation of Heidegger's silence that does not rely on these assumptions. I will examine three aspects of Heidegger's postwar silence and argue that it was an opportunistic attempt to insulate both himself and his work from unwanted criticism.

The most obvious aspect of Heidegger's silence has already been mentioned: his almost complete refusal to comment publicly on the Holocaust or any of the other mass crimes perpetrated by the Nazi state. But Heidegger did, in fact, make at least three references to the SS extermination camps after the war. Although these references have already been discussed in the recent secondary literature,[8] an historically informed reading can provide further insight into Heidegger's postwar perspectives on both Nazism and the Holocaust. The first of these references was made in a letter to Herbert Marcuse. This letter was written in response to Marcuse's demand that Heidegger clearly distance himself from his past political association with a regime that had killed millions of Jews and that had elevated terror to a condition of daily life.[9] Heidegger's letter, dated January 20, 1948, contains the following passage:

> I can only add that instead of the word "Jews" [in your letter] there should be the word "East Germans," and then exactly the same [terror] holds true of one of the Allies, with the difference that everything that has happened since 1945 is public knowledge world-wide, whereas the bloody terror of the Nazis was in fact kept a secret from the German people.[10]

Today it requires some effort to identify the two politically charged deceptions contained in this sentence. The first lies in the attempt to equate the forced resettlement of ethnic Germans in eastern Europe after the war with the mass murder of Jews during the war. In areas under German occupation or influence, people who were identified by the Nazis as "Jews" were generally rounded up and deported to concentration camps. Ethnic Germans, on the other hand, were treated as potential citizens of the Nazi state and were offered inducements to emigrate to Germany.[11] Ethnic German men were also eligible for recruitment (or draft) into the German military, security services, and labor organizations.[12] In other words, during the war ethnic Germans were offered privileges and weapons by the Nazi regime while Jews were sent to the gas chambers. After the war ethnic Germans were treated as enemy nationals by most eastern European governments, and not without reason. According to Heidegger's view, however, east Germans and Jews were equally victims of unjustified persecution. What sense does this make? Why would Heidegger choose this particular comparision? Heidegger's remark makes very little sense, until one remembers the repeated assertions in Nazi propaganda that Jews were the driving force behind Soviet communism.[13] The Soviet Union, that "one of the Allies" within whose sphere of influence many ethnic Germans were expelled from their countries of origin, was a communist *and therefore a Jewish* power. Seen from this perspective, Heidegger's moral reduction has a certain logic that can be restated as follows: During the war Nazi Germans attacked defenseless Jews and now communist Jews were attacking defenseless Germans.

The second deception in this passage is contained in Heidegger's assertion that the German people had no knowledge of "the bloody terror of the Nazis" as it was happening. It is, of course, true that civilian access to SS death camps was restricted and there were no German newspaper or radio reports of their activities. But the construction and operation of the death camps during the war was the culmination of an extremely public process that began years before. For most Jewish and politically left-leaning Germans, "the bloody terror of the Nazis" began in 1933 when Hitler came to power, and took on ever more extreme forms in the years that followed. Had Heidegger perhaps forgotten his conversation with Karl Jaspers in May 1933, during which he affirmed his belief in the existence of a dangerous international Jewish "conspiracy"?[14] Is it conceivable that this belief would have motivated him to expressions of disapproving outrage when Jews in Germany and occupied territories were rounded up and deported during the war? The deception lies in the implicit assertion that the existence of the death camps came as a complete surprise *to him*, as if someone else had held the beliefs that justified their creation.

The following year, on December 1, 1949, Heidegger made two references to the extermination camps in lectures before a select audience in Bremen. The first of these remarks was made in a lecture titled "The Con-Figuration" ("Das Ge-Stell"):

> Agriculture is now a motorized food-industry—in essence, the same as the manufacture of corpses in gas chambers and extermination camps, the same as the blockading and starving of nations, the same as the manufacture of hydrogen bombs.[15]

Here Heidegger carefully extends the dehistoricized political judgment contained in his letter to Marcuse the year before. Each of the Allied powers is now held responsible for actions that are "in essence" the same as the "manufacture of corpses in gas chambers." The reference to "the blockading and starving of nations" has a double meaning; it would have reminded German listeners at the time of the blockade imposed on Germany by the western Allies after the First World War and the recently lifted Soviet blockade of Berlin.[16] Despite possible confusion caused by his reference to hydrogen (instead of atomic) bombs, Heidegger also reminded his listeners that two of the Allied powers had invested billions in the development of weapons of indiscriminate mass destruction. The Soviet Union had recently tested a nuclear weapon and the Americans had already used them.[17] With these comparisons Heidegger achieves some measure of moral balance between victors and vanquished in their shared willingness to use indiscriminate violence, and he does this as a backdrop to a remark about an entirely different subject. The ironing out of the wrinkles of historical and political responsibility is thus completed in an apparently depoliticized context. The death camps now belong in the pantheon of morally equivalent crimes committed by the world's major powers; the "essence" of their actions is to be found a priori in a shared relationship to the world, a relationship that is also allegedly visible in the "essence" of the "motorized food-industry."[18] This move wards off any possible discussion and/or condemnation of particular atrocities with the assertion of an unspecified universal "essence" common to all of them. This assertion enables Heidegger to confirm the dehistoricization of the legacy of the extermination camps by elevating the discussion to a level at which historical detail loses all meaning. Because the death-camps and the SS are instantiations of some universal condition, there is no reason to address them specifically. Most significantly, there remains no reason for Heidegger to address his relationship to the political institution responsible for creating them.[19]

Heidegger's third reference to the death camps was made later the same day in a lecture titled "The Danger" ("Die Gefahr"). Here he made the following remarks:

> Hundreds of thousands die en masse. Do they die? They succumb. They are done in. Do they die? They become mere quanta, items in an inventory in the business of manufacturing corpses. Do they die? They are liquidated inconspicuously in extermination camps. And even apart from that—right now millions of impoverished people are perishing from hunger in China.
>
> But to die is to endure death in its essence. To be able to die means to be capable of this endurance. We are capable of this only if the essence of death makes our own essence possible.[20]

In this passage Heidegger once again makes a politically charged attempt to suppress historical memory and qualify the legacy of the Holocaust. He begins with several references to those who were "liquidated inconspicuously in extermination camps." The horror of these references, which German listeners at the time would no doubt have understood as references to Jews, is subsequently tempered with the mention of starving masses in *communist* China.[21] With this juxtaposition Heidegger attempted to show his audience that Germany was not the only country in which the mass "liquidation" of human life had occurred, and that elsewhere (i.e., under communist rule) it was happening on a scale even greater than that achieved by the SS. The latter point is made by his contrast of the "hundreds of thousands" killed in the camps with the ongoing death of "millions" in China. The final three sentences of this passage contain an apparently mysterious reference to the "essence" of death, an essence that is allegedly missing from the mass "liquidations" he had just mentioned. "They" did not really die because "they" could not "endure death in its essence." What does this mean? The beginning of the answer is to be found in Heidegger's earlier work. In section 74 of *Being and Time* (1927) he argued that the "anticipatory resoluteness" of Being-toward-death is the necessary precondition for authentic existence. That existence cannot be realized by isolated individuals; it can only be realized in and through an historical community in which individual fates are bound together in a common destiny.[22] In *The Self-Affirmation of the German University* (1933) Heidegger subsequently resolved this tension between individual fates and collective destiny with the help of "transcendental forces" found in the "spiritual world" of a people.[23] This spiritual world is that which is common to all of its members, "the forces stemming from earth and blood as the power which most deeply moves and profoundly shakes our being."[24] Although each people has its own spiritual world, according to Heidegger the spiritual world of the German *Volk* has given it a unique historical-spiritual mission to renew the possibility of authentic existence.[25] This means that the possibility of authentic existence depends upon, and is thus reserved for, those who share the German spiritual world. In the passage from the Bremen lecture quoted above, Heidegger explicitly distinguishes between "we" (i.e., himself and his German audience) who are capable of enduring death and "they" (the liquidated non-Germans) who are not. Read against the background of these earlier texts, the meaning of this passage can be more easily discerned: Those who were murdered could not *really* die because as non-Germans they never had the potential for "authentic" existence in the first place.

Thus, to refer to Heidegger's "silence" about the Holocaust without qualification is misleading. He did in fact comment on the work of the SS extermination camps to a limited number of people, and these comments were made in a manner that was consistent with his earlier, more public commitment to Nazism. In each of the references quoted above, Heidegger attempts to reduce the scale of Nazism's criminal legacy. His attitude in this matter is not noticeably different from that of many other Germans who resisted the notion of there being anything particularly horrible about the conduct of the Nazi government. The first two comments are also completely compatible with the belief, then as now widely held in Germany, that all of the dead should be considered "victims" of the war, regardless of whether they were murdered or had been murderers.[26] Another dimension of Heidegger's comments comes to light when one examines the time frame in which they were made. Heidegger's letter to Marcuse and lectures in Bremen took place during the short period (1947–50) of his banishment from the university and university teaching.[27] His statements during this time thus did not reflect directly on the university, which meant that he could more easily afford to make comments of a kind he was never to repeat after the teaching ban was lifted.[28] From then on, he kept quiet and he did so, according to his own account, in the interest of his career and to avoid conflicts that might alienate future students.[29]

Heidegger also displayed this concern for his professional reputation with politically motivated editing of some of his manuscripts prior to their publication after the war. In doing this he was not alone; many other German philosophers with pro-Nazi political backgrounds also made a considerable effort to remove or revise passages that might have become professional liabilities.[30] In Heidegger's work this problem becomes evident when one examines different editions of the published texts of some of his lectures. For example, several editions of the first Bremen lecture mentioned above do not contain his reference to the extermination camps.[31] A further example is provided by a particularly well-known passage in the *Introduction to Metaphysics*, which was first delivered as a series of lectures in 1935. In those lectures he made a remark that has since been much discussed:

> The works that are being peddled about nowadays as the philosophy of National Socialism but having nothing whatever to do with the inner truth and greatness of National Socialism—have all been written by men fishing in the troubled waters of "values" and "totalities."

This is the original version of his remark. As the lectures were being prepared for publication in 1953, two of Heidegger's students asked him to remove this passage from the manuscript. Instead, Heidegger struck out the second mention of National Socialism, substituted the term "movement," and added an explanation in parentheses that did not appear in the original text: "namely the encounter between global technology and modern man."[32] The original version is an attack on leading philosophers of the German Philosophical Society, which earlier had held meetings organized around each of these concepts.[33] This version is also an unqualified endorsement of

Nazism. The altered version is an attempt post hoc to place his support for Nazism in the context of his later criticism of modern technology. It is therefore a retroactive attempt to qualify his earlier support for Nazism. After its publication in 1953, the altered version became the object of tremendous speculation in the secondary literature about the nature of Heidegger's relationship to Nazism in the mid 1930s.[34] The full extent of the problem of such politically motivated manipulation of the texts is not yet known, because Heidegger's original manuscripts are only being made available to researchers once the text has been published in the collected works.[35] This matter is of particular importance to those who depend on translations for access to Heidegger's texts, because in some cases the English translations of his work have been made from altered German "originals."[36]

Finally, Heidegger's "silence" was reinforced by his suppression of texts that might have raised questions about his relationship to Nazism. At his express wish, many of his texts from the Nazi years were not published during his lifetime and have only recently begun to appear in print.[37] Here too Heidegger's actions were by no means unique; other German philosophers also withheld politically "untimely" texts from publication and did not list them in personal bibliographies.[38] In Heidegger's case this suppression of potentially relevant material extends to his correspondence as well.[39] This suppressed material includes both major philosophical texts and lectures. In 1989, for example, a previously unknown text, *Contributions to Philosophy (of the Event)*, was published for the first time.[40] Written in 1936–38, this text provides fascinating insight into Heidegger's relationship to Nazism and has already been widely discussed.[41] And at least two other major philosophical works by Heidegger remain unpublished.[42] An example of the suppression of lecture texts was provided recently with the publication of "Europe and German Philosophy." In this lecture, which he delivered in Rome in 1936, Heidegger argued that Europe was in danger of destruction, and he asked his audience to look to German philosophy as the source of its deliverance. He explained this situation as follows:

> Our historical existence experiences with increasing urgency and clarity that its future is reducible to the simple either-or of Europe's rescue or destruction. The possibility of rescue, however, demands two things:
> 1. The protection of the European peoples against the Asian.
> 2. The overcoming of their own rootlessness and fragmentation.
> Without this overcoming such protection cannot be realized.[43]

How was this second condition to be fulfilled? Here one must remember Heidegger's previous announcement, in *The Self-Affirmation of the German University*, that the German *Volk* had a unique historical-spiritual mission to renew the possibility of authentic existence. Since only the German spiritual world could bring forth this possibility, one can reasonably conclude that only the "forces stemming from earth and blood" within the German spiritual world would be capable of overcoming Europe's "rootlessness and fragmentation." This means that only Germany was capable of protecting "the European peoples from the Asian." This message was not particularly strange at the time; in fact, it echoes Hermann Göring's earlier judgment about the challenges facing the Nazi "revolution." One also finds very similar arguments repeated in later Nazi propaganda that sought to explain the wartime dangers facing German-occupied Europe.[44] That Heidegger should not have wanted such a text published during his lifetime is understandable, particularly given his above-mentioned desire to avoid conflicts that might jeopardize his career or alienate potential students.

In a conversation with Rainer Marten in the late 1950s, Heidegger expressed concern about the renewal of "Jewish" influence in German philosophy. Marten recalls that Heidegger "counted on his fingers the number of Chairs in philosophy that had already been reoccupied by Jews."[45] He did not express the same concern about possible Catholic or Lutheran influence in German philosophy; he was concerned about the alleged influence of that group that had been selected for extinction by the political organization he had long supported.[46] This concern about Jews at German universities recalls his remark to Jaspers in 1933 about the existence of a dangerous international Jewish conspiracy. It suggests continuity, and also calls attention to the fact that Heidegger was not the only person in postwar Germany to retain long-established political opinions. The attitude toward the death camps expressed in his few postwar comments is not essentially different from that expressed by those Germans whose main objection to Nazi Germany's conduct of the war was that it lost. Any public expression of such an attitude was inopportune in postwar Germany; for Heidegger such expressions could only bring problems, perhaps even of the kind he had experienced from 1947 to 1950. To avoid such problems, he postponed a public discussion of his political attitudes until after his death. This he did by avoiding further comment after 1950 on Nazism's gruesome legacy, by engaging in unacknowledged political editing of some of his manuscripts, and by withholding a number of politically revealing texts from publication.[47] Heidegger was, in fact, not silent about the death camps, National Socialism, or ethnic Germanic chauvinism. He simply refused to reject them.

NOTES

1. "Es gibt doch eine gefährliche internationale Verbindung der Juden." Heidegger to Karl Jaspers, May 1933, in response to the latter's question as to how anyone

could endorse the nonsense contained in the *Protocols of the Elders of Zion*. See Jaspers' *Philosophische Autobiographie* (Munich: Piper Verlag, 1977), p. 101.

2. See, for example, George Steiner's article "Heidegger, Again," in *Salmagundi*, No. 82–83 (Spring-Summer 1989). pp. 31–55.
3. George Kovacs, "On Heidegger's Silence," in *Heidegger Studies*, 5 (1989), p. 143.
4. "Heidegger's Silence," a paper delivered at the APA Central Division meeting in Chicago, April 22, 1993.
5. Theodore Kisiel, "Heidegger's Apology," in Tom Rockmore and Joseph Margolis (eds.), *The Heidegger Case: On Politics and Philosophy* (Philadelphia: Temple University Press, 1992), p. 17.
6. Philippe Lacoue-Labarthe, *Heidegger, Art and Politics* (Oxford: Basil Blackwell, 1990), p. 136.
7. Note that the Allies encountered this silence even before the war was over. See, for example, Stefan Heym's text from April 1945, "Ich bin nur ein kleiner Mann!" in his *Reden an den Feind* (Frankfurt/M: Fischer, 1986).
8. See, for example, Thomas Sheehan, "Heidegger and the Nazis," in *The New York Review of Books*, June 16, 1988; Victor Farías, *Heidegger and Nazism* (Philadelphia: Temple University Press, 1989); George Leaman, *Contextual Misreadings: The US Reception of Heidegger's Political Thought* (Doctoral dissertation, University of Massachusetts/Amherst, 1991); James R. Watson, "Why Heidegger Wasn't Shocked by the Holocaust: Philosophy and Its Defense System," in *History of European Ideas*, 14, 4 (1992); and Hugo Ott, "Biographical Bases for Heidegger's 'Mentality of Disunity,'" in *The Heidegger Case*.
9. Marcuse's letters to Heidegger, dated August 28, 1947, and May 5, 1948, appear in Bernd Martin, *Martin Heidegger und das "Dritte Reich"* (Darmstadt: Wissenschaftliche Buchgesellschaft, 1989).
10. Quoted in Sheehan, "Heidegger and the Nazis," p. 42.
11. Ethnic German immigrants were to be resettled in Germany's new "eastern territories" captured from Poland and the Soviet Union. These territories were to be "Germanified" with new settlements and imported ethnic German populations. The execution of this policy is discussed in: *Deutsches Blut kehrt heim*, Sonderdruck des Haupschulungsamtes der NSDAP, 1941.
12. In fact, any ethnic German serving in the German army, police, Waffen-SS, or the so-called organisation Todt automatically became a German citizen as of May 19, 1943. From that date on, any ethnic German who joined (or who was drafted) into any one of the above entities was also given German citizenship. *Reichsgesetzblatt*, I, No. 53 (May 25, 1943), p. 315.
13. "Im russischen Bolschewismus haben wir den im zwanzigsten Jahrhundert unternommenen Versuch des Judentums zu erblicken, sich die Weltherrschaft anzueignen, genau so, wie es in anderen Zeitperioden durch andere, wenn auch innerlich verwandte Vorgänge den gleichen Ziele zuzustreben suchte." Adolf Hitler, *Mein Kampf* (Munich: Zentralverlag der NSDAP, 1940), p. 751. See also "Die Juden als Anstifter der bolschewistischen Revolution," in *Judentum und Bolschewismus*, Scriftenreihe zur weltanschauliche Schulungsarbeit der NSDAP, Heft 27 (Munich: Zentralverlag der NSDAP, 1943).
14. See Note 1. For a more existensive discussion of Heidegger's relationship to Jews and Jewishness, see my *Contextual Misreadings*, pp. 138–150.
15. Quoted by Sheehan, "Heidegger and the Nazis," pp. 41–42.
16. Domenico Losurdo provides an excellent discussion of this passage and its context in "Heidegger and Hitler's War," in *The Heidegger Case*.

17. The Soviet Union detonated its first atomic weapon on August 29, 1949, three months before this lecture. The United States used atomic weapons against Japanese cities on August 6 and August 9, 1945. The reference to hydrogen (*Wasserstoff*) bombs is somewhat puzzling since the hydrogen bomb did not then exist; the first hydrogen bomb was detonated by the United States on November 1, 1952.
18. Note that Heidegger was not concerned about "motorization" as such. During his lectures titled "Der europäische Nihilismus" in 1940, Heidegger explicitly defended the complete "motorization" of the German armed forces. See Domenico Losurdo, "Heidegger and Hitler's War," in *The Heidegger case*, p. 148, and Martha Zapata, *Zur Rezeptions- und Wirkungsgeschichte der Philosophie Friedrich Nietzsches im deutschen Faschismus* (Innauguraldissertation am Fachbereich Philosophie und Sozialwissenschaften 1 an der Freien Universität Berlin, 1993), p. 198.
19. Heidegger became a member of the Nazi party on May 1, 1933, and remained a member until it was disbanded by the Allies in 1945. In the vernacular of the party bureaucracy, Heidegger had a "clean" membership; his membership card on file at party headquarters in Munich had no marks on it since he always paid his dues on time and was never subject to any kind of disciplinary proceedings by the party courts. It should be understood that membership in the Nazi party was not something that was available to anyone who wanted to join; membership was considered a privilege bestowed upon worthy (i.e., politically reliable and racially "pure") individuals. See Hans Buchheim, "Mitgliedschaft bei der NSDAP," in *Gutachten des Instituts für Zeitgeschichte*, 1 (Munich, 1958), p. 315. It must also be remembered that Heidegger's ties to the Nazi party predated his actual membership (see Hugo Ott, *Martin Heidegger: Unterwegs zu seiner Biographie* (Frankfurt/M: Campus, 1988), p. 141, and Leaman, *Contextual Misreadings*, pp. 133–135), and that resignation from the party was possible at any time (interview with Hans Semrau, Berlin Document Center, November 24, 1993).
20. Sheehan, "Heidegger and the Nazis," p. 42.
21. Heidegger's reference to tragedy in China would clearly have reminded his West German listeners of the recent victory of the Chinese Communists in the Chinese civil war. The creation of the People's Republic of China on October 1, 1949, consummated that victory and was widely believed to be a major triumph for "international communism."
22. Martin Heidegger, *Being and Time* (New York: Harper & Row, 1962), pp. 384–385.
23. See Leaman, *Contextual Misreadings*, p. 182.
24. Martin Heidegger, *The Self-Affirmation of the German University*, cited from Karsten Harries, "Heidegger as a Political Thinker," p. 315, in Leaman, *Contextual Misreadings*, p. 179.
25. See Leaman, *Contextual Misreadings*, p. 182.
26. This belief was publicly reaffirmed in Germany at the Bitburg military cemetary in 1985, when Chancellor Helmut Kohl and President Ronald Reagan together paid homage to German war dead. The ceremony caused a minor scandal because soldiers from the Waffen-SS were among those buried in the cemetery; after questions were raised about the appropriateness of honoring dead SS men, the German government took the position that these soldiers had also been "victims" of the war and were therefore deserving of ceremonial remembrance. This failure to differentiate between victims and victimizers was also displayed

in the recent remodelling of a monument in east Berlin that had once honored the victims of "fascism and militarism." The new inscription allows a somewhat larger group of people to be honored. It reads: "To the victims of war and despotism" ("Den Opfern vom Krieg und Gewaltherrschaft").

27. On December 12, 1946, the committee charged with the denazification of the university decided to strip Heidegger of his professorship and prohibit him from exercising any other function at the university. His pay was terminated at the end of the following year. This punishment was revised on May 18, 1949, by the university Senate, which voted (7 to 5) to grant Heidegger the status of emeritus professor. Once in effect, the Senate's decision restored both his retirement benefits and his right to teach at the university; the decision took effect at the beginning of the winter semester of 1950–51. See Ott, *Martin Heidegger*, pp. 324–340.
28. In advance of the vote in the university Senate, the philosophy faculty attempted to influence the outcome in Heidegger's favor with an approving reference to the "extreme discretion" ("ausgesprochene Zurückhaltung") Heidegger had exercised since his removal from the university. See Ott, *Martin Heidegger*, pp. 336–337. The philosophy faculty obviously made this reference because its members were, like everyone else in postwar Germany, acutely aware of the public postures that were viewed with approval by the occupation authorities and the new German bureaucracies. That Heidegger continued to exercise this "extreme discretion" after the close Senate vote is an indication that he understood which posture would allow him to pursue his own self-interest.
29. See Hans Sluga, *Heidegger's Crisis: Philosophy and Politics in Nazi Germany* (Cambridge: Harvard University Press, 1993), pp. 234–236.
30. For example, Arnold Gehlen also engaged in such political editing of his work prior to postwar republication. See Leaman, *Contextual Misreadings*, pp. 228–229. In a letter to me dated September 30, 1990, the philosopher Otto F. Bollnow addressed both this problem and its solution: "As for additional changes made in post-war editions of books by German philosophers, in which they have removed traces of a susceptibility to National Socialist ideas: such changes have been made. To investigate this, one would, in every instance, have to make a comparison of the different editions. . . . I know of no discussion of this matter." Hans-Georg Gadamer also addressed this problem in a letter to me dated May 2, 1990: "It is true that some authors. . . . later made slight changes, so to speak 'denazifying' their writings. . . . Whoever is curious [about this] could and can determine what changes have been made by comparing different editions." This problem, and both of these letters, are discussed in more detail in Leaman, *Contextual Misreadings*, pp. 227–234.
31. This lecture was published under the title "Die Frage nach der Technik," and at least three German editions (1954, 1962, 1967) do not contain the sentence in question. This has been discussed by Sheehan, "Heidegger and the Nazis," p. 42.
32. Rainer Marten, one of the two students in question, revealed the details of this episode in his article "Ein rassistisches Konzept von Humanität," in *Badische Zeitung*, December 19–20, 1987, p. 14. Also see George Leaman, *Heidegger im Kontext: Gesamtüberblick zum NS-Engagement der Universitätsphilosophen* (Berlin/Hamburg: Argument-Verlag, 1993), p. 125.
33. These meetings were held in 1930 and 1933 respectively. See Leaman, *Heidegger im Kontext*, p. 125.

34. An excellent discussion of this matter is provided by Tom Rockmore, *On Heidegger's Nazism and Philosophy* (Berkeley: University of California Press, 1992), p. 239.
35. Hermann Heidegger, conversation with the author, June 26, 1993. The collected works (*Gesamtausgabe*) are being published on the basis of the original manuscripts. Earlier editions of many texts, however, were prepared under Heidegger's editorial supervision and the original manuscripts were not made available.
36. For example, Sheehan pointed out that the English version of "The Question Concerning Technology" in David Krell's collection *Martin Heidegger: Basic Writings* (New York: Harper & Row, 1977) does not contain the reference to the extermination camps made in the original lecture in Bremen. See Sheehan, "Heidegger and the Nazis," p. 42.
37. Heidegger gave his son careful instructions as to the order in which his work was to be published after his death. Hermann Heidegger, conversation with the author, June 26, 1993.
38. For example, Alfred Baeumler wrote several texts during the Nazi years that were never published and can now only be examined with the written permission of his widow. See collection ED–315 (Sammlung Alfred Baeumler) at the Institute für Zeitgeschichte in Munich. One of these texts, *Das Kampf um das Eigentum* (1944), has been sealed because of the prevailing "anti-fascist environment" until the year 2003. The philosopher Hans Freyer did not alter new editions of his most compromising texts; he simply let them vanish from public view. He rewrote the bibliographical entries to some of his works so there would be no mention of those texts that would have been unacceptable in postwar Germany. See Leaman, *Contextual Misreadings*, pp. 227–228.
39. For example, Heidegger engaged in an extensive correspondence with Ernst Jünger during the Nazi years. Although these letters have survived and are now stored at the Deutsches Literaturarchiv in Marbach, access to them is closed (*gesperrt*). Upon asking when this correspondence might be examined, Victor Farías was told that the answer to this question was privileged information. Victor Farías, conversation with the author, November 26, 1993.
40. *Beiträge zu Philosophie (vom Ereignis)* (Frankfurt/M: Vittorio Klostermann, 1989).
41. See, for example, Rockmore, *On Heidegger's Nazism and Philosophy*, and Leaman, *Contextual Misreadings*.
42. Dieter Thomä, *Die Zeit des Selbst und die Zeit danach* (Frankfurt/M: Suhrkamp, 1990). pp. 761–762.
43. Martin Heidegger, "Europa und die deutsche Philosophie," in Hans-Helmuth Gander (ed.), *Europa und die Philosophie* (Fanfurt/M: Vittorio Klostermann, 1993), p. 31 (my translation).
44. Hermann Göring, "Der Kampf gegen Marxismus und Separtismus," in *Almanach der nationalsozialistischen Revolution* (Berlin: Brunnen Verlag, 1934), pp. 155–160. An excellent example of the propaganda which asserted a unique German ability to protect Europe from "the danger in the east" is provided by Otto Kriegk, *Die Geburt Europas* (Berlin: Verlag Scherl, 1943), p. 224: "Die in diesem Kriege Schuldigen haben mit dem Verbrechen der Vernichtung unersetzlicher Werte Europas das Verbrechen der Mobilisierung des Bolschewismus verbunden. *Nur wir* können die Welt vom Bolschewismus befreien. *Nur wir* vermögen die neue Ordnung zu schaffen" (my emphasis).
45. Rainer Marten, "Heidegger's geist," in Jürg Altwegg (ed.), *Die Heidegger Kontroverse* (Frankfurt/M: Athenäum, 1988), cited in Leaman, *Contextual Misreadings*, p. 150.

46. See note 19.
47. Note that Heidegger allowed the now famous interview with *Der Spiegel* in 1966, but only on the condition that the transcript be published after his death. Heidegger died on May 26, 1976, and the interview was published May 31, 1976.

5

Heidegger *silentio*

WILLIAM VAUGHAN

We are poised to speak again regarding a thinker and his relation to events of extremity. The publishers have awaited completion of essays intended to advance the thinking on this issue. Another book will soon be published on Heidegger and Holocaust. We are not yet to the point of understanding the issues. Not enough has been said or written about such things. There is the obligation to continue to respond to an issue such as this. A feature of the appreciation of silence is related to this obligation of speaking. Silence has dropped from sight here. There is only the obligation to speak, and the saying bears no relation to the said other than protection and heroic preservation. Surely to move questioning from the obligation of speaking to the appreciation of silence risks betrayal.

What is it to have written in a holocaustic tone? Why here concern ourselves with tone, lest we dare speak only of a holocaustic tone and not the events themselves? Surely there is the danger here of a kind of high-brow Holocaust revisionism. Perhaps it is that such writing reveals its catastrophic displacements, its aftershocks whose sorrows are never fully disclosed, never wholly there but concealed and muffled in undecidability. There is something of the genre of the holocaustal, which reveals an approaching of the abyssal, which discloses the wish of being touched by it at a remove, in greatest tension with the demand that the truth of these events be made present and clear. Some have argued there cannot be a narrative capable of witnessing or testifying to what has happened without recovering it as an aesthetic construct betraying the historical truth whose immensity escapes stylistic mastery. Accordingly, such a telling must resist at every point the contamination of the banal recovery of sentiment; the artist must engage in an unqualified saying whose clarity and truth are triumphant, a saying encumbered by opacity and by the withdrawal or retreat from narrative itself which marks the abyss of the unsayable.[1]

The problem often is one of language being corrupted to the point where it has to be invented anew, a writing not with words but against them. Often this involves telling less, so as to make the truth more credible. Often it involves using the language of others as one's own, the piecing together of still-usable language like so many skin-grafts. The failure of language to grasp or articulate the event is a recurrent topic in post-Holocaust writing. It is a problematic that cuts across genres. In some, the difficulty of speaking and the impossibility of communication are not only subjects; these failures permeate their very textuality.

How does one give testimony to an event that to some degree negates the very assumptions of discourse that make possible such telling? The hermeneutic antinomy, if you will, is that failing to testify to the event is to condemn it to historical forgetfulness, the imperative to testify thus further intensifying this antinomy. To overcome the claim that the holocaustic exposes the impossibility of bearing witness, a strategy of restitution arises through the negative constitution of textuality. The testimony that it is possible to communicate the impossibility of communication is ironically made possible through the inscription of this very failure in discourse. Such a restitutional strategy risks, however, not banal recovery but obscene dilution, the blur of linguistic indeterminacy, following what some believe to be the failure of language not only as straightforward referential witness, but the rendering of even the tone of such witnessing.[2]

It is here where one is reminded of Paul Celan's invocations of cinders and ash, of smoke and dust and sand in his poetry. The atmosphere of decay in his works seems to deepen the dichotomy of remembering and forgetting; they are at once an illustration of the role of the artist and a comment on the paradox inherent in that role, engraving, as they seek to do, memories into poetic language in the hope that it may preserve them as an urn preserves ashes. But the images of ash and sand also remind poet and reader that in many ways nothing is left to be remembered. For some, ashes and sand are traces, not in the sense of an imprint, but in the sense of the moment of self-effacement inherent in language, sand being nothing but a residue of what is destroyed.[3]

Celan's writing was to have done with the description of horror by horror, a poetry of melodic nullity. His work is marked by a terrible difficulty in reading and translating, by the need for revision of even elementary categories of understanding and tropes of interpretation as well as their reciprocal self-exposure. The metaphorical prisms through which Celan's experiences are made to pass are expressed in a language which, having once belonged to the configuration of ordinary life, must now bear the disfigurement of concentrationary experience. He seeks to achieve what Heidegger and de Man do not, the vestiges of the commemorative within a holocaustic tone.

If anyone despaired of language and sank into madness it was Celan, whose works come as close to anguished silence as works can. His poetry made language re-enter the camps to chronicle an experience outside of human experience, and this constitutes a reaffirmation of the very bonds of humanity whose destruction it describes. Where most of Celan's works should resemble an inarticulate cry, they represent, however damaged, a purity of word, a clarity of voice, the transparency of an historical and ethical condition. It is here where it seems possible to mark to some degree how the traversals of extremity cross within the "post-holocaustal" thought of Celan and the "post-metaphysical." Indeed, the later Heidegger asks if these two modes of discourse should be read as one, since both share a preoccupation with the limits of representational discourse and employ many of the same strategies in order to inscribe these limits, this failure of speech.

In this paper I will only again trace the trajectories of the Celan-Heidegger encounter, remembering that to say of two figures that they share a similar trajectory is not to say they arrive in similar places. Part I will be a brief overview of some recent major statements of the encounter; Part II will present some examples of how Celan sought to encounter the word of Heidegger in his poetry; Part III will seek to illustrate how Heidegger perhaps encountered Celan. Part IV will be the conclusion. Perhaps the gathering of ideas and language here is both a betrayal of the obligation to speak and a betrayal of the appreciation of silence. Be that as it may, my purposes in comparing these two figures are not for political expedience, to call on the "poet of authentic Jewish holocaustic experience" to somehow get Heidegger off the political hook,[4] but to show how Heidegger's silences preserve what facile condemnations of his silence regarding the Holocaust overlook, and that by striking a tuning-fork to them, both Heidegger and Celan can be seen to be gathered in a similar *silentio*, a similar distress, which comes from a world lacking any divine authority, a world with the old gods dead and the new not yet born.[5]

I

Modernity for Heidegger is marked by destitution. Humanity's attempts to reconcile itself with the world by objectifying it through science in order to subordinate it to the categories of subjectivity lead only to a nihilism as it appears in unfettered world technology. This is no mere consequence of modernity, however, but is rooted in the metaphysical essence of the West as such. Technological modernity is but the latest chapter in the metaphysics of presence—the constant presence and luminosity Plato attributed to the intelligible core of reality has now been transmuted into the constant availability of natural objects. During this period of destitute time, Heidegger thought it possible for thinkers to entrust themselves to the re-orienting guidance of poets, and he turned to poets for whom the bonds of language had not ruptured. The errors of his own involvement with totalitarian National Socialism, and his searching efforts to come to grips with the totalizing stance of technology, provoked his deep engagement with poets, of whom he found Hölderlin to be the one who reaches into the abyss, who traces the lost trace of the holy and salvific. In exposing himself to the danger of the abyss, such a poet is nevertheless still sustained by the bond of language. This insight, to which only later was Heidegger able to give full expression, was that language is poetic in the essential sense because it lets beings become manifest as such. This bringing to manifestation derives from no arbitrary human doing; language is neither an instrument of human will, nor a conventional depiction of the inner display of ideas to consciousness, nor the natural behavioral expression of our communal needs. The power of language lies behind and beyond any human power to construe its effects in an orderly way. Insight into this "essence" of language allows a gesture toward what lies deeper than the universal imposition of technology. Though the "place" of this bond is one of extremity and need, those who follow the poet are not deprived of speech, of world, of community, but can hope to renew another beginning. Heidegger's thinking here is to be thought as sealing off the encroachment of language from technological nihilism and what might be called a "postmodern sensibility," which has suffered displacement and has gone through a devastation of meaning cutting any nurturing bond.

In much of his poetry Hölderlin turned to the ancient Greeks for inspiration. Heidegger looked to the Greeks for insight into the possibility of preparing for the advent of new gods. While recognizing that the Greek world could never be revived, Heidegger still at this time called for the initiation of a new beginning that was as radical and enduring as that carried out by the ancient Greeks. This new beginning was not to be some empty repetition of Greek culture in German dress but an authentic repetition of the world-founding act of the Greeks. Heidegger explained the essence of this creative act in terms of Nietzsche's Dionysian and Apollinian categories, but qualified Nietzsche's use of these terms by reading them through Hölderlin, who Heidegger believed had meditated upon their relationship more closely.

As Michael Zimmerman has recently pointed out, Heidegger believed every historical people has both an endowment and an anointed task.[6] The Greeks, existing within the mood of astonishment or wonder, were endowed with the Dionysian gift, one of "being touched by the might of being." For them, the anointed task was the subduing of the unsubdued in the struggle of the work; the grasping and bringing-to-stand of being. Struck by the Dionysian presencing of entities, the Greeks were compelled to shape that presencing in terms of Apollinian metaphysical categories, forms, and structures.

The basic mood for the Greeks was astonishment or awe; the basic moods for humanity within the technological epoch, according to Heidegger, were horror and boredom. Just as the Greeks initiated Western history by profoundly experiencing and responding to what was disclosed in their primal mood (awe), so too the Germans could initiate a new historical beginning if they experienced and responded appropriately to what was disclosed in their primal moods (boredom and horror). Heidegger at this time thought Hölderlin's poetry could enable the Germans to become accessible to the pain involved in the horror of modernity. Pain for Heidegger was the basic form of the knowledge of *Geist*. The "saying" of the poet could help transform the mood of horror into one of "holy affliction," mourning but prepared.

This holy affliction could not be explained in political terms, but called for a primal encounter with being. For Heidegger, being named the self-concealing presencing in light of which entities revealed themselves in their various ways. The Germans, like the Greeks, were in principle capable of experiencing the self-concealing presencing of being in a primordial way. Lack of such experience had deadened the Germans and had led them into technological nihilism.

Again, at this time, the mourning involved in experiencing the holy affliction (by which again was meant the departure of the gods and the concealment of being) would also be the event of experiencing being anew—the event which would prepare the way for the arrival of new gods. Only by becoming vulnerable to the horror and grief involved in technological nihilism could it be discovered that such nihilism was historical in character, so that an alternative disclosure of entities could be possible. The mood of holy affliction and surrender to the pain involved in the death of the gods would work to cast off the technological armor and cease to allow people to fall into the distractions of mass culture and myths of progress.

Lacoue-Labarthe[7] used Hölderlin's conception of tragedy to provide an interpretation of Heidegger's thinking along these lines in connection with Heidegger's own involvement in the war. According to Lacoue-Labarthe, Heidegger failed to apply the theme of the death of God to the Holocaust. He argues that God died at Auschwitz, in any case the Greco-Christian God, and the event of extermination emanated from the need to annihilate the witnesses to another God which impeded the program of the West. Auschwitz represents what Hölderlin called a caesura, a radical break in history which occurs when God and humanity become radically separated. Such a caesura for Hölderlin was a basic law of the tragic character of finite existence. Auschwitz reveals the "essence" of the West because in the death camps the Western drive toward total domination achieved its apogee: Humans disposed of other humans like industrial waste, burning them in crematoria custom-built according to the latest technology. The radical break between God and humanity which occurred in the Holocaust resulted from a hubristic humanity which tried to raise itself to the level of the all-powerful God. Lacoue-Labarthe maintains that, in the tragic caesura provoked by such *hubris*, God is revealed as an abyss, a total absence which signals either the possibility for a new beginning or else the end of all historical possibilities. Heidegger regarded the events of the Holocaust not as instances of the caesura of which Hölderlin spoke but as symptoms or consequences of a real caesura: the death of God, which Hölderlin and Nietzsche had both previously surmised in the nineteenth century.

Lyotard[8] challenged Lacoue-Labarthe's use of Hölderlin's theory of tragedy to interpret the meaning of Auschwitz. Lyotard argued that Auschwitz cannot have represented a tragic caesura because nothing has really changed since the war: The West has not been released from its technological impulse. Germany's defeat was not sufficient to transform the impulse toward mastery and control. Drawing on the Western image of the Jews, Lyotard argues that the Jews died at Auschwitz because the Greco-Roman West had long resented them as reminders of those commercial, legal, military, and cultural projects whose aim is to deny human dependence on the nameless Divine. The Jews represent the memory of the unconquerable obstacle to the Western quest to make everything representable and controllable. As bearers of the memory of human finitude and dependence, the Jews had to be excluded. Their extermination was part and parcel of the global absorption into technological metaphysics.

Although Lyotard thinks Auschwitz cannot be conceived in terms of the artistic laws of tragedy, he agrees with Heidegger, up to a point, that Auschwitz exemplifies the dreadful "work of art" typical of the union of art and politics in the technological era. While an authentic work of art, such as a Greek temple, founded a world by letting entities present themselves appropriately and distinctly, the perverse technological work of art, such as the hydroelectric dam or a death camp, differentiates nothing, but rather reveals things indiscriminately as resources ready to use. A Greek temple and a hydroelectric dam are both instances of *techne*; both reveal entities; but whereas the former constitutes a world, the latter contributes to an un-world of modern technology.

The seeds of Lacoue-Labarthe's views in relation to Celan are sown in an earlier work, dealing more specifically with Celan's poetry,[9] in which Lacoue-Labarthe begins with two poems by Celan, "Tübingen, Jänner" and "Todtnauberg," the first an evocation of Hölderlin, the second an "account" of Celan's meeting with Heidegger in the Black Forest in July 1967. This choice is hardly innocent, positioning Celan as it does along the Greco-German lineage so described, which Hölderlin and Heidegger conceived as ending the barren and godless age of modernity. "Todtnauberg" has been widely discussed in this regard, as Celan's recording of Heidegger's having failed to hear the call of the destituted other and withheld the hoped-for "word" of atonement and halting consolation. In that poem, the meeting's apprehensive intensity of approach, its hope, and its unfulfilled parting are re-enacted. Even within the tranquil, rural scene, there is the insistent memory of senseless brutality and leveled mass graves lurking between poet and thinker that remains unaddressed. Lacoue-Labarthe reads Celan's work according to ontological categories taken from the later Heidegger, particularly the latter's lectures on Hölderlin, and takes the poem "Todtnauberg," Celan's poem "about" the silence of some "coming word" from Heidegger, to be symbolic of Heidegger's general refusal throughout the postwar period to explain his involvement with National Socialism. He sees Heidegger as having intuited the "categorical retreat" of God, an absence of the divine which is also an appearing. That God and the divine are missing is an absence, an absence which is not nothing, but the presence of the hidden plenitude of that which was and which, thus gathered, is. Celan, for Lacoue-Labarthe, functions as the ironic repetition, the latest and terrible degree of this Hölderlinian problematic.[10]

II

Lacoue-Labarthe was on target with the connections made between Heidegger and Celan regarding the absence of the divine, but does not go far enough, either with Heidegger or Celan, in showing how both poet and thinker here are moving toward the abyssal, although what that means takes different forms in each. The abyss is not merely that of the withdrawal of being or the failure of the holy, but is the abyss with which the atrocities of this century have opened up beneath poet and thinker, the deprivation of the assurance of meaning by a kind of internal marking, a signalling of a prior condition of negation or torsion within the language employed. Perhaps no commentator has established this phenomenon of "abyssal inversion" in Celan in connection with Heidegger as conclusively as Véronique Fóti. Consider the poem "Largo," dating from the 1960s.

"Largo"	"Largo"
Gleichsinnige du, heidegängerisch Nähe:	You of the same mind, moor-wandering near one
über- sterbens- gross liegen	more-than- death- sized we lie

wir beieinander, die Zeit- lose wimmelt dir unter den atmenden Lidern,	together, the time- less teems under our breathing eyelids,
das Amselpaar hängt neben uns, unter unsern gemeinsam droben mit- ziehenden weissen	the pair of blackbirds hangs beside us, under our whitely drifting companions up there, our
Meta- stasen	meta- stases.

Celan's poetry is marked by interlingual puns, bizarre neologisms, oblique personal references, and intentional misquotations. The title of this poem refers to a broad or slow movement of music. In the first line, "heidegängerisch" is an inescapable allusion to Heidegger. This reference is underscored by the use of some of the central words from his philosophical writings: "Nähe" and "Zeit." Indeed, Celan and Heidegger are "of the same mind."

In the third stanza, there are the two blackbirds. These are of course stock figures in fairy tales, who speak in riddles and bring bad tidings. In the German one reads "Amsel"—the poet's real name was Paul Antschel, which he changed to Celan after the war. Celan might also have been alluding to Grass's novel *The Dog Years*, which chronicles the love-hate relationship between a Jew and a Nazi during the war. The Jewish character in the story is named Amsel, and throughout the book there is a deadly pastiche of the "metaphysical jargon" of Heidegger.

Toward the end of the poem, the presence of "our whitely drifting / companions up there" is a reference to the Jewish victims of the war: the smoke of the bodies burned in the crematoria. This is a common image in Celan's poetry—one might think of the lines from his most famous poem, "Death Fugue" ("he gives us a grave in the air"). The Jewish dead in Celan's work inhabit the air, are the very substance we are condemned to breathe: souls turned into smoke, into dust, into nothing at all—our "metastasis."[11]

According to Fóti, in Celan's abyssal poetry, language not merely conveys violation but is the enactment of violation itself, a performance of what it is about. Faced with the uncircumventable condition of enacting and inscribing the unspeakable, Celan engaged in a disruption of language which could allow for the expression of a violation unable to be spoken of in the intact language. This laminate fissioning of language makes the violative bringing-to-word possible. It is a restitutional movement, for if language shows itself only to be self-referential, if it brings nothing really to word, if no truth can step into its midst, then the anguished self-implication has failed in its aim.

One of Celan's chief means of semantic destabilization is the trope of paronomasia, which exposes every word in the text to the possibility of being an alteration of a lost paradigm resolutely drawing back from rational or divinatory reconstruction.[12] The withheld word is not merely the forgotten word (such as Heidegger's name being absent from "Todtnauberg"). It may also be, to use Fóti's own analysis, "the dreaded word or name which lurks unrecognized in seemingly innocuous speech ("heidegängerisch" or "Amsel") which opens up a vista upon another scene of language. The paronomasia is an abyssal inversion by eroding not merely the monosemy of the word or name, but also metaphor and other linguistic tropes which depend upon a reasonable stability of linguistic entities." Celan's "heidegängerisch Nähe" is no enriching metaphor but a kind of torsioning. For Celan, a re-poisoning of language by such encrypting may yet have accomplished restitution.[13]

Celan sought to encounter Heidegger's thinking using less cryptic measures as well. The poem of most direct engagement with the philosopher is perhaps "In der Luft":

IN DER LUFT, da bleibt deine
Wurzel, da
in der Luft.
Wo sich das Irdische ballt, erdig,
Atem-und-Lehm.

Groß
geht der Verbannte dort oben, der
Verbrannte: ein Pommer, zuhause
im Maikäferlied, das mütterlich bleib,
sommerlich, hell-
blutig am Rand

aller schroften,
winterhart-kalten
Silben.

Mit ihm
wandern die Meridiane:
an-

gesogen von seinem
sonnengesteuerten Schmerz, der die
Länder verbrüdert nach
dem Mittagsspruch einer
liebenden
Ferne. Aller-
orten ist Hier und ist Heute, ist, von
Verzweiflungen her,
der Glanz,
in den die Entzweiten treten mit ihren

IN THE AIR, there your root lives
on, there,
in the air,
Where the earthly emballs itself, earthy,
breath-and-clay.

Tall
he walks, the banished one up there, the
burnt one: a Pomeranian, at home
in the may-bug song which stayed
motherly, summerly, bright-
blooded at the edge

of all the jagged,
cold hard-winter
syllables.

With him
the meridians walk:
at-

tracted by his
sun-steered pain, which brothers
countries under
the noonday-spell of a
loving
horizon. Every-
where is Here and Today, is, born of
despairs
the radiance
into which the divided ones step with their

geblendeten Mündern:

der Kuß, nachtlich,
brennt einer Sprache den Sinn ein, zu
der sie erwachen, sie—;

heimgekehrt in
den unheimlichen Bannstrahl
der die Verstreuten versammelt,
die
durch die Sternwüste Seele Geführten,
die
Zeltmacher droben im Raum
ihrer Blicke und Schiffe,
die winzigen Garben Hoffnung,
darin es von Erzengelfittichen rauscht,
von Verhängnis,
die Brüder, die Schwestern,
die
zu leicht, die zu schwer, die zu leicht
Befunden mit
der Weltenwaage im blut-
schänderischen, im
fruchtbaren Schoß, die lebenslang
Fremden,
spermatisch bekränzt von Gestirnen,
schwer
in den Untiefen lagernd, die Leiber
zu Schwellen getürmt, zu Dämmen,—
die

Furtenwesen, darüber
der Klumpfuß der Götter herüber-
gestolpert kommt—um
wessen
Sternzeit zu spät?

blinded mouths:

the kiss, nightly,
brands the meaning into a language to
which they awaken, they—:

returned home into
the un-homely banishment
which gathers up the scattered ones,
the
ones lead through the star-desert Soul,
the
tentmakers up there in the space
of their glances and ships,
they, the tiny sheaves of Hope
in which archangels wings rustle, and
doom,
they, the brothers, the sisters, those
found
too light, too heavy, too light,
with
the world-weighing scales in
their incestuous, their
fruit-bearing lap, the lifelong
strangers,
spermatically garlanded with stars,
heavily
resting in the shallows, their bodies
towering up to thresholds, to dams,—
the

ford-folk, across whom
the club-foot of the gods comes
stumbling,—by
whose
star-time too late?

The expressionist metaphors for destruction in the poem are linked to biblical allusions: the "breath and clay" of line 4 recalls passages on the emergence of life from the book of Genesis; "durch die Sternwüste Seele Geführten" might refer to the wanderings of ancient Jews in the desert (Exodus); the motif of violence and destruction (line 8) recalls the children's song from the Thirty Years' War: "Maikäfer flieg, /Der Vater ist im Krieg, / Die Mutter ist im Pommerland, / Und Pommerland ist abgebrannt" (May beetle fly, / Father is at war, / Mother is in Pomerania, / And Pomerania is burned away). In line 38, the "Weltenwaage" recalls the Last Judgment; yet the subsequent "und der Klumfuß der Götter" (line 45) evokes not a biblical god but Hephaestus, the god whom Zeus expelled from Olympus.

The various syntactic structures create a tension between fusion and displacement in the poem. The opening line asserts that the roots are no longer in the earth but in the air; and the verb "bleiben" emphasizes that they will remain there. But the air is no transcendent realm nor a vacuum; it has become a place of encounter, inextricably linked to earthly things. The image of the burned traveler turns the air into a grave, recalling the vivid death imagery from "Largo" and "Death Fugue." This poem refers not only to Jewish pogroms, however, but also to the suffering and devastation of the German region of Pommern (Pomerania) during the Thirty Years' War. The traveler from Pomerania is familiar not only with this song ("zu Hause im Maikäferlied"), but also with the destruction it laments. By contrasting the "motherly" song to "cold and wintry" syllables, Celan's text also points to the tension, inherent in poetic language, between the world's fragility and its hardness.[14]

The traveler's suffering and pain become forces of attraction that draw together all the displaced and uprooted. As these forces are guided by the sun, they assume cosmic dimensions. Like meridians, the geographical circles that link distant regions, they fuse past and future, transforming distant realms into a point-like presence. They reconcile the countries and those who have been separated. Through their union (here a kiss), language attains meaning and sense.

The subsequent stanza brings to life the vision of a people scattered in the desert of the universe: the souls who wander in it become companion of the stars. Like the ancient Jews wandering in the desert, the cosmic tentmakers carry hopes and misfortunes with them. The souls of these brothers and sisters have been weighed on the "world-weighing scales," as on the day of the Last Judgment; their bodies, like corpses in the death camps, are now towering up to thresholds in the deep. The last lines engage in questions of divine justice and protection but leave them unresolved. Even Hephaestus, the god of artists and craftsmen, of the banned and the exiled (Heidegger again, perhaps?), arrives too late at the site of destruction. The bitter irony and resignation inherent in these images counteract the apparent ambiguity of the final question.

Celan is exploring the bond between victims of violence and destruction in ancient and modern times, but here insists that to have one's roots "in the air," to be homeless and displaced, has become a recurrent human condition, a disruption which has turned into a continuity. The notion of Dasein as displacement is linked to the idea of a constant movement forward: The traveler follows a path in the air, and the souls wander in the desert. The image of the foreigners points to Heidegger's "Language in the Poem," which associates the word "Fremd" with the Old German "fram" in the sense of "to be on the way." Celan is connecting the idea of both displacement and being in motion with the metaphor of a meridian which turns poetry into a gathering point for the displaced.[15] Indeed, the entire poem is an engagement with Heidegger's fourfold. The earth and sky, mortals and divinities, are here, in the air in which smoke whirls and stars guide; in the mortality of the burnt bodies of the dead and the pain of their memory; in the references to the world, to home, to the earth and clay where none are buried; in the divinities that are white archangels and club-footed gods; and all of this united in the horizon of the meridian to which Celan's poem appeals.

We mentioned how Heidegger thought Hölderlin's poetry made possible the elementary emergence of human existence and its world. He even analyzed the inferiority of other poets in relation to Hölderlin.[16] Could Celan have filled this role for Heidegger? Indeed, it seems as though Celan was moving in this direction precisely as Heidegger was moving away. In many respects Heidegger's later thinking on language signals a movement away from the privileging of Hölderlin, or even poets generally, and eventually toward an event in language itself. Just as Heidegger contrasted Hölderlin with Nietzsche, in that Nietzsche remained rooted in modern metaphysics whereas Hölderlin presaged the overcoming of all metaphysics, and, in preparation for the new beginning at the end of philosophy as metaphysics, Heidegger turned away from the language of metaphysics to the language of Hölderlin's poetry, so Heidegger moves on from the language of Hölderlin's poetry to how an everyday thing "worlds world." The essays in the 1950s explore the possibility for a non-subjectivistic, non-anthropocentric encounter with things. He argued that the abstract "space" of the subject must give way in favor of the concrete "place" of things. Heidegger maintained here that virtually anything can play the role of opening up the place on which things can encounter each other. A footbridge is not set into a pre-existing place, but rather helps to gather into a shared place the constituents of the fourfold: earth and sky, gods and mortals.

Heidegger's most famous example of an everyday thing which gathers together the fourfold elements of a world is the jug. The jug "works" by holding open a void in which wine may be held. For Heidegger this "void" is not an empty nothingness but instead the self-concealing source in terms of which all things appear. Meditating on the curious character of the jug discloses that the jug somehow draws upon the same "nothingness" which constitutes the temporal-linguistic transcendence of human existence. The jug can play the ontologically disclosive role once assigned almost exclusively to the work of art. As the bearer of wine, the jug gathers the elements of the world—earth and sky, gods and mortals. The jug reveals that the wine comes from grapes nourished by the warmth of the sun, and that the wine enlivens the mortals who inbibe it and provides a libation for the gods. The jug allows earth and sky, gods and mortals, to come near to each other, to manifest themselves to each other in a mirroring play which lets each come into its own. Rational cognition, Heidegger maintained, is simply incapable of understanding the event which makes possible the worlding of the world constituted by the interplay of the fourfold. The mutual appropriation of the earth and sky, gods and mortals, both takes place within and gives rise to the "region" which constitutes a particular world. "Dwelling" describes the mode of existing involved in the mutual play in which everything is allowed to show itself appropriately.[17]

In addition to the fourfold, the idea of a motion forward, which Heidegger uncovers in Trakl's poetry, is also present in Celan's "In der Luft." In contrast to Trakl's travelers, the autumnal soul, Groddek, Elis, through the twilight of poetic language, Celan's "Verbannte" and "Verbrannte" bear the memory of the Jewish dead. For Heidegger, Trakl's verse conceives pain as a fundamental dimension of life, associating it with truth and good. Pain is understood here ontologically, as the fundamental trait of the soul's nature. It is the animator of the forward movement of Trakl's poetry. Pain was of importance to the later Heidegger, in that the appearance of pain means the emergence of something which escapes universal technological control and mastery. Authentic experience of pain confronts the *Gestell* with something which defies it. In Celan's "In der Luft," pain is the motor of the movement as well, but it is the suffering of the survivor which gathers the displaced, the burned, and the exiled into the meridian.

Celan's later Meridian speech sheds additional light on his notion of the meridian.[18] At the end of the speech, Celan evokes a return to the *topos* of his cultural origins, the Bukovina. But the text underscores this region to no longer exist. The search for the *topos* of the origin is undertaken on a map of childhood, implying the imaginary character of both the map and *topos*, but the quest for origins leads to the discovery of the force of which his "In der Luft" speaks, the force that draws together past, present, and future, disparate elements, and those that have been separated. It is a meridian, an immaterial but terrestrial system, which displays remarkable similarities to language. It is the loosest of structural principles, and undergoes a movement between still existing and ceasing to be. A geographical circle, it embodies the idea of a constant turn, a symbol for the constant semantic transformations that poetic language undergoes.

For Heidegger, Hölderlin was the poet who in his verse not only uncovered the dwelling of mankind as dwelling but also posited the new time, of the gods which have fled and the gods that are coming. Perhaps, after the war, to recover the question-worthiness of the holocaustal, one could make recourse to a *mythos* in which the truth of beings could again be secured in such a way that it could open up the way of a new dwelling on earth. Such was the Hölderlinian *mythos*. Celan at once attains to the Hölderlinian position and wreaks bitter, ironic havoc with the idea. For "In der Luft" also awaits a future and posits a time. This, however, is a time of despair. The bodies of exterminated Jews in the death camps are piled up to dams, to fords, to thresholds, yet for these gods they are nothing but a mere hindrance across which they stumble. The concluding metaphors of Celan's poem mark the crucial difference between his own negative attitude toward God and the much more affirmative beliefs of other Jewish thinkers, such as Buber and Scholem. Again and again Celan's works exhibit doubt regarding the existence of any divine protection. Heidegger and Celan are united, not only in their negative theological anticipation and despair of the absent God, but in the question of how to speak of a transgression otherwise than in the language the transgression was itself dedicated to exceeding.

That language could serve humanity and being as the meridian-like gathering of these now-sundered aspects is prevalent in many of Heidegger's works. In "The End of Philosophy and the Task of Thinking," for example, the word "Vollendung" is advanced to characterize the end of philosophy.[19] In Heidegger's essay "Logos (Heraclitus Fragment B 50)" the Greek word "legein" undergoes an encounter with the Latin "legere," which means to collect, to gather together, to pick, or to read. His question, "What lay originally in 'legein' as 'legen?'" concerns "legere." Yet in the essay the Latin verb speaks by means of its German counterparts "lesen" (to pick, to read) and "Lese" (gathering).

> *Legen ist lesen.* ["To place is to gather."] . . . The gleaning at harvest time gathers fruit from the soil. The gathering of the vintage involves picking grapes from the vine. Picking and gleaning are followed by the bringing together of the fruit. So long as we insist on the usual appearances, we are inclined to take this bringing-together as the gathering itself or even its termination. But gathering is more than mere amassing. To gathering belongs a collecting which brings under shelter. Accommodation governs the sheltering; accommodation is in turn governed by a safekeeping. . . . The safekeeping that brings something in has already determined the first steps of the gathering and arranged everything that follows. . . . The sheltering comes first in the essential formation of the vintage.[20]

What Heidegger comes to in *An Introduction to Metaphysics* is that language is uncontainable within a theory of the *logos*. Language is mystified in the sense of becoming radically other, utterly different than romantic imagination. Heidegger concentrates this otherness in the Greek word "deinos," which he picks up on from its appearance in the famous chorus from Antigone about the strangeness of man. This word is taken, not in the still human sense of "fearful" or "terrible" but as "Überwaltigung" and "Unheimlich," overpowering and uncanny. "Deinos" becomes an event of incomprehensible violence that shakes the human loose from everything safe and familiar, which disconnects him from his ground and transports him into a realm of otherness.

Truly poetic language is language impinging or impacting on human existence, laying it open, exposing it to the uncanny, estranging it from its comfortable fixities, disclosing Dasein as "deinotation," strangest of all. "Dichten" is an event of radical estrangement in which Dasein is shattered against the uncanny. Heidegger suggests that the Greeks tried to register their encounter with the uncanny in tragedy; tragedy is the first representation of the "Unheimlich," a first taming, a first governing. This appropriating of the uncanny is the work of the *logos*. The *logos* is the way Dasein brings the overpowering and the strange under control—an overpowering of the overpowering. But Heidegger seeks to show language is not *logos*, not wholly identifiable or reducible to it; rather it is excessive and uncontainable, although there could be no *logos* without it. Language as *logos* is gathering, ordering, controlling, making sense. Language as the "poetic" is something else—"Überwaltigung," "Unheimlich," "adike." It is something other, language resisting its own gathering, withholding itself, refusing itself, threatening to explode its own forms.

What Heidegger gives us is a criticism of the *logos* as that which overcomes language, tames it, bends language to human use. "It is by no means evident that language is *logos*." *Logos* here means that which gathers, orders, makes sense of things; it is that which makes possible the unity of being in the construction of logical categories. It makes possible the building of the proposition, or the language of the ethical, or the tone of grief. Hence the logical function of the sign, which is to take over what language gives it and to hold it in place, stabilizing it, fixing it for the assertions and frameworks of the *logos*.

> The word, the name, restores the emerging being from the immediate, overpowering surge to its being and maintains it in this openness, delimitation, and permanence. Naming does not come afterward, providing an already manifest being with a designation and a hallmark known as a word; it is the other way around: originally an act of violence, the word sinks from this height to become a mere sign, and this sign proceeds to thrust itself before the being. Originary saying opens up the being of the being in the structure of its collectedness. And this opening is collected in a second sense: *the word preserves what was originally collected and so administers the overpowering power.* Standing and active in *Logos*, which is ingathering, man is the gatherer. He undertakes to govern and succeeds in governing the power of the overpowering.[21]

Consider now how this is taken up in Celan's "Die Winzer" . . .

Die Winzer

Sie herbsten den Wein ihrer Augen,
sie keltern alles Geweinte, auch
dieses:
so will es die Nacht,
die Nacht, an die sie gelehnt sind, die
Mauer,
so forderts der Stein,
der Stein, über den ihr Krückstock
dahinspricht
ins Schweigen der Antwort—
ihr Krückstock, der einmal,
einmal im Herbst,
wenn das Jahr zum Tod schwillt, als
Traube,
der einmal durchs Stumme
hindurchspricht, hinab
in den Schacht des Erdachten.

Sie herbsten, sie keltern den Wein,
sie pressen die Zeit wie ihr
Auge,
sie kellern das Sickernde ein, das Geweinte,
im Sonnengrab, das sie rüsten
mit nachtstarker Hand:
auf das ein Mund danach dürste,
später—
ein Spätmund, ähnlich dem ihren:
Blindem entgegengekrümmt und gelähmt
ein Mund, zu dem der Trunk aus der
Tiefe emporschäumt, [indes]
der Himmel hinabsteigt ins wächserne
Meer,
um fernher las Lichtstumpt zu leuchten
wenn endlish die Lippe sich feuchtet.

The Vintagers

They harvest the wine of their eyes,
they crush out all the years' weeping,
this also:
thus willed by the night,
the night, which they're leaning
against, the wall,
thus forced by the stone,
the stone, over which their crook-stick
speaks away
into the silence of answers—
their crook-stick, which just once,
just once in fall,
when the year swells to death, swollen
grapes,
which just once will speak right
through muteness, down in-
to the mineshaft of musings.

They harvest, they crush out the wine,
they press down on time like their
eyes,
they cellar the seepings, the weepings,
in a sun-grave, which they ready
with night-toughened hands:
so that a mouth might thirst for this,
later—
a latemouth, like to their own:
bent toward blindness and lamed—
a mouth, to which the draught from
the depth foams upward, meantime
heaven descends into waxen seas,
and
far off, as a candle-stub, glistens,
at last when the lip comes to moisten.

translation by John Felstiner

The opening pronoun refers of course to vintagers, common figures in German Romantic poetry. In their being evoked again and again, there is an unmistakable reference to a people. As John Felstiner explains:

> Other commentators, sure that "Die Winzer" chiefly concerns the poetic process itself, have identified its primary subject, they who "harvest the wine of their eyes," as poets who take on humanity's pain and transform

it for us. Such a reading is plausible, but it neglects those subjects who first found voice in Celan's "Deathfugue," and whose wartime suffering was mixed into European earth. It's they, a buried people, who are leaning against night in "Die Winzer," and who "speak . . . into the silence of answers."[22]

At issue here, amid the paradox of death and the fullness of swollen grapes, is whether such suffering and death can yield speech. One might also read a secret allegory of Heidegger's view of language and humanity in a relation of gathering, only included now in what is harvested is the "cellared seepings, the weepings,/in a sun grave, which they ready/with night-toughened hands," of a people who before being shot had to hand-dig the ditches into which their bodies would be thrown. The Heideggerian view of language may obviate referential witnessing, but "they" harvest the wine of their eyes, manifesting the accreting of time that goes into making wine and remaking grief; silence may be the only proper response, but "they" yet gather so that mouths might thirst for such as this later; where there is only the slightest moisture on the lips about to speak, there will one day perhaps be speech. The moistness of the lip recalls here as well the "moisture" of the "Feuchtes, / viel" at the end of "Todnauberg," where Heidegger and Celan's conversation is metonymically likened to their unfinished walk through wretched, wet moors. No clarity here, only dampness, the disturbingly amorphous "much" articulating a lyric voice on the edge of drowning in the vegetative landscape through which it travels. Again Celan voices the haunted unvoiced in the Heideggerian account of the origin of the *logos* and of the sign as that which designates, fixes, and stores; for there is as well the storing away of a vintage of terrible suffering, not voicing any hope but the frail word spoken in utmost extremity, only to those "late-mouths" come drastically late to the events in question, thirsting for utmost speech.

III

One can pursue the explication of the internal resources for Heidegger's possibly looking to Celan to appropriate the Hölderlinian *mythos* by an appeal to their beginnings. Starting with the essay on "The Essence of Truth" (1930) and more specifically with the essay on "The Origin of the Work of Art" (1936), the work of art for Heidegger appears as a "setting-into-work of the truth," insofar as truth is the opening of the historical horizon in which every verification of a proposition becomes possible, prior to or more fundamentally than the correspondence of the proposition to the thing. That is to say, it is the act by which a certain historical and cultural world is instituted, in which a specific historical "humanity" sees the characteristic traits of its own experience, defined in an originary way. For Heidegger, the work is an "exhibition" of a world and a "production" of the earth. Heidegger emphasizes the notion of exhibition in the same terms we might use for "putting on" an exhibition in a museum or gallery, for instance; for it implies that the work of art has the function of founding and constituting the outlines which define an historical world. A society or social group—in short, an historical world—recognizes the constitutive traits of its own experience of the world (for instance, the implicit criteria for distinguishing good from evil, truth from error, and so forth) in a work of art. This idea affirms the inaugural nature of the work; in the work of art, the truth of any historical epoch is revealed. The essential element here is not so much the inaugurality of the work, or a "truth" which could be opposed to error, as the constitution of the fundamental outlines of a given historical experience.

Put in depreciatory terms, the aesthetic function here is one of an organization of a consensus. In the work, each individual's sense of membership in a historical world may be recognized and intensified. The work as a "setting-into-work of truth"—in its exhibition of a world—is the place where a sense of membership in a group is made recognizable and is intensified. The notion of a work of art as a "setting-into-work of truth" can be understood only by examining its other aspect as a "production" of the earth. In the 1936 essay, the idea of the work as a "Herstellung" of the earth is associated with both the materiality of the work and, especially, the fact that by virtue of this materiality the work occurs as something which is always kept in reserve. In the work, the earth is not strictly speaking matter; it is the presence of the work as such, namely, its concrete appearance as something which always calls attention to itself. The earth is that of the earth, to which each new interpretation always returns and which always leads to new readings and therefore new possible "worlds."

Where Heidegger speaks of the earth in the Greek temple as being in relation to the seasons, to the natural decay of matter, and so forth, or where he speaks of the conflict between world and earth as that in which truth opens up as *aletheia,* one sees that the earth is the dimension which in the work connects the world as a system of discrete and unfolded meanings to its "other," the *physis,* if you will, which sets in motion the tendentially immobile structures of historical/social worlds through its rhythms. In short, the work of art is the "setting-into-work of truth" because in it the opening up of a world as a context of referrals, like a language, is permanently connected to the earth as the "other" of the world.

Heidegger's conception of truth in art as bringing into unconcealment is perhaps analogous to a productive conception of truth in science. A work of art reveals a world in a way analogous to the way in which a paradigm or research program institutes an object domain, providing a concept of an object in general, and hence unifying scientific practice by providing guidelines for inquiry, criteria for theory evolution, and so on. A work of great art can reveal the horizons of a world in just the same way that a scientific framework institutes the horizons of a scientific world. Great art for Heidegger transports human beings out of their ordinary realm, in a negative way. In modernity, art is peripheral, its significance limited to pointing to or gesturing at the normative center without being able to invade it. Art is at the periphery and technology is at the center. A nature poem by Hölderlin, the painting of a pair of peasant shoes by Van Gogh; these works claim and solicit us to a mode of revealing that we cannot validate or sustain. The value of art for Heidegger seems to be just this distance, the gap between solicitation and validation. He is not merely archaizing, merely pining for a return to worlds that works of art can still present. Rather, art enacts a world disclosure it cannot deliver, especially in technical modernity; it lives in its failure to attain its ownmost possibility of revealing. Art's essential impossibility within the technological epoch reveals that epoch. Through its failures we come to experience the sense of the periphery, and thus the meaning of the holding-sway of the center. In other words, art's distance reveals technological modernity in that we experience art as a mode of understanding unavailable to us. This unavailability itself signifies and is meaningful to us.

There is a peculiar completeness to the leveling accomplished in this age of the *universal imposition* of technology.[23] Even the dominant subjectivity Heidegger once diagnosed disappears into the general availability of things to be ordered. There is no first being that grounds all the rest. Everything is functional. This for Heidegger is the culmination of the West's metaphysical drive: The meaning of reality is pure available presence. There are no hidden dimensions that are anything more than a lack of information. Everything is in plain view, humans included: humanity just belongs within universal imposition and is not its source. Humanity acts within possibilities and a mode of temporality that solicits and challenges it to further activity.

The later Heidegger wavered between being hopeful and being unremittingly pessimistic about this state of affairs. Universal imposition is thought to be a nihilism so dark that it lacks the light even to see itself as darkness and instead conceives itself as Enlightenment. At times his thinking is quite clear on the negative point about human incapacity in this regard, that any such effort only produces a new form of objectification. At other times his thinking is quite unclear about how we might escape from the interlocking systems of technological thought and practice in which our lives are enclosed. In places, the only hope he offers lies in the possibility that the danger by which man is threatened may come to be understood as danger. Heidegger is often condemned for not having a political theory or moral theory. It is at least consistent with his view, however, that what was at the bottom of these pursuits was the universal homelessness and alienation that gives rise to an unbearable uncertainty and insecurity, which in turn motivates the goings-on of technology and the universal objectification of everything. Political and moral disputes only reinforce the same striving for predominance and the same pursuit of universal objectification that is the source of the conflict itself.[24]

Universal imposition affects us immediately and overall, but it is not the last word. There is a possibility that our experience of being challenged within technology could turn us toward something more basic. Heidegger wants to locate this imposition in the place where it is made possible. The universal imposition of technology is not ultimate; something more primal speaks through it. The epoch of technology is complete in itself, but there must be something more to say than just describing universal imposition. Heidegger says: "What we experience in universal imposition as the constellation of man and being through the modern world of technology is a prelude to what is called the event. . . . In the event the possibility opens for us of overcoming the simple dominance of universal imposition in a more original happening."[25]

David Kolb has described this thinking with eminent clarity. Because the modern world presents everything as open to view and available to understanding, because it takes nothing to be hidden that cannot be revealed by getting more facts, we are ironically in a better position to recognize the conditions that make any world possible. If we think everything has been made present and available, then nothing remains hidden or beyond our world to account for it. In this situation, we can recognize that there is nothing to ground our world but its happening, the happening of a world. There is only the emerging, the event, the coming into unconcealment, the clearing that opens a space for humans to live a certain way of being human. Recognizing this is "emancipatory"—we can know the limits of our world and refuse to accept as ultimate any of the grounds or measures or principles it offers.

In other words, because of the dominance of universal imposition, which plays out and levels out the metaphysical impulse to search for causes and grounds, we are especially situated to experience the event on its own. But this is the most dangerous of situations, for that which most threatens is also the necessary key to overcome that threat. What is devastating is that it is not far from this view to a view which holds that the greater the threat, the better chance there is of recognizing it. Surely this is a linchpin of the later Heideggerian dynamic, the ironic notion that technology dominates us, yet it is only through the most extreme form of such domination that we can even see the domination. Just how we are led to an understanding of the event is the motor for Heidegger's thinking, taking the form of a kind of negative theology on this issue. He variously considers art, poetry, everyday things, and eventually language in general as ways through which the event is intimated.

The most important thing to say about the event, taken on its own, is that there is almost nothing to report about it. Heidegger speaks of it as "withdrawing," and elsewhere as the "photographic negative of the Gestell." The opening of this free space for the appearance of things is not some event that happens elsewhere. It happens not beyond or behind beings but, as it were, in front of them. Yet that happening is not obvious. The forgetfulness of the event that Hiedegger finds throughout the Western tradition is not due to inadvertence on man's part. The very nature of that event is to make beings open and available but not to intrude itself. The event is hiddenness itself. It is therefore not surprising that the event has nothing to show for itself. This is so in several senses. As an opening of the space for the encounter with beings, a transcendental enabling condition (although Heidegger would vehemently deny this Kantian-sounding function), the event allows things to rise out of the darkness of universal imposition. If the event had qualities of its own, they would need to be made available, unconcealed. It would be some kind of entity among other entities, and the event of unconcealment would be missed. The event itself cannot be an entity or relation among other entities. To think it as an entity is to make presence itself present, to perform the metaphysical transposition of the wonder of unconcealedness into the question about grounds and causes.

If it is not an entity in its own right, the event does not have a structure, inner necessity, or law, or anything about it that could come to presence on its own. This means there is nothing in it or related to it that serves as a foundation for its occurrence. Therefore there is nothing about it to understand, as the word "understand" is commonly used. There is nothing hidden in it to be ferreted out, nothing to be analyzed, nothing to be used as a first principle or ground or as basis for explanation.

All of this is played out in regards to language. In the art essay, we are told that to comprehend the essentially poetic character of all art we need the "right concept of language." This "right concept" will demand of us a surmounting of the traditional functional and linguistic approaches to language. Language understood as a vehicle of communication, or as an object of linguistic science, although containing its own legitimacy, is not the language of the poetic and will not reveal the event. Language as communication is the verbal and written exchange designed for the imparting of information. This is language approached in terms of its function and viewed as an instrument for defining, explaining, deducing, and drawing inferences pertinent to objectifiable matters of fact. The linguistic and metalinguistic approaches to language are of the same cloth as in the instrumental approaches to language. In the science of linguistics, language becomes an object with a complex of morphemes, parts of speech, and syntactical and semantic rules. Language understood in this way is an especially complicated and powerful tool, making possible the improvement of numerous cooperative practices that constitute human culture.

In the later reflections on language, Heidegger discusses the faltering of language by way of the meaning of "Zeigen" (showing) that is radically irreducible to a representational and "technological" concept of language. It is precisely this representational concept of the relation between language and things which is subverted by the "showing" of the originary word that occurs in the poetic. The faltering of language, at which Heidegger says reflection on the nature of language arrives, is to be understood as a "showing"; but rather than fall back into a metaphysical concept of language as a sign for something, this "showing" subverts both our usual referential way of understanding the word-thing relation and our own relation to language itself. To experience language as "Zeigen," or as "Sage" (originary saying), means that language is not a mere faculty of man. It ceases to be something with which we as speaking human beings have a relation; it is instead the relation of all relations, the universal medium through which anything becomes meaningful at all. Language is "Zeigen" not by being an instrument for showing things; rather, "Zeigen" means "Erscheinen lassen"—that is, to "make appear," particularly in the sense of making each thing be reflected in the mirror-game of the fourfold.

The showing in which the word falters is not a reference back to the thing, but rather a positioning of it in proximity to or in the framework of the regions of the world, the four regions of the fourfold, earth and sky, mortals and divinities, to which it belongs. Yet humanity belongs to the fourfold insofar as it is mortal, as it experiences death as death. The faltering of the word in the "Zeigen" of originary saying finds a precise point of reference in one of the constitutive dimensions of Heidegger's early existential thought, the being-toward-death, which had a central function in his analysis in *Being and Time.* It is not merely a matter of poetically evoking the halo of the world's regions around the thing, which would remain imprecise and leave the "poetic" with all the ornamental vagueness it has always had within the metaphysical tradition. The connection between language and mortality suggests that the faltering of the word in originary saying and in poetry is not to be understood in terms of referential or prophetic provisionality but as being defined by its relation to the constitutive mortality of Dasein. The latest of later Heidegger still seems faithful to the authenticity of existence being defined by its explicit projection toward death. Whereas in *Being and Time* the "existentiell" significance of the anticipation of death is left undefined, the connection between originary saying and mortality now seems to supply elements for thinking through the meaning of authentic existence and its decision for death in a way which emphasizes language and deemphasizes Dasein. For the later Heidegger, the anticipation of death upon which the possibility of authentic existence depends is the experience of the connection between language and mortality, the faltering of the word in the originary saying of poetry.

The non-technological language of the poetic plays an indispensable role in the event; indeed, only insofar as our language is the language of the poetic are we able to witness and participate in the event appropriately. The character of discourse provides the horizon for the possibilities of understanding everything out from under technology, because the contextual place opened up and articulated by the event is a "language place." The language and expressions of metaphysics, logic, technology, and ethics operate according to principles which displace and shut out the full, self-concealing character of this event, in effect alienating themselves from their own source. Heidegger's own late essays furtively resist such "technological" language, in doing so surely matching the abyssal inversions of Celan. His discussions are presented in bits and pieces, in hints and metaphors and etymological maneuvers, in dialogue form and meditations on poems. The natural inclination is to try to picture some unifying concept that will resolve the mixtures into a whole, but this will not do, for the idea is not to produce anything resembling an allegory of ideas. The effect of Heidegger's efforts is to block any attempt to reduce this "poetic saying" to a unitary concept. The effort to say what it is is misguided. In the end, it is not a portable concept to be taken from Heidegger's texts. If one wanted to say what the "poetic event" is, one must say all of what Heidegger says, and perhaps in no particular order.

Poetry or the "poetic" for Heidegger is thus best to be understood when defined negatively, from the standpoint of the goings-on of technology. But "negatively" is meant here in a very qualified sense, as is the reference to the "right concept of language" and "non-technological thinking." The poetic cannot become its own object of scrutiny. The opposition technological/non-technological cannot become the object of a strict, rigorous, serious analysis without one of those terms determining the value of the discourse itself. The thinking here must work at not becoming an integral part of the object it claims to follow. Like raising the question of technology, our thinking must seek constantly to avoid the certainty of traditional concepts of language. What happens here is that we are in a position of not knowing what to say about language. We are maneuvered out of the theoretical attitude with respect to language. We are farther than ever from getting a fix on it. And yet it is precisely because language, wherein we witness the happening of the origination of that which it is the task of thought to think, is poorest at pointing to and speaking out itself that this event has gone unthought in the history of thought, even though it is precisely this languaged event which first lets there be a history of thought whatsoever. This is why Heidegger's later work takes the forms it does, and why he finds poets who have given themselves over to listening to the claims and possibilities of language to be closer to the call of the "event" than philosophers, who have insisted upon the language of rigorous categories and of logic. The original identity to which both man and being belong is found in the way in which each belongs to language in this special sense of opening.

Heidegger's thinking on art is directly related to the "poetic." At the end of the art essay, he makes the claim that all art is essentially "poetic." This "poetic" is to be understood not in the narrower sense of poetry, the poem as a particular linguistic work. Rather, the "poetic" is now to be thought of as just that form of thought which thinks non-technologically. As commemorative and responsive, it is a "letting-be" of a primal reality. It neither objectifies nor manipulates the primal reality. Thinking the "poetic" antedates the split between subject and object and the increasing technification of thought. It is neither localized in an epistemological subject nor is it geared to an objectification of its thought. Such a thinking furrows an opening to the encountered realities and keeps these realities from being congealed into scientific objects. Nor is it to be thought of as a kind of couch-potato passivity, but rather a difficult posturing or comportment that makes possible a disclosure other than that of universal imposition.

If, on the basis of Heidegger's texts, we try to clarify that obscure element which opposes the world in the work of art, we encounter the earth of the fourfold to which Dasein belongs as something mortal. Poetry can be defined as that language in which a world of unfolded meanings opens up, and in which our terrestrial essence as mortals reverberates. The faltering of the word lets being appear, but of course putting it this way is already misleading; being does not occur as something beyond the word or as something which was already there independently of it; rather, it occurs as an effect of silence. Perhaps faintly echoing the breakdown of the tool in *Being and Time*, the idea of poetry as the site of the "setting-into-work of truth" is an effect of silence linked to the earthliness and mortality of Dasein. One can thus assign to the faltering of the word in Celan's works the meaning of becoming a *monument* in the Heideggerian sense. It is not a means of intensifying the fullness of the word, but a weakening and an approximation of the figure of death. Celan's is a sumptuary monument, not merely to indicate or witness need but to function so as to put one, by way of language, at the mercy of a need of limitless loss. The accent is placed on a loss that must be as great as possible in order for the activity to take on redemptive meaning.

To return to our central questioning. Is the holocaustal the advent of the event? Can Celan's poetry constitute this epochal bringing-to-word? Celan's poetry converges with Heidegger's poetic insights in that the poetry could be singled out as a privileged site, in regard to the common experience of where language arises, as that which "zerbricht," as that which falters or breaks up. Celan combines the abyssal inversion of language with those events which cannot come to word by any alchemy of inversion so as to yet bring-to-word. The poetry stands as an enactment and a self-cancelling of the figure of inversion. The figure oscillates throughout Celan's poetry and seeks both to attain and to undo commemoration by frustrating closure. In so doing, language assimilates itself to the very movement of temporality as relentless alteration, with no possible response to the resulting loss.

When Heidegger speaks of the work of art as "the setting-into-work of truth," he explains that it is such insofar as it sets up a world and sets forth the earth. The setting up of a world is the meaning of the work's historical opening. This function of the work as setting forth of the earth is the fact of bringing the earth into the open as the obscure element upon which every world takes root and from which every world draws vitality, but without ever managing to bring it out of obscurity. The earth later is seen as one of the fourfold of the world, which is unfolded in earth and sky, mortals and divinities, and it is clear that the earth is inhabited by human beings insofar as they are mortals. From the earth we are sent back to mortality. The work of art is a "setting-into-work of truth" because it sets up historical worlds, inaugurates and anticipates, as an original linguistic event, the possibility of historical existence, but always only in reference to mortality. Celan was aware of such inaugural aspects but cut to the bone of their abstractions, reminding one of the costs. As a "letting-dwell," Celan's "In der Luft" uses Heidegger's metaphors and ideas both with and against Heidegger. No longer is the earth the site of dwelling, but the air, the grave of the Jews burned alive in Auschwitz. Not only do mortals gather in such a home, but also all those exiled and murdered. No divinities, only their absence and negation. No sky, but the desert of stars through which the separated and murdered travel. Celan's poem is historically situated in the dwelling place of its own dates and the horrors of the Holocaust, and serves to connect past, present, and future, the dead and survivors, by burning them into language.

IV

Connections between the genre of Holocaust art and Heidegger's views on art and language are simply trampled when we rush to judgment about silence regarding the Holocaust, or when we simply raise questions in accusation against silence, having already calculated the answer in advance. Perhaps there is something here more extreme even than moral and political condemnation, something which does not leave moral condemnation behind but allows its creative reinheritance that exceeds it in claim. Perhaps on only one side of the silence here is there not sound. Perhaps there is silence as possible restitution. If there is, for Heidegger it must certainly be an *interrupted restitution*; just as we cannot analyze art by starting from the metaphysical categories of thing or equipment, since both those categories become accessible only in and through the work of art itself; just as we cannot analyze Being or presencing with the help of any other category, since all categories pertain to beings not Being, and presencing itself never comes to presence (since in all categories Being is already understood); just as we cannot analyze technology with the help of any other category, since all categories appear only in the mode of thought which is itself technological; just as we cannot approach the event in anything like a traditional way; so too we cannot analyze language with the help of any other category, since all categories appear only in language. We cannot grasp the essence of language by speaking about language. We cannot speak of it, we can only speak so as to listen out of it, as it were. Everything appears to us in and through language, but language as a whole does not appear. Only a listening can emerge for the later Heidegger, a reticent, deafening listening which is not the absence of speech but the condition of its possibility, a needful silence that belongs to language. Perhaps, in turn, we cannot grasp the holocaustal as well. Perhaps such witnessing does not occur in the fullness of the poet's expression, nor is even about the power of language so much as our relation to it. It is about the breaking off of such, the abdication, a secret allegory of *Gelassenheit*.[26]

Heidegger's later thinking concerning the poetic and "Ereignis" came to supplant even the individual poet. Could Celan and Heidegger both have come to see the myth of the hoped-for word, the myth of the political, of the hero-poet, of the holocaustal tone as world-instituting, of the Hölderlinian-Celanian axis? In Todtnauberg could they both have come to see the myth of the holocaustically founded saying? Perhaps this too is to mythologize, to narrativize where it is no longer proper to do so. For as the myth is formulated, as soon as it is at stake as myth, it is already over, already interrupted and failed. The poeticity of the holocaustic is itself a myth, a poetizing projection. The very appeal to the Holocaust as the historical founding of the parameters of a people is itself a myth in the sense of a fiction.[27]

These two figures passed each other at the end, going in opposite directions. Celan, after the death-camp experiences which marked him as a writer, started from a point of the abyssal, and as he advanced in the direction toward whatever crumbs of redemption could yet be had in the Heideggerian views of art and language, met Heidegger going the other way, retreating from the instituting myth that "In der Luft" was written to sustain. Heidegger surely was moving in this direction of retreat, although De Beistegui sees it as Heidegger's greatest failure not to have fully arrived. To appeal to the myth as myth, to appeal to its necessity as myth, is already to formulate the impossibility of its presence. As soon as the mythic becomes an object of thought and debate, as soon as it appears as a solution to a historical-political crisis, it can no longer operate as myth. It begins to *function*, to work. It is the staking out of a place, place-setting, an arresting. The power of the myth cannot be anticipated, but only thought of once it is no longer operative. To that extent the creation of the myth is itself a myth. De Beistigui is surely right about this; despite Heidegger's criticism of the one-track thinking of modernity, to take Celan to forward some meridian of the holocaustal, to function as an object for scrutiny and manipulation and redemption, would be but to forward the grid by a meta-narrative which itself would qualify as a leading candidate for thinking within universal imposition. It is a gesture which re-encloses one within the code of technological thinking all the more.

Against Heidegger, but also because of Heidegger, against the forbearance or reverent intimacy or solicitous regard, the holocaustal itself must be interrupted. Celan's abyssal inversions, however cryptic, imply a controlling of language. His *function* as the ironic, world-instituting poetic-event must be interrupted. This signals not a destitution that has not yet come to experience, but the final closing of the Hölderlinian lineage, the failure of the poet-myth. What arrives is not the advent of the concealed promise of the event, but the marking precisely of the impossibility of a mythic humanity. This is the collapse which Heidegger had no means to forestall, for it would sever the tie of art and language to human existence altogether in favor of a self-contained formalism. Heidegger tried to steer between the Scylla of failed-mythic humanity and the Charybdis of the deconstructive abyss, and his thought did not have the resources to succeed.

Heidegger ought to have presided over the failure of the Hölderlinian logic of which Celan was the last installment. To inquire into the holocaustal, to discourse on its epochality, is primarily to inquire into the *mythos* through which it may be founded. The myth, the expression and sharing, is the opening and founding gesture of the dreadful work of art. It is that through which the community of the suffering-others could be revealed to itself. The possibility for the holocaustal-meridian and Celan's restitutive inversions would constitute one of the most rigorous enactments of Heidegger's Hölderlinian dream; it was probably the very rigor of the enactment which pushed Heidegger away. One must keep in mind that for Heidegger each historical epoch is determined by a unique dispensation of being, by the appearance of a particular sort of nothingness or aporia that directs man's speculations and activity in a new direction and thus establishes a new ontology. All other ontological possibilities and the ethical and political standards they entail are subsequently reinterpreted within this new ontology, and hence lose any independent claim to truth. Each age thus believes that it has the truth and consequently regards all others as mere superstitions or speculation. Moreover, each age is *right*; it *does* have the truth. History is the collection of the various projections of that which is incomprehensible upon temporality, each being unique and incommensurable with all others, yet each being an expression of the "destiny of being." And if we think of historical epochs not as sequential occurrences but as something like object domains in science, or like "genres" that arise and overlap, the genre of the holocaustic, however historically situated, gives insight into "that which genres," the event of unconcealment of being. For is this not the same as to talk, as Heidegger does, of the genre/epoch of nihilism as it appears in our time, the night after the sunset of being (God and metaphysics) and before the sunrise of Being itself? The world-midnight for Heidegger is a moment of revelation into the worlding of any world. The historical world of the Jewish Holocaust is revealed in the light of metaphysics. The source of the light itself remains unilluminated and hence concealed. When monumental darkness can be perceived as a source of light, the highest truth appears not as the conclusion of an arduous historical development but as the mysterious beginning that establishes the horizon of such a development. The fact that Celan chose to write strictly in German, the literary language treasured by his family, but also the language of the murderers of his family and race, also responds to Heidegger's privileging of that language, perhaps to inoculate it against obscene silence, to renew it as yet a possible source of meaning. He sought to rupture the connection of the inaugural art-work with re-poisoning, not for clarity but for the damaged conservation of traces and witness. Yet Celan's poetry must fail to accomplish even this instituting and founding, for such instituting of the holocaustic tone itself would risk being co-opted by universal imposition. Celan's is always poetry as encounter, dialogue, conversation, after all, and so rooted in subjectivity. Celan's inversions frustrate the redemptive power of his poetry, not in order to renounce restitution but to accomplish it all the more. To renounce restitution would be to deny a voice to the very victims Celan purports to commemorate. Such an accomplishment fails, however, in the sense that all such revealing of the necessarily occlusive event must fail.

Heidegger's silences are something more than a mere political strategy of denial, and something less than Felman's de Man-as-heroic-deconstructor. His silences are not that of the heroic image of tragedy, but of one realizing that all facets of human redemption are sometimes victim to the sclerosis of language. This is no assumption of historical responsibility. This is no exultant pulling back from the instituting of the holocaustal; not so much an act of courage as of forbearance or reverent intimacy and solicitous regard. Not that this means that we will therefore or henceforward know what has happened, or that we can come away with some insight which neatly underwrites what has been at work here; on the contrary, given Heidegger's views of language and the event, we may well be less in a position than ever before to witness what has happened, or what is happening now. But this is not merely to deny the possibility of any referential witnessing. The books and articles accumulate on the subject of Heidegger, silence, and the Holocaust. They make for a certain genre themselves, with rhythms of speech and demonstration principles, copyright restrictions, and royalty agreements. To domesticate, to circumvent, to publish, to politicize, is perhaps to remain deaf alongside the unheard-of. The themes of which we speak, the need for limitless loss and the need of its witnessing, send us down a path which has precisely anticipated discourse respecting it. To say of Heidegger's *silentio* that it has a similar trajectory is not to make of Celan some seamless exemplar of Heidegger's subject-less, post-metaphysical thought, nor call on Celan as the moral witness against the philosopher's political errors. Celan's poetry records the failure of the coming to word of healing, a missed interlocution not merely with Heidegger, but with the "thousand darknesses of death-dealing speech" that no amount of re-poisoning could heal.[28] For Heidegger, in the failure of the coming to word of healing, the destruction of the age remains withheld. Faced with the holocausts of the death-camps, and those of technological-holocaustal-deconstructional modernity now certain to come, he failed to give word no word could come. What was such a silence if not the attempt to move already beyond the horizon of the technological noon and the holocaustic eve, a movement beyond which eludes us still? What was this if not a light not always seen in the middle of such a day, a darkness not always such night?

NOTES

1. Two examples of whom might be Theodor W. Adorno, *Negative Dialectics* (New York; Continuum Publishing Company, 1983), and Maurice Blanchot, *The Writing of the Disaster* (Lincoln: University of Nebraska Press, 1986).
2. The present discussion is colored by Shoshana Felman's stunning 1989 essay on Paul de Man's silence regarding his having written 150 articles for the fascist newspaper *Le Soir* in occupied Belgium. Felman's central thesis is that the Holocaust was about the inevitable failure of referential language, and since any attempt to bear witness to it would only repeat its crimes, de Man is not guilty of collaboration but is indeed one of the Holocaust's greatest victims, because silence is the only proper response to such extremity. De Man's works instead become for Felman an act of courage; the lifelong concealment of one's questionable past is the highest form of responsibility for that past. Indeed, de Man did not even write the offending essays; rather they were written by language

and ideology speaking through him. De Man's silence actually articulates the ethical impossibility of a confession that cannot take place. To use language referentially, to try to say something about the world, is not just linguistically naive but morally suspect, according to Felman. If what got de Man into trouble in the first place was the attempt to speak of something outside of language, to speak retrospectively of his wartime involvement would repeat the very error he committed in working as a journalist. See Shoshana Felman, "Paul de Man's Silence," in *Critical Inquiry*, 15.4. (Summer 1989), pp. 704–744.

3. Derrida reads Celan this way in "Shibboleth," in Geoffrey Hartman and Sanford Budick, *Midrash and Literature* (New Haven: Yale University Press, 1986), pp. 307–347.
4. The Heidegger-Celan encounter should not be compared too closely to the events surrounding the discovery of de Man's wartime writings. Felman even brings Primo Levi to de Man's defense: Levi as proto-deconstructor on the incapacity of language to bear witness. I want to spell out Heidegger's encounter with Celan in a way which does not make of their connection what Felman makes of de Man and Levi. As stated in the body of the paper, that Celan and Levi could make language reenter the camps to chronicle those experiences, experiences outside of human experiences, constitutes a reaffirmation of the very bonds of humanity whose destruction it describes. Nor do I wish to thoughtlessly equate Heidegger's situation as Rector in Germany with that of concentration camp survivors, as if Heidegger was a victim of events in a similar way to Celan. Voluntary silence is perhaps in many respects never comparable to mute affliction. Throughout this essay, the issues are not that the Holocaust was a myth, or that holocaustal events did not occur, or could not be remembered or expressed, but that such a situation of not recognizing or remembering their occurrence and the difficulties of their expression could ever have arisen in the first place.
5. In the words of Babette Babich's excellent recent article, "Questioning Heidegger's Silence: A Postmodern Topology," in Arleen Dallery, Charles Scott, with P. Holley Roberts (eds.), *Ethics and Danger* (Albany: SUNY Press, 1992), pp. 83–106.
6. Michael Zimmerman, *Heidegger's Confrontation with Modernity* (Bloomington: Indiana University Press, 1990), pp. 115–131.
7. Philippe Lacoue-Labarthe, *Heidegger, Art, and Politics* (Oxford: Basil Blackwell, 1990).
8. Jean-François Lyotard, *Heidegger and "the jews"* (Minneapolis: University of Minnesota Press, 1990).
9. Philippe Lacoue-Labarthe, *La Poésie comme expérience* (Paris: Christian Bourgois, 1986).
10. Celan's "Todtnauberg" has received extensive recent commentary. The best recent interpretations in relation to Heidegger are J. D. Golb, "Celan and Heidegger: A Reading of Todtnauberg," in *Seminar*, 24.3 (September, 1988), pp. 255–268, and Mark M. Anderson, "The 'Impossibility of Poetry': Celan and Heidegger in France," in *New German Critique*, No. 53 (Spring-Summer 1991), pp. 3–18.
11. See Paul Auster, "The Poetry of Exile," in *Studies in Twentieth Century Literature*, 8.1 (Fall 1983), pp. 108–110. For a discussion of "Death Fugue," see John Felstiner, "Paul Celan's *Todesfuge*," in *Holocaust and Genocide Studies*, 1.2 (1986), pp. 249–264.

12. Paronomasia is normally understood as any play on words. This particular example is one of antonomasia, a related figure of speech in which an epithet, or name of an office or dignity, is substituted for a proper name. The single most concentrated reading of this trope in any writer would have to be the "Genet-side" of Derrida's *Glas* (Paris: Galilée, 1974). The limits of discourse to represent the Holocaust are figured as well in ellipsis (omission), aposiopesis (the breaking off of speech as if unwilling or unable to go on), and aporia (talking about the impossibility of speech). For a detailed analysis of paronomasia throughout Celan's poetry, see Warner Hamacher, "The Second of Inversion: Movements of a Figure through Celan's Poetry," in "Lessons of Paul de Man," *Yale French Studies*, 69 (1985), pp. 276–311.
14. I owe this and the remainder of my discussion of this poem to Amy Colin's fine book on Celan, *Paul Celan: Holograms of Darkness* (Bloomington: Indiana University Press, 1991), pp. 133–140. (See the introduction for a discussion of recent Celan commentary and bibliography.)
15. In "Language in the Poem," Heidegger understands "fremd," strange, as "fram"—forward to somewhere else, underway toward something, onward to the encounter with what is kept in store for it. The affinities of Celan's poems to "Die Sprache im Gedicht" are not surprising because, according to Otto Pöggeler, the poet studied this essay precisely at a time when he worked on this poem. See Martin Heidegger, "Language in the Poem," in *On the Way to Language* (New York: Harper & Row, 1971), pp. 162–163, and Otto Pöggeler, *Die Spur des Worts: Zur Lyrik Paul Celans* (Munich: Verlag Karl Alber, 1986).
16. I am thinking of Heidegger's treatment of Rilke in the essay "What Are Poets For?" in *Poetry, Language, Thought* (New York: Harper & Row, 1971).
17. Celan's notion of poetry as a dwelling place brings to mind a variety of philosophical and literary traditions, from Hegel and Heidegger to Hölderlin and Träkl. Udoff's essay "On Poetic Dwelling" sets Celan's poetry against the horizon of Hegel's, Heidegger's, and Fackenheim's notions of dwelling. From the vantage point of the Holocaust, Udoff emphasizes, Celan's poetry is a "letting-dwell," which discloses the memory and silence of Auschwitz. See Alan Udoff, "On Poetic Dwelling: Situating Celan and the Holocaust," in Amy Colin (ed.), *Argumentum e Silentio: International Paul Celan Symposium* (Berlin: Walter de Gruyter, 1987), pp. 320–351.
18. Paul Celan, "The Meridian," in Celan, *Collected Prose*, trans. Rosmarie Waldrop (Riverdale-on-Hudson, NY: The Sheep Meadow Press, 1986), pp. 37–55.
19. Martin Heidegger, "The End of Philosophy and the Task of Thinking," in David Krell (ed.), *Martin Heidegger: Basic Writings* (New York: Harper & Row, 1977), p. 375.
20. Martin Heidegger, "Logos (Heraclitus, Fragment B 50)," in *Early Greek Thinking* (New York: Harper & Row, 1984), p. 61.
21. Martin Heidegger, *An Introduction to Metaphysics* (New Haven: Yale University Press, 1959), p. 144. The German original is particularly important here: "wonach das Wort das ursprünglich Gesammelte bewarht und so das Waltende, die phusis, verwaltet." Notice the Greek word, "phusis," which Ralph Manheim leaves out of his translation.
22. John Felstiner, "Repetition and Restitution: Translating Celan's 'Die Winzer,'" in *Prooftexts*, 10 (1990), p. 163. Felstiner mentions that, a month before writing this autumn poem, Celan read Heidegger on Hölderlin's 1801 elegy, "Bread and Wine."

23. This is David Kolb's translation of Heidegger's "Gestell." See David Kolb, *The Critique of Pure Modernity* (Chicago: The University of Chicago Press, 1986). I follow his argument closely here.
24. "Agriculture is now a motorized food industry—in essence, the same as the manufacturing of corpses in gas chambers and extermination camps, the same as the blockading and starving of nations, the same as the manufacture of hydrogen bombs." This is Thomas Sheehan's translation of the phrase, from Heidegger's 1949 lecture, "Das Ge-stell," in his "Heidegger and the Nazis," in *The New York Review of Books*, June 16, 1988, pp. 41–42. The sentence was deleted from the version of this lecture published as "The Question Concerning Technology." This now infamous statement by Heidegger equating death-camps with modern agriculture follows from his view that great danger exists not only in the manifestation of death-camps, but also in the delusion of tranquility of mechanized agriculture. The horrors of the Holocaust are at least apparent, whereas the motorized food industry is cloaked with the benign aspect of progress. The "solution" that is modern agriculture for Heidegger further intensifies insecurity; the blunt remark about the death-camps follows from his views on technology in that an *equal evil* (to Heidegger) exists in apparent prosperity, which conceals the nihilism of world technology. The desolation of everything is compatible with the attainment of the highest living standards for human beings. Entirely too much has been made out of this statement, as is the case with Heidegger's claim that "only a God can save us" in his *Spiegel* interview.
25. Martin Heidegger, *Identity and Difference* (New York: Harper & Row, 1969), p. 36. I follow Kolb's discussion of this issue, as well as his translation of "Ereignis" merely as the event.
26. Since the god that is spoken of in the *mythos* is perhaps never to come, in a time of distress marked by the absence of gods, it can only be a matter of freeing the space for the hypothetical coming of a new god. That God is missing is an absence, but an absence which is not just nothing, but the presence which one must first take hold of, of the hidden plenitude of that which was, and which thus gathered, is. The very appeal to the god remains as the only alternative, that only a god can save us, that new humanity can arise only out of relations to the divine, and this can be done only under the condition that the people be ordered to the founding saying of the poet.
27. I follow the lines of the argument spelled out by Miguel de Beistigui in "Heidegger's Mythocentrism," in *Research in Phenomenology*, 21 (1991), pp. 21–35.
28. The quote is from Paul Celan, *Gesammelte Werke* (Frankfurt/M: Suhrkamp, 1983), Vol. 3, p. 186.

6

Todtnauberg[1]

OTTO PÖGGELER

In 1967, Paul Celan gave a poetry reading in Freiburg-im-Breisgau. The following day, July 25, he met with the philosopher Martin Heidegger in the latter's hut in Todtnauberg, in the Black Forest. He entered these lines into the hut's visitors' book: "Into the hut's visitors' book, with a view of the well's star, with a hope of a coming word in the heart. July 25, 1967/ Paul Celan." However, the walk on the Horbach moor which Celan had requested had to be interrupted because of wetness. On the return trip to Paris, Celan, in Frankfurt, wrote the poem "Todtnauberg" (dated August 1).[2] It appeared separately in 1968, in a limited edition of fifty, and was subsequently published in the volume *Lichtzwang*. Heidegger enjoyed displaying the attractive volume, however Celan reported that both the visit and Heidegger's letter of thanks deeply disappointed him: What Celan had expected from this meeting, which he had put off for such a long time, was not fulfilled. Celan, who remained interested in Heidegger's thinking, met the philosopher again in March 1970, without their coming to a further understanding. Did Heidegger simply not understand what the hermetic poet had conveyed to him, or was there insufficient time to approach the questions which truly needed to be considered?

What precisely did Celan want in this forest, which is called black, in the tiny place whose name must have reminded him of the mountain as well as of death? In 1922, Heidegger built a simple vacation home near the small spa town. Greek philosophy emerged in colonial territory, and was there presented to the rest of the world. In Athens it was subsequently urbanized; brooks and plane-trees outside were, for Socrates, already places where one could be tempted by the dark voices of nature. This situation changed in Roman times: Cicero and Plotinus wanted to have influence in the capital, but for them the country estate was a place of retreat and tranquillity. When

Rousseau sought refuge at Lac de Bienne or went to the hermitage near Paris, it was because he wanted to return to nature and transform his sensibility and thought, so that he could load a new world upon his shoulders (as Hölderlin emphasized).[3] Nietzsche let Zarathustra put a curse on the big city and seek the loneliest loneliness in the mountains. For Heidegger, the hut was not simply a place to spend summer vacations and ski, it was also a place of retreat and concentrated work which remained connected to life in those simple, but marked relationships out of which the philosopher emerged.

In 1933, Heidegger abandoned the work on the pre-Socratics which had occupied him during a sabbatical semester in order to descend from the hut to the city and his engagement on behalf of Hitler. He did not merely refer to the new martyr of the movement, Albert Leo Schlageter, with whom he saw himself bound as a man of the land and as one who was rooted in the soil of the Black Forest; in the autumn of 1933, the new Freiburg rector also organized a National Socialist education camp in Todtnauberg. But, by this time had not everything to do with the land finally lost its innocence, insofar as remote locations were made to serve as concentration camps (for example, in that same year 1933, Heuberg or Kislau near Karlsruhe)? After 1945, when Heidegger had to justify his prior political conduct, the hut became a place of refuge. The monograph *Aus der Erfahrung des Denkens*,[4] which was written in the hut and first issued privately in 1947 in an edition of fifty, seeks, like a kind of convalescence after a serious illness, a new beginning in the most simple things: the course of the day and the seasons, the flowers of a mountainside and a star. Soon young Frenchmen—members of the resistance—came to the banned thinker and pilgrimaged to his hut out of a "cry of distress" (a mountain there bears this name, but Nietzsche's Zarathustra also hears the people's "cry of distress" in one of his last temptations). When Celan also finally came to the hut, for him January 20 was not simply the day of Lenz's departure from Goethe's Strasbourg, it was also the day of the Wannsee Conference, which introduced the "final solution of the Jewish question." Celan confronted Heidegger as a survivor and an escapee, whose mere existence was already a cry of distress and an unavoidable question.

Celan's poem "Todtnauberg" records what struck the poet during the visit. It names with the help of substantives, which are broadened through appositions or relative clauses and supplemented by details of place and time. The ordered lines of the poem are not once disturbed by a semicolon; there is merely a period at the end. The poem is, however, divided into eight stanzas, which generally have two lines, in two cases, three. Only one stanza, the third, extends to ten lines and incorporates a parenthesis with a question mark. This stanza concerns the poet's central gesture, the inscription in the hut's visitors' book, and makes the meaning of the gesture explicit: the poet's hope of a word from one who genuinely thinks.

The first stanza names the flowers on the mountains: arnica, the *compositae*, from which a remedy for hemorrhages can be made, and eyebright, the *labiatae*, whose expressive name already says that it is used to sooth the eyes. Celan then takes a draft from the "well with the starred die above it" (well known from many photographs). He was a guest of Heidegger's, whose out-of-the-way lodgings made do with water supplied from a spring, connected to the dark depth of the earth as well as the star of the night sky. "Moving towards a star," reads the hut's visitors' book, but the star obtains its power of orientation by rising out of the immeasurable depth of the night. When Heidegger, in 1944–45, at the end of the conversation on a country path *Zur Erörterung der Gelassenheit*, speaks with Nietzsche of the act whereby human beings have unchained the earth from the sun, he posits the night as that which, out of its distance and depth, brings the constellations close to human beings. In the difficult years 1946–47, Heidegger, while at the hut, had begun to translate Laotse with the help of a Chinese acquaintance. The text *Grundsätze des Denkens* cites Hölderlin's description of wine as a dark light in a cup from his late poem "Andenken," but also Laotse's saying, "He who knows his brilliance covers himself in his darkness." He appends a truth to this of which it is said that everyone knows it, but few are capable of following it: "Mortal thinking must descend into the darkness of a well's depth in order to see the star during the day." (This text appeared in 1968, in the *Jahrbuch für Psychologie und Psychotherapie*, as a gesture of thanks to the psychiatrist von Gebsattel, who had cared for Heidegger in a sanatorium when he suffered a collapse before the denazification tribunal.) Did Celan really enter this world as a guest? He came from another world and remained in another world. Hence he also saw what Heidegger hardly did. When the arnica blooms yellow, the language of the yellow spots was clear to Celan. Eyebright is used for eyes which are wounded, darkened, and blinded by what they see. (In the *Poems 1938–1944*, the early poem "Herbst" speaks of eyebright, while the poem "Mystische Lied" asks for the eyes to be healed.) The well speaks of the land of the well, and this, for Celan, is the lost homeland. In the starred die also speak the playing hands of Mallarmé, the ever elusive seven, and the stubbornly sprouting starflower. Can poetry retrieve what is lost by orientating itself to the impossible? (A poetic typographical error in *Lichtzwang* turned the starred die once again into a die of stone.) In every case Celan's star remains separated by an entire world from the eight-pointed star that Heidegger chose for his tombstone.

The second stanza distributes three words among two lines, and thereby accentuates the determination of place: "in the/hut." However, a hesitation, an alarm, also resonates: Is the poet permitted to enter this hut? In his publications the philosopher made the hut into a sign of identity with the homeland, a rootedness in the land that maintains itself even in the present world civilization. Whenever Celan himself speaks of a hut, it is of a hut that belongs to another world. The poem "In eins," from the volume *Niemandsrose*, unites the revolutionary *peuple de Paris*, the workers' uprising of February 13, 1934, in Vienna, and the Spanish opposition to fascism, with the poetry ventured by Mandelstam and others in *Petropolis*-Petersburg.[5] When the end of the poem demands "Peace to the huts!" Celan reworks an old formula, "War on the palaces!" and thus declares his solidarity with the poor inhabitants of the huts who want to win peace without declaring new hostilities. The poem "Hüttenfenster" from the same volume speaks of those who were scorned, persecuted, and exterminated, of the East European Jewry out of which Celan emerged.[6]

The long third stanza poses—just before the entry in the hut's visitors' book—the question whose names have already been recorded in this book. Certainly this is not merely a question provoked by curiosity; fear also plays a role, for does the poet not place his name behind names which were perhaps entered here in 1933? Dare he, who had reproached Buber for meeting with Heidegger without genuinely expressing himself, do that? After the inquiring parenthesis the book is divested of its neutrality and becomes "this" book. However, it is precisely in this book that Celan writes the lines telling of a hope for a word. Is a hope in the heart for the word from one who thinks meant, or a hope for the word in the heart of one who thinks? The interpretations ventured hitherto allow for both possibilities. Normal linguistic usage speaks in favor of the first solution, which nevertheless remains trivial—in any case, the hope is a hope in the heart. The rhythmic order of the word groups supports the second solution, but also that Celan, as Heidegger's guest, would take account of Heidegger's manner of speaking. No longer being and time, but the truth of being and the word; already in the 1930s, Heidegger had reformulated his fundamental question in this way. Since Augustine and Meister Eckhart, one speaks of a word in the heart, which, at the same time, signifies the re-birth of a person. Heidegger traces this tradition back to the problematic of *logos* in Heraclitus, which he ultimately links with Laotse's discussion of the path. The monograph *Aus der Erfahrung des Denkens*, written at the hut, expresses it thus: "As soon as we have the thing before our eyes, and in our heart an ear for the word, thinking prospers."[7] A few months before Celan's visit, on April 4, 1967, Heidegger had concluded his Athens lecture "Die Herkunft der Kunst und die Bestimmung des Denkens" with the following verses from Pindar: "But the word, more durable in time than action, determines life, if only with the favor of the Charites/it retrieves language from the depths of the contemplative heart." In the lecture course entitled *Was Heißt Denken?*[8] Heidegger links the *Zu-denkende* that enjoins us to think with a thinking that is both gratitude and memory; in this way he was able to refer to that thinking in the heart of which Pascal spoke. According to the New Testament, Mary is moved by a word in the heart after the Annunciation. Celan often articulated these relationships between thinking, remembrance, and gratitude, as well as those between heart and word. The one who thinks, whose word is expected in our poem, is certainly also someone who ponders and reflects; the heart is the watchful conscience that does not seek to avoid guilt by means of some excuse. Celan, moved by the forceful pensiveness of Heidegger's attempts at thinking, would like to look into such a heart in which the expected word is there, leaving nothing unsaid. Celan did not forget that Heidegger avoided all hasty attempts to reach a solution, and wanted to withdraw with his merely preparatory thinking before the one to whom the liberating word would prospectively be granted. But Celan persisted and urged that we must resolve the difficulties which confront us within our finite lifetimes. Thus a variant of the poem speaks of the "imminently" coming word.

The second half of the poem consists of five short stanzas. The first names a wooded marsh[9] and orchis.[10] It appears once more to accord with Heidegger's talk of country ways and paths of the beginning, the aporetic wood paths which are, nevertheless, ways to the source. Marshes are tracts of wet, grassy land; here they are uneven, evidently completely so, since they were formed within the wooded moor and its cycles of growth and decay. The orchis is the *Knabenkraut* of the high moors, a kind of orchid.[11] When orchis stand next to other orchis, but each one singly by itself, one is reminded that for the Chinese—and in the language of Zen Buddhism—the orchis names one who composes poetry or thinks, who in his solitude is completely himself. Our poem speaks of the way in which these solitary individuals relate to one another. However, the uneven marshes also remind us of the hills of cemeteries; Celan certainly did not forget that the knacker's yard is also called a "marsh"[12]—that place of death, where expired, flayed animals are hastily buried. The natural landscape can also remind us of something shameful; in any case, the marshes remain uneven, distinct from the factories of Auschwitz, where entire areas together with their indentations can be levelled with the ashes of the dead. The beautiful orchid had already been mentioned in the poem "Von der Orchis her,"[13] from the volume *Atemwende*. It refers there, as the "Knaben-Kraut," to the childhood in the five mountains which still guided the young man and provided him with a homeland. From that place the poet grasps the hand of that You who grants him language and destiny, far removed from those foreigners who play with language on the Paris quay (like the followers of Mallarmé and the surrealists). The orchid is called orchis or *Knabenkraut* because its roots are similar in appearance to a testicle. The poem "Radix, Matrix,"[14] from the volume *Niemandsrose*, equates gender in this sense with the chain of generations, and asks about that "murdered" generation that looms "black in heaven." The poem "Auch mich,"[15] from the volume *Lichtzwang*, is able, in a similar manner, to bring together an almond and a testicle (not only on the basis of their shape) and conclude: "the almond-testicle/storms/and blooms." The view of this storm is also in the image of the orchis that stands next to another orchis, woven together by concealed threads.

The last stanzas speak of the ride in the car and the interrupted journey into the moor. During the ride "coarse stuff" becomes clear; the contrast between what is raw, uncooked, barbaric, undigestible, incomprehensible and what is clear is overcome. Do the forest and the moor show the travelers the face of cruelty and danger? From the fact that the subject of the very next stanza is overhearing, it becomes clear that what is meant by "coarse stuff" are the coarse, not easily understood remarks to be found in Heidegger's later writings, which are now clarified in conversation. Just as Celan never forgets those who quietly and unpretentiously help others—the cabinet-maker who took Hölderlin in, and Lucile among the revolutionaries—so here he singles out the driver of the car who overhears. However, when he is referred to as "the man," this is not merely an informal expression, but is also meant in the sense that he is a witness of the attempted meeting and conversation. The journey into the high moor, however, is soon interrupted; the wooden paths remained only half trodden. These paths represent Heidegger's attempts, at a time when he was extremely threatened, to nevertheless see a trail, to keep old paths passable, to find new paths and to recover. Here, however, these paths upon which wooden switches[16] are overlaid to protect one from sinking, lead over the raised, decaying, or metamorphosed former life on the moor. In the case of the wooden switches, one should not forget that they can also be used to beat victims of persecution and prisoners. Celan's intention to traverse the moor together with Heidegger was not realized. The rain adds new moisture to the wet matter that rises up from under the moor. The land and the moor need the rain. However, too much wetness reminds one of the great flood, if not of the sulphur storm over Sodom, the "yellow flood."

Everything noted by Celan is sharply and precisely observed; at the same time, it is given a particular significance in this context. But the significance was not at all the same for Heidegger and for Celan. During the visit in Todtnauberg, Heidegger wanted to consider the commonality in their resistance against an alienated world (and Celan, according to his report, acknowledged that the hope of such a resistance was indeed shared). But Celan did not want to forget the corpse under the table, and it is precisely for this reason that he wanted to go into the moor. Since the path which led to the moor could not be traversed, Celan sought to cultivate an understanding of the nature of his concern among a small number of people: In addition to a limited edition of the poem "Todtnauberg," the year 1968 saw the publication of the volume *Fadensonnen*. There the last poem, "Denk dir,"[17] speaks of the "moor soldier of Massada." In earlier volumes of poetry, Celan had spoken of the heath, the coast, and the beach, for example, but not of the moor. In the poems from the volume *Fadensonnen*, he frequently began to speak of the moor soldier of Massada, but then reserved these verses for the concluding poem. "We are the moor soldiers"—that was the song of the inmates of the concentration camp Papenburg-Börgermoor (Wilhelm Langhoff had already reported on this in his 1935 book *Die Moorsoldaten*). If now, after Massada, the moor soldier is transported to the Dead Sea, it is with the hope that the new Israel could be the guarantor of continued life in memory after the Holocaust.

In the volume *Lichtzwang*, the poem "Für den Lerchenschatten"[18] names the "moos victims" (*Moos* being a south German variation of *Moor*). The poem "Wetterfühlige Hand"[19] speaks directly of a path into the moor. The hand, as the organ of writing, may stand for poetry; this hand is "weather-feeling," and can let itself be shown the nocturnal path through the wooded moor by the pool of water that has collected there. A word, a stanza in itself, speaks of "luminescence"—that cold glow produced when vegetable matter decomposes in the moor. The poem concludes with a peculiar stanza:

> Whoever now operates the bellows of the peat-organ, one-
> legged, he
> wins a bright beam
> loss.
>
> Wer jetzt die Bälge der Torforgel tritt, ein-
> beinig, der
> gewinnt einen Starkstrahl
> Verlust.

The bellows supply air to the organ, which produces sound in the pipes (in a peat-organ the bellows might, at the same time, remind us of the hides[20] from a knacker's yard). In any case, the bellows of an organ, like the pedals of a bicycle, can only be operated with two legs. But here the impossible is to occur: These bellows are to be operated by a single leg, by one, unaided, who is injured and handicapped! The organ is a peat-organ; its sound rings out when dead plants, deprived of air, are transformed into peat. Can something dead produce a sound—perchance in the poem's act of remembrance? Whoever was to realize this impossibility would not simply encounter luminescence, he would also come to possess a "bright beam loss," that profound light which comes from that which is irretrievably lost. The moor that becomes peat is not only a site of cruelty, it is also the site where we ask just how it is that the murdered and the dead affect us today. Thus the poem "Irisch,"[21] from the volume *Fadensonnen*, speaks of the desire to "cut peat," but "on the heart slope."

If one considers the different worlds from which Celan and Heidegger approached one another, the question arises of whether a meeting—so late and forestalled—could be thought at all. Could a philosopher who thought from the site of Greek tragedy and Heraclitus meet with a lyric poet who translated the poets of the Russian Revolution, and who incorporated Jewish mysticism into his poetry? Could a thinker who, with Cézanne, finally sought other beginnings in the perfection of that which is most simple, meet with a poet for whom each and every thing exposed a gaping wound? Could a German who bore some responsibility for the events of 1933, and a Jew who only narrowly escaped the extermination operations, commonly strive for a "word"? One should not forget that Celan was a Jewish-German poet, and also wanted to be one. Is it not disturbing to see how the young Celan, who drew heavily on Rilke's *Cornet*, would later, using the song of the Nibelungen, bring together war and extermination in the monstrous image of the last survivors at Etzel's estate, quenching their thirst during the great fire with blood drunk from helmets (as described in the poem "Russischer Frühling" from 1944)? On the other hand, Celan must have also seen—and experienced—that the path of the new Russian lyric poets, for example that of Mandelstam, led to exile and death, that Isaak Babel had correctly formulated the question, "Where is the sweet revolution to be found?" to say nothing of the way in which Ivan Goll's lyric poetry was literarily and politically misused! Wherever fundamental change is sought, it is always possible that it will become entangled in the naked struggle for domination of the world or be perverted in some other manner, and philosophy, like lyric poetry, is not excluded from these entanglements.

In the poem "Wenn ich nicht weiβ, nich weiβ,"[22] from the volume *Fadensonnen*, Celan alludes to Hölderlin's formulation "And no one knows." Hölderlin, in the ode "Rousseau," says of the time of fundamental change and transition: "and no one/Knows to indicate the allotted path."[23] The second stanza of the elegy "Brot und Wein" says of the "marvellous" favor of the heavenly one: "and no one/Knows what it is or whence comes all she does and bestows."[24] The poem fragment "Heimath" begins with the words, "And no one knows." Celan says of the headless and mindless ones that they eulogized the "race of the You-less" with "Aschrej"—a word devoid of meaning that effaces everything.[25] Did the expressions "Happy is he who" or "Happy are you, Israel,"[26] not reverberate in the "Heil" that a dictator claimed as his own? Against all perversions Celan places that You which alone keeps him securely orientated on his path—in those conversations in which the You, in the form of the persecuted, the murdered, but also the one who unselfishly helps others, lends a divine radiance to the world. When the meeting with Heidegger did not produce that word for which Celan had hoped, Celan did not take refuge in a poem, but bequeathed to us a task in this poem, which must also have been recognized then, even if it could not be accomplished.

Translated by Wayne Klein

NOTES

1. This essay is excerpted from Otto Pöggeler's book *Spur des Worts. Zur Lyrik Paul Celans* (Freiburg: Alber, 1986) pp. 259–271. There are no footnotes in Pöggeler's text; all footnotes are mine—Trans.
2. As will soon become clear to the reader, Pöggeler's interpretation of "Todtnauberg" depends upon an intimate knowledge of the poem's structure and organization, including the position of individual words. In light of this it seemed important to provide the text of "Todtnauberg" so that the reader would have easy access to it, and hence could more easily follow Pöggeler's train of thought. The nature of Pöggeler's interpretation has also necessitated some departures from Michael Hamburger's excellent translation. In most cases in which I have provided my own translation of a term or line, the reason has been to maintain terminological consistency within Pöggeler's text, or to take account of a distinction made by Pöggeler which would otherwise be lost. Hence an explanation of these changes is almost always to be found within Pöggeler's text itself. Translations from poems other than "Todtnauberg," when available, are taken from Michael Hamburger's *Poems of Paul Celan* (London: Anvil Press, 1988), henceforth cited as PC. References to the original German texts are taken from Paul Celan, *Gesammelte Werke*, ed. Beda Allemann and Stefan Reichert (Frankfurt/M: Suhrkamp, 1983). This text is cited as GW, followed by volume and page number.

Todtnauberg

Arnica, eyebright, the
draft from the well with the
starred die above it,

in the
hut,

the line
—whose name did the book
register before mine?—,
the line inscribed
in that book about
a hope, today,
of a thinking man's

coming
word
in the heart,

woodland sward, unlevelled
orchid and orchid, single,

coarse stuff, later, clear
in passing,

he who drives us, the man,
who listens in,

the half-
trodden wretched
tracks through the high moors,

dampness,
much.

(PC, 293/GW, 2.255)

3. The reference is to Hölderlin's poem "Der Rhein." Hölderlin's ode to Rousseau is discussed below.
4. This text has been translated under the title "The Thinker as Poet," in Martin Heidegger*: Poetry, Language, Thought*, trans. Albert Hofstadter (New York: Harper & Row, 1971).
5. PC, 207/GW, 1.270.
6. PC, 213/GW, 1.278.
7. "The Thinker as Poet," p. 5.
8. *What is Called Thinking*? trans. J. Glenn Gray (New York: Harper & Row, 1968). Gray translates Heidegger's expression "das Zu-denkende" as "that which must be thought about," p. 7.
9. The word here translated as "marsh" is the German *Wasen*. As Pöggeler notes further along in this paragraph, Celan plays on the polysemy of *Wasen*, which is also German for "knacker's yard."
10. Pöggeler, following Celan, uses the German Orchis.
11. *Knabenkraut*, which literally means "boy-plant," is derived from the testicle-shaped roots.
12. *Wasen*.
13. GW, 2.64.
14. PC, 186/GW, 1.239.
15. GW, 2.311.
16. The word here rendered as "wooden switches" is *Holzknüppel*. In his poem Celan uses the expression "Knüppel-/pfade" to describe the "half/trodden" path which he and Heidegger take through the Horbach moor. As Pöggeler explains, a *Knüppelpfade* is a path, usually running through moist or wet land, upon which wooden switches are placed in order to prevent one from sinking.
17. PC, 282/GW, 2.227.
18. GW, 2.305.

19. GW, 2.309.
20. The term translated as "bellows" is *Bälge*, which, as Pöggeler notes, can also be used to designate the hide of a dead animal.
21. PC, 278/GW, 2.189.
22. GW, 2.154.
23. Hölderlin, "Rousseau," trans. Michael Hamburger, Friedrich Hölderlin, *Poems and Fragments* (Ann Arbor: The University of Michigan Press, 1967), p. 129; translation modified.
24. Hölderlin, "Brot und Wein," ibid, p. 243.
25. *Aschrej* is a Hebrew word meaning "happy." Pöggeler's citations in the following line indicate that the source is most probably a brief text recited before Psalm 145 during Jewish prayer services. The text reads as follows:

    Happy are they that dwell in Thy house;
    They will ever praise thee.

    Happy is the people who thus fare;
    Yea, happy is the people whose God is the Lord.

    Source: *Sabbath and Festival Prayer Book* (New York: Rabbinical Assembly of America, 1946), p. 76.
26. Because the lines cited by Pöggeler do not accord precisely with the English translation, I have translated them directly from the German text.

7

Heidegger and Holocaust Revisionism

TOM ROCKMORE

This is not a paper about either Heidegger, his theory, or the Holocaust, but about the link among them. It has two presuppositions. First, I will presuppose that any adequate discussion of the Holocaust has to grasp its historical specificity even to begin to understand it. Second, I will presuppose that Heidegger never directly considers the Holocaust as a problem either in his published writings or in his *Nachlass*.

Any examination of Heidegger and the Holocaust does well to begin from the astonishing fact that Heideggerians have continued to be attracted to revisionist views of the Holocaust. I will contend that this is not an accident since Heidegger's own theory makes it difficult, perhaps even impossible, to grasp the specificity of this historical event. In that sense, Heidegger's students have been true to Heidegger's thought.

Now, there is an obvious difference between what Heidegger did, which is basically to ignore the entire problem of the Holocaust, and what he could have done on the basis of his thought. Important philosophical theories are important in virtue of their capacity to speak to questions that are not addressed by their authors. The problem here is whether Heidegger could have addressed the Holocaust, or whether his students can now address it on the basis of his thought. I don't wish to contest the importance of Heidegger's theory, since that would be to deny what is obvious. Heidegger is a powerful thinker whose theory, like those of all important writers, has insights beyond the explicit intentions governing it. Nor do I wish to deny that elements of Heidegger's theory can be lifted out of it to illuminate piecemeal various aspects of the Holocaust. I merely wish to deny that the theory as a whole can illuminate an event that it cannot grasp and that it prevents anyone who thinks within its limitations from grasping.

1. PRESUPPOSITIONS EXAMINED

Let me begin by arguing for my presuppositions. I am presupposing that an adequate discussion of the Holocaust must grasp its historical specificity, and that Heidegger never addresses the topic directly. A frequent theme in the discussion is the claim that the Holocaust is incomparable with other events, no matter how terrible, and even uncognizable.[1] To find terrible events, we do not need to consult human history in general since our own century will do nicely. Yet, although this century has been filled with human tragedy, including the slaughter of the Armenians, the use of the atom bomb in Japan, the war in Cambodia, or the war now under way in the former Yugoslavia, the Gulag in the Soviet Union—the list is very long—there is perhaps nothing in this or any other period, no matter how terrible, even approaching the immensity of the Holocaust. Despite arguments to the contrary in the German *Historikerstreit*, for instance in Ernst Nolte's celebrated effort to relativize the Holocaust as merely one event among others,[2] to which I will return below, this seems a reasonable claim. But it is a mistake to hold that if an event is incomparable, it is also uncognizable. On the contrary, I subscribe to the view that the Holocaust is cognizable but unique, as all events are unique. Otherwise, something like the covering law model of history proposed by Carl Hempel would be true, and there would be historical laws[3] but no lessons to be learned. The problem, obviously, is to go about learning whatever lessons can be learned in order to prevent other similar events from occurring.

The much-debated claim for uncognizability transforms the discussion of the Holocaust into something like noumenology in the Kantian sense of the term "noumenon." Ever since Kant, who held that all knowledge begins with experience, distinguished between the phenomenon or appearance and the thing-in-itself, philosophy has been engaged in describing the ineffable. Examples include the Kantian view of the sublime, Kierkegaard's account of existence beyond reason, and most recently Levinas's idea of the unknowable other. The point is that we must be able to know the Holocaust, to cognize it, in order to make claims about it at all. Strictly speaking, we fall into dogmatic skepticism when we maintain that it cannot be known. At most, we can claim that we do not yet know it since none of our techniques has yet been able to grasp it and that we do not see how we can know it. But we cannot claim that it is unknowable without availing ourselves of knowledge that we claim that we do not possess and that no one has or could have.

Now it is an assumption, subject to correction, that Heidegger's corpus does not directly discuss the Holocaust. We can only report that there are no, or almost no direct, references to the Holocaust in the writings published during his lifetime or after his death. Since access to his *Nachlass* is unfortunately still restricted and there are, equally unfortunately, at present no plans to publish his letters, we cannot rule out the possibility that his view of the Holocaust will come to light at some later date. Yet, for reasons to be cited below, that seems unlikely since Heidegger later made changes in his theory to suggest the need not to come to grips with this or any other aspect of National Socialism.

2. Heideggerian Revisionism

Revisionism, or the effort to provide a radical revision of or even to deny the existence of the Holocaust, is a disturbing dimension of the Holocaust discussion.[4] Holocaust revisionism assumes various forms that may or may not be associated with extreme types of antisemitism, as in the infamous "Protocols of the Elders of Zion."[5] For present purposes, it is sufficient to distinguish two distinct forms of Holocaust revisionism: the radical denial that there ever was a Holocaust, the attempt to deny that it occurred; and the somewhat milder effort to relativize the event by arguing that it is either comparable to, or less significant than, other historical events. The former is a feature of the French discussion, where revisionist historians such as Robert Faurisson simply deny the existence of the Holocaust on the grounds that there are no former deportees able to testify to the existence of gas chambers.[6] The latter view emerged in the German *Historikerstreit*, in which a group of historians, most prominently Ernst Nolte, argued that the Holocaust was called forth by, and needs to be understood against the background of, the even worse, so-called Asiatic event of Stalinism in the former Soviet Union.

Holocaust revisionism is an obviously extremist point of view, mainly associated with Nazi apologetics. The astonishing interest of a number of prominent Heideggerians in Holocaust revisionism is a striking fact in the Heidegger discussion. The point is not to brand all Heideggerians, or even a certain kind of Heideggerian, as either a witting or unwitting Nazi apologist but to remark and interrogate the remarkable gravitation of certain Heideggerians, including Nolte or Jean Beaufret, to this extremist view. It goes without saying that many other Heideggerians, including those closely identified with the master's thought, such as Jacques Derrida and Philippe Lacoue-Labarthe, have no links to Holocaust revisionism and criticize Heidegger for his failure to confront the problem of the Holocaust.

Beaufret, who later arguably became the most orthodox of all the Heideggerians, was the recipient of the "Letter on Humanism" in 1947, at a time when Heidegger, in trouble after the war, when he was called to account for his actions as the Nazi rector of the University of Freiburg-im-Breisgau, was seeking allies in France. Beaufret quickly rallied to Heidegger's cause, becoming Heidegger's most important representative in France. He defended Heidegger's person and thought tooth and nail, from roughly 1947 until his death in 1982. Although a fine expositor of Heidegger's writings, his devotion to them would not have sufficed for his unusual importance in the French context that derived mainly from the particular structure of French education, in which students who later go on to the *grandes écoles* tend to study in one of several Parisian *lycées*. It is worth noting that a large number, perhaps the majority of those who later became important in the French Heidegger discussion, were earlier students of Beaufret.

In his many writings, Beaufret constantly sought to deny or otherwise to minimize the nature and significance of Heidegger's political involvement with Nazism. He typically maintained that Heidegger never did anything that could justify the allegations raised against him.[7] It is but a short step from the view that all the objections brought against Heidegger were wide of the mark to the further view that the events alleged never even existed. Toward the end of his life, Beaufret became interested in Faurisson's revisionist view that the Holocaust did not exist. When Faurisson aroused passionate objections, Beaufret rushed to defend him.[8] At least two letters from Beaufret to Faurisson exist detailing Beaufret's support of Holocaust revisionism.[9]

Nolte, a one-time Heidegger student, is an important German historian, well known for his studies of the Third Reich. More recently, he has published a biography of Heidegger in which he seeks to relativize a number, although not all, of the objections raised against Heidegger. He acknowledges that Heidegger turned to Nazism on the basis of his philosophy,[10] and later maintained his faith in the ideal that Nazism continued to represent.[11] But for Nolte, the fact that Heidegger rallied to Nazism is not significant. According to Nolte, Nazism, although bad, is better than Bolshevism;[12] and in the 1930s there was only a choice between these two extremes. For this reason, he maintains that all former Nazis should now be rehabilitated.[13]

3. Holocaust Revisionism and Heidegger's Theory

The striking attraction of some among Heidegger's students to Holocaust revisionism can be explained through a variety of factors, such as the understandable desire to defend Heidegger's person and thought that apparently led Beaufret to support what can only be seen as a wild interpretation simply denying historical reality, if that term has any meaning at all. Nolte represents a rather different approach. Many Heideggerian students, for instance Beaufret, Pierre Aubenque, François Fédier, and others, seek to drive a conceptual wedge between Heidegger the man and Heidegger the great thinker, in order to save, if not the man, at least his theory.[14] In the United States, this attitude is represented by such as Charles Scott, who manages to read the famous *Rektoratsrede* in a way that frees it from any Nazi taint in order to appear as a defense of the Greek idea of science.[15] Others, such as John Sallis, go even farther in warning against the very idea of evoking Heidegger's political commitment as incompatible with grasping his theory, or reading his texts.[16]

The refusal, widely present in the orthodox Heideggerian discussion, to make any effort to comprehend Heidegger's theory against the context of his times, is consistent with the traditional philosophical view of knowledge as unrelated to either time or place, but inconsistent with Heidegger's own contextualism. To his credit, despite his strongly orthodox brand of Heideggerianism, Nolte properly recognizes that Heidegger the man and Heidegger the thinker are one and the same person, and that Heidegger the man and the thinker must be understood in the context of his times.[17] He relativizes the event of the Holocaust on similar grounds.

Holocaust relativism is not incompatible but rather compatible with the general thrust of Heidegger's own later theory. Heidegger distinguishes between beings, or entities, and being in general, roughly the being of beings. *Being and Time*, his first and greatest book, is a treatise on the problem of being. According to Heidegger, this problem was first posed authentically in early Greek thought and then later forgotten. In his later thought, beginning with his Nietzsche lectures, in his famous 1938 lecture on "The Age of the World Picture," and later in his papers on technology, Heidegger develops an influential critique of modernity on the twin levels of metaphysics and technology. According to Heidegger, modernity is defined by an indifference to the true thought of being that has given way to a worldview (*Weltanschauung*) concerned with beings as opposed to being, the decline of metaphysics in the legitimate sense of the term, and the increasing dominion over beings on display in modern technology. The latter is no more than the direct result of faulty metaphysics following from the forgetfulness of being.

Heidegger's critique of modernity is not only compatible with but in fact necessarily leads to Holocaust relativism. Whatever the merits of this critique, it clearly does not allow for distinctions to be drawn between different events in the modern period that all fall under the same heading. If all modern events are explicable in terms of the fall away from being, if they are all the same in that crucial respect, then obviously the Holocaust and all other events lose their historical specificity. From this angle of vision, as Bentham would say, pushpin is as good as poetry since nothing essential distinguishes them. From the Heideggerian angle of vision, it is not possible to pick out the Holocaust as a particular event unlike others in the modern period. From Heidegger's exalted perspective, all modern events are like all other modern events.

4. HEIDEGGER'S COMMENTS ON THE HOLOCAUST

Anyone who takes up the topic of Heidegger and the Holocaust must be struck by the relative lack of direct or even indirect references to this event or series of events in Heidegger's corpus as it is now known. Although Heidegger never directly addresses the Holocaust, we cannot infer that he was unaware of it. One of the defensive strategies employed as early as the 1940s to defend Heidegger the man and the thinker from the consequences of his enthusiastic adhesion to National Socialism was the claim that as an intellectual he was unaware of and basically unconcerned with politics.

This line presupposes that well-known view that philosophers in general are only distantly aware of the outside world. The classical example is Thales, who thought all is water and proverbiably fell into a well. Yet Heidegger was not the ivory tower intellectual he is often thought to have been, unaware of anything except philosophy. Like his colleague Karl Jaspers, he was concerned with practical matters from the very beginning of his career. Typically, his first series of lectures is in part concerned with the reorganization of the German university.[18] When Heidegger became a Nazi, he was deeply concerned with the practical *Gleichschaltung* of civil servants in the university, going so far as to organize concentration camps for intellectuals.[19] Heidegger was keenly aware of political details, and even recommended Göring , the Reichsminister and after Hitler the second political figure in the Nazi hierarchy, as the ideal of the new German man.[20]

The Holocaust resulted directly from the application of Nazi government policy.[21] Heidegger served as the Nazi rector of the University of Freiburg im Breisgau from spring 1933 until summer 1934, resigning quickly after the assassination of Ernst Röhm, head of the SA, on June 30, 1934. Nazism was an effort by Adolf Hitler and his followers to acquire political power in Germany and, through aggressive military actions, the entire world. It did not understand itself as a serious intellectual theory, and even less as a theory of ontology that rivaled Heidegger's theory. Heidegger later claimed that in his Nietzsche lectures he broke with and criticized Nazism.[22] This claim has been accepted at face value by some of Heidegger's students as indicating a complete break with Nazism.[23] But inspection of his writings reveals that his occasional criticism of Nazism is always directed against its possible pretensions as a rival theory of being, but, so far as I know, was never directed against the practical results of its policies. Even when Heidegger mentions a practical result, such as the emphasis on *Blut und Boden*, or race as the real historical subject, it is not to denounce the practical results of Nazi politics; it is rather to denounce a supposedly mistaken, metaphysical view of history.[24]

In Heidegger's writings published during his lifetime and in those that have so far appeared from his *Nachlass*, with the exception of a letter to

Herbert Marcuse, his former student, to the best of my knowledge only two late passages from his lectures on technology directly mention the Holocaust. In a letter dated August 28, 1947, Marcuse asked Heidegger to comment on the Holocaust. In his response, in a letter dated January 20, 1948, Heidegger defended himself against the charge that he had failed to respond to the Holocaust on four distinct grounds: He could not make a public and clear confession without inviting the destruction of his family; in his work from 1933 and 1934 he took a clear stand against Nazism; it would be humiliating to confess in the manner of former Nazis; and for the claims about Jews one could put East Germans.[25]

Heidegger's response is entirely inadequate to Marcuse's request that he finally take a stand on the Holocaust. It is correct that during the war it was not possible to make a confession without serious personal risk, although that was certainly possible later on. But there is no record that Heidegger ever took a clear stand against Nazism in the period he mentions. Some of the lecture courses are missing, notably the lecture course on logic from summer 1934. The partial transcription of this course, based on the notes by Helene Weiss, his student, has recently been published in a bilingual edition.[26] It reveals that in this period, far from criticizing National Socialism, Heidegger was attempting to provide a philosophical grounding for Nazism. Certainly, the possible humiliation due to admitting a mistake is not commensurable with the destruction of the European Jews as the direct result of a political regime Heidegger himself favored. And, as Marcuse himself pointed out in his response to Heidegger's letter, whatever hardships the East Germans suffered were in no way comparable to the fate of the Jews.[27]

In the wake of his correspondence with Marcuse, Heidegger gave four lectures on technology in Bremen on December 1, 1949. Two passages in these lectures, of which one was retouched in the published version, address the Holocaust indirectly, but as clearly as Heidegger ever did so. In a passage in a still unpublished lecture on technology, he wrote:

> Hundreds of thousands die en masse. Do they die? They succumb. They are done in. Do they Die? They become mere quanta, items in an inventory in the business of manufacturing corpses. Do they die? They are liquidated inconspicuously in extermination camps. And even apart from that, right now millions of impoverished people are perishing from hunger in China.
>
> But to die is to endure death in its essence. To be able to die means to be capable of this endurance. We are capable of this only if the essence of death makes our own essence possible.[28]

In a lecture that appeared during Heidegger's lifetime as "The Question Concerning Technology," his published text reads, "Agriculture is now the mechanized food industry." This is vastly different from the passage in the lecture Heidegger delivered. Heidegger was obviously aware of the importance of this passage, whose original wording reads as follows: "Agriculture is now a mechanised food industry, in essence the same as the manufacturing of corpses in gas chambers and extermination camps, the same as the production of hydrogen bombs."[29]

These passages, particularly the latter one, have attracted attention in the literature. Karsten Harries notes that Heidegger understands the extermination camps as factories of death that preclude the authentic appropriation of death as a human possibility.[30] Lacoue-Labarthe has denounced the scandalous insufficiency of Heidegger's remark in the latter passage, which he regards as revealing the essence of the West.[31] The deeper problem that reflects on Heidegger's theory is that from his angle of vision this statement, as Pöggeler points out,[32] is literally correct—since in terms of the forgetfullness of being all forms of technology are equally mistaken—but, as already mentioned, clearly inadequate to grasp the historical specificity of the Holocaust. This is not a psychological difficulty but rather a philosophical limitation of Heidegger's theory.

5. Interpretations of Heidegger's Silence

We cannot merely be indifferent to the Holocaust. The Holocaust can be understood as representing a direct challenge to modernity, including the modern view of progress that comes to us from the Enlightenment. Heidegger's later thought contains a critique of modernity. How can we explain the extraordinary absence of more than passing comment on the Holocaust in Heidegger's writings?

Different analyses have been proposed to account for Heidegger's failure to provide more than a couple of indirect comments in the wake of his exchange of letters with Marcuse. Heidegger was a professor in Freiburg im Breisgau, which after the war, when Germany was occupied, fell into the French occupation zone. After the war, the so-called Oehlker commission, charged with removing former Nazis as well as Nazi collaborators from the German university in the French occupation zone, asked Karl Jaspers, Heidegger's colleague, for an opinion. In his report to the Oehlker commission, which removed Heidegger from the university in 1945, Jaspers maintained that Heidegger was evasive, unwilling to face such questions as antisemitism, and further maintained that a change of opinion about Nazism after June 30, 1934, was essentially meaningless.[33]

The occasions to face Nazism in general, or at least to comment directly on the Holocaust, were not lacking. After the war, Heidegger repeatedly declined invitations from the theologian Rudolf Bultmann,[34] the poet Paul

Celan,[35] and the philosopher Karl Jaspers to excuse himself in public or at least to come to grips with the Holocaust. At most he was willing to say to Jaspers in private that the individual is responsible for his or her actions, and that even as late as the end of the war he did not see the political consequences of his actions in 1933.[36] Silvio Vietta has suggested that when the Heidegger Archives are opened to the public, it will become clear that Heidegger was deeply ashamed.[37] But the archives are not open and at present only those who have the approval of the Heidegger family and their allies have unrestricted access to the unpublished material. Derrida suggests that if Heidegger had only said he was sorry we would not still be discussing the problem, but Heidegger was just not capable of it.[38] Harries maintains that there was essentially nothing that Heidegger could or should have said since he was not responsible for the Holocaust.[39]

These commentators agree at least in noting the psychological problem of whether Heidegger was later personally up to the task of accepting personal responsibility for his earlier identification with Nazism. Doubtless Heidegger's unusual personality is a factor. His mental health seems to have been fragile.[40] He exhibited a strange combination of overweening pride in his philosophical ability—he eventually came to believe that the only "philosophers" of importance were Heraclitus, Anaximander, Parmenides, and himself—as well as a reluctance to assume responsibility for his actions, the capacity to denounce colleagues when it suited his purposes, and so on. Yet Heidegger was not only an individual but a philosopher, who viewed the world, including Nazism, through the lens provided by his philosophical theory.

Two aspects of his philosophical theory relate to his failure to take up the challenge of the Holocaust. One that has already been mentioned is Heidegger's undifferentiated rejection of modernity as such, which prevents a grasp of the specificity of the historical event of the Holocaust. This insensitivity to the historical specificity of the Holocaust is in evidence in the simplistic, infamous, but strictly correct equation, correct from Heidegger's angle of vision, drawn between the extermination camps and agricultural technology. The other aspect that has not so far been mentioned is the theory of silence, or *Schweigen*, that accompanies, underlies, and even justifies Heidegger's own silence regarding the Holocaust.

In retrospect, Heidegger's writings contain an ever shifting theory of silence that appears suspiciously like a form of psychological rationalization. It is as if he revised his theory to provide a philosophical basis for his personal actions. In *Being and Time*, Heidegger describes silence and hearing as possibilities of discursive speech.[41] He specifically identifies the possibility of authentic silence in genuine discourse, as distinguished from mere silence.[42] In the account of conscience, he maintains that the call of conscience is silence.[43] In the initial cycle of Hölderlin lectures, immediately after the rectorate, when the problem of coming to grips with this problem became a real possibility, he inverted the relation between silence as a form of speech and speech in order to ground speech in silence.[44] In the *Beiträge zur Philosophie*, he maintains, following the revised understanding of silence announced in the Hölderlin lectures, that speech is grounded in silence. According to Heidegger, silence is the measure since it first provides the standard.[45] On the basis of this text, we can infer that Heidegger kept silent about the Holocaust and Nazism in general for the reason that to do so is supposedly to engage in an authentic form of genuine discourse by maintaining the standards of rigorous thought based in silence.

6. Reading Heidegger against Heidegger

Like Husserl, Heidegger emphasized the need to go to things themselves (*zu den Sachen selbst*). Although Heidegger never directly confronts the Holocaust, his later theory is sharply critical of modernity. The preceding discussion has identified psychological and philosophical reasons explaining Heidegger's silence with respect to the Holocaust. Now we can distinguish provisionally between Heidegger's theory and the use he makes of it. It remains to be seen whether Heidegger's theory can be read against Heidegger in order to face the event that he was unable to face. This strategy is by no means unprecedented. Kant distinguished between the spirit and the letter of a theory. Following Kant, Hegel opposed the letter of the critical philosophy through its alleged spirit in order to complete the Copernican Revolution in philosophy. Husserl claimed to take up the hidden secret of modern times in his theory. In his ontological reading of the critical philosophy, Heidegger claimed to complete Kant's theory in his fundamental ontology.

We can be brief here, since the foundations for the analysis of this question have already been provided. I have already conceded that I do not wish to deny that aspects of Heidegger's theory can be abstracted from it and employed to construct an understanding of the Holocaust. I only wish to argue that the result is not Heideggerian but anti-Heideggerian since it runs against the main thrust of Heidegger's theory.

My skepticism about the residual resources of Heidegger's theory to capture the Holocaust derives from the deepest distinctions of the theory itself. Heidegger is basically a dualistic thinker, but the historical specificity of the Holocaust cannot be captured within the dualistic Heideggerian framework. Heidegger's entire theory of being is predicated on the seminal ontological distinction between beings and being. This distinction enables him to exclude mere ontical questions about beings to concentrate on the theme of being that traverses his thought from one end to the other. In his later thought, most visibly in the *Beiträge zur Philosophie*, Heidegger gives up fundamental ontology, but not the concern with being, to make a new beginning based on a theory of the event (*Ereignis*). But he conserves throughout his dualistic distinction between being, understood as the single event obscuring/determining world history, and beings or events.

Yet this very distinction that makes it possible for him to focus on being makes it impossible to focus on beings, or even a single event, no matter how unusual, such as the Holocaust. And it is not possible to do so from within a dualistic framework in which beings or events are not measured comparatively against each other but absolutely with respect to being or the event of being. If this is correct, then short of abandoning the ontological distinction that underlies Heidegger's theory, short of transforming his theory into a view alien to it, there seems to be no way to read it in another, different way to analyze the Holocaust. For the unresolved and in my view unresolvable tension between the dualistic framework from which the theory springs and the object in question—in other words, a disparity between the conceptual framework and the historical event—prevents the Heideggerian theory from grasping the historical specificity of the most terrible event in our century.

7. Conclusion

This paper has examined the link among Heidegger, his theory, and the Holocaust. I have argued that Heidegger did not address the Holocaust for psychological and philosophical reasons, following from his conviction that it was authentic not to speak, namely, to be silent, and that his dualistic theory prevented him in any case from doing so. I have further expressed my skepticism, in virtue of the dualistic structure of the theory, that it can be read in independence of or even against Heidegger in order to come to grips with the Holocaust.

I come now to the conclusion. Heidegger's brilliant theory of being has been widely influential, among the most influential philosophical theories of our time. But, as the discussion of his failure to address the Holocaust has shown, the difficulty is not only or even mainly psychological but philosophical. Philosophically, even when Heidegger's theory is read against Heidegger, there are simply no resources to come to grips with the Holocaust within the wider framework of the theory. Heidegger intended his theory to cast light on being; but it attracted attention in virtue of his fantastic ability to capture the concerns of the German people as the Weimar Republic came slowly to an end. Yet, although his theory reflected the times, it was inadequate to know them, to grasp them on the level of thought. Although he was led toward Nazism on the basis of his theory, it was insufficient to shed any light, however dim, on Nazism or on the Holocaust to which it gave rise.

The weakness at the heart of Heidegger's theory is not simple nor unimportant, but important if philosophy is concerned with concreteness and if the Holocaust is one of the most momentous problems of our troubled time. David Krell, long one of Heidegger's most ardent American supporters, now claims to detect *ein Versagen des Denkens*[46] in his thought. Yet the problem is not the failure of thought in general, as Krell so grandly suggests, but rather the failure of Heidegger's thought.

The issue can be framed but not resolved in two points. First, as Derrida points out, the study of Heidegger requires us to think his theory and political commitment without relinquishing our political responsibility.[47] So far this attempt has not often been made. The very difficulty of this task is shown by Derrida's own, recent problems in defending Heidegger[48] and Paul de Man.[49] Second, we need to reexamine our normative conception of philosophy as indispensable for or at least relevant to the good life. Heidegger renewed this claim in a number of places in his work, including his request for leave in 1943, where he suggested that the completion of his work was essential to the future of the West,[50] and in his account of a new, allegedly deeper humanism in the "Letter on Humanism." Yet, since there is no way from a concern with being to the problems of human being, since such enormous problems as the Holocaust can no longer even be raised from this perspective, it follows that Heidegger's inability to confront the Holocaust points to a clear choice between two normative views of philosophy: a continued flight from the ontical level, from the despised *doxa*, to the ontological plane that is largely irrelevant to human concerns; or a qualified return to the practical plane as the basis and goal of our philosophical thought.

NOTES

1. See Alan Rosenberg, "Was the Holocaust Unique? A Peculiar Question," in Isador Walliman and Michael N. Dobkowski (eds.), *Genocide and the Modern Age: Etiology and Case Studies of Mass Death* (Westport, CT: Greenwood Press, 1987).
2. See *Forever in the Shadow of Hitler? Original Documents of the Historikerstreit: The Controversy Concerning the Singularity of the Holocaust* (Atlantic Highlands, NJ: Humanities Press, 1993).
3. See C. G. Hempel, "The Function of General Laws in History," in Herbert Feigel and Wilfrid Sellars (eds.), *Readings in Philosophical Analysis* (New York: Appleton-Century-Crofts, 1949).
4. For a summary of recent revisionist readings of the Holocaust in English, see Lucy Dawidowicz, *The War against the Jews: 1933–1945* (New York: Bantam, 1986), pp. xxi–xxxii.
5. See Norman Cohn, *Histoire d'un mythe: La "conspiration" juive et les protocoles des sages de Sion* (Paris: Gallimard, 1967).

6. For this view, see Jean-François Lyotard, *The Differend: Phrases in Dispute* (Minneapolis: University of Minnesota Press, 1988), p. 3.
7. See Jean Beaufret, *Entretiens avec F. de Towarnicki* (Paris: PUF, 1984), p. 87.
8. For a discussion of the link between Beaufret and Faurisson, see Michel Kajman, *Le Monde*, January 22, 1988, pp. 1, 18.
9. See *Annales d'histoire révisioniste*, 3 (Autumn-Winter 1987), pp. 204–205.
10. See Ernst Nolte, *Martin Heidegger: Politik und Geschichte im Leben und Denken* (Berlin: Propyläen, 1992), p. 277.
11. See Nolte, *Martin Heidegger*, pp. 168–169.
12. Ibid., pp. 115, 123.
13. Ibid., p. 150.
14. For a discussion, see Tom Rockmore, *On Heidegger's Nazism and Philosophy* (Berkeley: University of California Press, 1992), Chap. 1: "Revealing Concealed Nazism," pp. 15–27.
15. See Charles E. Scott, *The Question of Ethics: Nietzsche, Foucault, Heidegger* (Bloomington: Indiana University Press, 1990), pp. 148–172.
16. See John Sallis, *Echoes after Heidegger* (Bloomington: Indiana University Press, 1990), p. 11.
17. See Nolte, *Martin Heidegger*, p. 277.
18. See Martin Heidegger, *Zur Bestimmung der Philosophie*, *Gesamtausgabe*, Vol. 56/57 (Frankfurt/M: Vittorio Klostermann, 1987).
19. See Hugo Ott, *Martin Heidegger: Unterwegs zu seiner Biographie* (Frankfurt/M: Campus, 1988), pp. 214–223.
20. See Ott, *Martin Heidegger*, pp. 146–148.
21. See Raul Hilberg, *The Destruction of the European Jews* (New York: Harper & Row, 1961).
22. See "Only a God Can Save Us: Der Spiegel's Interview with Martin Heidegger," in *Philosophy Today* (Winter 1976), p. 274.
23. See Pierre Aubenque, "Encore Heidegger et le nazisme," in *Le débat*, No. 48 (January–February 1988), p. 121.
24. See Martin Heidegger, *Beiträge zur Philosophie (Vom Ereignis)*, *Gesamtausgabe*, Vol. 65 (Frankfurt/M: Vittorio Klostermann, 1989), p. 493.
25. The letter, together with Marcuse's response, is cited in Victor Farías, *Heidegger and Nazism* (Philadelphia: Temple University Press, 1989), pp. 284–285.
26. See Martin Heidegger, *Lógica: Lecciones de M. Heidegger (semestro verano 1934) en el legado de Helene Weiss* (Madrid: Anthropos, 1991).
27. See Farías, *Heidegger and Nazism*, pp. 284–286.
28. Cited in Rockmore, *On Heidegger's Nazism and Philosophy*, p. 242.
29. Cited in Rockmore, *On Heidegger's Nazism and Philosophy*, p. 241.
30. See his "Introduction" to Günther Neske and Emil Kettering (eds.), *Martin Heidegger and National Socialism: Questions and Answers* (New York: Paragon House, 1990), pp. xxix–xxx.
31. See Philippe Lacoue-Labarthe, *La Fiction du politique* (Paris: Christian Bourgois, 1987), pp. 58–63.
32. See Otto Pöggeler, "Heidegger's Political Self-Understanding," in Richard Wolin (ed.), *The Heidegger Controversy: A Critical Reader* (New York: Columbia University Press, 1991).
33. See Jaspers' report, cited in Ott, *Martin Heidegger*, pp. 315–317.
34. See Ott, *Martin Heidegger*, pp. 163–164.
35. See Otto Pöggeler, "Todtnauberg," in this volume.

36. See his letter of April 8, 1950, to Jaspers, in Martin Heidegger/Karl Jaspers, *Briefwechsel 1920–1963* (Frankfurt/M, München, Zürich: Vittorio Klostermann and Piper, 1990), pp. 200–203.
37. See Silvio Vietta, *Heidegger's Kritik am Nationalsozialismus und an der Technik* (Tübingen: Niemeyer, 1989), p. 101.
38. See Jacques Derrida, "Heidegger's Silence," in Neske and Kettering, *Martin Heidegger and National Socialism*, p. 146.
39. See Harries, "Introduction" in Neske and Kettering, *Martin Heidegger and National Socialism*, pp. xxxi–xxxii.
40. See Hugo Ott, "Biographical Bases for Heidegger's 'Mentality of Disunity'" in Tom Rockmore and Joseph Margolis (eds.), *The Heidegger Case: On Philosophy and Politics* (Philadelphia: Temple University Press, 1992).
41. See Martin Heidegger, *Being and Time* (New York: Harper & Row, 1962), ¶ 34: "Being-there and Discourse. Language," pp. 203–211.
42. Ibid., p. 208.
43. Ibid., p. 342.
44. See Martin Heidegger, *Hölderlins Hymnen "Germanien" und "Der Rhein," Gesamtausgabe*, Vol. 39 (Frankfurt/M: Vittorio Klostermann, 1980), p. 218.
45. See Heidegger, *Beiträge zur Philosophie*, ¶ 281, p. 510.
46. See David Farrell Krell, *Daimon Life: Heidegger and Life-Philosophy* (Bloomington: Indiana University Press, 1992), p. 138.
47. See Derrida, "Heidegger's Silence," in Neske and Kettering, *Martin Heidegger and National Socialism*, pp. 146–147.
48. See Thomas Sheehan, "A Normal Nazi," in *The New York Review of Books*, January 14, 1993.
49. See Jacques Derrida, "Like the Sound of the Sea Deep within a Shell: Paul de Man's War," in Werner Hamacher, Neil Hertz, and Thomas Keenan (eds.), *Responses: On Paul de Man's Wartime Journalism* (Lincoln: University of Nebraska Press, 1989).
50. See his letter of July 17, 1943, to Prof. Schuchardt, dean of the philosophy faculty, cited in Farías, *Heidegger and Nazism*, pp. 268–269.

8

Heidegger's "Silence" about the Holocaust: An Attempt at a Reconstruction

RAINER ALISCH

1. The Discussion of the "Silence"

In those remarks which have so far come to light, Heidegger relativized the crimes committed in the concentration camps. He compared them with the forced displacement of the "'East Germans'" by "one of the Allies,"[1] which is to say, by the former Soviet Union. Moreover, by homogenizing technology to the degree that it becomes evil itself so that all distinctions disappear before it, Heidegger equated these crimes to "agriculture" as "mechanized food industry," to the "blockade" of Berlin, and to the "manufacture of hydrogen bombs."[2] However, in spite of the expectations of some of his interpreters, students, and friends, and the demands of his critics that he explicitly distance himself from the Holocaust by morally condemning the crimes or attempting "to think Auschwitz," Heidegger never did. Together with the refusal to acknowledge his own National Socialist past,[3] this has become the "silence" and has, ever since, been an object of an independent discourse[4] and a part of the confrontation concerning the "case" of Heidegger. The concept itself is ambiguous. What is called Heidegger's silence has less to do with the man himself than with his readers; for as Silvio Vietta has emphasized, Heidegger certainly expressed himself "on the linguistic level which was at his disposal as a thinker and a philosopher, on the level of a critique of metaphysics and of the history of being."[5] In addition to that which is recognized as Heidegger's silence, there is another manifest "silence," namely, that in his statements.

In the interim there have been a multiplicity of opinions, explanations, or interpretations of what is called Heidegger's silence. Approximately four positions can be distinguished. The first can be considered part of the tradition of those who deny "Auschwitz." It is propagated by Polacco de Ménasse,[6] for example, in connection with Robert Faurisson, the French revisionist "historian," to whom Jean Beaufret, one of the key figures in the French interpretation of Heidegger, wrote letters of encouragement.[7] A second position can be attributed to Ernst Nolte, whose book on Heidegger, which seeks to reconstruct the political context in which Heidegger acted, deserves special mention. As part of his attempt to rehabilitate all of those who, like Heidegger, worked for a "small scale solution"—that is to say, fascism as a preventative measure against the Bolshevik world revolution—Nolte also rehabilitates Heidegger's silence and hence sees no reason for an "admission of guilt."[8] The third position takes Heidegger's work and biography to be a closed totality which contains within itself all the explanations for his silence. George Steiner interprets Heidegger in this manner, seeing his life and work as both a "consequence of Heidegger's particular view of German destiny" and as a psychological consequence of Heidegger's "petty character," with its "deeply rooted and agrarian traditions of secrecy and exploitation."[9] Dieter Thomä understands Heidegger's silence on the basis of a "double necessity," which springs from the immanent pressures of Heidegger's "path of thinking" as well as from the "necessary denial of what was at issue during the period of his engagement with National Socialism."[10] Finally, George Kovacs' sweeping attempt to interpret Heidegger's silence, which is similar to Vietta's, also belongs to this position: that Heidegger, after his political "error," remained "faithful to his primordial and unrelenting work on the question of being (*Sein*) in silence." At that time he spoke from a position of an "essentially ontological-phenomenological analysis," which means "that he is not really silent (that his silence is limited and not meaningless) for those who are willing to listen."[11] As represented by Jacques Derrida, Jean-François Lyotard and Philippe Lacoue-Labarthe, the final position distinguishes itself from the foregoing one, above all, by means of the fact that for them "silence" loses its feature of merely demanding "understanding," and instead acquires the character of an empty site, something at one's disposal. Silence is understood as the task of replacing the emptiness with one's own discourse. Insignificant even in comparison with Heidegger's actual National Socialist engagement, it is precisely the moral abnormality of a silence that cannot be excused by means of understanding, that is considered to be "unforgivable," "inexcusable," or "something leaden,"[12] which appears to make this further thought essential. In a play of hypothetical questions and answers, Derrida makes perfectly clear what is at issue: What would have happened if Heidegger had excused himself for "Auschwitz" and had then received "absolution"?

We "would not be in the position of needing to ask ourselves what the experience of Heidegger's thinking might contain in affinities, in synchronizations of thought, in commonalities of provenance and the like, with that still unthought phenomenon which National Socialism represents for us."[13]

Derrida's transformation of the moral indignation over Heidegger's silence into the question of the unthought of National Socialism is also shared by Lyotard and Lacoue-Labarthe.[14] They attempt to determine the relationship between Heidegger's philosophy and National Socialism, and at the same time to denazify the philosophy in order, by means of it, to "think" National Socialism. With regards to the initial step, Lacoue-Labarthe had distinguished himself above all from Theodor W. Adorno. In a "postscript"[15] he reacted in a manner analogous to Derrida and Lyotard to the new investigations of Heidegger's National Socialist period, which, in contrast to the usual practice up to that time, which was to deny any connection,[16] rehistoricized this problematic anew.[17] At issue is the material that Hugo Ott had brought to light on the occasion of the new edition of Heidegger's *Rektoratsrede* published in 1983,[18] but above all the publication of *Heidegger and Nazism* by Victor Farías in 1987. Adorno and Farías answered the question, what is the relationship between Heidegger's philosophy and National Socialism, in a reductive manner. Adorno declared Heidegger's philosophy to be "fascist to its innermost core," while Farías found an "unreserved agreement with the generic foundation of National Socialism."[19] Derrida, Lacoue-Labarthe, and Lyotard dehistoricize Heidegger. This is the case insofar as they oppose the main weaknesses of reductive thinking—its inability to make sense of the discontinuities in Heidegger's philosophy and the fact that it seeks to establish that Heidegger's philosophy has an essentially fascist element[20]—with the thesis that there is an immanent split within Heidegger's philosophy. In his "late philosophy," it is argued, Heidegger not only broke with his own subjective, that is, metaphysical Nazism,[21] and thereby—as his own critical remarks are said to demonstrate—proceeded to distance himself from and oppose National Socialism, but in his "Overcoming Metaphysics," he developed a problematic whose scope extended beyond historical National Socialism.[22] This is said to offer, for the first time, an adequate way of approaching National Socialism, and to open up the possibility of thinking National Socialism, as well as the Holocaust, "with" Heidegger.[23] In this sense, Derrida integrates the Holocaust into Heidegger's philosophy of "spirit," which stretches back to the Hebrew "ruah" and the Aristotelean "pneuma," and suggests even *the* "gas" itself.[24] Lacoue-Labarthe traces the extermination of the Jews back to an ancient model, as a consequence of which the political is constituted on the basis of art, one of the *topoi* which occupied Heidegger during and after his so-called turn.[25] Lyotard denies that it is necessary to have recourse to the Ancients by citing Hegel's verdict that the

Jews were barred from the ancient stage because they were not tragic subjects. Their fate can better be understood with Hegel: Because their God does not allow himself to be *aufgehoben* into spirit, "they must . . . finally be *aufgehoben*."[26]

In fact, concepts such as "art" and the "tragic," as well as the name Hölderlin, the category of "spirit," and the invocation of the "ancients," represent something like an unthought National Socialism insofar as they recall the material on the basis of which the national, conservative elite, to which the majority of philosophers belonged, conceived their project of a "national" revolution,[27] or, like Heidegger, dreamed the "dream of a 'people's religion.'"[28] Next to the fascist "movement," understood in a narrow sense, this was the second column of true National Socialism, which, in the absence of this elite, would have been possible neither in Italy nor in Germany. After 1945, this "column"[29] was for the most part left untouched by the allies' measures. Integrated into the political culture of the emerging Federal Republic, its cooperation with National Socialism remains invisible. What is termed Heidegger's silence is a variant of the way in which this process was carried out.

What follows is an investigation of philosophical form. At issue is to understand why that which is interpreted as Heidegger's silence—the remarks on the crimes of the National Socialists are also a part of this—does not rest on an internal mistake in his thinking, as Lyotard and Lacoue-Labarthe believe,[30] and is therefore not a failing that can be corrected within the premises of Heidegger's own thinking. Instead, "silence," which can be described as the refusal to make morally formed or socio-analytical statements, is understood as an element that structures this thinking. It results from Heidegger's self-positioning within the philosophical tradition, that is, from his rejection of what he calls "representational" thinking. This means that it wasn't only after 1945 that "silence" informed Heidegger's thinking, thus accommodating a majority political culture that was marked by a need to forget, but that this had already been the case before. It also means that Heidegger's silence in regard to the Holocaust loses its exclusivity. It is a part of Heidegger's frequently reiterated refusal to speak about the "times" in any form other than "philosophical."

The first of the two following sections will focus on the forms in which Heidegger's colleagues treated the Nazi past after 1945. The second section will study the functionality of the philosophical form on which Heidegger's silence is based. The guiding thesis is the idea that it is the philosopheme of criticism of the subject which lies at the root of his silence; that enables Heidegger to advocate the fascist transformation of the university while at the same time attacking its politicization. In a similar fashion, he can criticize Nazism and at the same time paralyze resistance against it. After 1945, he continues this criticism, but the form in which he criticizes Nazism becomes part of the general "silence" about the Nazi past, and thus contributes to the integration of elements of Nazism into the new West German society.

2. The Context of "Silence": West German Philosophy, 1945–50

For the public life of German academic philosophy, the end of the Second World War meant, first of all, that the universities were closed. The philosophical societies had suspended the normal course of philosophical conferences with the beginning of the war; the most important academic journals ceased to appear years before the end of the war. If we compare this situation with the one that obtained after the First World War, in which there was no such disruption, apart from the amount of destruction and of human suffering, it was completely new with respect to the question of guilt which was then being raised. In addition the "state," with which German philosophy traditionally had a special relationship, was in ruins. In spite of the differences, the break of 1945 cannot be understood apart from that of 1918 (this is true on the basis of the continuity in personnel alone); even less can it be understood without considering the preceding period of National Socialism, above all the "national awakening" of 1933.

In his attempt to evaluate both world wars with respect to their production of "metaphysical-poetic discourse," George Steiner has made reference to the greater productivity of the period following the First World War, which was principally due to academic outsiders. But the fact is that also after 1945 there were publications which satisfied the criterion of the "arrogant striving for totality"[31] that are not, however, mentioned by Steiner: Popper's *The Open Society and Its Enemies* (1944/57); Adorno and Horkeimer's *The Dialectic of Enlightenment* (1947); the first volume of Bloch's *The Principle of Hope* (1954); Lukács' *The Destruction of Reason* (1954); but also Löwith's *From Hegel to Nietzsche* (German edition, 1950).

The truth of these omissions lies in the fact that "out" in this case meant emigration. In addition, apart from particularly prominent Nazis such as Ernst Krieck and Alfred Baeumler, who because of their "peasant" origins were never truly accepted as members of the guild, in the Western zones a majority of the recently released members of the Nazi party were accepted back into the academic philosophy establishment without delay.[32] For this reason, attempts to disturb the virtually unbroken hegemony of the "elders" were hindered.[33] Accordingly, the emigrants began to be influential—for example, as analysts of fascism—only in the altered political constellation of the 1960s, whereby the impression rightly arose that in this respect there was nothing in the years after 1945 comparable to the upheaval of the 1920s, but rather simply continuity. Moreover, the period after 1945 was not in fact the moment of new ideas. As with Bloch, Lukács, and the other emigrants whose work was still in part based on the crises and constellations of the 1920s, so too the views of Arnold Gehlen, Hans Feyer,[34] or Heidegger, whose *An Introduction to Metaphysics* (from 1935, first published in 1953), were determined by works from the years prior to 1945.

What was, however, emphasized by the texts of National Socialist philosophers published immediately after 1945 was the lack of that unmediated relationship to the state which was characteristic of the end of Weimar and the subsequent period of National Socialism. Nevertheless, there could be no doubt that philosophers remained in the service of the state.

In Heidegger's *Rektoratsrede* of 1933, the "state-philosophical function"[35] of philosophy found its expression, among other things, in the summons toward the unity of science: "All science is philosophy, whether it knows and wills it—or not." Behind this was the view that only under the leadership of philosophy could science occupy the "innermost determining center of the entire existence of people and state."[36] In addition to the National Socialist student body, the traditional scholarly class, which Fritz K. Ringer has designated the mandarin class (*Mandarinat*), could also recognize itself in the demand for unity.[37] For the debate over the "crisis of science," into which Heidegger had thus intervened, belongs, along with catchwords such as "dissolution," "specialization," and "positivism," to the discussion concerning the "cultural crisis." It is within the context of this discussion that the "educated" expressed their position, which had become precarious as a result of societal upheavals.[38]

The unity of science in philosophy also determined Nicolai Hartmann's discussion of the "uncrowned king of philosophy"[39] during the first postwar meeting of philosophers in Garmisch-Partenkirchen in 1947. The intended unity was to arise out of a "decisive critique of the theoretical presuppositions" of science. The impulse for this came, among other sources, from an interpretation of National Socialism which regarded it as a degeneration of the guiding values of scientific reason: "How could a dogmatic metaphysics of race become widespread, which did not at all accord with actual biology?"[40] For the field of philosophy in the period immediately following the war, dominated by the positions of the old elite, this way of speaking can be considered as prototypical. It was easy to appeal to transhistorical values insofar as, already before 1945, the "times" were, from the standpoint of these values, increasingly viewed critically; also one's own activity in the historical moment of 1933, in which these values appeared to be realized, was thereby obscured.

In 1933 the task fell to nationalistic, conservatively attuned philosophy to deliver to the "new" state that segment of the population whose "spirit" it represented. In 1945 a comparable accomplishment seemed impossible without some further effort, if only for the reason that there was no longer any agreement within the philosophical community; this is reflected in the fact that Georgi Schischkoff, one of the organizers of the philosophy conferences, deemed it necessary to make precise recommendations for the organization of the subsequent conferences.[41] Even the self-appointed task of representing the *Zeitgeist* proved overwhelming.[42] The spirit of the times was not the one embodied in philosophy. Fritz J. von Rintelen, for example, in the opening address to the second philosophy conference in Mainz in 1948, complained that "respect for intellectual greatness" has been lost, and that education amounted to a "craftsmanship of the intellect" and led to the "ignorance of the specialist." During the concluding discussions on "The Relationship of Philosophy to Contemporary Events," which took place in Deidesheim, he observed that the war youth have "essentially [not] made any spiritual progress," and that we need to first "shake [them] up" "so that they [will be] capable of expressing their opinions."[43]

Speaking very broadly, one can say that, with respect to the confrontation with the problem of the "times," two positions crystallized during the first three conferences (the third took place in Bremen in 1950, and it was here that the Allgemeinen Gesellschaft für Philosophie was founded). The first falls back upon the ever present "eternal questions"[44] and values of philosophy, that is, "those highest values . . . in contrast with which the events of decades and of generations are unimportant,"[45] as Erich Rothacker put it, who, in addition to Hans Heyse, was the second prominent Nazi to appear in Mainz. The other position sought to confront the times insofar as they articulated themselves "philosophically." It reacted to a type of philosophy which, aside from Marxism, corresponded to the times like no other, but was criticized precisely on this account.[46] For it put into question the timeless validity of those values which now were being summoned up against "defeatism," "isolation," and "specialization"—reason, humanism, and Christianity—and appeared thereby to correspond exactly to that which, after 1945, one believed to recognize in National Socialism, namely, "nihilism."[47] What is meant is existentialism. Because its main representatives, Heidegger and Karl Jaspers, were not present at the conferences, the controversy over existentialism was in the first instance played out by Bollnow and von Rintelen as a form of shadow boxing.[48] And both agreed that existentialism was derived from the isolation and irrational attunement of life-philosophy and energetically called for it to be overcome.[49] Bollnow conceded that the French variant, as represented by Sartre, was a "truly existential matter" with "political significance" in virtue of its close relationship to the resistance; while in Germany it was a matter which concerned "no event that could be understood on the basis of the internal movement of the German spirit,"[50] but was rather solely an issue of fashion. The political significance which the central concepts "decision" and "resoluteness" had for the unleashing of fascist subjectivity[51] remained unnamed. Also unnamed was the fact that the danger that existentialism could "degenerate into a flight into the all too private sphere"[52] had already once been encountered, namely, in that the "total state had assumed . . . total responsibility"[53] for individualized existence.

If one adopts a socio-analytical standard, then in neither the first position nor the second was National Socialism an object of discussion. In expressions such as the "events," "the events of decades," the "last 10 years,"[54] the "frightful events of the last decades,"[55] National Socialism remained in this sense unthematized. "It is not surprising that in Bremen there was little discussion from the organizers of the recent history of the National Socialist dictatorship, of the genocide and the extermination of the European Jews, for this did not occur at the previous conferences either. Even less could one expect that a large number of speakers would have felt compelled to speak about their own specific philosophical and scientific-political contributions to these events."[56]

In contrast with the silence of the conferences, a text by Jaspers stands out in which he turned to one of the gravest questions which the Germans then had to pose to themselves, the question of guilt.[57] This text was part of a series of lectures Jaspers delivered in 1946 at the University of Heidelberg, and, like a text of Spranger's which at that time remained unpublished, it emerged against the background of the Nuremberg Trials. Against the "superficiality of the chatter about guilt," Jaspers develops a succession of levels of guilt: "The Germans" as such are not guilty, rather criminal, moral and metaphysical guilt concerns only the individual; a people can collectively only be made responsible in a political sense. Jaspers' reflections aim at an "inner reversal"[58] of the individual, upon which alone a renewal of the whole can rest. Already in 1948, in the climate that prevailed in the Western-zones, which aimed at an intellectual and political restoration (under which his Jewish wife particularly suffered), Jaspers considered his entreaty a failure and retreated to Switzerland.[59]

Jaspers' concentration on the single individual is directed against a way of coming to terms with guilt that, because it "lacks real commitment, withdraws from the task of realizing this process in the heart of the individual's sense of self." In this way it secures "in a new manner a false, collective feeling of self worth." What Jaspers has in mind is the tone Heidegger adopted with him after he had sent him a copy of "The Question of Guilt" in the hope of such an inner transformation: "The guilt of the individual remains, and remains even more, the more individual he is. But evil has not yet run its course. It is only now entering a true world stage."[60]

3. An Attempt to Make Heidegger's "Silence" Speak

It is clear from this brief examination of the founding events of West German philosophy that the attitude toward the National Socialist era is inadequately described by the concept of silence, understood as an explicit non-thematization. On the one hand, silence appears to be an inherent element of a particular type of philosophy, a view which is still held today. This type of philosophy denies the particulars of its involvement in everyday affairs and instead sticks to "timeless" thematics.[61] On the other hand, we see that the "past" was—and is—entirely capable of being thematized in the imaginary constructions of philosophy[62] as the "decline" of values, placed in confrontation with existentialism, or as a morally conceived attempt to work through "guilt."

In this second sense, Heidegger's silence (that which is evident in his texts) can be understood from three perspectives. First, in relation to a phenomenon which Hermann Lübbe has termed "communicative silence."[63] Second, from the manner in which Heidegger's philosophy itself is political, although it differentiates itself at the same time from "the political." And third, from the way in which Heidegger seeks to distance himself from his own political activity as well as from National Socialism in general. These last two points are directly connected with what is called Heidegger's turn.

In 1983, on the occasion of the fiftieth anniversary of Hitler's coming to power, Hermann Lübbe, reacting to the reproach of "repression," retrospectively described the procedures which governed the universities after 1945 as a national necessity. To all those involved, "porter and professor," the "students who in 1945 were still young enough to be members of the youth movement," as well as the "professorial colleague returning from flight or hiding," the facts of the recent past were known: "They knew it from one another." However, the "certain silence" which reigned was a necessary means of dissimulation, so to speak, "necessary in order to integrate the subjects of this history, but not the history itself, into the new state."[64] The silence, reciprocally maintained,[65] did not merely assure the continuity of personnel, it also safeguarded—to extend Lübbe's train of thought—the ability of thinking itself to adapt to the new circumstances, while at the same time helping to shape them.[66] Bollnow transformed existence philosophy into the "new security," while Joachim Ritter, whose influential school Lübbe also belonged to, "made the ancient concept of the *polis* into a bourgeois notion, in order to provide an Aristotelian foundation for the newly developing bourgeois order."[67]

In one respect Heidegger's thinking produced its effect in this silence in a similar manner, but in another sense it was rather atypical. Jürgen Habermas confirms that *Being and Time* has enjoyed a completely untarnished reception since its publication. It has a "position of such eminence in the philosophical thinking of our century that it is a mistake to think that the substance of this work could be discredited, more than five decades later, by political assessments of Heidegger's engagement with fascism."[68] What is true of *Being and Time*,[69] however, appears to be somewhat more difficult for other parts of Heidegger's philosophy. Otto Pöggeler's assertion that Heidegger's thinking lacks "a 'practical' philosophy,' but not a political dimension,"[70] owes less to the conviction that Heidegger's thinking does not allow for a political praxis, than to a desire to defend this praxis. And there, where it is a question of the theoretical constitution of political praxis, this assertion should be understood as a defense of the kinds of thinking which underlie Heidegger's praxis.[71] The fact that Heidegger's "thinking of the origin" after the war could still be widely influential—even when circumstances favored parliamentary democracy—not as "political philosophy,"[72] is due, paradoxically, to the ways in which Heidegger "non-politically" politicized his philosophy—with the result that it came into conflict with the National Socialist authorities, who took themselves to be the official trustees of the political.

The process of this formation can be observed in 1933. Like Gehlen, Freyer, Baeumler, and Krieck, Heidegger also constructed his philosophy around the concept of "action," whose specific characteristics Baeumler prototypically formulated: "Action does not mean, to decide in favor of . . . for that assumes that one knows what one is deciding in favor of; rather, action means: to follow a path, to take sides, on the authority of a fateful mission, on the authority of one's 'own right.'"[73] In relation to a philosophy that is merely contemplative, reflexive, autonomous, and hence distant from any conception of praxis, this is considered to be "political."[74] Heidegger's move toward an explicitly practical philosophy is also linked to a rejection of academic thinking: "We have renounced the idolization of a groundless and impotent thinking. We are seeing the end of philosophy that is subservient to it."[75] The demand that is implicitly contained in this statement—to make oneself "subservient" to power rather than to "impotent thinking"—considered as a "purely" philosophical event, means to subordinate oneself to an "originary power" in order, by means of a "turning," to put an end to the "groundlessness" of the metaphysical tradition of thought.[76] By claiming that he is "led" by "being" itself,[77] Heidegger immunizes himself against criticism; and that which prepares the "ground" for thinking in this way has the exact opposite effect once it is translated into the sphere of political thought. It removes "the metaphysical grounds of political philosophy hitherto and thereby undermines the foundation which it had provided to politics."[78] The "internal" abolition of the "political" from Heidegger's philosophy, evidenced, for example, in his critique of value philosophy—the values, universally invoked but absent, pave the way for the destruction of the

Jews—echoes the abolition of political spontaneity, which from 1933 was carried out "outside" as real politics, be it repressively or be it by means of free choice.

Thus Heidegger acted politically as a philosopher, and not merely in the actions he took as rector.[79] This is so even when Heidegger not only did not understand the effect of his philosophical activity as "political," but also had a predominantly negative relationship to the political, as is clear from those statements which have hitherto been made public.[80] The attempts Heidegger made to distance himself from politics, including those from the postwar period, contain sufficient truth to explain his opposition. In 1933 the concept "political" functioned, among other ways, as a means of bringing the universities into line. This was demanded by the nationalistic, conservative professors, as well as by the National Socialist professors and the National Socialist student leadership, who were in union with them.[81] Hence Heidegger's declaration that the essence of the university cannot be "determined on the basis of 'politics' or some other set of purposes"[82] was motivated by a clear resistance to the instrumentalizing grip of the state. However, this can by no means be understood—and this is precisely what is at issue in 1933—as a rejection of the university becoming fascist. Heidegger was simply concerned that those initial measures, which remained caught in "external matters" or mere "organizational issues" and hence were still trapped within the bounds of subjectivity, should correspond to the "inner" essence of the university and science. That is to say, Heidegger conceived of them as ideal, autonomous acts of submission, which could be understood "purely" philosophically as a return to the "beginning" and the "end."

By 1933 the most important elements in Heidegger's thinking had already taken shape, through which—if in a different form—he would orient himself to the National Socialist past after 1945. It is a thinking that understands itself as a stage of "being," that produces a reverential effect—a will for that which ought to be—and that distances itself from all forms of the political understood as an "autonomous" sphere.

But which path does Heidegger take? Do we, as Tom Rockmore assumes, have "the curious situation of a philosopher who initially insisted on the social role of philosophy, and who, on his own account, was led by his philosophy to Nazism, but who later denied a social role to thought while continuing to insist on the interest of an authentic form of National Socialism"?[83] Against the assumption of a "break," Heidegger himself suggests that there is continuity, at least so far as the immanent development of his thinking in this period is concerned. In his view, the "turn" in his thinking was already completed at the beginning of the 1930s.[84] And the "curious situation" referred to by Rockmore appears to be caused primarily by the fact that he interprets Heidegger's philosophy in light of the history of ideas and concepts. Rockmore sees a "social" or "political role" there, where he describes Heidegger's philosophy as "a form of Platonism in which politics follows from philosophy." The point at which Rockmore believes Heidegger abandons "his prior insistence on a political competence of the philosopher," namely, in his discussion of the opposition between philosophy and thinking, he interprets as "an almost Aristotelian version of the social inutility of pure philosophy."[85] But even if one questions the direction taken by Rockmore's interpretation, the assumption that there is a difference between the texts he cites is correct. For, although the first sentence of the "Letter on Humanism"—the first text in which Heidegger expresses his desire to speak once more—promises something different, it begins with remarks which, in comparison with the activist gestures of the *Rektoratsrede*, seem actually to retract that which might refer to a "social role" for philosophy: "We are still far from pondering the essence of action decisively enough." Instead of action being elevated to a theme in what follows—perhaps in connection with *Being and Time*—it is reduced to a type of "thinking" that no longer understands itself as philosophical or scientific, a thinking that solely "acts insofar as it thinks," not however in a "practical" sense, but rather only as a "thinking of being," which "belonging to being, listens to being."[86]

Finally, in the "Letter on Humanism" there are also the philosophical method and rhetorical gestures which lure the "understanding" into a trap; just as in the *Rektoratsrede*, where the external circumstances, rather than the inner diction or the content, refer to the National Socialist character.[87] If we reject the inner-philosophical perspective preferred by Rockmore in favor of one in which the political aspect of philosophy is reflected in the question, What effect is produced by this philosophy?—irrespective of whether the author understood himself as a Nazi or not—then the "later" philosophy, including that subsequent to 1945, maintains its political, action-oriented impetus, and in precisely the same form as in the *Rektoratsrede*. Likewise, Heidegger's statements in 1945 essentially constitute a reinterpretation of the possibilities for action which lie in the future, as a "destiny" that will destroy everything if a transformation of "thinking" is not successful in the near future. This amounts to a blanket delegitimization of all forms of political praxis, including those in which Heidegger recognized National Socialism; not National Socialism itself, but rather the "true" National Socialism is meant.

The manner in which Heidegger is able achieve this dual effect can be understood by tracing the different ways in which he represents the overcoming of "subjectivity," which is also one possible description of the "turn." In the texts written in 1937–38 on the subject of "Die Bedrohung der Wissenschaft,"[88] Heidegger argues entirely from the perspective of 1933. The "essential threat to science [comes] neither from any political measures taken against it, nor from the new, practical goals prescribed for it, but rather principally and exclusively from itself, which is to say, from its inability and reluctance to effect an inner renewal and transformation."[89] Heidegger in no way objects that "industry" has "taken over" science, but—in a manner corresponding to his critique directed at the "inner" state of science—that it is solely a question of an "external demand," which, like the "uniformity" produced in the interest of "profit," is "only accomplished externally" and hence brings about "no inner awakening and renewal and transformation" of science.[90] Against this—as in the *Rektoratsrede*—Heidegger opposes the "task of the second beginning," a "meditation" on a "more originary" knowledge which has not yet been "unfolded." This should also enable each individual science, which, because it "is based upon results, [makes itself] practically indispensable," to achieve something that will unify the people. This occurs insofar as science itself, "as a spiritual reality, [begins to have] a creative and educational" influence.[91]

In the lecture given a few months later, "Die Begründung des neuzeitlichen Weltbildes durch die Metaphysik" (1938),[92] Heidegger's interest has shifted. It is no longer focused upon the question of how a science, which in the course of war preparations becomes "practical" to a hitherto unknown degree, still remains true to its "origin." Rather, Heidegger directs his attention to the representation of the tendency immanent within science as it manifests itself in technologies—"atomic physics," "the airplane," and "radio"—whose development was aided by the modernization drive carried out under National Socialism. Science is "one of the pathways upon which the modern age rages toward fulfillment of its essence, with a velocity unknown to the participants."[93] Words like raging and driving[94] describe a condition of blindness or unconsciousness. The causes of this condition, according to Heidegger's astonishing explanation, lie in the forms assumed by rationality in modernity, which represent the exact opposite of this unconscious process in the "representative" or "calculative" thinking of the "subject." The dynamic unleashed by these forms leads to paroxysm: "As soon as the gigantic in planning and calculating and adjusting and making secure shifts over out of the quantitative and becomes a special quality, then what is gigantic, and what can seemingly always be calculated completely, becomes precisely through this, incalculable." By "shifting over" into the "incalculable," the "gigantic" is "withdrawn from representation"[95]—this is one of the formulae by which Heidegger holds out the prospect of a return of the "origin."[96]

The idea of a "timeless" process, ever overcoming itself, which eludes the grasp of human beings to the degree that it destroys the possibility of being grasped, did not by any means emerge from the mind of a philosopher removed from this world. To its background belongs, for example, the conflict laden "non-simultaneity" (Ernst Bloch) of technical modernization and a nostalgic romanticism for the land.[97] Heidegger's work concerned one of the variants in which religion, art, literature, and philosophy, as "secondary politicizations of the cultural sphere," "[were] politicized to the degree that the existing contradictions, displaced from the sphere of their regular articulation ('politics'), return in deferred form."[98]

Heidegger's achievement consists in the fact that he does not direct these "contradictions" "inward" in a moral manner—where, as conflicts of conscience, they become "insoluble"—but rather brings them to a philosophical "solution," somewhat analogously to the literary, eschatological utopias in which the agrarian aspect of National Socialism triumphs over its technical aspect.[99] This did not simply allow the most diverse forces to come together and to be mobilized within National Socialism, at the same time it allowed for "critique" and polemics. Heidegger turned against National Socialism insofar as he was able to reveal that its practices and ideas were still subject centered and caught within representative thinking: "Man as a rational being of the age of Enlightenment is no less subject than is man who grasps himself as a nation, wills himself as a people, fosters himself as a race, and, finally, empowers himself as lord of the earth."[100] However, this was an immanent critique, which measured National Socialism according to its own claims, as if it had simultaneously set out to promote anti-Cartesianism.[101] Indeed, it was not a form of resistance. On the contrary. Heidegger's critique of the subject paralyzed the forms of understanding which would have made resistance possible.

In "The Letter on Humanism," Heidegger extends his vision of a subjectivity freed from technology, which, already at the beginning of the 1940's through the period immediately following the war, he had declared to be "a reality reigning through everything, the basic reality of the history of the world rolling on and on into its most modern modernity."[102] National Socialism, which manifests itself as "biologism," "nationalism," or vanishes within "technology,"[103] at the same time, together with its conception of humanity, [104] the entire phenomenon of the world war and the new "isms"[105] (for example, existentialism), becomes part of the interplay between the withdrawal and event of "truth" that has existed since Plato.

Perhaps Heidegger could have called a lack of correspondence to this "truth," as for example occurs in its "forgetting," a "human failure,"[106] but not guilt, because it is here a question of a "destiny within the history of being."[107] An attempt to come to terms with the past in moral terms as, for example, Jaspers had proposed in the form of a discourse on guilt, is unnecessary. In Heidegger's eyes such an attempt also rests upon a fiction promoted by philosophy and consciousness, namely, that of a subject who is responsible for his own actions.

Heidegger himself retreats to the purity of thinking itself: "In order to learn how to experience the aforementioned essence of thinking purely, and that means at the same time to carry it through, we must free ourselves from the technical interpretation of thinking."[108] A thinking that "listens to being" guarantees that no "idle talk about 'the truth of being' and the 'history of being' is set in motion," but above all, that the past is not spoken about. For that speaking which accords with being now demands less "precipitous expression than proper silence. But who of us today would want to imagine that his attempts to think are at home on the path of silence?"[109] With this conclusion Heidegger does not enter into the "silence" diagnosed by Lübbe, but rather first brings it about.

Translated by Wayne Klein

NOTES

1. Letter to Herbert Marcuse of January 20, 1948, cited in Victor Farías, *Heidegger und der Nationalsozialismus* (Frankfurt/M: Fischer, 1989), p. 374. [Translator's note: Heidegger's writings are cited with reference to the original German text and the English translation, when available. Secondary sources are cited as they appear in the notes to Alisch's German text. Because of the difficulty in correlating references to works written in French and cited in German translation, I do not refer to English editions of these texts. All unattributed translations are my own.]
2. "Das Ge-Stell," unpublished lecture from January 12, 1949, cited from Wolfgang Schirmacher, *Technik und Gelassenheit. Zeitkritik nach Heidegger* (Freiburg: Alber, 1983), p. 25. See the unpublished lecture "Die Gefahr," also given in Bremen on January 12, parts of which are cited by Thomas J. Sheehan in his essay "Heidegger and the Nazis," *New York Review of Books*, 15.6 (1988), p. 41.
3. The hopes of Paul Celan and Herbert Marcuse for a "word" from Heidegger are well known. See *Martin Heidegger und das "Dritte Reich." Ein Kompendium*, ed. Bernd Martin (Darmstadt: Wissenschaftliche Buchgesellschaft, 1989), p. 156, and Hugo Ott, *Martin Heidegger. Unterwegs zu seiner Biographie* (Frankfurt/M: Campus, 1988), p. 342. Explicit attempts by Heidegger to distance himself from his National Socialist past have been handed down solely from private sources. See Dieter Thomä, *Die Zeit des Selbst und die Zeit danach. Zur Kritik der Textgeschichte Martin Heideggers 1910–1976* (Frankfurt/M: Suhrkamp, 1990), p. 662; Heinrich W. Petzet, *Auf einen Stern zugehen. Begegnungen und Gespräche mit Martin Heidegger 1929–1976* (Frankfurt/M: Societas, 1983), p. 43, and Heidegger's letter to Karl Jaspers dated March 7, 1950, in *Martin Heidegger/Karl Jaspers. Briefwechsel 1920–1963* (Munich: Klostermann, 1992), p. 196.
4. A preliminary overview can be found in *Antwort. Martin Heidegger im Gespräch*, eds. G. Neske and E. Kettering (Pfullingen: Neske, 1988), p. 134, and George Steiner, *Martin Heidegger. Eine Einfür hung* (Munich: Hanser, 1989), pp. 33ff.
5. Silvio Vietta, *Heideggers Kritik an Nationalsozialismus und an der Technik* (Tübingen: Max Niemeyer, 1989), p. 101.

6. See R. G. Dommergue Polacco de Ménasse, *Auschwitz: Das Schweigen von Heidegger oder Kleine Einzelheiten* (Kritik Verlag, 1990), p. 4. His work comments upon a French radio broadcast about Heidegger in which A. Glücksman, G. Steiner, M. Cazenave, J. P. Faye, and F. Fédier participated. De Ménasse presents numerous "proofs" that the crimes perpetrated upon the Jews at best occurred only on a minor scale, and imputes that Heidegger also held this view.
7. See Ott, *Martin Heidegger,* 15, and Farías, Heidegger, 376. Tom Rockmore distinguishes two variants within the attempts to dismiss Heidegger's engagement with National Socialism. There is the variant which denies "Nazism as Nazism," as represented by Beaufret, following Faurisson, and then there is one represented by François Fédier, which asserts that "the essence of Nazism was hardly recognizable in the beginning," "Heidegger und der National Sozialismus: eine dreifache Kehre?," in *Zur philosophischen Aktualität Martin Heideggers,* Vol. 1, Philosophie und Politik, eds. D. Papenfuss and O. Pöggeler (Frankfurt/M: Klostermann, 1991), p. 410. Abel O. Pugliese also employs the latter argument to deny Heidegger's Nazism. A connection between Heidegger's thinking and his biography, i.e., his engagement with National Socialism, cannot be made because the means of terror which were employed after 1933 were at that time "not yet capable of being divided up into periods according to contemporary, objectively political criteria, of being criminalized, and, as a consequence, recognized as processes which were capable of being corrupted" "Heideggers Denken und der Nationalsozialismus," in Papenfuss and Pöggeler, p. 362.
8. Ernst Nolte, *Martin Heidegger. Politik und Geschichte im Leben und Denken* (Berlin: Propyläen, 1992), pp. 296, 267.
9. Steiner, *Martin Heidegger*, 34, 37.
10. Thomä, *Die Zeit* 628.
11. George Kovacs, "On Heidegger's Silence," in *Heidegger Studies,* 5 (1989), pp. 137, 145.
12. Jacques Derrida, *Vom Geist. Heidegger und die Frage* (Frankfurt/M: Suhrkamp, 1988), p. 159; Philippe Lacoue-Labarthe, *Die Fiktion des Politischen* (Stuttgart: Edition Patricia Schwarz, 1991), p. 164; Jean-François Lyotard, *Heidegger und die "Juden"* (Wien: Passagen, 1988), p. 56, cf. pp. 65, 87. See also Steiner, Martin Heidegger, 27, 29 and Nolte, Martin Heidegger, 261.
13. Derrida, "Heideggers Schweigen," in Neske and Kettering, *Antwort,* 159f.
14. See Lyotard, Heidegger, 86, 69, 72, and the concepts of "the unforgettable" and "the forgotten"; Lacoue-Labarthe, *Die Fiktion,* 59ff, 79f, 144, 149f.
15. See Lacoue-Labarthe, *Die Fiktion,* 13, 149ff, 167ff.
16. On these strategies see Thomä, *Die Zeit,* 475ff.
17. See Pierre Bourdieu's remark that "The philosopher always thinks in relation to history, even when he does not believe this of his own thinking. I have reconstructed this political context." (Bourdieu is here referring to his *Die politische Ontologie Martin Heideggers* [Frankfurt/M: Suhrkamp, 1988]). "And only with such a rehistorization of Heidegger's thinking can his true project be understood": " . . . ich glaube, ich wäre sein bester Verteidiger," *Das Argument,* 171 (1988), p. 725.
18. First published in the journal of the Breisgau Historical Society, "Schau ins Land," nos. 102 and 103, and the *Zeitschrift für die Geschichte des Oberrheins,* no. 132; later in Ott, *Martin Heidegger.*

19. Cited from Lacoue-Labarthe, *Die Fiktion*, 149, 186. The German edition of the Farías book no longer contains the passages cited by Lacoue-Labarthe.
20. See Farías, *Heidegger*, 44: "In contrast with the numerous attempts to trivialize the significance of Heidegger's relationship to National Socialism, the present investigation comes to the conclusion that Heidegger's thinking is articulated in and through this relationship, in accordance with its own past and that of an entire epoch, and that in this relationship the later development of his thinking is determined in essential respects." See Lyotard, *Heidegger*, 77.
21. See Lyotard *Heidegger*, 86. Rockmore holds the view that the interpretations of Derrida and Lacoue-Labarthe are guided by an assumption of an "epistimological-theoretical break," similar to that introduced by Althusser in his interpretation of Marx, "Heidegger's Nazism and the French debate," in *Martin Heidegger, Critical Assessments*, ed. C. Macann, Vol. IV (London: Routledge, 1992), pp. 60f. On the other hand, Pierre Aubenque suggests that Althusser's "anti-humanistic" reading of Marx was influenced by the French reception of Heidegger, "Heideggers Wirkungsgeschichte in Frankreich," in *Martin Heidegger—Faszination und Erschrecken. Die politische Dimension einer Philosophie*, ed. Peter Kemper (Frankfurt/M: Campus, 1990), pp. 120ff.
22. Naturally this can only be asserted if, in turn, National Socialism is itself transformed into a timeless phenomenon. Cf. Lyotard, *Heidegger*, 102.
23. See Jacques Derrida, "Die Hölle der Philosophie," cited from *Die Heidegger Kontroverse*, ed. Altwegg (Frankfurt/M: Athenäum, 1988), p. 84f.
24. See Derrida, *Vom Geist*, 116ff.
25. See Lacoue-Labarthe, *Die Fiktion*, 65ff.
26. Lyotard, *Heidegger*, 104.
27. See also the essays on Eduard Spranger, Theodor Litt, Nicolai Hartmann, and Joachim Ritter in *Deutsche Philosophen 1933*, ed. Wolf F. Haug (Berlin: Argument, 1989), as well as Gadamer's essay " . . . die wirklichen Nazis hatten doch überhaupt kein Interesse an uns," *Das Argument*, 182 (1990), and Teresa Orozco's article, "Das 'Bild der Antike' und der NS-Staat. Fragen zum Interview mit Hans-Georg Gadamer," from the same volume.
28. Gadamer, "'Zurück von Syrakus?'" in Altwegg, *Die Heidegger Kontroverse*, 177.
29. See Wolf F. Haug, *Vom hilflosen Antifaschismus zur Gnade der späten Geburt* (Berlin: Argument, 1987), pp. 175ff.
30. Lyotard speaks of a "deconstructive slip," *Heidegger*, 86, cf. 78, 110; cf. Lacoue-Labarthe, *Die Fiktion*, 39, 44, 55ff on Heidegger's "'thought' accident" and "error."
31. Steiner, *Martin Heidegger*, 9, 10.
32. For example, Arnold Gehlen, Otto F. Bollnow, Fritz J. von Rintelen, Joachim Ritter, Erich Rothacker, and Helmut Schelsky. For the dates of their careers, see George Leaman, *Heidegger im Kontext. Gesamtüberblick zum NS-Engagement der Universitätsphilosophen* (Berlin: Argument, 1993).
33. See Thomas Laugstien, *Philosophieverhäatnisse im deutschen Faschismus* (Berlin: Argument, 1990), pp. 12ff, and Konrad Lotter, "Exil und Rückkehr. Deutsche Philosophie vor und nach 1945," *Widerspruch*, "Restauration der Philosophie nach 1945," 18 (1990). Silvia Markun reports that in 1950 the *Zeitschrift für philosophische Forschung* still refused to review the section of Bloch's *Prinzip Hoffnung, Freiheit und Ordung, Abriß der Sozialutopien*, which had been published by Aurora-Verlag, *Ernst Bloch. Mit Selbstzeugnissen und Bilddokumenten* (Reinbeck: Rowohlt, 1977), p. 38.

34. See Gerwin Klinger, "Freiheit als 'freiwillige Aufgabe der Freiheit'. Arnold Gehlens Umbau des Deutschen Idealismus," in Haug, *Deutsche Philosophen*, 191. Cf. Leaman, *Heidegger im Kontext*, 11f.
35. Cited from Laugstien, *Philosophie verhältnisse*, 44; cf. 69.
36. Martin Heidegger, *Die Selbstbehauptung der deutschen Universität* (Breslau: Korn, 1933), pp. 8, 10; "The Self-Assertion of the German University," trans. Karsten Harries, *Review of Metaphysics*, 38 (1985), pp. 472, 473; translation modified.
37. See Rainer Alisch, "Heideggers Rektoratsrede im Kontext," in Haug, *Deutsche Philosophen*, 86ff, and Fritz K. Ringer, *Die Gelehrten: der Niedergang der deutschen Mandarine* 1890–1933 (Stuttgart: Klett-Cotta, 1983).
38. See Ringer, *Die Gelehrten*, 228ff, 243, 316.
39. Cited Alex Demirovic, "Symphilosophein—oder die organisierte Philosophie. Die Allgemeine Gesellschaft für Philosophie in Deutschland und ihre Veranstaltungen 1947–1951," *Widerspruch*, 18 (1990), p. 33. Hartmann was also the keynote speaker at the first philosophy conference held after Hitler's assumption of power, October 2–5, 1933. See Wolf F. Haug, "Nicolai Hartmanns Neuordung von Wert und Sinn," in Haug, *Deutsche Philosophen*.
40. Nicolai Hartmann, "Ziele und Wege der Kategorienanalyse," *Zeitschrift für philosophische Forschung*, II (1947), pp. 499f. Hartmann's reference to National Socialism with the word "race" can still be considered typical, because it is quite correct to equate National Socialism with biological racism. However, for those academic philosophers schooled in idealism—here one could name Gehlen, among others (cf. Gerwin Klinger, "Freiheit," 192ff.)—including notorious Nazis such as Krieck and Baeumler, the "accent [was] on the concept of discipline" whereby "race [was] in the final analysis a product of will and of the spiritual determination of goals" (cited from Leaman, *Heidegger im Kontext*, 73, from a report of the SS to Rothacker). After 1945, Rothacker was able to use this report to present himself as an opponent of National Socialism.
41. See Georgi Schischkoff, *Zeitschrift für philosophische Forschung*, III (1948), p. 424. Ways of counteracting the "chaos of the diverging specialties" were discussed in Bremen during the symposium. See Helmut Plessner, *Symphilosophein. Bericht über den Dritten Deutschen Kongreß für Philosophie Bremen 1950*, ed. Helmut Plessner (Munich: Leo Lehnen, 1950), p. 9.
42. See Heinz L. Matzat, "Der Philosophiekongress 1947 in Garmisch-Partenkirchen," *Zeitschrift für philosophische Forschung*, II (1947), p. 383.
43. Fritz J. von Rintelen, "Zur gegenwärtigen Stunde der Philosophie," *Philosophische Vorträge und Diskussionen. Bericht über den Philosophen-Kongress, Mainz, 1948*, special issue no. 1 of the *Zeitschrift für philosophische Forschung*, ed. Georgi Schischkoff (Wurzach: Pan-Verlag Rudolf Birnbach, 1949), pp. 13ff. For a discussion of the proceedings at Deidesheim, see p. 198.
44. Erich Kaufmann, ibid., 200. Further on we read that "philosophy is the only bond left to us by means of which to combat the danger of specialization in the sciences and among human beings." Cf. Litt, who calls for "self-examination" following "fanatical self-obsession and nihilistic self-sacrifice" (cited from Schischkoff, *Zeitschrift*, 22), and Spranger, whose harmless sounding theme, "cultural encounters as a philosophical problem," sets forth the task of striving for cultural hegemony as "co-bearers" of the "spiritual-moral, supra-individual powers," following military defeat (ibid., 32ff).
45. Rothacker, cited from Schischkoff, *Zeitschrift*, 199. See Theodor Litt's concluding remark: "The philosopher must truly assume a timeless standpoint, to

see in a certain manner with the eye of God" (ibid., 196).

46. See Matzat, "Der Philosophie kongress 1947;" 393; Schischkoff, *Zeitschrift*, 14, 22ff, 195f, 198ff.
47. In his essay, "Martin Heidegger und die Universität Freiburg nach 1945. Ein Beispiel für die Auseinandersetzung mit der politischen Vergangenheit" (*Historisches Jahrbuch*, 1985, pp. 116f), Ott quotes from a 1947 letter from the then editor of the Catholic monthly *Hochland*, F. J. Schönigh, which makes the following connection: "Perhaps this remedy appears *ad ovum* to many to be all too radical, but it would seem to be necessary in order to prevent the shocking nihilism of, say, Heidegger or Sartre from being seen simply as a reflection of a political catastrophe, which it certainly is, but it is not essentially that. In Heidegger and Sartre the European spirit has reached that point to which it has been drawn for centuries, where it stands before nothingness. You are all familiar with Heidegger's political past. If I mention it, it is really only because in this way the connection between nihilism and National Socialism can be made immediately clear." Cf. Heidegger's letter to Jaspers dated April 4, 1950 (*Briefwechsel*, 202).
48. In Bremen there was a symposium on the topic of "Situation and Decision" (see Plessner *Symphilosophien*,), in which the questions raised by existentialism were discussed. Demirovic refers to a report of the Frankfurt Institute for Social Research in which it is conjectured that part of the reason why Bremen was chosen as the site of the conference was that the South German supporters of existence philosophy would not be able to make the expensive journey to Bremen (Demirovic, "Symphilosophein," 33).
49. See Otto F. Bollnow, "Deutsche Existenzphilosophie und französischer Existentialismus," lecture given at the philosophy conference in Garmisch-Partenkirchen, *Zeitschrift für philosophische Forschung*, II (1947), pp. 239ff, as well as his essay, "Zur Diskussion über die Existenzphilosophie auf dem Philosophischen Kongress in Garmisch-Partenkirchen," ibid., p. 588; and Fritz J. von. Rintelen, "Endlichkeit—Existenz—Transzendenz," lecture given at the philosophy conference in Garmisch-Partenkirchen, *Zeitschrift für philodophische Forschung*, III (1948), pp. 179, 191ff.
50. Bollnow, "Deutsche Existenzphilosophie," 233.
51. Alone from von Rintelen do we read that "to such a dynamic posture of resoluteness already belongs an appeal in favor of truly questionable goals and tasks," "Zur gegenwärtigen Stunde," 13. On the use of the category of "Entscheidung" in Heidegger's election appeal of November 12, 1933, see Laugstien, *Philosophieverhältnisse*, 32ff, and Alisch, "Heideggers Rektoratsrede," 85f.
52. Bollnow, "Zur Diskussion," 593.
53. Herbert Marcuse (1934), cited from Laugstien, *Philosophieverhältnisse* 46.
54. Cited from Schischkoff, *Zeitschrift*, 197, 199, 200.
55. Von Rintelen, "Endlichkeit," 184.
56. Demirovic, "Symphilosophein," 33.
57. At the first conference the question of guilt was at least posed as a task. Cf. Matzat, "Die Philosophie kongress 1947," 383.
58. See Eduard Spranger, "Die Frage der deutschen Schuld" (1946), in *Staat, Recht und Politik, Gesammelte Schriften*, Vol. 8, ed. H. J. Meyer (Tübingen: Niemeyer, 1970), and Karl Jaspers, *Die Schuldfrage. Von der politischen Haftung Deutschlands* (Munich: Pieper, 1987), pp. 18, 16.
59. In a letter to Heidegger dated March 25, 1950, Jaspers initially mentions that,

in contrast with two other texts, all the copies of *Die Schuldfrage* have not been sold. He then adds: "The students certainly filled the lecture hall; it was a sensation. But like my fellow countrymen, they otherwise have shown very little interest in these debates. For me at that time a great deal rested upon my attempt, which saw itself crippled after only a year" (*Briefwechsel*, 199).

60. Jaspers, *Die Schuldfrage*, 79f; Heidegger's letter to Jaspers, dated April 8, 1950 (*Briefwechsel*, 202).
61. If one accepts Matzat's report (see Matzat, "Die Philosophie kongress 1947," 383ff), then perhaps two-thirds of the conference in Garmisch-Partenkirchen was devoted to debating subjects such as "The problem of the one and the many in Plato's *Parmenides*."
62. For a critique of the dominant forms of philosophical attempts to come to terms with the past, see Haug, "Philosophie im Deutschen Faschismus," in Haug, *Deutsche Philosophen*, 14ff, and Laugstien, Philosophie vorhältnisse, 17f.
63. Cited from Haug, *Vom hilflosen Antifaschismus*, 190. Lübbe himself was accepted into the NSDAP, member number 9.952.954, on April 20, 1944. Cf. Leaman, Heidegger im Kontext, 144.
64. Cited from Haug, *Vom hilflosen Antifaschismus*, 189f.
65. How this functioned can be seen from the case of Max Müller. Denounced by Heidegger in 1938 (see Müller, in Martin, *Martin Heidegger* 107f), he nevertheless maintained the official form of address until his 70th birthday. In a retrospective look at the affair, Heinz Hülsmann writes that "The relationship appeared clear. . . . Whoever chose the master, whoever the master elected, he chose his memory," "Philosophie studieren," *Widerspruch*, "Philosophie im deutschen Faschismus," 13 (1987), p. 114.
66. See Hartmut Längin, "Das Problem einer Überwindung des Existentialismus. Otto Friedrich Bollnows 'Neue Geborgenheit,'" Widerspruch, 18, (1990).
67. Wolf F. Haug, "Gramsci und die Politik des Kulturellen," *Das Argument*, 167 (1988), p. 45, note 4.
68. Jürgen Habermas, "Heidegger—Werk und Weltanschauung," in Farías, Heidegger, 14; "Work and Weltanschauung: The Heidegger Controversy from a German Perspective," trans. John McCumber, *Critical Inquiry*, 15, 2 (1989), p. 435; translation modified.
69. For a critique, see Wolf F. Haug, "Philosophie," in Haug, Deutsche Philosophien, 18ff.
70. Otto Pöggeler, "Einleitung," in Heidegger und die praktische Philosophie, ed. Annemarie Gethmann-Siefert and Otto Pöggeler (Frankfurt/M: Suhrkamp, 1988), p. 7.
71. Pöggeler represents exactly that compromise which takes account of the view, which Kovacs has once again revived (Kovacs, "On Heidegger's Silence," 143f), that Heidegger's philosophy is to be understood as a completely apolitical thinking of foundations, as well as Alexander Schwan's unqualified, rigorous rejection of the later Heidegger: "Heidegger's stereotypical analyses of the present age and political events are completely inadequate; moreover, in their self-certainty they are dangerous," Alexander Schwan, "Zeitkritik und Politik in Heideggers Spätphilosophie," in Gethmann-Siefert and Pöggeler, Heidegger, 105.
72. Otto Pöggeler, "Heidegger und die politische Philosophie," in Papenfuss and Pöggeler, *Zur philosophischen Aktualität*, 349.
73. Alfred Baeumler, *Männerbund und Wissenschaft* (Berlin, 1934); cited from Laugstien, *Philosophieverhältnisse*, 45. See Heidegger, "Die Universität im nationalsozialistischen

Staat" (1933): "To become historical means to act in accordance with the great powers of being [*Dasein*] which are invested in the state" (cited from Martin, *Martin Heidegger* 180). See Alisch, "Heideggers Rektoratsrede," 87ff.

74. Likewise Baeumler: "The theoretical human being and the political human being" differ in that the latter is not determined in his "being" by the fact "that he participates in a higher 'spiritual world' . . . but rather in that he is an originarily acting being" (cited from Laugstien, *Philosophieverhältnisse*, 45).
75. Martin Heidegger, "Bekenntnis zu Adolf Hitler und dem Nationalsozialistischen Staat," cited from Guido Schneeberger, *Nachlese zu Heidegger. Dokumente zu seinem Leben und Denken* (Bern: printed privately, 1962), p. 149.
76. In addition, compare Walter Schulz's interpretation of the "turn," which can be read in contraposition to that of Derrida, Lyotard, and Lacoue-Labarthe. Schulz here maintains, among other things, that "self-assertion" is to be understood as the "necessity of shattering," "an event that is 'made necessary' by being itself." The "shattering" in the act of self-assertion does not rest upon a "willed denial," which would still be a metaphysical position," "Über den philosophiegeschichtlichen Ort Martin Heideggers," in *Heidegger. Perspektiven zur Deutung seines Werkes*, ed. Otto Pöggeler (Königstein: Athenäum, 1984), p. 138f, note 10.
77. Cf. Heidegger's statement: "The essence, however, gains clarity, rank, and power only when first of all and at all times the leaders are themselves led—led by that unyielding spiritual mission that forces the fate of the German people to bear the stamp of its history," *Selbsbehauptung*, 5; "Self-Assertion," 470.
78. Alexander Schwan, *Politische Philosophie im Denken Heideggers* (Cologne: Westdeutscher Verlag, 1965), p. 11.
79. This question differs from that which asks how Heidegger's philosophy determined his political activity.
80. Only in his lecture to the Tübingen student body does Heidegger, in association with the model of the "worker" fashioned by Ernst Jünger, use this concept affirmatively. The "new" student knows that he himself is called to action as "a worker" "for carrying out the political demands of knowledge" (cited from Farías, Heidegger, 207). The "demands of the will" cited by Martin (Martin, *Martin Heidegger* 181), is a transcription error from the original.
81. Cf. Laugstien, *Philosophieverhältnisse*, 47ff, 67ff.
82. Martin Heidegger, *Das Rektorat 1933–34*, in *Die Selbstbehauptung der deutschen Universität. Das Rektorat 1933–34*, ed. Hermann Heidegger (Frankfurt/M: Klostermann, 1983), p. 29; "The Rectorate 1933–34," trans. Karsten Harries, *Review of Metaphysics*, 38 (1985), p. 489; translation modified.
83. Tom Rockmore, "Heidegger after Farías," *History of Philosophy Quarterly*, 8, 1 (1991), p. 97.
84. Cf. Heidegger, *Über den "Humanismus,"* in *Platons Lehre von der Wahrheit. Mit einem Brief über den 'Humanismus,'* 3d ed. (Bern: Franke, 1975), p. 72; "Letter on Humanism," trans. Frank A. Capuzzi and J. Glenn Gray, in *Martin Heidegger, Basic Writings* (New York: Harper & Row, 1977), p. 208.
85. Rockmore, "Heidegger after Farías," 97.
86. Heidegger, *Über den "Humanismus,"* 53ff; cf. 104f, 111ff; "Letter on Humanism," 193ff; cf. 231f, 236ff.
87. See Jaspers' letter to Heidegger dated August 23, 1933, in which he declares the address to be "the only evidence hitherto of a contemporary academic

will," *Briefwechsel*, 155. Although he later revises this view, he holds on to the "aura of the philosophy," ibid., 258.

88. In Papenfuss and Pöggeler, *Zur Philosophischen Aktualität*, 5ff. Part of the background can be deduced from the text itself and the notes of the editor, Hartmut Tietjen. See Ott, *Martin Heidegger*, 272ff, and Monike Leske, *Philosophen im "Dritten Reich." Studie zu Hochschul- und Philosophiebetrieb im faschistischen Deutschland* (Berlin: Dietz Verlag, 1990), pp. 95ff. For Vietta, Heidegger's "critique of National Socialism" begins at this point in time (Vietta, *Heideggers Kritik*, 19ff).
89. Heidegger, "Die Bedrohung," 11.
90. Ibid., 9, 18.
91. Ibid., 25, 12f. The main opponent named here by Heidegger is Ernst Krieck, who wanted to "do away with" philosophy and replace it with a national, political anthropology, described in a book of the same name written in 1936–38. See "Die Bedrohung," 23ff, and Laugstien, *Philosophieverhältnisse*, 72ff, 104ff.
92. Published as "Die Zeit des Weltbildes," *Holzwege*, 4th ed. (Frankfurt/M: Klostermann, 1963); "The Age of the World Picture," trans. W. Lovitt, in *The Question Concerning Technology and Other Essays* (New York: Harper & Row, 1977).
93. "Die Zeit des Weltbildes," 87; "The Age of the World Picture," 135.
94. In the "*Beiträge zur Philosophie*, written in 1936–38, Heidegger describes his procedure at that time as the "other way" to a "meditation on science." "[N]ot a mere description of an objectively subsisting condition, but the setting forth of a process, insofar as it aims at a decision concerning the truth of science," *Beiträge zur Philosophie, Gesamtausgabe*, Vol. 65 (Frankfurt/M: Klostermann, 1989), p. 144.
95. Heidegger, "Die Zeit des Weltbildes," 87f, 104; "The Age of the World Picture," 135f, 154.
96. See the much discussed passage from *An Introduction to Metaphysics*: "The works that are being peddled about nowadays as the philosophy of National Socialism but have nothing whatever to do with the innner truth and greatness of this movement (namely the encounter between global technology and modern man) have all been written by men fishing in the troubled waters of 'values' and 'totalities,' "*Einführung in die Metaphysik* (Tübingen: Niemeyer, 1953), p. 152; *An Introduction to Metaphysics*, trans. Ralph Manheim (New Haven: Yale University Press, 1959), p. 199. Because it is certain that Heidegger later added the passage in parentheses (cf. Ott, *Martin Heidegger*, 277), in 1935—in contrast to 1938—he was still of the opinion that it was the task of National Socialism to "arrest the decline and transform it into a . . . condition in which the long concealed originary truth of being would occur once more," Winfried Franzen, *Von der Existenzialontologie zur Seinsgeschichte* (Meisenhein: Hain, 1975), p. 93.
97. On the "two poles" of National Socialism, see Albert Speer, *Der Sklavenstaat* (Berlin: Ullstein, 1984), pp. 123ff.
98. Laugstien, *Philosophieverhältnisse*, 60. On the specific influence of philosophy on National Socialism, see 65f, 114ff, 144ff.
99. See Jost Hermand, *Der alte Traum vom neuen Reich. Völkische Utopien und Nationalsozialismus* (Frankfurt/M: Athenäum, 1988), pp. 235ff, 253ff.
100. Heidegger, "Die Zeit des Weltbildes," 102; "The Age of the World Picture" 152.
101. This is the title of a book by Franz Böhm, a student of Krieck's, published in

Leipzig in 1938. See Konrad Lotter, "Zum Begriff der deutschen Philosophie. Franz Böhm: *Anti-Cartesianismus. Deutsche Philosophie im Widerstand.* Leipzig, 1938," *Widerspruch*, 13 (1987).

102. Heidegger, *Platons Lehre von der Wahrheit. Mit einem Brief über den "Humanismus,"* 3d ed, (Bern: Franke, 1975), p. 50; "Plato's Doctrine of Truth. John Barlow, in *Philosophy in the Twentieth Century*, ed. William Barrett and Henry D. Aiken (New York: Random House, 1962), Vol. 3, p. 269.
103. Heidegger, *Über den "Humanismus,"* 67, 88f, 104; "Letter on Humanism," 204, 220f, 232.
104. See Heidegger, *Platons Lehre*, 48ff ["Plato's Doctrine," 268ff], Farías, *Heidegger*, 347ff, and Ott, *Martin Heidegger*, 268ff.
105. Heidegger, *Über den "Humanismus,"* 56; cf. 58; "Letter on Humanism," 195; cf. 197.
106. See Martin Heidegger, "Nur noch ein Gott kann uns retten," *Der Spiegel*, no. 23 (1976), p. 201; "'Only a God Can Save Us': The *Spiegel* Interview," trans. William J. Richardson, in *Heidegger: The Man and the Thinker*, ed. Thomas Sheehan (Chicago: Precedent Publishing, 1981), p. 52.
107. Heidegger, *Über den "Humanismus,"* 88; "Letter on Humanism," 219.
108. Heidegger, *Über den "Humanismus,"* 54; "Letter on Humanism," 194.
109. Heidegger, *Über den "Humanismus,"* 57, 92; "Letter on Humanism," 196, 223; translation modified.

9

Self-Destruction

HENRI CRÉTELLA

One half-century after having been committed, the genocide perpetrated against the Jews by the Nazis has yet to be reflected upon. This does not mean that it has yet to be historically demonstrated, juridically prosecuted, and morally condemned. For all of this has, essentially, been accomplished. But the fact that, under the cover of "revision," a shameless attempt at effacing the facts has been able to develop, and that more recently—in a manner otherwise serious and decent—there has been a tendency toward a "relativization" of the facts, demonstrates in a doubly decisive way that we have until now eluded what is presently at issue: namely, the *singularity* of the Extermination.

Nothing, however, would serve better than the current debate on the subject to demonstrate that there is a gulf between a question passionately discussed and the same question properly treated. Having been situated exclusively in the domain of historical information and of moral protest, the discussion could do nothing other than oscillate as it has between the Charybdis of a well-documented confusion and the Scylla of a censure accompanied by the most deplorable return of the repressed. One should therefore be pleased to have avoided until now the one danger as well as the other. But this is no reason to remain in an oscillation that threatens to deliver us up to such dangers at any moment. We are therefore faced with the decision to exit from this situation by entrusting ourselves to what is above all at issue in the question: namely, the meaning of *reflection*.

It is only by this means, indeed, that it becomes possible to escape the double reduction—historical and moral—that has prevented us for so long from disclosing what precisely was at issue in "the final solution." At issue was not a particular genocide, but quite literally a total destruction. The madness of the project should not dissuade us from thinking it—if only for the simple reason that there is no other way to oppose its repetition. For madness signifies unreason personified, not the mere incapacity to reason. It is therefore necessary to specify positively what this aberration consisted in, this aberration which led so furiously to "unreasoning with reason" ["déraisonner avec la raison"], to use an expression coined, I believe, by Rousseau.

The same author, in any case, provides the first tools which allow us to characterize the phenomenon under consideration. For what is Nazism if not the most horrific refusal in regard to the Other to sympathize with him, that is to say, to exercise what Rousseau called pity? And what is Nazism in itself, then, if not the most unbridled affirmation of what Rousseau called a denatured self-love ["amour de soi"], or, in other words, the reduction of a community to the pure expansion of its self-preservation? What is most horrific in Nazism lies in its exclusion of all considerations other than those of the conditions for preserving a determinate community. No other dimension, including that of pride ["amour-propre"], intervenes to trouble this basic project. It is solely concerned with survival. With the Nazis, there was no vanity whatsoever, only the strictest concern for utility. It is only an appearance that they seemed seized by "delusions of grandeur" ["la folie des grandeurs"]; in reality, they were never animated by anything other than the most gigantic will to efficiency. Hence the brutality which defines the Nazi phenomenon. The monstrosity of this phenomenon thus seems to consist in the hypertrophy of the tendency toward the mere preservation of existence. This allows us to explain why the phenomenon was able to menace, and continues to menace, highly developed societies. The reason for this is that such societies have quite simply made survival their goal, and so they have made utility the medium of their "progress."

The Nazi phenomenon should therefore not be reduced to "a past historical fact." It should be considered, rather, as the true, *unique* danger which confronts humanity, especially in technologically advanced societies. The singularity of this danger resides in the fact that it menaces humanity in its *dignity* by inviting humanity to exchange this dignity for mere survival. Unlike an ordinary danger, where it is a question of "saving one's life," what this danger turns on is the calamity of conserving life after life has lost its dignity. In other words, what must be avoided here is not seeing one's life terminate, but rather the second death of indignity. For it is to this second death that the Nazis would have liked to be able to condemn those whom they attempted to exterminate. And it is to this second death that they themselves, in their madness, submitted. Thus they inflicted upon themselves the evil to which they succumbed—definitively.

But we still need to specify what would have happened if, disastrously, the Nazis had not failed—in other words, if they had not been the only ones to succumb to the evil which they endeavored to administer. For it should be obvious from now on that this evil continues to threaten us. The second death, however, is independent of the fact of passing from life to the beyond. We should also recognize that this absurdity should by no means be connected to the extinction of humankind, but rather to a process of self-destruction ["autodestruction"] capable of unfolding without the physical disappearance of humanity. Indeed, the destruction of one's own existence ["du même"] is not equivalent to an assault against the *self* ["contre soi"]—an assault to which humanity unconsciously surrendered. This is so true that it has been, on the contrary, within the ambit of the exclusive concern for its preservation that humanity has historically been willing to expose itself to self-destruction. Thus may we summarize the terrifying lesson of Nazism. To forget it will condemn us to ensuring its perpetuity. It is only on the strict condition of not shutting ourselves up in our selves ["*en soi*"] that humanity will succeed in escaping the repetition of a process of self-destruction whose *stupefying* effect it has experienced for a first time.

Stupefying effect—because it places us in a double impossibility of thinking. This leads us to the question: How are we to confront this impossibility of thinking whose terrifying effect Nazism has revealed? This is precisely the special challenge which Heidegger has enabled us to take up.

And yet, for the sake of this challenge, Heidegger had to be the first to endure the sharp necessity to which the ordeal finds itself ordained. On the experience of thinking, Heidegger has pointedly asserted that, "Whoever thinks greatly must err greatly."[1] This is the paradox which we must constantly confront if we wish to measure properly the greatness of Heidegger's contribution to the history of thought. For there is greatness, as no one will seriously contest. But in reality, this is a double greatness: a greatness in errancy as in recovery—the one relating to the other like the two sides of a coin. This is what we need to understand: not its shadowed aspect or its hidden face—there is nothing, on the contrary, more obvious in this case than errancy—but rather the necessary experience thanks to which alone a true recovery can take place. And this would be a recovery as long and difficult in its realization as its character of *im*possibility is astonishing.

For experience is negative in its essence, and even doubly so. Not only is it the case that "experience is the name that each gives to his errors," but, beyond errancy, experience has no other meaning than that of delivering us from the illusion of a "truth" which could be construed positively. This means that what applies to truth applies to real experience: Such experience leaves us more defenseless than we were as long as we remained in illusion. More defenseless, and at the same time more embarrassed, for we then find ourselves confronted with a second sort of impossibility, which is difficult to endure in a sense quite different from the impossibility which preceded it—whence the temptation to fall back into illusion. For example, we fall into illusion when we turn to the error opposed to one we have just abandoned, without bothering to analyze the impulse to which we had first given way. This allows for a renewal of irresponsibility. It allows us to neglect, therefore, what we should have learned from the previous error, namely, not the rectification of an isolated error, but the correction of the spiritual disposition which has given rise to errancy. This errancy should not be reduced to a merely useless residue which must be eliminated from "the production of truth."

It is necessary, on the contrary, to conceive of error—or rather, of errancy—as the necessary first moment of this double experience of impossibility which defines humanity. We must conceive of errancy properly, to be sure. For there are two ways of failing to do justice to the conception of errancy. The first consists in fleeing from it. Not at all by making a mistake, but rather—and this is much more uncanny—by not bothering oneself with it. It is a matter of emphasizing that there is no fault in this case, not yet—no "errance," not even an omission ("carence"), but rather a strict deficiency. Error, fault, or "sin" all presuppose that one has distanced oneself from a prior state—not a state of innocence, but rather of elementary lack of consciousness. What is surprising in the human species is that its humanity seems singularly alien to what humanly defines it. And, in fact, it is proper to distinguish between two notions of humanity. The one is merely "specific," and the other is ethical. It is precisely this difference which allows us to explain the *Shoah*, giving due regard to what constitutes its "specificity." For if the horror of the *Shoah* was literally absolute, it is because this horror derives from two conceptions of humanity, one of which is characterized by a complete insensibility for what it treated as a mere object. This insensible humanity was so distinct in all ways from the other one, which it ignored so "definitively," that it was led to exterminate the representatives of this other humanity. And so, rather than speak of an opposition, we must speak here of an absence of relation. We must speak of a separation—a separation which manifested itself by a will to segregation which did not have to wait for Nazism to declare itself. Nor did this will disarm itself along with the collapse of Nazism. In particular, this separation is of a piece with the oblivion of what is human, an oblivion from which humanity must perpetually tear itself away. Yet the problem—in respect to the *Shoah*—is that we find that this oblivion, along with Modernity, is quite learnedly defended. This does not mean scientifically legitimated. One should not confuse scientism with scientificity. Scientificity is characterized by a scrupulous lucidity regarding its subject matter, and this brings it under the ethical order. But scientism ignores the limit of validity of all truly scientific knowledge, and so scientism has led to the conception of humanity as a species defined biologically, whose development obeys laws of the same type as those which rule the other "mechanisms of life." Racism has never been anything other than a particularly aberrant consequence of this reduction, and Nazism its monstrous "application."

Monstrosity, nevertheless, is not equivalent to simple culpability. This is, really, the whole difficulty of the question we have before us. Indeed, the criminality defined by the deliberate rejection of what properly constitutes humanity shows itself to be more serious than any mistake, more injurious than any culpability. Such humanity consists in being conscious, without fail, of humanity's omissions and of its errancies. To be conscious in this way has the effect of remedying such omissions and errancies. Without a doubt, this is the sense of the *felix culpa*, which nevertheless no one should pronounce without dread and trembling—especially here. For it is necessary to justify this *felix culpa* in every instance—which, one will agree, is a particularly delicate matter when it is a question of the *Shoah*. . . . Indeed, it is necessary to explain how Heidegger could have made so overt a mistake and to have then made amends so discreetly. To present the question in this manner, however, is not obvious. Heidegger's adversaries will object that he did not make a mistake, but rather that the Nazi crime is, at the very least, not prohibited by his philosophy. And—they will add—the proof of this is that he never truly made amends: his lack of self-criticism, his contempt for democracy—in short, the silence concerning the *Shoah*, which, for all practical purposes, he never broke. Does not this suffice to demonstrate that his most intimate convictions remained fundamentally the same as at the moment of his engagement? The indictment thus divides into two distinct parts: First of all, this is not a circumstantial error but rather a criminal tolerance or potentiality which renders "the thought of Heidegger" objectionable; and, in the second place, his enduring harmfulness is emphasized. Our task is then fully delineated: We must steadfastly show that incriminating someone's thought is an absurdity, and, additionally, we must show how the proper rectification of this thought has led Heidegger to the point of—enabling *us* to think the *Shoah*.

These two strands of our task, moreover, should not be separated in this exposition. For, what the rectification of the thought has contributed is the sense of the errancy which it necessitated. This is explained by the difficulty which constrained Heidegger to withhold publishing the third division of *Being and Time* and, more generally, as F.-W. von Herrmann has reminded us, its "second part."[2] This means that until the end of his life—and even beyond, because "the interruption" did not end until 1989, with the publication of the *Beiträge zur Philosophie*—Heidegger preferred to leave indeterminate the manner in which he brought about the turning (*die Kehre*) to which his breakthrough work was connected. We now know for what essential reason. Nothing will better demonstrate that this reason is in precise relation with the *Shoah* than the logic of composition of this second great work, or rather of these contributions which are the *Beiträge zur Philosophie*. Heidegger signified this with the term *Götterung*, that is to say, purely formally, manifestation of god—the manifestation of this god very precisely designated as the ultimate or the last (*der letzte Gott*) and, sometimes even as the god of gods (*der Gott der Götter*). Indeed: for what other reason were the Jews exterminated if not for having observed the law of this unique "God," long after the time when faith was proposed to the whole of humanity? It is hardly possible, for anyone who wants to consider the means of revelation, to doubt that it is the same God for Heidegger as for Christianity and Judaism. For it is a matter of language in the three cases: for faith, for law, and for thought.

It is therefore no accident that "the last book" by Heidegger was, as Jean Beaufret has remarked, *On the Way to Language* (*Unterwegs zur Sprache*, 1959), whose title in French, *Acheminement vers la parole*, translates so well the literal sense of the German. François Fédier has explained the difficulty clearly: language ["*la parole*"] is not speech ["*la langue*"], and even less a speech decreed to be superior and inspired. Language is not speech but rather what speech says, for what speech says is never expressly but rather always silently. It was necessary, therefore, to find the right way to express this insight. Heidegger did not come to this way until he had renounced presenting his thought in the classic form which he had adopted in his breakthrough work. What is new in the *Beiträge zur Philosophie* consists precisely in that this renunciation takes place in a reflective manner. But the manuscript had to remain unpublished through his lifetime, and this has meant that Heidegger's decision to pass from the previous mode of presentation to the formulation of his unthought thought could only be noticed, but by no means explained. For, the formulation of this unthought thought itself remained without relation to the project of the turning (*Kehre*), which "the second part" of *Being and Time* should have fulfilled. It has been reserved for posterity to be able to reconstitute this second part, thanks to the previously unpublished manuscripts, notably the lecture courses. These confirm for us that, in his lifetime, Heidegger expressed only "the first part" of his project. For it is the second part of this project which enables us to explain Heidegger's errance as well as everything which he left us which will prove to be even more significant.

Let us begin by indicating what the errancy consisted in. It was not, as has been the ceaseless accusation, the application of a philosopher's thought to an aspect of reality—that aspect of reality which seemed to have the task of verifying such thought. It was, quite to the contrary, an omission of thinking which the engagement served to fulfill in a manner as faulty as it was erroneous. What was at issue for Heidegger in this unhappy engagement with the Nazis? Essentially, what was at issue was to give to a reality which demanded revolutionary change the task of dealing with a problem which could by no means be addressed in this manner. This problem is, indeed, the problem of philosophy, and it will open up on the unthought thought of philosophy. This unthought thought here took the name of theology. For theology, and precisely this theology, constituted the second half of the project which *Being and Time* was expected to complete. This may be readily verified by a reading of pages 171 to 202 of the lecture course held at Marburg during the summer semester of 1928. But what relation, one might object, exists between this theological project and the one which the Nazis fomented? What relation, indeed, other than an erroneous one? Nevertheless, the relation in question was that the scope of *Being and Time* was not just "Being" but Being's foundation in beings. It was precisely this task—"to found Being in beings"—which devolved to theology as a task for theology to perform. Moreover, this will remain theology's task, but in modes which will effectively have been thought through. This signifies that errancy did not reside in the project but only in its omission, or in the incapacity to think it at one particular time.[3]

This time, in any case, came to an end with Heidegger's resignation of his position as rector in April of 1934. The errancy was over, consequently, before Nazism revealed itself for what it was in reality. This limits Heidegger's fault to what he recognized it to be: a fault of thinking, but nothing which could in any way be compared with the crimes committed by the Nazi regime. Nevertheless, we should characterize this errancy more precisely. It consisted in a first encounter with the impossibility of thinking. This encounter was faulty in that the impossibility was not faced up to properly. The function of the engagement was, in effect, that of a postponement—of a postponement which was, moreover, clearly hopeless. Heidegger never really believed in the successful outcome of his engagement. But, nor did he "just pretend". The proof of this is his lack of disavowal, and this was of such a kind that we can explain his errancy only by an impossibility—an impossibility of thinking how to avoid such errancy. What makes an impossibility endured in such a manner into an experience which remains to be appropriated is quite precisely the fact of not having reflected upon it in its negativity—the fact, in other words, that the impossibility has not been grasped as such, but rather only suppressed. Had the impossibility been properly apprehended *as* impossibility, its errancy would not have happened. It is then surely a matter of a fault by default of thinking, and not by excess. In other words, we must insist that the fault consists in the deed—or, rather, in the misdeed—of *not* thinking, and not in "thinking too much." To think badly is to think not enough, and not the reverse.

Having now formally characterized Heidegger's fault, it is important to specify right away that no one other than Heidegger himself could have instructed us in the task of imputing this fault to him in this way. But this should not proceed without a precise, existentiell objection. For it was Heidegger who taught us—in *Being and Time*—that death is the encounter with impossibility. Not to have properly apprehended impossibility, in the case in question, amounts to fleeing in some manner from this encounter with truth. Let those who cannot desist from making their accusations go on doing so; but let us recall that the existeni*al* sense of errancy resides precisely in this mortal discovery of one's own impropriety (*Uneigentlichkeit*), of one's "inauthenticity," as Heidegger's term was first translated in French (and in English). When Heidegger wrote—and this has the weight of a confession—that whoever "thinks greatly" cannot but "err greatly," he both recognizes and indicates that he himself had to go to the limit of his inauthenticity. It was only at this price that the turning (*die Kehre*) could transpire, the turning which enabled him "to think greatly"—as he did. This is therefore the first encounter with impossibility: an improper, "inauthentic" encounter, but one which can be properly ended by the turning which allows us to discover its necessity. For "authenticity," or "propriety" (*Eigentlichkeit*) is never anything but the discovery and the transformation of a previous impropriety: an operation, therefore, on the order of conversion.

This means that we now cannot neglect to consider this in the dimension which causes the principal difficulty. We must not consider it in its individual aspect, but in its spiritual import. We cannot, after all, realistically explain Heidegger's fault, or the correction of this fault, if we close ourselves up within the limits—whether existential or formal—of the "first part" of "his" thought. In this completely formal context, therefore, Heidegger was able to avoid every occasion for personal shortcoming. The opportunity for such shortcoming presented itself only in one very particular place in the second part of his path of thinking: in precisely that place where ontology, having remained formal up until that point, must concretize itself in theology through a sudden turning ["retournement"]—*Umschlag* or *Kehre*. The difficulty of this turn ["tournant"] thus explains a good deal more than errancy. For it was preceded by quite a long period of hesitation—six years to be exact, during which the crossing-over of the turn remained in suspense. Given this suspended hesitation, we must no longer fear to assert that, paradoxically, it was his year of errancy (1933/34) which led Heidegger to carry out this turn effectively. This then allowed him, along with "the event" (*das Ereignis*), to discover the second part of his thought. We can even date the time of this correction fairly precisely. Its decisive formulation is contained in the *Beiträge zur Philosophie* (1936/38), whose "appropriate subtitle" is precisely *On the Event* (*Vom Ereignis*).

For, if Heidegger had to hesitate for so long and to make so great a mistake before being able to articulate this thought of the event, it is because the difficulty which must be faced is revealed to have an unsuspected character—to the point that the thinker preferred to reserve for posterity the care of discovering the fullness of the event and to measure its rigor. This could not have been attempted until half a century after he had expressed his thought. Thus we are only at the very beginning of the attempts which will allow us to discern the difficulty in a fresh light. What has changed—in this case—between Heidegger and us can be summarized as follows: On one side, it lies in what he has given to us, and, on the other, in what he is reproached for. We must rediscover the sense of what he has given us to think, while demonstrating the illegitimacy of the trial to which he has been subjected. In this ex-plication (*Aus-einander-setzung*), or this "debate," the principal question must bear very clearly upon that which, in respect to the *Shoah*, could very well teach us about the thought of the event. The term self-destruction has seemed to me the most appropriate for signifying this, and for reasons which have been renewed since I proposed it (*Etudes Heideggeriennes*, 8[1992] p. 151.

It has been necessary, furthermore, to give this expression a double explanation. It is a matter of addressing the problem posed by the double signification of the prefix "self-" ["auto-"] in the expression "self-destruction" ["autodestruction"]. One must understand that this expression also requires an elucidation: On the one hand, we have the "self" of the "subject"—in German, *das Selbst*, and, on the other hand, the "same" or "identity"—in German, *das Selbe*. The whole difficulty consists in having to articulate these two senses of the prefix which are in apparent opposition. Here is precisely what allows the thought of the event to take effect, but on the condition of making explicit what is doubly unthought in the thought of the event.

Let us begin with what is most immediately pressing, namely, the role played by the self or the subject (*das Selbst*) in the conjunction of the event. This role is at once decisive and derivative. It is derivative because the role is assigned by the conjunction of the whole, the "structure," in other words, of the event. This is unified in the fourfold (*das Geviert*): heaven, earth, divinities, and mortals. In order to indicate the manner in which Heidegger concretely rethought the "*logos* of the cross"—which he chose to designate with the name of Christianity (*Christlichkeit*) so as to distinguish it from institutionalized Christendom (*Christentum*)—I have proposed to call the logic which the fourfold obeys staurology, from the Greek *stauros*: cross. Here we find ontically translated that which devolves to theology in the unthought thought of philosophy. Until now, no one has paid any attention to this, remaining fascinated by an "ontology" against whose abstraction Heidegger had warned us on the next to last page of *Being and Time*. It is therefore necessary to insist that the project of "fundamental ontology" pursued by Heidegger was never one of a "pure science of Being" but rather was articulated from the first as an onto*logy* which must be founded on an on*tic*, which means that the guarantor of the "sense of Being" is nothing other than the comportment of a certain kind of being: the being which we ourselves are. In other words, ontology rests upon an ethic, which inscribes itself in a staurology in which Heidegger has expressed, not the science—general and special—of Being, but rather the crucial experience of beings.[4]

This crucial experience is undergone by the self or subject, which this experience consequentially defines as "the crucified." This is the source of the relation with the *Shoah*, which we will endeavor to understand and which will then illuminate the Jewish essence of "Christianity." But here the adjective Jewish does not designate an ethic group. On the contrary, it signifies that there is not true humanity without being related to divinity—as the Jews have shown us. In other words, it is not blood and soil which properly defines us, but rather the possibility of emancipating ourselves from this very blood and soil. The "sense of the Earth," then, should be subordinated to "the call of Heaven"—but this certainly will not happen without a struggle. Strange struggle, always beginning again, and one which the victim can only win. But at what a price! This is the testimony of the *Shoah*—a testimony like never before. Yet, who would dare claim that the message has sufficed? For this, it would be necessary to deprive it of that which constitutes the spirit of the message, namely, that humanity may only be assured of its extreme fragility.

But here we must not make a mistake. The fragility in question has nothing to do with a flaw in the constitution of humanity. It pertains, rather, to the nature of the subject which we must embody. This fragility takes its measure, indeed, from the difficulty of the task imposed. It is a matter of forming a humanity which peacefully adjudicates its own differences, but which is at the same time capable of safeguarding beings as a whole. In other words, it is a matter of constituting the self or the subject (*das Selbst*), which is able to assume, as it must, the same or the identity (*das Selbe*) that is crucially entrusted to it. As it must—this means: in a manner appropriate to the different manifestations of the truth. Heidegger distinguishes five, and in an order which should not be ignored.[5] He begins, we should recall, with "the work of art" and ends with "the questioning of the thinker." Between these two are placed successively "the act which founds the state," "the proximity" of the divine designated as "the being that above all *is*" ["le plus étant dans l'étant"] and, finally, "the essential sacrifice." I have already had occasion elsewhere[6] to indicate the reason why "the work of art" is given first rank: the work of art allows that element to come forward by which the four following modes can find the way to manifest themselves. Without language, in fact, whose essence is silence, no other manifestation of the truth could deploy itself. Of the four following modes, "the essential sacrifice" is, of course, the one which we should focus on here. The fact that it should be situated between, on the one side, the proximity of the divine, and on the other, the question of thinking, cannot be overlooked. This signifies, on the one hand, that "the essential sacrifice" is determined by divinity, but, on the other hand, as well that it very closely conditions the act of thinking. What is there to say, then, about the putting to death of an entire people, in particular when it was ordered by "the master criminal" who began his abuse without opposition?

It is a question, similarly, of not neglecting any of the expressions of the "questioning of the thinker," no matter how apparently private. Thus it should have been recalled, as is now beginning to be done, that, from 1935 on, Heidegger had the habit—granted, with only a select few—of referring to Hitler as "the master criminal" (*der Hauptverbrecher*).[7] Given this, could one formulate his rejection more energetically? Without a doubt, this denunciation never had the public notoriety from which the *faux-pas* which preceded it had unfortunately benefited. But there were a number of ways for Heidegger to indicate his opposition, none of which were without some danger. While inconspicuous, their efficacy was no less determinative. What is essential in this deed was, not to expose his abhorrence of the Führer, but rather to disclose the conditions of Hitler's criminal operation. On this view, the name of master criminal—*Hauptverbrecher*—allows us, surprisingly, to summarize what remains to be thought. For this is by no means the unreflective expression of simple spite. Quite the contrary. It is enough to place in evidence the composition of the word and to underline the prefix—*Haupt-verbrecher*—to see right away what this otherwise inconspicuous first element offers us as a matter for thinking. Indeed, how could it be possible now not to evoke the unfortunate *Selbstbehauptung*, which led to the *faux-pas* committed by Heidegger at the time of his rectorate? But how could we not also oppose to Heidegger the rectification, brought about ten years later, of what we must consequently call his capital error, his *Hauptfehler*![8] Since the true nature of this error and the difficulty in rectifying it have been, until today, largely ignored, we should scrutinize the different effects of this delusion, with its multiple consequences.

The first of the effects of this delusion affects the self or the subject, which is reduced to subjectivity. This subjectivity, certainly, is singular in the final analysis, but it is linked up to an indefinite aggregate of groups, which demand to be understood as so many persons endowed with a boldly domineering "me." Thus the self is no longer the unassignable intimacy to which all experience cannot but be allocated; it seems, on the contrary, highly differentiated by the exclusive particularity of individuality, singular or collective, which presumes to embody it. The self ["le 'soi'"] is thus replaced by the me ["le '*moi*'"], whether this be that of the Führer, or of the People, or of Humanity, or, moreover, of the Party, the Army, or even the University. It is capable, as well, of being more abstract, of calling itself God, Reason, or the Revolution. In each of these cases, it functions in the same way—by means of command and oppression—but not with the same degree of indignity. It should not be, therefore, a question of erasing the differences which exist between diverse forms of domination. What constituted the Nazi horror amounts to this: that the principle of oppression was deprived of any universality. It was, when all is said and done, the whim of an individuality which imposed itself with its measureless hatred of everything which differed from it. Hence the madness of a regime which has shown as never before what the word tyranny means. What should concern us, meanwhile, it not so much the singular figure of the master criminal as the common delusion by means of which he succeeded in perpetrating his crimes. This delusion is that of subjectivity, of the isolated me, shut up in its unicity and submitted to its commands, whether this unicity be "transcendental," "social," "racial," or quite simply "libidinal." It is astonishing that Heidegger—who was the first to oppose to the pretenses of this egology his precise analyses of Being-in-the-world with the Other—should have allowed himself to be ensnared by the most glaring form of the delusion from which he liberated us. The reason for this is, as has been indicated, that during the period when the trap closed shut, Heidegger had not yet elaborated the staurology which was the only thing which would have allowed him to avoid this trap. The analysis of the self, with which the published part of *Being and Time* ends, needs to be completed by a determination of the "same" which must be reconciled with the self. This required nearly ten years finally to emerge—from 1936 onwards—in the thinking of the event. Moreover, this thinking remained unpublished in its full form for more than fifty years. This is the cause of what has been called the Heidegger affair; it is entirely due to an ignorance of the second part of the thought of the event, in other words, of the neglect of the necessary contribution, at once ontical, theological, and ethical—in short, staurological—which must be brought to bear as much on the analyses proposed in the breakthrough work as on the purely ontological determination of the event which has supplemented—without replacing—the unpublished part of *Being and Time.*

This now allows us to understand the cause of the second effect of the delusion which Heidegger was not able to dispel until after having made his sacrifice to it in the most astonishing fashion. This second effect no longer has to do with "the subject"—*das Selbst*—but rather with "the same"—*das Selbe*—with which it must be reconciled. We are no longer concerned at present with the effects of the egological isolation imposed by the delusion in question, but rather with the ontological reduction to which the delusion is allowed to proceed abusively, first by simplication, then by classification. The simplification consists in the confusion between two questions—that of *Being* and that of *beings*—whose respective specificity and mutual articulation are thus ignored. Consequently, in the place of considering the "things themselves"—*Being* and *beings* taken in the difference *and* their belonging to one another—a "logic" imposes itself in the form of a classification by degrees of the diverse kinds of essences or natures of things. In the confusion of *Being* and *beings*, "logical" organization then confers the uniform, "rational" appearance of a pure ontology. When the same of identity—*das Selbe*—finds itself, as it does here, reduced to the dimension or a whole, characterized by its unique uniformity, the determination of a principle of order becomes essential. Hence the importance—which is ontological prior to being political—of the "leadership principle" (*Führerprinzip*), which allows the formal ordering of a logically pulverized aggregate of all beings. Under these conditions, there is no question which cannot be, or, rather, which must not be taken up by the channels of administration. Included here, then, are the questions of population. It is in such a rationalized framework that we must comprehend Nazism in what allows us to characterize it, namely, racism and, above all, antisemitism. Racism, indeed, constitutes a "principle of classification" of populations, which enables the administrative regulation of their relations—without the least passion. The matter may have seemed less obvious in respect to the Jewish question, but, examining things closely, this issue simply presented a higher degree of complexity. Jewishness, for the Nazis, did not properly represent a race, but, rather, the anti-race itself. The "Jew" was mélange incarnate, and thus the opposite of the principle of race defined by its purity. Hence the necessity of eliminating the Jew—a necessity just as rational as racial. This necessity was thus able to authorize "the administrative crime," as Hannah Arendt has described this crime against humanity.

Therefore, Nazism is something entirely different from a simple aberration which violates "the principle of reason." Consequently, one ought not to be surprised that this movement raged on in the nation that has, in some sense, been chosen by philosophy. Nor is it an accident if the thinker who was called upon to discover what is unthought was not able to avoid being seduced for a moment by the idea of overturning, from the inside, the rationality of this most dangerous movement. "Where the danger is, grows the saving power also," he would recall later. But, in that moment, what carried him away was the delusion of an "action"—political, administrative—able to supplement the task of thinking. Therefore, we must characterize the evil which he could not resist for the better part of a year as a *will not to think*. This is the essence of evil—among human beings at least. In its initial stage, it appears in that instant—as brief as a swoon—in which we choose to set aside the urgency of thinking, or, in other words, the urgency of questioning. And so Heidegger set aside the Jewish question. This does not just mean that he did not consider the Jewish question a sufficient justification to avoid compromising himself with a movement when he could not overlook what the Führer thought of Jewishness. It also means that he prevented himself from making explicit the question of humanity as it presented itself concretely. For the question of humanity is precisely the question of the self or the subject (*das Selbst*), and this question is crucially articulated along with the question of the same or identity (*das Selbe*). It is, to summarize, the question of beings as a whole which, once again, was left unarticulated.

Once again—because it was left unarticulated a first time with the suspension of the publication of *Being and Time*, a publication, which, as we know, did not get past its second division. We should then not be too surprised that the thinking toward which Heidegger led us has until now barely been grasped in part. The reason for this is that he never entirely communicated it while he was alive. And, with respect to the previously unpublished manuscripts which have been published to date, if these allow us to reconstitute the whole of the project and its principal articulations, they nevertheless do not give us the full grasp of Heidegger's thought which we would wish to have. And for good reason, because the desire for this realization should not be fulfilled. For "the time for systems is past," as Heidegger has pointed out at the very beginning of the *Beiträge zur Philosophie*. This is, without a doubt, the reason for the interruption of *Being and Time*. But it is by no means the same as a renunciation either of the project itself or of the rigor of its accomplishment. In particular, the kind of thinking which is called upon to succeed "systems" is no less exigent than they; on the contrary, it is more rigorous. It is a matter of replacing the unidimensional bondage to logic with the free jointure signifying the four dimensions of beings. In other words, staurology must succeed ontology. Only on this condition will self-destruction be set aside. This is, in any case, the teaching of the *Shoah*.

This teaching is inscribed in the Hebrew name which we are slowly learning to give to what we have called, for a longer time, genocide, Holocaust, or extermination. None of these last three terms, of course, should be discarded for the sake of some linguistic purity. It is a matter, on the contrary, of conserving such usages, for each one allows us to specify that which we must think. Thus, genocide expresses the racial determination of what Holocaust reveals in its sacrificial character. As for the term extermination, this soberly indicates the fury of the project. *Shoah*, however, has the singular merit of precision in designation—truly a double merit. It was not just any population which was the object of the extermination, nor was it in just any civilization that this took place. It occurred precisely in that civilization whose "Hebrew heritage" constitutes one of its two principal determinations. Hence the term *self*-destruction, which has seemed to me capable of expressing the true scope of the operation whose absurdity—paradoxically—gives us the most to think about.

This term seems to signify formally that the project was destined to fail. But it is precisely this failure which was so furiously pursued as it took place, and it was pursued in such a manner that a particular impossibility reveals itself here to be the condition of the operation. We must determine this condition in its essential contradiction. Considering the matter carefully, it appears to be doubly constituted, for it is necessary to distinguish between the contradiction internal to the project and the external contradiction against which it hurled itself voluntarily. The first, inward contradiction allows us to explain the madness of the project, and the second, its fury. The former having determined the latter, we must then begin by characterizing the madness. Much more than a simple error about oneself, it consisted in a false consciousness *of* the self (*das Selbst*). Not only did the Nazis consider themselves a race essentially lacking in any community with the rest of humanity, but, more profoundly, they detached the human species from everything of which the Jews were, by contrast, the living testimony—namely, that humanity has its sojourn on earth but is at the call of heaven, and that humanity finds itself linked to a language to which the event constitutes the response. This means that humanity is bound to divinity in such a way that the self or the subject must not be reduced to human subjectivity, but rather intimated as the crossroads ["entrecroisement"] of the four dimensions of beings. This crossroads cannot be assigned, but it is more intimate for each of us than what properly defines us.

Nazi antisemitism thus appears to us as a crime against humanity conditioned by contempt for the exigencies of spirit. Hence the intimate contradiction which defines the madness of the extermination—madness in that the crime was tantamount to recognizing, in order to suppress its own madness, that which the criminals pretended did not exist, namely, the humanity of those whom they murdered. Otherwise they would not have used dissimulation, for, as we know, such dissimulation was hardly lacking in their project. Indeed, the principal characteristic of the Final Solution resides precisely in the extraordinary secrecy with which it surrounded itself. Today, this secrecy allows some to persist in denying the crime. After what has just been said, we should not underestimate this phenomenal fantasy, for it attests to an enduring hatred of the spirit, a hatred whose resurgence manifests its fury. For the moment, certainly, this fury is largely impotent, but it is nevertheless seriously menacing. We should connect this fury to the chain of aberrations in which the denial of the extermination is nothing but an "historical" link. This link in the chain is surely quite visible, but certainly not the most important. What is most important is found earlier—at the very beginning of the chain, precisely in the place where this chain is attached to the deepest part of the human soul.

But what about this deepest part of the soul, and how should we understand its constitution? Here exactly is what the staurology which Heidegger bequeathed can teach us. Again, we must not make a mistake, for he has bequeathed it to us in the manner which La Fontaine's laborer spiritually revealed a treasure to his children—on the condition that we ourselves should know how to cultivate the terrain prepared by his efforts. Indeed, we are not inheriting a doctrine, but a question—and a question, moreover, linked to a logic of impossibility. On one hand, there is the criminal impossibility to which Nazism gave the unbearable proof of reality. Its principle is generalized segregation: the segregation, in other words, of one "race" from the bosom of humanity, but a segregation of humanity from the bosom of the fourfold as well. Impossibility here means enmity, a hatred hidden in the pretense of superiority. This superiority is that of the master over his subordinates, a superiority multiplied downwards by these subordinates over the rest of humanity; it is a superiority, in the end, of the human racial principle and the usurpation by this principle of the role of divinity. Hence the decision to do away with the people who have taught us a completely different conception of divinity. Therefore, the sacrifice imposed upon this people was structurally a part of the Nazi religion. For, it is indeed a matter of religion which is at issue, a religion whose seductiveness alone allows us to explain how coldly the crime was administered. Such religion is reduced to the narcissistic worship of one's own preservation. No transcendence here, only the cult of German blood, a cult which, moreover, did not need to be broadly confessed; it sufficed that the ritual be mechanically observed. And so, to participate in the crime which was committed, it sufficed simply not to think about it. To participate, however, does not mean to perpetrate. Indeed, it is necessary to distinguish between culpability and criminality. The incontestable culpability of the participants—which extends beyond the Germans!—should not be assimilated to a true criminality. The designation of criminality should be reserved strictly for those responsible for the event, namely, those who, in order to carry it out, shared in "the terrifying secret." It is necessary, therefore, to limit criminality to the master criminal and to those who personally assured him of their active complicity.

Even if the act had been committed by the great majority of the population, no murder could be committed without the determination to do it. The lack of consciousness which is sufficient to constitute culpability is thus opposed to the deliberate character of criminality. Hence the spiritual malignity of the deed in itself, because it is a matter of willing what contradicts the elementary exigency that rules its very life. But it is a matter of spirituality, too, as we know. The proof of this is the effort exerted to escape the consequences of the act committed, an escape which must begin with the effort required to erase reality. On this point, the Nazis surpassed everything one could have imagined. Nevertheless, they could not avoid finding themselves confronted in turn by the impossibility which Heidegger enables us to interrogate. The criminal side of the impossibility is only the inverse of what constitutes the essential issue, namely, its sacrificial character. Impossibility does not primarily mean enmity, therefore, but rather an astonishing activity of liberation. Let us say, in order to declare it, that this liberation consists in thinking negation in a reversed manner. Consequently, we should not think of negation as a secondary process of opposition, but rather as an act whose accomplishment has original primacy over all positing. For there is no positing which does not derive from a fall from which negation properly allows it to right itself. Thus there is not less but more in the negation of possibility than there is in its realization. There exists, then, a "possibility of impossibility" higher than all reality, for it is precisely such a possibility which, in *Being and Time*, defines death when it is taken on freely. The relation between this death and the one which later will be called the essential sacrifice cannot be accidental.

One freely consents to the essential sacrifice with one's own life. Life, then, manifests the self-donation to which life is linked. This self-donation ["autodonation"] constitutes the original negation of what self-destruction ["autodestruction"] imposed. It consists precisely in this donation of the self (*das Selbst*) which reveals for us the essence of the same (*das Selbe*). The *Shoah* has given its horrifying testimony in demonstrating the true necessity of this subject for uniting the whole of what is. We should give thanks to the people in whom humanity has recognized itself.

Translated by Gregory Fried

NOTES

1. Martin Heidegger, "Wer gross denkt, muss gross irren." Cf. *Aus der Erfahrung des Denkens, Gesamtausgabe*, Bd. 13, p. 81.
2. Cf. F.-W. von Herrmann, *Heideggers "Grundprobleme der Phänomenologie." Zur "Zweiten Hälfte" von "Sein und Zeit"* (Frankfurt am Main: Vittorio Klostermann, 1991).
3. The course in Marburg referred to in this passage was published in 1978. Cf. *Gesamtausgabe*, Bd. 26. [For an English translation, see Martin Heidegger, *The Metaphysical Foundations of Logic*, trans. Michael Heim (Bloomington: Indiana University Press, 1984), pp. 136–159.—trans.]
4. I have attempted to present this *Staurology* (under this title) in a text whose complete version has appeared in *Etudes Heideggeriennes*, 9 (1993).
5. Cf. Heidegger, *The Origin of the Work of Art*, third section, *Der Ursprung des Kunstwerkes*, in *Holzwege, Gesamtausgabe*, Bd. 5, pp. 49–50.
6. Cf. footnote 4, above.
7. Cf. the letter of December 17, 1945, to René Le Senne from Louis Sauzin, a French officer charged with what he himself calls "the Heidegger affair," his "greatest concern." This letter was published in *La règle du jeu*, 4 (May 1991).
8. I have given the evidence for Heidegger's *Hauptfehler*—as well as for his self-correction—in an article entitled "Penser le danger," which appeared in *Cahiers philosophiques*, 53 (December 1992).

10

Heidegger's Essentials: Appropriations and Expropriations

JAMES R. WATSON

> What difference does it make to this murderous society, whether it have one member more, or less? Will its laws, its manners, its customs be vitiated? Has an individual's death ever had any influence upon the general mass? And after the loss of the greatest battle, what am I saying? after the obliteration of half the world—or, if one wishes, of the entire world—would the little number of survivors, should there be any, notice even the faintest difference in Things? No, alas. Nor would Nature notice any either, and the stupid pride of man, who believes everything created for him, would be dashed indeed, after the total extinction of the human species, were it to be seen that nothing in Nature has changed, and that the stars' flight had not for that been retarded. Let us continue.[1]

> Agriculture is now a motorized food industry: in its essence it is the same thing as the manufacture of corpses in gas chambers, the same thing as blockades and the reduction of a region to hunger, the same as the manufacture of hydrogen bombs.[2]

Appropriation perverts, no matter the rights set forth in justification for this violence. Philosophy privately manipulated by secretive hands always fashions badly those to whom it does not belong—the Other of its appropriation. The sacred task of an appropriating retrieve/rescue from the clutches of the spiritually disabled requires a secret way, a way of language unbeknown to the chattering others without proper kin(d).

Appropriated philosophies are always taken from the texts of the public realm with the violence of appropriation (*Ereignis*). Snuggled in a *Heimat*, appropriated philosophy speaks much less ambiguously, more forcefully, and, above all, becomes "purified" in and through the rescuing retrieve from the public muddle of human plurality. Only the truly great thinkers—those who think only one thought—are resolute enough to poke this spiritless corpus of impotent texts and extract what remains unthought in it. Philosophy is too great and powerful a thing to leave in public hands: "Far from the market place and from fame happens all that is great: far from the market place and from fame the inventors of new values have always dwelt."[3]

> But because Dasein is *lost* in the "they," it must first *find* itself. In order to find *itself* at all, it must be "shown" to itself in its possible authenticity. In terms of its *possibility*, Dasein *is* already a potentiality-for-Being-its-self, but it needs to have this potentiality attested.[4]

Consider, for example, the public image of the Marquis de Sade—a wicked pervert who practiced and wrote despicable things. In return for which he was sentenced to a total of thirty-two years and one month in prison. His heinous crimes were spanking a prostitute in Paris, giving aphrodisiac sweets to girls in Marseilles, seducing his sister-in-law, annoying his powerful in-laws (probably his second greatest "crime"), allowing "moderates" to escape during the Terror, and attacking Bonaparte's entourage.[5] And he did *publish* some obscene books—the greatest crime of all. Sade spent thirty years of his scandalous libertine life in various kinds of confinement. In prison (during the years of transition from the Monarchy to the Republic and from the Terror to the Consulate and then to the Empire) he became a writer-in-solitude.

Heidegger's case is somewhat different. He never published what most would regard as an obscene book, nor as far as we know did he ever practice the things Sade recommended for all true libertines. Certainly there are no references to Sade or his texts in any of Heidegger's published works or available lecture transcripts. Sade, it seems, was not on Heidegger's list of major thinkers. Yet there are certain lines of thought that can and should be drawn from Sade to Nietzsche, and certainly from Nietzsche to Heidegger, and then back from Heidegger to Sade. Such a drawing, admittedly a complex, multidimensional figuration, might help us see crucial aspects of an oscillating modernity, especially if it were then juxtaposed with the unimaginable one called Auschwitz. The complexity of mixed images of different lineage is precisely the stage of modern actors.[6]

Alongside one another, the prescient and horribly prosaic statements of Sade's "old Pope" seem puny in contrast with Heidegger's easy assimilation of mass murder. Sade's "Pius VI" (Giovanni Angelo Braschi) speaks to Juliette of global destruction and mass murder in his great apologia for murder. Here is a segment of the dialogue between Juliette and Pius VI:

> "Oh, Braschi!" I exclaimed during a moment of lucidity, "what would they say, the people upon whom you professionally impose, if they could see you in the midst of these turpitudes?"
>
> "They would express for me the same contempt I have for them," Braschi answered, "and despite their pride they would own to their absurdity. But no matter! let's continue to dazzle and dupe them: the reign of error shall someday come to its end, we must enjoy it while it lasts."
>
> "Why yes, yes indeed," I concurred, "let us fuddle and fool mankind, it asks for no greater service. . . . Braschi, say now, shall we not immolate a few victims in the temple whither we are soon to go?"
>
> "Of course we shall," the Holy Father replied, "blood must flow before orgies are satisfactory. Seated on Tiberius' throne, I imitate his voluptuous practices; and I too know no more delicious discharge than that expelled in echo to the plaintive accents of the dying."[7]

Within the inner greatness of this privatized philosophy of murder is there a secret bond of criminality between Pius VI and the later Pius XII?[8] The former, who claimed murder as one of Nature's laws, and the latter, who chose to remain silent (Veritatis Splendor?) during the murder of six million Jews? And then Heidegger, who chose to withdraw his very sparse lecture references to the mass murder of Jews from the published version of his 1949 Bremen lectures?[9] Is there also a kind of inner, secret law protecting the spiritually great from ordinary standards of decency? To date, neither Hitler nor any of his SS members who were Catholic have been excommunicated because of their deeds: The murder of Jews constitutes no formal heresy. And then Heidegger, who proclaimed in 1935 that Christian dogma and the question of Being could not be brought into relation,[10] yet "remained a Catholic on the tax rolls all his life and in the end received a Catholic burial."[11] Secret bonds among those whose greatness elevates them above the doctrines and creeds for the masses?

While still under the captivating influence of Wagner and his musical theater, Nietzsche wrote:

> Whenever one acts, in small things as well as great, one always has in view this correspondence between deed and receptivity; and he who gives must see to it that he finds recipients adequate to the meaning of his gift.[12]

Perhaps, and this has been subtly suggested,[13] Heidegger resonated with this counsel when he decided to withhold his 1949 Bremen lectures' comments (which, we should note, do not use the words murder and Jews as such) from public consumption. According to this version of the "withdrawal," Heidegger understood that the public is simply incapable of dealing with such a stark formulation of the "truth." The public, then, does not include those (philosophers) who are capable of withstanding exposure to the stark truth.

Whatever the case, Heidegger saw no need to begin again the task of thought in the face of the death camps. On the contrary, for Heidegger the death camps were simply instances of global technicity's unquestioned sway, in which service one of the Allied Powers "exterminated millions of [East Germans]" after the war.[14] His thought, carefully coded in an appropriated philosophy, was such that it already encompassed and opposed what was revealed at Auschwitz. No need, then, to begin anew: "When ye are willers of one will, and when that change of every need is needful to you: there is the origin of your virtue."[15] The resolute ones stand apart from the shameless proliferation of public images, each immodest to the point of indecency, and each and all "tiresome" for those select few called to essential thought.[16] Whence this call to the few?

Like the identificational recruitment apparatus of aestheticized "politics," appropriated philosophy works to produce subjects/adherents whose self-interests have been reduced to that allowable within the event of appropriation itself (*Ereignis*). Strictly and essentially speaking (the only way appropriated philosophy speaks), the event of appropriation is the symbolic destruction of others who do not belong—*das Man*. What may seem to be a radical phenomenological undertaking to set forth something beyond the traditional (modern) subject-object dualism—Being-in-the-World—might instead be a radicalization of specific socio-historical structures. If, for instance, "the roots of the existential analytic, on its part, are ultimately existentiell, that is, ontical,"[17] can the question of Being be anything other than the horizon of an identificational recruitment for the purpose of articulating the recruitment's "basic structures" and thus providing an ontological-existential justification for these "invariant" features of its "authentic" (private) life?

There is another parallel between Nazi "politics" and appropriated philosophy: The invariant, essential structures of those belonging within the event of appropriation are articulated in opposition to some indiscriminate/indifferent mass that threatens their relationship to their essential being. In 1935 Heidegger attributed the collapse of German Idealism in the first half of the nineteenth century (the democratic, bourgeois revolutions and the industrialization of Germany) to the predominance of technical intelligence:

> The prevailing dimension became that of extension and number. Intelligence [*Intelligenz*] no longer meant a wealth of talent, lavishly spent, and the command of energies, but only what could be learned by everyone, the practice of a routine, always associated with a certain amount of sweat and a certain amount of show. In America and in Russia this development grew into a boundless etcetera of indifference and always-the-sameness—so much so that the quantity took on a quality of its own. Since then the domination in those countries of a cross section of the indifferent mass [*Gleichgültigen*] has become something more than a dreary accident. It has

> become an active onslaught of what we call the demonic [*das Dämonische*] (in the sense of destructive evil). There are many indications of the emergence of this demonism, identical with the increasing helplessness and uncertainty of Europe against it and within itself.[18]

The demonic grows in tandem with the growth of what can be learned by everyone, led by that cross section of the indifferent mass forming the American and Soviet intelligentsia, and organized against an uncertain Europe with Germany as its (spiritual) center—"the nation with the most neighbors and hence the most endangered."[19] The danger is both external and internal. Not only is essential Germany surrounded by those who have learned what "anybody" can learn, there is an internal infestation of its spiritual center—"the evil within."

Why "the demonic"? If Heidegger had chosen to enter the fray of political contestation, he simply could have said "our enemies." But, for Heidegger, before this "enemy" can be met on the battlefield, its internal infestation of recruited spirits must be eradicated by other than ordinary political means. The cleansing of spirit is preparatory for battle.[20] Only when the spirit is revived will Germany have any chance of defeating the delusional demonism of technocratic America and Russia.[21] This is what Heidegger advocated in 1935, when there were already well over sixty concentration camps in Germany to deal with infestations by other than ordinary political and legal means.

Up to this point, it may seem that I am making a case for the claim that Heidegger's "appropriation" of philosophy simply got it wrong; that is to say, that his "violent" interpretations of the great thinkers are more idiosyncratic distortions than accurate readings. And, yes, I do want to say that. But I also want to say that Heidegger's idiosyncratic distortion is very much of a piece with what constitutes a large part of the philosophic tradition. Heidegger, in other words, is heart and soul part of a tradition that oscillates from encouraging the very appropriations which distort its own appropriative distortions to "de-constructing" or "dis-owning" its own appropriations. The *secretum* of philosophy does indeed separate insiders from outsiders, but what yet remains problematic is whether this separation has anything to do with the discernment of thinking-through this separation.[22]

After Plato's melodramatic (and partly unconvincing) stories about Socrates' sad end in and by democratic Athens fell into hands that preferred private over public screenings, the anti-political "philosophy" of the *Republic* was set forth as the *Urtext* of (political) philosophy, not however in the realm of the public but in the privacy of academies and their select initiates. Under covers (Plato's metaphor for the poisonous, seductive product of writing),[23] the truth was taught by a few (older men) and "transmitted" to another selected few (younger men). This securing appropriation of truth and its good old boys' symposiums was and is a tribal attack on the political/public realm. The "tragedy of appearance," the manifestation of *who* one is, is possible, however, only within the artifice of the latter.

> Although nobody knows whom he reveals when he discloses himself in deed or word, he must be willing to risk the disclosure, and this neither the doer of good works, who must be without self and preserve complete anonymity, nor the criminal, who must hide himself from others, can take upon themselves. Both are lonely figures, the one being for, the other against, all men; they, therefore, remain outside the pale of human intercourse and are, politically, marginal figures who usually enter the historical scene in times of corruption, disintegration, and political bankruptcy. Because of its inherent tendency to disclose the agent together with the act, action needs for its full appearance the shining brightness we once called glory, and which is possible only in the public realm.[24]

The tribal attack on the public realm of unique personal revelations, the manifestation of who we are within the realm of human plurality, is directed against the power of this public disclosure. Tribalism sustains itself against the political with techniques of reproduction/representation that effectively reduce revelations of unique (kind-less) personal identity to typologies of physical and/or mythological identity: Racism is prototypical in tribalism. From the perspective of political disclosure, however, dia-tribes are wastes of time. Which is not to say that political disclosure is without considerable risk, as it also faces the insistence of tribal identification recruitment. When Alexander, for example, put on "barbaric" dress in Persia, the Aristotelian tribe knew it had a problem that only violence could solve.

By the time of the New Church and its *Adversus Judaeos* tradition, the tribal guardians of truth were able to teach the *Republic* together with the *Protagoras*—which raises and addresses the question of the political quite differently than the former—with no unsettling consequences. A new election had occurred. Thereafter, the old elect, the Jews, would be allowed to remain as proof of falsehood and its rightful punishment. Philosophy, tribally secured by a clan tracing itself to that of the Aristotelian one, had become firmly proprietary. For all of his radical hermeneutical tendencies, Heidegger would never break with this proprietary tradition and its Christian anti-Judaic identificational recruitments.

In his 1935 lectures on metaphysics, Heidegger explicitly refers to this crucial period of appropriation, without however mentioning its antithetical and anti-Judaic roots. The reading that Heidegger gives here of the New Testament concept of the *logos* attributes the determination of this concept to "the Jewish philosophy of religion developed by Philo," which then comes to signify "*kēryx*, the *angelos*, the herald, the messenger, who hands down commands and commandments; *logos tou staurou* is the word of the cross.

The proclamation of the cross is Christ himself; he is the logos of redemption, of eternal life, *logos zōēs*. A whole world separates all this from Heraclitus."[25] In a few sentences Heidegger shows how a whole world lies between the writers of the New Testament and the pre-Socratic philosophers, but without ever mentioning the contentious "world" in which Philo's "reversal" of Platonism was developed in opposition to those who desired "to abandon the letter of the Torah for a 'purely spiritual religion' [and] imagine it can dispense with the outward observance. . . ."[26] By connecting Philo's spiritualizing *midrash* with the New Testament interpretation of *logos* as "the word of the cross," Heidegger erases Philo as a Jew. And that is precisely how the new elect have always dealt with Jews and their alleged spiritual inability to interpret the meaning of scripture/texts.

When Heidegger began turning toward the neighborhood of art/poetry and thinking, he did so without abandoning either previous attachments or the appropriative equipment that had secured them. Despite the preparations for and subsequent executions of state-sponsored mass murder and inappropriate death, Heidegger's thought remained attuned to "mineness" and "appropriate death" as it turned toward the primacy of Being and Dasein's "shattering on Being."[27] Such a proper closure, however, belongs only within a specific (proprietary) neighborhood of thinking and poetry. Eight years after Philo's erasure as a Jew, Heidegger snuggled his retrieving thought in the Swabian territory of Hölderlin's poetry. It was a private time of commemoration for the gathering of kinsmen.

The proprietary neighborhood of 1943 is a mimetic scene, a kind of self-presentation by Heidegger in and through his 1935 reading of Hölderlin's reading of *Oedipus Rex* juxtaposed with his reading of Hölderlin's "Heimkunft / An die Verwandten" and "Andenken."[28] The result is a complex series of images within images with Heidegger self-positioned in the Oedipal figuration of unconcealment and shattering. The first in this series begins in 1935. With one eye/I too many, Heidegger says:

> Our relation to everything that makes up being, truth, and appearance has long been so confused, so devoid of foundation and passion, that even in our manner of interpreting Greek poetry and *making it our own* we barely suspect the power wielded by this poetic discourse in Greek being-there [*Oedipus Rex*]. Karl Reinhardt's recent interpretation of Sophocles (1933) comes appreciably closer to Greek being-there and being than all previous attempts, because Reinhardt sees and questions the tragic process on the basis of the fundamental relations between being, unconcealment, and appearance.[29]

Thrown out of certain appearances, Greek and German Dasein is shattered on Being. The tragedy of appearances exemplified by Oedipus is taken as a requisite for an essential German relation to the Being of beings. Is there a parallel or, more precisely, a certain parallax between Oedipus' fall from King to murderer and Heidegger's "unconcealment"?

Despite the language of revealment and disclosure, Heidegger's Oedipal figuration is not political in the sense of a disclosure within the space of "sheer human togetherness." In Heidegger's reading of Reinhardt's reading of Sophocles, Oedipus is revealed/rescued tribally; that is, Oedipus is "hurled out" of his (political) glory (doxa) into his "embodiment of Greek being-there" (*Gestalt des griechischen Daseins*).[30] Oedipus blinds himself when *who* he is (public being) is subordinated to *what* he is (private being). Greek Dasein, for Heidegger, is essentially the same as all Dasein—tribal: the essential Being of being-human is tribal.

Another series of images (poetic dwelling, naming, and manifestation, the one *Gespräch* whereby Being comes into words, and "Angels"), grouped around *die Weile des ausgeglichen Schicksals* (the sojourn of balanced destiny),[31] is added in 1943 by weaving Hölderlin's poem "Andenken" within the fabric of Heidegger's appropriation. Regarding this intricate tapestry, I could not even begin here to improve on Véronique Fóti's insightful and critical interpretation of Heidegger and the poets. Instead, I want to remark her crucial point concerning why Heidegger was unable to read/appropriate Hölderlin's last hymn, "Mnemosyne":

> Heidegger's own understanding of temporalization (*Temporalität des Seins*). . . does not accord with Hölderlin's treatment of the destinal or tragic moment as sheer "counter-rhythmic interruption," empty of all content and therefore refractory to (re)presentation. Heidegger's emphasis, even in his reading of Hölderlin's late poetry, is on "the infinite interconnection of the entire relationship" and on historicity as configuration rather than disfiguration. More importantly still, he does not countenance the possibility of a disaster that is bereft of saving power and that lies outside the sphere of tragedy and brings with it the failure of commemoration if not the erosion of language itself.[32]

And it is precisely this self-inflicted "blindness" that underlies all of Heidegger's willful figurations in the face of the unimaginable. Resting in its "own" element, Heidegger's *ausgeglichen Schicksals* is an adamantine refusal to admit the possibility of a shattering of *both* beings and Being. In the monstrous shadow of that anti-political wisdom which is Auschwitz, such hardness forms the "spiritual" foundation of measures to continually eradicate whatever and whoever is perceived as a threat to the balance of tribal destiny. Just as Himmler maintained idealism in the face of the disfiguration called "cleansing,"[33] Heidegger refused his own *public* disfiguration with the withdrawal of his 1949 Bremen lecture remarks on the death camps.

How, then, do we stand with Being after Auschwitz, after state-sponsored mass murder and the shattering of Jewish communities, the distortion of language, and the strengthening of tribalism under the cover of "business as usual"? If we continue to speak tribalized language in what remains of the public realm, then a generalized and unintentional lying in public will become the completion/end of the anti-political philosophical tradition of appropriation. Instead of a place for the revelation of our unique personal identities, the public realm becomes the arena of warring social clubs and their secretive plots. Consider what Berel Lang says about the distinctive literary figure contrived by the Nazi clan and "their" language of genocide:

> A person who denies having done something he knowingly did is lying—but it is not the language that then does the lying, it is the speaker. Calling the Nazi genocide a "Final Solution" [*Endlösung*], by contrast turns the phrase itself into a lie—as calling Achilles a "lion" discloses the latter term to be a metaphor. The figurative lie links two contradictory literal references ["solution to a problem" and "murderous annihilation"]; it also attempts, in asserting the connection, both to deny the contradiction and to conceal it.[34]

An appropriated and thus privatized/coded language can lie in public even when its speaker does not. Did Heidegger understand that "his" language and philosophy would never be read the way he intended after Auschwitz and its disclosures? Did Heidegger understand that his refusal to face that disfiguration was essentially a refusal to submit his philosophy to the revelation of public disclosure? I think he did.

But, even if Heidegger did understand all of this and deliberately chose to guard the *secretum* (the essentials) of his philosophy (the *Archiv* story), and although his private intentions and desires may be respected by tribal loyalists, his published works can no longer stand apart in such guarded security. Heidegger's philosophy must neither be ignored nor simply reiterated in its "own" terms. Heidegger's philosophy may well remain *heimlich* for its "insiders," but Paul Celan's poem "In der Luft" turns Heidegger's sense of (Hölderlin's) *Heimkunft* (home-coming) and *das gedichtete Geheimnis der sparenden Nähe* (the poeticized mystery of sparing nearness)[35] into an *unheimlichen Bannstrahl* (un-homely preserve).[36] In Celan's poetry, Heidegger's images within images are disfigured by impossible figurations of the barrier to imagination—Auschwitz. Celan does not permit Heidegger's philosophy to stand apart from that which it refuses. Although Heidegger refused Celan a "thinkers' dialogue," Celan did not refuse to com-plicate Heidegger.

Texts, unlike their bindings or fittings (*Fuge*) between sheltering covers, are always com-plicated: texts are *un-heimlich*. In a sense, Celan's "In der Luft" expropriates certain of Heidegger's appropriations:

> No longer is the earth the site of dwelling, but the air, the grave of the Jews burned alive in Auschwitz. Not only do Mortals gather in such a

home, but also all those exiled and murdered. No divinities, but Absence and Negation—no sky, but the desert of stars through which the separated and murdered travel. As a dwelling place mindful of its own dates and the horror of the Holocaust, Celan's poetry opens up a wound that violence and war burned into language. And it is this wound which ultimately connects past, present, and future, the dead and the survivors.[37]

What Celan does not do, however, is privatize or proprietize his expropriations. All of us, not just a select few, have this new site of dwelling. All of us, including the select few, are this wound speaking us as we speak.

Heidegger is not to be forgotten: *Schimmelgrün ist das Haus des Vergessens.*[38] But neither can we wounded ones afford to leave his texts in their fittings. Instead I would suggest un-kin(d) mixings of the type Celan-Heidegger.[39] What Heidegger left unsaid in his sojourning solitude is precisely what *his* thought could not say. But that unsaid is not the same as what the man Heidegger chose to say and not say. If Heidegger had said, "In the face of what has been disclosed, I will have to begin again the task of a thinking that may prove impossible," all of his compromising political involvements and philosophical counterparts would have paled by comparison with such a great move. But Heidegger chose otherwise. Unlike Heidegger's political choice in the face of disclosure, something can be done about Heidegger's texts that will take them away from their "belongingness" to that shameful choice. After Auschwitz is the time of improprietary thinking.[40]

NOTES

1. Marquis de Sade, *Justine, Philosophy in the Bedroom, and Other Writings*, trans. Richard Seaver and Austryn Wainhouse (New York: Grove Weidenfeld, 1990), pp. 332–333. Hereafter JPB. This is from the famous section of *Philosophy in the Bedroom* entitled "Yet Another Effort, Frenchmen, If You Would Become Republicans."
2. This is Wolfgang Schirmacher's citation from the second of Heidegger's 1949 Bremen lectures, as quoted by Karsten Harries in his Introduction to Gunther Neske and Emil Kettering, *Martin Heidegger and National Socialism* (New York: Paragon House, 1990), p. xxx.
3. Friedrich Nietzsche, *Thus Spoke Zarathustra*, trans. Walter Kaufmann (New York: Penguin Books, 1978), p. 52.
4. Martin Heidegger, *Being and Time*, trans. John Macquarrie and Edward Robinson (New York: Harper & Row, 1962), p. 313. *Sein und Zeit*, 11th ed. (Tübingen: Max Niemeyer, 1967), p. 268.
5. Jean Paulhan, "The Marquis de Sade and His Accomplice," in JPB, p. 7.
6. See Jean-François Lyotard, *The Postmodern Explained: Correspondence 1982–1985* (Minneapolis: University of Minnesota Press, 1992), p. 84: "It is clear now, after the event, that the works produced by the artistic avant-gardes for more than a century are involved in a parallel process of complexification. This

complexification bears on the sensibilities (sight, hearing, movement, language), not on expertise or knowledge. But the philosophical import of these works, or their power of reflection if you like, is as far-reaching in the order of receptivity and 'taste' as is the import of technoscience in matters of knowledge and practice."

7. Marquis de Sade, *Juliette*, trans. Austryn Wainhouse (New York: Grove Press, 1968), pp. 764–765.
8. This is not to imply an uninterrupted philosophic continuity from Pius VI to Pius XII. Pius XI was of a different cast. See John K. Roth and Michael Berenbaum, eds., *Holocaust: Religious & Philosophical Implications* (New York: Paragon House, 1989), p. xvi.
9. I have suggested the reasons for Heidegger's "withdrawals" in "Why Heidegger Wasn't Shocked by the Holocaust," *History of European Ideas*, 14/4 (1992), pp. 545–556.
10. Martin Heidegger, *An Introduction to Metaphysics*, trans. Ralph Manheim (New Haven: Yale University Press, 1959), p. 7, *Einführung in die Metaphysik*, 3d ed. (Tübingen: Max Niemeyer, 1966), p. 5. Hereafter IM and EM respectively.
11. Theodore Kisiel, "Heidegger's Apology," in Tom Rockmore and Joseph Margolis, eds., *The Heidegger Case: On Philosophy and Politics* (Philadelphia: Temple University Press, 1992), p. 20.
12. Friedrich Nietzsche, *Untimely Meditations*, trans. R. J. Hollingdale (New York: Cambridge University Press, 1992), p. 197.
13. See Jacques Derrida, "Heidegger's Silence," *Martin Heidegger and National Socialism*, eds. Günter Neske and Emil Kettering (New York: Paragon House, 1990), p. 147–148. In my estimation Heidegger's philosophy alone is incapable of coming to terms with National Socialism. However, I certainly agree with Derrida that today we must "read Heidegger the way he did not read himself." That Heidegger's 1949 lecture comments were "zu kraβ" for public consumption was suggested to me by Professor Reinhardt Maurer (Freie Universität Berlin) in a letter critical of my article" Why Heidegger Was Not Shocked by the Holocaust."
14. See Victor Farías, *Heidegger and Nazism*, trans. Paul Burrell and Gabriel R. Ricci (Philadelphia: Temple University Press, 1989), p. 285. In his response to Herbert Marcuse's request that Heidegger offer a response to the *Shoah*, Heidegger says, "To the severe and justified reproach that you express 'over a regime that has exterminated millions of Jews, that has made terror a norm and that transformed everything connected to the concepts of spirit, freedom, and truth into its opposite,' I can only add that instead of the 'Jews' one should put the 'East Germans,' and that is even more the case for one of the Allied Powers, with the difference that everything that happened since 1945 is known to all the world, while the bloody terror of the Nazis in reality was kept secret from the German people."
15. Friedrich Nietzsche, *Thus Spake Zarathustra*, trans. Thomas Common (New York: The Heritage Press, 1967), p. 70.
16. See Martin Heidegger, *What Is Called Thinking?* trans. Fred D. Wieck and J. Glenn Gray (New York: Harper & Row, 1968), pp. 28–29.
17. Heidegger, *Being and Time*, p. 34.
18. IM, p. 46; EM, p. 35.
19. IM, p. 38.
20. These comments in the 1935 lectures resonate with certain passages in the 1953 essay "Die Sprache im Gedicht: Eine Erörterung von Georg Trakls Gedicht," *Unterwegs zur Sprache* (Pfullingen: Neske, 1971), p. 60; *On the Way to Language*, trans. Peter D. Hertz (New York: Harper & Row, 1971), p. 179: "Evil is

ghostly in that it is the revolt of a terror blazing away in blind delusion, which casts all things into unholy fragmentation and threatens to turn the calm, collected blossoming of gentleness to ashes."

21. See Otto Pöggeler's excellent discussion of this aspect of Heidegger's writings and lectures in his essay "Heidegger, Nietzsche, and Politics," in *The Heidegger Case*, especially pp. 132–139.
22. See Sissela Bok, *Secrets: On the Ethics of Concealment and Revelation* (New York: Vintage Books, 1984), p. 6.
23. Plate, *Phaedrus*, 228–231.
24. Hannah Arendt, *The Human Condition* (Chicago: The University of Chicago Press, 1958), p. 180.
25. IM, pp. 134–135.
26. Rosemary Ruether, *Faith and Fratricide: The Theological Roots of Anti-Semitism* (New York: The Seabury Press, 1974), p. 37.
27. EM, p. 135.
28. Heidegger's *Erläuterungen zu Hölderlins Dichtung*, 4th ed. (Frankfurt am Main: Klostermann, 1971).
29. IM, p. 107–108. Emphasis added—JRW.
30. IM, pp. 106–107; EM, p. 81.
31. Heidegger's *Erläuterungen*, p. 122.
32. Véronique Fóti, *Heidegger and the Poets: Poiesis/Sophia/Techne* (Atlantic Highlander, NJ: Humanities Press, 1992), p. 74.
33. "While eliminating a germ, when all is said and done, we do not wish to become infected by the germ and to die from it. I will not allow the least zone of infestation to form or to become established. Whenever it is formed, we shall burn it out altogether. Although, however, we can say that we have accomplished the most difficult task for the love of our people. And we have not sustained any damage to our inner self, our soul and our character"—as quoted by Saul Friedländer, *Reflections of Nazism: An Essay on Kitsch and Death*, trans. Thomas Weyr (New York: Harper & Row, 1984), p. 103.
34. Berel Lang, "Language and Genocide," *Echoes from the Holocaust: Philosophical Reflections on a Dark Time*, eds. Alan Rosenberg and Gerald E. Myers (Philadelphia: Temple University Press, 1988), p. 350.
35. Heidegger, *Erläuterungen*, p. 30.
36. Paul Celan, *Gesammelte Werke*, Vol. I (Frankfurt am Main: Suhrkamp 1983), p. 290; hereafter GW. Amy Colin translates *unheimlichen Bannstrahl* with "unhomely banishment"—see her superb study *Paul Celan: Holograms of Darkness* (Bloomington: Indiana University Press, 1991), p. 135. This is certainly part of the sense of *Bannstrahl*, but the Swiss sense of a "[forest] preserve which protects against avalanches" is also part of Celan's attempt to employ *Bannstrahl* for conveying both the sense of the "ex-communication/expulsion" of Jews and the only kind of security left to survivors after Auschwitz. Thus *Bannstrahl* can also be read as a counter-image to Heidegger's *Holzwege*.

    Also compare the "Wayward Winds" section of my *Between Auschwitz and Tradition: Postmodern Reflections on the Task of Thinking* (Amsterdam: Rodopi, 1993).
37. Colin, *Paul Celan*, p. 139.
38. GW, 3, p. 46: "Mouldy green/fresh is the house of oblivion." The active forgetting of Auschwitz, for example, permits "fresh starts," but all of them are still mouldy, i.e., repetitions of what led to Auschwitz. After Auschwitz, business-as-usual (including philosophy-as-usual) is *Schimmelgrün*.

39. To com-plicate the type even further, a mixture of Celan-Kiefer-Heidegger would be an even better start for saying what the solitaire Heidegger left unsaid.
40. See my "Improprietary Thinking: No More Ours or Theirs," *Contemporary Philosophy*, XII/12 (November/December 1989), pp. 30–32.

11

Comrade Heidegger

JOSEPH MARGOLIS

You must not suppose I have forgotten the Holocaust. Of course not. But it has faded in a certain natural way. For me it has lost its primacy, because it has lost a good part of the power of its original presence. It remains, of course, the perfect horror that it always was; but I have other favorites now, or rather there are other horrors that possess me. At the moment it seems to be the Bosnian adventure gathered at Sarajevo, which, in this interval, waits to fall and waits for its final winter. I think I am able to hold on to what is unspeakable in the Holocaust because I have found it so easy to hold on to the same in Bosnia. And before that, the same in Somalia. There are too many darlings of this sort, too many insistent surrogates. It's not a question of the validity of human suffering or evil. It's the unbidden living presence of the event in collective memory. No one pays attention to that. For example, to be an American, *now*, is to be a bit "ready," subliminally, for the possible redemption of that great calamity of the "Indians'" fatal history in their own land. (The sense of necessity is gathering in some of us—slowly. It may never come to anything.) I begin to feel it only remotely, I'm sorry to say, although I am certainly clever enough to find the brave words for its acknowledgment—and I do believe them. Occasionally, a scene in a weak movie shows me that it is still a source of collective shame. The mechanism is a little like pornography, and the sense of recovered presence is a sort of serial infatuation. I think if I insisted on the Holocaust's primacy, it would be a complete sham. It is already too distant for that: not burned out, it's true, but I should need a spiritual pump for a full erection. The Cambodian slaughter is more recent, but it was always too remote, too abstract, for me; though a few newsclips here and there, a few stray lines of a journalist's description, have, I admit, brought me occasionally to a full and secret presence even there. And I have wept without moving. Anyone who understands the kindness of pornography will understand that.

In this sense, I cannot possibly treat the lively outrage against a toad like Martin Heidegger seriously. It offends against the constant urgency of the latest horrors of our world. Whatever do they mean, those who still complain that Heidegger never openly acknowledged the actuality of the Holocaust, the obscenity of his own metaphor about the gas chambers, his final stupid silence about his obvious complicity in the glory days of the Nazis? *That* had its very feeble presence once upon a time, I don't deny. But that we all have been cheated by Heidegger's refusal to make a public confession, that we are still cheated, what is that supposed to mean? Misplaced zeal, I'd say; staged piety. The juxtaposition is suspicious and the thoughtful perseveration borders on the monstrous.

There is a deep illiteracy about these matters, particularly in the United States. Someone asks you: Well, and what is your opinion of the way the Turks slaughtered the Armenians? You answer with a fatigued smile and an appropriate hint that shows that you know the facts, that it was of course another unspeakable horror. You are right. But you are conspiring with appearances. The conversation is a fake. Because chatting in Philadelphia over coffee, in the August of 1993, you cannot seriously suppose that, except for a very few ancient Armenians in the neighborhood, or others somehow genuinely touched by a finger of memory, that slaughter has a presence *there and then*. What is missing is collective outrage, collective suffering, collective judgment, collective revenge. It is a mystery, of course, but you cannot miss its absence: Its presence is the nerve of history. It is palpable in Bosnia on every side. You feel it though you are not a part of it. Or rather, the embarrassment of Bosnia is that we feel enough of it, peripherally, to want to share it at a safe distance—all of us, collectively, through the entire Western world at least—and we cannot. We are embarrassed by the need for outrage in the presence of inaction. We cannot make ourselves feel what we can only feel together. Think of sharing at a distance the early days of *Solidarnosc*. *That* worked for a while: a surrogate identity, an infatuation with a short-lived alien ethos. I *was* there, though I was safe at home.

We can always act, of course. A civilized world cannot afford to depend entirely on the fickleness of such a sense of presence. But it also cannot act effectively without it.

The Holocaust has had its long inning. It is still an *unanime*, a persisting membership. There are Auschwitz survivors after all, and they have their families, their comrades, their comrades' comrades. Some of the rest of us are still touched by that enormity. We feel in our bones a membrane of connection that no one or two of us could possibly produce at will. Heidegger, I say, must have been aware of the same. He knew that the collectivity that was the Nazi *Volk* was mortally shattered by the defeat of the Third Reich. He was thereupon cast free of his spell: made utterly alone. Under the circumstances, anything *he* might say was already too late to be the continuing voice of that same collective presence. He fell out of his trance when it made no sense to continue to speak as if in the presence he once had shared. I don't deny that you can feel Nazism and antisemitism gathering again: You feel it to be a kind of deathless phoenix. But it needs time to come to life once more as the tacit second nature of any people. I think Heidegger realized full well that he had shaped his own private voice so compliantly that he could no longer—for instance in the *Spiegel* interview—speak in anything but a transparently false way apart from the ventriloquism he practiced on himself. He could no longer command his public voice. He bears witness to that, failing in the prudence of his own silence. But *that* means that *we*, haranguing forever about Heidegger's refusal to acknowledge the error of his ways, his inability to answer the decent questions Marcuse and Jaspers and other so awkwardly and generously fed him, are ourselves too busy with contriving to stop the normal seepage of the Holocaust's first vigor.

I was in Washington, D.C., a little while ago. My Iranian cabbie asked me, with more wit than he knew, whether I had seen the new Holocaust Museum. I had not. (I don't need it. I believe I don't, but I'm not entirely sure.) My driver was on to the mounting killings in occupied Palestine within Israel. I had been pondering how to write the very lines I am writing, and I realized instantly that *he* spoke out of a Muslim presence that *I* could not deny *I* shared. At the same time, I could not deny the contrary grip of the Holocaust. I am all these things therefore: a Somali at the end of life, a cousin of a dead Palestinian boy, an Armenian and an Azeri patriot at once, an Israeli dreading the next holocaust, an American uneasy in an airconditioned vacuum, a Vietnamese immigrant puzzled by my preoccupation. My sense is that I can no longer have the one without the other. My Israeli friends, one dear man in particular, have concocted an argument to show that if one (that is, a "Jew") hesitates to affirm that the Holocaust was and is the sui generis horror of the human race's history, then one is a complete apostate to whatever is genuinely human. I deny it. Israel is certainly one of the seismic centers of the Holocaust's continuing tremor. I admit it collects me in a way I cannot disregard. But it has paled in my lifetime. It is remembered but it pales. It pales in its collective power. And it must. It must make room for the crowded vitality of the West Bank and the Gaza strip that saps the theme of the other; it must make room for the treacheries of South Africa, for the new terrors of the peoples of the old Soviet Union, for the ominous energy of the Khmer Rouge. (I can tell you that I had put these lines down before the signing of the peace accords between the Israelis and the PLO.)

You cannot escape the sense of collective presence. It is the sine qua non of human life. Language and custom in the shape of latent power: neither good nor evil, nothing but the permanent possibility of each. It is as available to the Nazi as it is to the Jew and the Gypsy—and the black and the brown. You dare not trust it for an acceptable life, but you cannot live without it. It is an artifact that no one quite invents; but in inventing what we do, we find we have reinvented our own collective life—*and* ourselves. Heidegger was peculiarly sensitive to the calling of his ethos, and he was gifted the way a shaman is—unstable, pliant, shameless, willing to be used, skilled at using himself in the same way, and then perhaps frightened by the sudden knowledge that, in Germany's inevitable defeat, he could never scramble back to claim a saving allegiance. Except by literally doctoring his own words. A kind of paper prosthesis, you might say. In defeat, Heidegger lost the power to rejoin the collectivities the Nazis had thought to murder. And *we* ignore them.

His trivial silence, therefore, has nothing to do with the grandeur of history's presence, which, ironically, he understood better than his honorable self-blinded critics. He was a brilliant fool and an ensorcelled knave, but *we* risk losing the meaning of history in kicking his dead ass.

There's the business of his philosophy, to be sure. It's hard to admit his conceptual powers: We think *we* may be tainted if we admit them. But his gifts are there, his conceptual discoveries cannot be denied. We *are* tainted, but we *were* tainted before Heidegger, as well as through Heidegger, and even after Heidegger. That's why the punctuated judgments of so many solemn scholars working after the fact in their book-lined studies confuse the issue. They pretend there is a true sensibility we can draw on to confirm (in the isolation of pure reason, you see) the certainty of Heidegger's violation. *But there are no such norms*! None that belong to the collectivities of our living world. Look around you.

It's odd that John Damjanjuk should have been acquitted in Israel, just now, of being "Ivan the Terrible." Imagine that! It speaks well for Holocaust sensibility. It may survive a little longer for it. But Heidegger and Damjanjuk are linked by holy history. Those who share its living presence have resisted false witnesses—in Israel. Those who still labor at keeping the memory of Heidegger's banality alive (deliberately confusing it with the Holocaust) risk the pornographer's trade. Heidegger and Damjanjuk are minor players after all. I don't know whether Damjanjuk was at Sobibor. He was not at Treblinka. I don't know whether Heidegger's archival papers will show that he was racked with guilt. It's a question of a horrid pathology in either case. I am thinking of our own deformed understanding. We have abandoned our collective history and we would revive it by some sort of bookish hocus-pocus. It won't work.

We were not Nazis, I admit. But we ignore the continuities that bind us to the Nazis. They are alive in us, after all. Politics is an art form by which humans conspire to be shaped collectively. They cannot shape themselves, except by opening themselves to influence. You deaden the possibility, wasting your time with your accountant's calculus. Heidegger cheated us, you say. Meanwhile *you* fail to sense the Holocaust's continuation in another guise, and you insist it's not true. That's why the guardians of the Holocaust cannot be trusted. *Summum malum*, they say, favored the world but once—*in us*: "How dare you compare the Bosnian episode to that?" (Or, the useful chaos of the West Bank, for that matter?)

The importance of defining Heidegger's guilt depends on the supposed singularity of the Holocaust. Well, of course, if you believe *that*, then you are right. But you cannot then grasp the mechanisms of history. You compartmentalize events in a lawyer's way. You disallow the shaping of that temperament that might still diminish the Holocaust's continuance. I say you must allow the Holocaust to dissolve. You must, to preserve its force. You must enter into the memory of every such evil. You must be shameless in your proxy griefs. You must teach yourself to belong to each. You must. . . . that is, we must. There's nothing natural about it. It's a choice we cannot make by choice. That's what the Heidegger industry obscures— on all sides. Give it up. Only the living suffer and die. The fuse of history and outrage is there. The other is worse than necrophilia.

I don't say these scourges will never end. But I doubt it. They have their charm: the cleansing of the world, for instance. The Nazis had a genius for it. There's the trick. It's not remembering that counts: it's remembering in order to resist all those futures that will be continuous with that past. The Heidegger business is a self-deception. It eats up the collective testimony that still dreams of an end to holocausts. The point of remembering is to bring the Holocaust to an end. Can that be done? What has the condemnation of Heidegger to do with that? It confuses a misguided single life with our own sly blindness. We cannot see the Holocaust's continuation in other forms.

I am not one of those who believe in rational systems of morality. I don't deny the game. But I have no confidence in single cases or universal rules of justice. The practice may be needed, for all I know, I don't deny it. But it never awakens the terrible powers of the Nazis or the terrible powers of the victims of the Holocaust—*in us*. It cannot. It would betray itself if it did. Nevertheless, the others are also human powers—horrific powers. We have no idea how to harness them.

We lack the wit to redirect such energies. We remember them and then stupify the gift, retelling such stories as Martin Heidegger's and (even more trivially) Paul de Man's. They are tales of the dead, I think, utterly detached from genuine mourning. Perhaps we need these sacrificial goats. We're not prepared to face the raw forces of our moral world.

Heidegger, after all, is the caricature of our own deception. He was that dangerous creature, a gifted man of the academy, who sensed he could give direction to the spiritual forces of his own world. Hitler was intellectually more marginal. Heidegger sensed the fact. He even wondered in his modest way whether German destiny would finally oblige *him* to serve as the *Führer* of all the *Führers*. He was apparently prepared to submit to whatever a *volkisch* duty might there require. Brave man! But Hitler grasped the forces Heidegger never fathomed. They swept him away even at the moment of his Rector's Address at Freiburg (May 1933). The slaughter of the Röhm faction must have frightened him. He became more prudent but he never gave up the vision that his own philosophy—an academic toy, after all—might still control the currents of collective life. He never grasped the point of the ventriloquism he practiced in his shallow way. The puppet-master must be the supreme puppet, after all. Hitler had the gift for it, make no mistake. Marx had his Lenin; Lukács was overwhelmed by Stalin. We, on the other hand, caviling at Heidegger's betrayal, ignore at our peril the question of how our own detached verdicts are linked to the same forces that produced Heidegger as a minor distraction. They are alive, you see. They are in the world's veins, in our veins.

You sense the pulse in Bosnia. The Western world watches, transfixed in inaction. It cannot fathom the ancient furies that must exhaust themselves. It dares not act. Well, it will not act. It cannot manage such a primal storm. Its temperature is too cool for that, too low for intervention. It can only bleat. It would have had to act (if it could) out of a code of decency like the one we bring to bear against Heidegger. It's a question of political entropy. We miss the lesson, narrowing our sights, condemning Heidegger each time more brilliantly and more decisively than before. Meanwhile, elevating the Holocaust to impossible heights, we ignore the holocaust itself. It was (is) a volcanic phenomenon, largely subterranean, internal to our own chthonic energies. It would (will) never have submitted (submit) to executive reason at the point of maximal eruption. That's what we ignore, turning to label Heidegger's tepid evil.

I recall some pertinent irrelevancies here (affording a little relief from my own insistence). I personally dislike great patriotic parades, the massing of people for political and ethnic functions. I shall never be a leader of men. I sense too quickly the incipient violence in the anonymous crowd. I am afraid of crowds; and I remember the thirties too well though I was only a boy. I count the political crowd a force of nature, a force of second nature. I know it cannot be eliminated from the human condition. But I also have no illusions about its ever being rationally harnessed. It is not a fiction, and it is never negligible.

Heidegger seems to have believed its energies could be harnessed. That was his *hubris*. In a similar sense, those who are content to judge him *still* (however rightly), those who still insist he violated their own safe codes, are, like Heidegger, the somnambulists of our age. I count myself, rather, a citizen of the world. What I mean, of course, is that, devoting myself to what I call my work, I have deliberately detached myself in a risky way from local roots. It's a widespread practice in the West, of course, utterly impossible to perfect because its perfection would undermine the very viability of social existence.

Human life is collective at its core. It's an artifact that, as second nature, functions as if it were our first. It is language and custom in a political guise. It is the brute source of holocausts and the memory of their victims—*and* the exercise of those reflective powers by which we imagine we can break free of those original energies. We cannot—in the aggregate.

We share with Heidegger the presumption of autonomy. He saw what we do not: how that judgment serves collective life, how it grows historically, loses its originating intuition, acts and then discovers by surprise the cunning of how it had been tethered all along. He dared to dream he could control its source—for an interval at least. We, on the other hand, are infinitely less alert, less active, tracking Heidegger's presumption in our cerebral tunnel, neglecting its deviousness in ourselves.

I suppose I am an "intellectual," the hothouse product of something like the great musical intelligence of the Western world. It's a bit like being surprised at Bartok's instant recovery of the folk melodies of his own people, while puzzling over the uncertain liberties of the twelve-tone scale. What I mean is, you cannot help but sing with the first, whether or not you compose with the second. You make no music if you detach yourself from the sources of the first.

I remember very distinctly, as a young university teacher living in a genteel corner of Brooklyn, sitting on the steps of my house, minding my first-born in the afternoon sun, being engaged in a short conversation with two kindly spinster ladies, next-door neighbors who shared a sense of family from time to time, saying to them that I had no home at all, nothing but a transient dormitory for a life that needed no more for its own purpose. They had hardly lived anywhere but the one-block street we shared, except of course for their extensive travels abroad, something one could imagine out of a Henry James novel. They exaggerated a kind of shock at hearing my admission, but in a way they warned me of my mistake. I now understand what they meant to say.

But it's not altogether a mistake. It's a division of labor. I *am* as detached from the local and the collective as anyone could possibly be. (So was Heidegger, really.) But I now respect the significance of that loss of instinct. (Heidegger did so more promptly.) It *is* now largely lost in the political sense but not (I think) in the cultural. I have never been tempted by Heidegger's presumption, scribbling at all hours alternative academic recipes for a new generation of aspirants intended to serve the destiny of a mystic *Volk*. But Heidegger *did* indeed grasp, in Freiburg, the presence of a living cord I could not even dream of in lower Brooklyn. My own work has demanded a slower recovery of that meaning. I find myself therefore in Heidegger's debt. Better: *His* grave mistake helps to correct the deeper mistake of academics (like myself) who have no bearings at all, no sense of how to join their (our) percipient powers to the collective torrent we don't even hear. And yet we would be judges.

Bosnia and the rest afford the same lesson, but less eccentrically. You will think it unfair that the partition of the region should have had to wait for the exhaustion of the resisting Muslims and the impotence of the rest of Europe, and you would be right. But such resolutions always depend on such exhaustion. (We are witnessing the beginning of the same in the Middle East.) The collective loyalties involved can only decay. They cannot be rationally managed at their white heat. They cannot support any semblance of reasonable justice. History will always correct their corrections in some equally terrible future. There is no other way. We are forever the witnesses of a Greek tragedy. (I don't mean this in a bookish way.) It is a blind extravagance on our part to be repelled by Heidegger, if we also reject his own remarkable discovery. Because it is a clue of sorts. It's the reason, I say, you have to let the Holocaust go. There are always too many such flowers for the picking. It's a monstrous sincerity that claims a divinely appointed suffering for the Jews. At the close of our millennium, we are members of one another or we are nothing.

I must tell you a joke. (Another stab at relief.) It's not mine of course. It's probably not anyone's, but I heard it first from a friend who is known for an exceptional wine cellar of such jokes. I hope I won't ruin it. Have patience. It seems a certain rabbi was unusually pious, forever marvelling at how he was less than nothing in the sight of God. Every day, he was moved to rediscover that truth as if for the first time. And his assistant, somewhat more worldly, saw enough of its validity to chant the same lesson in a tactful refrain. A black man, the Sabbath Goy of the synagogue, who was genuinely moved by the rabbi's purity, uncontrollably blurted out on one occasion: "I am nothing, nothing at all, less than nothing." Whereupon the rabbi's assistant exclaimed: "Huh, look who thinks he's nothing!" The custodians of the Holocaust are in the same boat. You must see the dark comedy of the thing.

There's a great puzzle in political history that we may never solve, namely, when and how to intervene effectively to avert a holocaust, even a small one, to bring the entire syndrome to an end. It cannot be done from within any ethnic loyalty and it cannot be done by intellectuals detached from such loyalties. That's what joins the stories of Damjanjuk and Heidegger. Because the acquittal of Damjanjuk was achieved in the middle of a collective space in which one might have expected an academic judge to yield to the imagined insistence of collective revenge. Instead, we have been offered a heroic correction—a small one but a sign of a larger possibility. It was a verdict arrived at by applying a code of decent conduct prepared in a cool interval within the collective intensities of the same people that had bound their fate to the Holocaust forever. If the Old and New Testaments have any meaning at all, then here is a verse from the last unfinished book.

The lesson is this. The intellectuals are the scribes (certainly not the only ones) who, from time to time, history permits to rewrite the collective vision of their own people. They act in a symbiotic way: serving energies they cannot invent, composing utopias their comrades may inexplicably fuse (some day) with the fire of their own lives. Heidegger was on to that possibility. Who knows what blinded his own judgment and instinct? But his academic critics miss the implied instruction of his life: They divide political judgment and political instinct; they have no grasp at all of collective life. John Damjanjuk, I venture to say, is a herald of sorts. (I have no shame in milking the image, you see.)

I'll add one last intemperate thought. The Holocaust is nothing but another such mistakenly detached clue. What it signifies is that bearing witness to the great episodes of human suffering—the despairing lives of whole peoples, whether by starvation or murder—is the sole occasion on which to fuse our codes of justice (such as they are) with the newest forms of our collective energies. We are, everywhere, the witnesses of *summum malum*, but we are also, *everywhere*, its victims. To ignore the lesson is the obverse side of Heidegger's stupidity, the glibness of insisting that, here and now, no one has suffered or will ever suffer as "we" have. Judging these matters—Heidegger's case or Damjanjuk's—is readying ourselves for those intervals of calm when the holocausts of any particular day are spent; when it becomes possible again to fuse the perceived forms of justice (drawn from various ancestral sources) with the energies of incipient collectivities that out-flank the past's. I see no other way to escape the movable holiday of the Holocaust, though I have no reason to believe we ever shall.

12

Heidegger at the Nuremberg Trials: The "Letter on Humanism" Revisited

HANS SEIGFRIED

After World War II, there were altogether thirteen Nuremberg Trials. They were conducted against leaders of the Third Reich, and they lasted from November 20, 1945, to April 14, 1949. The trial of major figures such as Hermann Göring was held before the International Military Tribunal, made up of representatives of the four Allied Nations.

On August 8, 1945, the Allies signed the London Agreement, which governed the conduct of the Nuremberg Trials. Nineteen other nations also subscribed to it. In Article 6 of its Charter, the following acts were listed as crimes "coming within the jurisdiction of the Tribunal for which there shall be *individual* responsibility": crimes against peace, war crimes, and crimes against humanity. Outside the courtroom, none of the crimes listed got more attention than the crimes against humanity, either then or later.[1] The Charter defines them as "murder, extermination, enslavement, deportation, and other inhuman acts committed against any civilian population, before or during the war, or persecutions on political, racial or religious grounds in execution of or in connection with any crime within the jurisdiction of the Tribunal, whether or not in violation of the domestic law of the country where perpetrated."[2] With this definition the Charter clearly established an inroad into the received understanding of absolute state sovereignty and exclusive domestic jurisdiction. The principles on which the Tribunal acted were subsequently endorsed by the General Assembly of the United Nations on December 11, 1946,[3] although they were already discussed earlier that year during the drafting sessions of the Charter of the United Nations in San

Francisco and considered as inherent in the Charter.[4]

On October 6, 1945, indictments were handed down against Göring and others by the prosecutors. The First Nuremberg Trial (The Trial of the Major War Criminals) began on November 20, 1945, and its sentences were announced on October 6, 1946. Twelve among the defendants were condemned to death. They were executed on October 16, 1946, except for Göring who escaped hanging by committing suicide on October 15.

Earlier, on June 26, 1945, the United Nations was formed in a concerted effort "to save succeeding generations from the scourge of war, which twice in our lifetime has brought untold sorrow to mankind, and to reaffirm faith in fundamental human rights, in the dignity and worth of the human person, in the equal right of men and women and of nations large and small."[5] In light of the worldwide publicity, such as it was, surrounding the formation of the United Nations and the Nuremberg Trials, it is difficult to imagine that the issues on the table at the Nuremberg Trials, chief among them "crimes against humanity" and "individual responsibility," were not on everybody's mind, especially on the mind of philosophers. In a grand style, Sartre was the first to speak his mind on the matter in "Existentialism Is a Humanism." The lecture was fittingly remembered as "the cultural event of 1945."[6] It was delivered only two weeks after the indictments were handed down and a month before the First Nuremberg Trial began.

While reports about the monstrosity of "inhuman acts" committed during the war spread despair, and information about the overwhelming power of regimes and the pervasiveness of collaboration threatened to paralyze a whole generation, Sartre defended humanism and optimism about our condition. He rejected philosophy as mere contemplation, advocated action, and insisted on complete individual responsibility for our immediate past and immediate future. He allowed no excuses, not even in the cases of a military leader acting under higher command and Abraham acting under the command of God.[7]

When stating "the first principle" of his account of the human condition, namely, that "man is nothing else but that which he makes of himself," Sartre referred to Heidegger's analysis of facticity.[8] Shortly after his lecture, and about two weeks before the beginning of the First Nuremberg Trial, Sartre invited Heidegger to privately discuss with him the matter in Baden-Baden, in preparation for a public debate. When Heidegger received the invitation in the beginning of October, he was embroiled in "denazification" hearings in connection with his application for reinstallment at the University of Freiburg. He was called on to explain his actions in support of the regime in which terror was the rule and "inhuman acts" were considered morally praiseworthy.[9] These hearings and negotiations with the University of Freiburg and the French Military Government continued until

1949. Today, there can be little doubt that they would have been much briefer and more devastating for Heidegger had the extent of his collaboration, for instance, in "Operation Sternheim," been known then.[10] For reasons unknown to me, the meeting between Sartre and Heidegger did not take place. Others, among them Max-Pol Fouchet, the editor of *Revue Fontaine*, approached Heidegger around that time for permission to translate some of his works into French, or better yet, for an essay on the current state of affairs, or on the philosophical discussions in France.[11]

For the time being, Heidegger declined to write such an essay, but must have given his permission for the translation of his paper on "Plato's Doctrine of Truth." The translation was being prepared by Josef Revan while the philosophical discussion in France was focused on the issues being raised in the Nuremberg Trials. As pointed out earlier, it took the International Military Tribunal about a year to arrive at its conclusions.[12] The death sentences of the First Nuremberg Trial were carried out on October 16, 1946. Only a few weeks after the hangings took place, on his front lawn, so to speak, and the Second Nuremberg Trial (The Doctors' Trial) had begun on October 26, Heidegger received Jean Beaufret's letter of November 10, pressing him for more concrete answers to questions that arose during work on the translation of his contribution to the French debate. Heidegger's response was mailed in early December. In it Heidegger finally dealt with the current state of affairs and directly addressed the issues, or so it seemed, that preoccupied the philosophical discussions in France, namely, the Nuremberg issues of crimes against humanity and individual responsibility.

The letter to Beaufret was written while Heidegger was awaiting final judgment in his own case. In its preliminary ruling, on October 5, the day before the sentencing in Nuremberg, the French Military Government barred Heidegger from teaching and all other activities at the University of Freiburg. The final decision, on December 28, 1946, was basically the same. During the following months Heidegger was revising the German text of his letter to Beaufret for publication in Switzerland. In the middle of it, on March 11, 1947, when he was officially informed about the decision of the French Military Government, Heidegger learned also that his income from the university would be cut completely by the end of the year. The revised version of the letter was finally published, six months after the original was mailed to Beaufret, as the "Letter on Humanism," together with "Plato's Doctrine of Truth."

The connection between the two texts needs some clarification, as does the relationship between "Plato's Doctrine of Truth" and Sartre's "Existentialism Is a Humanism." On the face of it, it seems to be odd that a paper on Plato's doctrine of truth should have anything to do with humanism, that is, with the understanding of the conduct of human affairs and individual responsibility. It is obvious, however, that in 1945 Heidegger wanted it to be his contribution to the French debate of the current state of affairs and the issues on the table at the Nuremberg Trial. And the fact that in 1947 he published his letter to Beaufret together with this paper indicates that he saw in the "Letter on Humanism" a mere footnote, or appendix, to this paper.

Aside from all such considerations, the paper on Plato's doctrine of truth has a most intriguing history.[13] It seems that an early version of it, based on Heidegger's lecture course "On the Essence of Truth" in the winter semester of 1930/31, was first read to the monks in the Abbey of Beuron, in the fall of 1931. The version we know, however, was written in 1940 and first published in 1942, against the fierce protest of Rosenberg's *Hauptamt Wissenschaft* and Goebbels's *Reichsministerium für Volksaufklärung und Propaganda*. Heidegger's remarks about humanism were considered to be irreconcilable with the officially endorsed "political humanism" of Wilhelm Brachmann. The paper was scheduled to appear in Ernesto Grassi's *Jahrbuch für geistige Überlieferung*, but the two offices tried everything to prevent its inclusion in the volume, or at least have Heidegger's remarks on humanism deleted from the paper. In the end, Grassi got permission to publish the paper in full, but only after Mussolini had intervened through his ambassador with Goebbels himself, and with strict orders from the *Reichsministerium* that Heidegger's paper must not be mentioned in reviews of the volume.

It is imperative that we briefly review the sketchy remarks on humanism at the end of the paper, little more than one of nineteen pages in the English translation, in order to understand both the fierce protest of the Nazi government against them and the fact that in 1945 Heidegger wanted the French to see in them an important contribution to the debate of the philosophical issues raised at the Nuremberg Trials.[14]

Among Heidegger experts it is commonly understood that Heidegger's central claim in this paper is as follows: In Plato's allegory of the cave we can see traces of a change in the understanding of truth. What before was experienced as the endless interactive process of the disclosure of the things in experience has become the mere mirroring of a distant but eternally fixed realm of things that we can only see with the eye of the mind. As mere mirroring, then, the disclosure of things in experience is, strictly speaking, a mere function of seeing, perceiving, and expressing what we see with the eye of the mind in propositions. As such a function, truth then remains rigorously controlled and firmly contained by what is perceived with the eye of the mind as the unchanging and eternally prefixed order of things. Truth is the agreement of our propositions with that order.

But, it seems to me, this is only part of the story told in the paper, and the less important one at that. After all, for Plato the allegory of the cave was a mere illustration for *paideía*, that is, for teaching what it means to be human and what position to take in the midst of things. What Heidegger was primarily concerned about, just as was Plato, was the impact of the understanding of truth on our struggle with and anguish about being human and finding a foothold in the flux of experience. In other words, the remarks on the change of truth were a mere setup for the discussion of the understanding of what it means to be human.

It is the anguish about being human and establishing a place in the midst of things that has kept alive our whole metaphysical tradition down to the present. What Heidegger tried to demonstrate, however, is that we still do not fully comprehend the impact of what happened early on in our tradition with the radical transformation of truth that can be traced to the Platonic theory of forms. In this theory the terms for answering all questions about what it means to be human have in principle been permanently fixed, and what is worse, they have been fixed in such a way that they cannot be challenged by experience. What we can do, what ends we must pursue, and what lives we must live have all been definitively inscribed into the grand design of things which, with proper training, we must learn to see with the eye of the mind and, with strict discipline, we must strive to imitate in life. Over the centuries, the promotion of such mirroring and mimicking of what we see with the eye of the mind has taken on many forms, such as the construction of a moral outlook and the organization of various programs for the salvation of immortal souls, the advancement of reason, the cultivation of manners, the development of the spirit of community, the maintenance of physical health and fitness, and so forth. And it was understood all along that what is perceived with the eye of the mind is just what it is. The true order of things, it was believed, did not depend on us; we had no say and no hand in the shaping of it. We could secure our place within such a true order of things only if we accurately mirrored it in our minds and faithfully mimicked it in our actions.

Clearly, then, with the Platonic theory of forms our anguish about what it means to be human and our efforts to secure our position within the scheme of things have been forced into a system that was closed, in principle. If for a moment we want to use the word "humanism" for the open struggle with our human condition, we could say that with Plato the struggle had ground to a halt, and humanism was perverted into an "ism" and ideology that has not been sufficiently challenged since then. For even today, while rolling into the "most modern" stage of world history, we still believe that reality has been basically fixed long ago and has consequently remained unchanged. We only need to behold this reality with the eye of the mind, tailor our behavior to it, and universal harmony must result of itself in accordance with the eternal laws of the preordained order of things. With the growing accuracy of the representation of reality and the spectacular efficiency of the new programs for the monitoring of human behavior and action, the received forms of humanism take on the character of extreme, unconditional, and totalitarian "positions." With nearly exhaustive information about reality at their disposal and powerful administrations at their command, it is tempting to believe that our leaders alone are in the position to determine what reality is and what we must accept as its law. His notorious plea for cooperation with the Nazi regime in 1933 shows that Heidegger himself could not resist this temptation and became a true believer for an unknown length of time.[15]

Heidegger's assessment of the received notion of humanism, then, turns out to be utterly devastating: All traditional forms of humanism are variations of the Platonic original and as such intrinsically totalitarian. Within a fixed scheme and preordained order of things we ultimately all end up puppets, no matter how we turn it, as Plato himself came to realize.[16] And so this realization must strike us and lead us to see that more is needed for understanding what it means to be human than finding out how things are in order to take our place among them. We must finally get around to subject the scheme of things itself to rigorous inquiry and learn to question what in Heidegger's technical language is called Being itself—that which determines what things are and on the basis of which we recognize and understand them, namely, the scheme of things.[17]

There is no need to dismiss Heidegger's concluding remarks in "Plato's Doctrine of Truth" as oracular. With his account of the Being of things as "contextual assignment" in his environmental analysis and with his searching existential-temporal interpretation of its meaning, Heidegger had already demonstrated that we unavoidably have a much greater hand in the scheme of things and its continuous revision than the traditional idea of a prefixed scheme and ready-made order of things allows for.[18] Naturally, human responsibility takes on a radically new meaning when we come to realize that we all unavoidably have an interest, a say, and a hand in this ongoing process in which it is determined how things are and how they are disclosed to us for the time being. The truth of propositions can no longer be understood as mere agreement with the way things are apart from this process. The basic acts of the received sense of being human, namely, the mirroring and mimicking of a preordained order of things that is removed from this process, lose all meaning.

It seems to be obvious by now why, in 1945, Heidegger could see in his paper on Plato's doctrine of truth a contribution to the French debate on humanism and human agency, inaugurated with Sartre's lecture, in the face of the Nuremberg Trial, although it remains to be seen where Heidegger could agree and where he would have to disagree with Sartre. But, perhaps, it has not yet become fully clear why, in 1942, high ranking officials of the

Nazi regime got nervous about Heidegger's remarks on humanism.

It seems that Heidegger's remarks did not fully agree with the official position of the regime. In its decision against "contemporary humanism," that is, the revival of Renaissance humanism promoted by Ernesto Grassi and others, Rosenberg's *Hauptamt Wissenschaft* had endorsed the "political humanism" of Wilhelm Brachmann. The revival of Renaissance humanism could only be seen as a preparation for what "political humanism" was supposed to do, namely, to re-establish and guard the heritage of ancient Greece as the great example of the blood-based achievement of Indo-Germanic peoples, ultimately in order to keep alive their sense of mission (*Schicksalsgläubigkeit*), the belief in their master-role.[19] Obviously, Heidegger's whole paper, not just the concluding remarks on humanism, somehow deviated from this officially endorsed objective. In "political humanism" the ancient Greeks were admired for what was regarded as a prerequisite for that Indo-Germanic belief, namely, their superior sense for self-determination and autonomy. In his paper on the Platonic doctrine of truth, however, Heidegger argued that in the Platonic setup self-determination turned into self-surrender, surrender to the pre-established order of things, best described with a phrase from one of his early theological writings as "self-sacrifice in the bright light of truth" (*Entselbstung im Lichtglanz der Wahrheit*).[20] Recognizing the Platonic perversion in its many variations down to the present—including Christian humanism, Renaissance humanism, "contemporary humanism," and the "political humanism" of the Nazi regime—could be the first step in the recovery of genuine self-determination on which human decency, dignity, and greatness depend.

It must have been difficult, indeed, for the Nazi bureaucrats to demonstrate conclusively that with his critique of Plato's doctrine of truth Heidegger had corrupted the spirit of the Nazi regime's official position on humanism or completely abandoned it. Of course, in hindsight we could say that Heidegger's critique of self-surrender in the name of truth could and should have been used as a basis for criticizing the concrete operations by which the regime brutally exterminated many millions of people who did not agree with it and who did not surrender to, or conform with, its truths. The Nazis believed that such truths as the superiority of the Aryans were established by the scientific study of the races. We don't know how much Heidegger knew, in 1942, about the magnitude of the crimes against humanity and inhuman acts committed against totally innocent people in the name of the Nazi regime. The fact remains that Heidegger did not connect his abstract critique of humanism with these concrete crimes and use it as a basis for criticizing them until the fall of 1945, when they were raised at the First Nuremberg Trial and in the French debate inaugurated by Sartre.

When pressed, in the fall of 1945, for a contribution to the French debate on humanism, human agency, and individual responsibility, Heidegger eventually gave his permission for the French translation of his paper on Plato's doctrine of truth, as I have pointed out earlier.[21] Read within the context of the French debate, Heidegger's paper was bound to raise questions such as these: (1) When dealing with the issues on the table at the Nuremberg Trial, can we still meaningfully talk about humanism? (2) Must we not broaden the study of the fundamental scheme of things (ontology) to include the search for directives for the conduct of human affairs—for deciding what is good and what is evil in the conduct of human affairs (ethics) (3) Without recourse to a fixed scheme and ready-made order of things, is it at all possible to avoid the bankruptcy of "anything goes"?

As a matter of fact, such questions did arise during work on the translation and were put to Heidegger in Beaufret's letter of November 10, 1946.[22] As we have seen, much had happened since the fall of 1945, both at the trials in Nuremberg and, in Heidegger's own case, at the University of Freiburg. The human condition, so it must have seemed to everyone, was much more complicated and vulnerable than anyone had been prepared to admit. Clearly, in the context of the French debate in the fall of 1946, the concluding remarks in the paper on Plato's doctrine of truth about the need for questioning the scheme of things must have appeared to be much too abstract, completely speculative, and utterly inadequate for dealing with the human condition. It seems to me that with his decision to address these questions in his response to Beaufret's letter, Heidegger, too, agreed that much more was needed.

Heidegger began his response by rejecting the idea of philosophical thinking as mere contemplation and theoretical analysis, just as did Sartre at the beginning of his lecture "Existentialism Is a Humanism." The relationship between thinking and human agency has turned out to be much more intimate and intricate than we were led to believe by the ocular philosophies of Plato, Aristotle, and their successors. In his earlier analysis of everyday existence, Heidegger had already extensively argued that we must radically revise our received notions of thinking and acting and come to see theory and practice as two forms of taking care of human affairs.[23] We could afford the aristocratic luxury of thinking of ourselves as *mere* spectators, as could Plato and Aristotle, only on the condition that all the so-called practical matters concerning us had already been taken care of, or were being taken care of for us by others, and that in a fit of forgetfulness we projected this care-free, exceptional condition onto the scheme of things. Without the detailed analysis of everyday existence in his earlier works, Heidegger's introductory remarks on thinking as realizing and performing would have remained as abstract and frustrating as the remarks on the need for questioning the scheme of things. The scheme of things—in Heidegger's technical language, the Being of things—determines what everything is in the midst of things. Consequently, what he seemed to be suggesting was that we should see thinking as the interactive and responsive realization, or performance, of this fundamental determination, rather than as the mere representation of some fixed assignments that hover somewhere above us and that we merely execute and reproduce in our actions, or have others do for us.

On the basis of this revised understanding of human agency, in light of his earlier analysis of everyday existence, Heidegger set out to discuss the issues raised by the three questions listed above. He devoted most space to the first question (36pp), much less to the second (9pp), and hardly any to the third (2pp), perhaps because the second and third were much harder to deal with than the first.[24]

The first question was: Does it still make sense to talk about humanism? In his lecture on "Existentialism Is a Humanism," Sartre proposed humanism as the remedy against the radical evils of totalitarianism, whereas Heidegger argued in his contribution to the debate that all traditional forms of humanism are intrinsically totalitarian. And yet, it was not obvious at all where they disagreed. Of course, Sartre would have had to reject with Heidegger all traditional forms of humanism if they turned out to be based on a fixed scheme of things. After all, the first principle of Sartrean humanism stated that we are completely responsible for what we are and that we are nothing else but what we individually choose to make of ourselves.

Heidegger's strategy for dealing with the problem was simple. He had to show that (1) the belief in a fixed scheme and ready-made order of things is intrinsically totalitarian, (2) all traditional forms of humanism are based on a variation of this belief, (3) we can have a say and a hand in the scheme of things and its continuous revision, and (4) the continuous revision of the scheme of things is a complex, interactive, and responsive process in which we play the role of a guardian, rather than that of a master. For the purposes of my paper, there is no need to rehearse all these moves. It is enough to point out that Heidegger agreed that it would be meaningful to use the word "humanism" for the basic belief that man can have a hand in the scheme of things and that this rebellious belief could be an effective antidote against totalitarian thinking. "Self-sacrifice in the bright light of truth" would lose its dehumanizing effect if we could remember that we can have, and insist that as a matter of course we actually do have, a hand in the scheme of things.

Of course, Heidegger was not claiming that the process in which things get placed within a scheme, such that they can appear and be apprehended as this or that—or if you prefer the light-metaphor, the process of illumination and disclosure—was dependent on the fact that we are simply around, but on the condition that we remain actively involved in it.[25] But Heidegger insisted, against Sartre, that it does not entirely, and perhaps not even decisively, depend on us as individuals and that we are, consequently, not completely responsible for it. After all, something like a new scheme of things could emerge, but not be entirely invented in what he had described as "ecstatic projection," if for no other reason than the fact that the projection must operate within the limitations imposed on it by previous assignments.[26] This is especially true if such assignments are accepted with religious fervor and closed off from reconsideration and renegotiation, no matter what mischief and harm they may have caused—in an attitude best described by the "Fiat iustitia et pereat mundus" of Ferdinand I.

The difficulties raised with the second question were much more serious. It seemed to be downright cynical and cruel to propose radical self-determination as an antidote against totalitarianism without at the same time giving precise directives and establishing binding rules for living a decent human life. By the fall of 1946, those who had escaped the horror had their confidence in everything that made life worth living shaken by the daily news from Nuremberg, with its dreadful disclosures of the massive crimes against humanity committed by civilized people. And those who had survived the terror were desperately trying to find a reason for still believing in human decency. In this condition it seemed to be much more sensible to "safeguard and secure the existing bonds even if they hold human beings together ever so tenuously and merely for the present," than to insist on questioning the scheme of things.[27]

Heidegger eagerly agreed that these were genuine difficulties and tried to address them, after explaining why what he was going to do was very preliminary and must not be mistaken as an attempt to construct an ethical theory with sets of rules for action on the basis of some readily available ontology. In order words, he admitted that he was unable to say much, if anything, about the question in this form: Must the new definition of humanism in terms of man's involvement in the scheme of things remain "mere theory" and pure speculation, or can we derive from it directions for "practical behavior [*das tätige Leben*]"?[28] He tried to show, instead, how his reformed thinking—thinking as placing things within a scheme, thinking as transaction—could help us to better understand the origin and nature of good and evil, and what thinking can do about them. It is quite impossible, however, to recognize this strategy for dealing with the second question in the standard English translation. Heidegger's intriguing and perhaps provocative discussion of good and evil has become a cryptic philosophy of healing with no traces of a struggle with the issues raised at the Nuremberg Trials.

Clearly, Heidegger thought that not much inquiry was needed for seeing that we do not simply invent the scheme of things such that we are totally responsible for it. Put metaphorically, we do not fabricate "the house of

Being" as spiders produce their webs. But, if by questioning the scheme of things we could see where we nonetheless have a hand in it, then, perhaps, we could also see where good and evil arise and get an improved sense for the good and evil of human agency.

The translators, however, made Heidegger's plain claim that his reformed thinking could help us to get to the root of good and evil utterly unintelligible. Heidegger introduced his discussion of *das Heile* and *das Böse,* or *das Unheil,* that is, of good and evil, with the following remarks:

> Gleichwohl schafft das Denken nie das Haus des Seins. Das Denken geleitet die geschichtliche Existenz, das heißt die humanitas des homo humanus, in den Bereich des Aufgangs des Heilen [the origin of good].
>
> Mit dem Heilen [with the good] zumal erscheint in der Lichtung des Seins das Böse. Dessen Wesen besteht nicht in der bloßen Schlechtigkeit des menschlichen Handelns . . . .[29]

The translators did not know the difference between *das Heile* and *das Heilen,* between "good" and "healing." Clearly, they were puzzled, but not puzzled enough to reach for their German dictionary and grammar. They obviously knew that the genitive form of *das Heilen* must end with an "s" and believed that it got lost at the end of the first sentence.

They consequently translated the word as "healing" and even inserted their supposed correction of the original German into their translation:

> And yet thinking never creates the house of Being. Thinking conducts historical eksistence, that is, the *humanitas* of *homo humanus,* into the realm of the upsurgence of the healing [*des Heilens*].
>
> With healing, evil appears all the more in the lighting of Being. The essence of evil does not consist in the mere baseness of human action. . . ."[30]

But there was no need for such a correction. *Des Heilen* is the perfectly correct genitive form of *das Heile.* As a result of this corruption, much of what follows has become utter nonsense—nonsense upon stilts, as Bentham would say—such as the remark about the appearance of evil with healing in the next sentence.[31] Obviously, the fake profundity of Heidegger's remarks in translation had its own attraction, for it generated quite a bit of equally "profound" work on Heidegger's philosophy of healing.

How, then, could questioning the scheme of things help us to get a better sense for good and evil? To begin with, Heidegger thinks, it seems to be obvious that evil is not simply the viciousness of human action but the hatred (malevolence) of intolerance, just as good is the kindness (benevolence) of tolerance. Both hatred and kindness, however, can ultimately arise only in the struggle over the scheme of things, that is, the placing of things within a scheme. In kindness we acknowledge, or affirm, what is placed within the scheme, and in hatred we reject, or negate, what threatens (to negate) things placed within the scheme. But both what we are kind to and what we hate can be experienced only within this involved struggle over the assignment of things. Both kindness and hatred are response-forms within this endless struggle. Basically, it is the ever emerging scheme of things that allows for the good (*das Heile*) to arise through our kindness, and the evil (*das Unheil*) through our hatred.[32] We are responsible, then, for good and evil to the extent to which we are involved in this ongoing struggle that determines what things are.

But what are the gains from this insight, such as it is, for dealing with the issues raised at the Nuremberg Trials and for the desperate search for directives and rules that would help "to save future generations from the scourge of war . . . and to reaffirm faith in the dignity and worth of the human person,"[33] as demonstrated in the Charter of the United Nations and the preparations for its Universal Declaration of Human Rights? Clearly, good and evil, as described by Heidegger, are not fixed standards hovering somewhere above us that could provide any guidance in the endless struggle for a new order of things and for measuring the humanizing and dehumanizing effects of human actions. But it would seem that all such standards and binding rules and laws for the direction of human action, above all for avoiding inhuman acts and crimes against humanity, would have to be functions of the emerging order, that is, temporary results of the interactions, transactions, and negotiations in our human associations that generate the order. Consequently, what is most important is that we find our way into this process and feel at home in it—"in [the bright light of] the truth of Being," where everything gets its place assigned in the provisional scheme of things.[34]

But, just as in the case of his concluding observations about humanism in his critique of Plato's totalitarian doctrine of truth, here, too, we would have to dismiss as oracular Heidegger's remarks on the origins of good and evil, together with his deliberations about the grounds for accepting rules and laws for the conduct of human affairs, had he not already furnished us with some elements of an analytical account of human existence that is required for dealing with these matters.[35] With his remarks on the postwar efforts to establish standards for the conduct of human affairs, Heidegger merely brings out and stresses points already argued in his existential analysis. These points are necessary for addressing the issues on the table at the Nuremberg Trials and for dealing with Sartre's claims about total individual responsibility. For the most part, Heidegger had argued, we operate and act within an inherited and prevailing context of assignments. What we perceive as option and obligation, as decent and indecent, as good and evil, is largely predelineated by this context. And yet, this context itself is not permanently fixed but is grounded in the concrete temporality of human existence, that is, in an anguished holding out of individuals, in endless struggles, for some daring vision of an unalienated mortal life. The extrapolation of the implications of this account was the great project which Heidegger had conceived as genuine empirical philosophy and fundamental ontology.[36] With the Nuremberg revelations about the horrors inflicted on us by Nazism and the hearings at the University of Freiburg about his own personal involvement in "the movement" of Nazism, the time had come for Heidegger to concretely demonstrate to himself and others the *Durchleuchtungskraft* of his phenomenological account of human existence: Can it help us to understand what happened and assist us in our efforts to save future generations from such inhumanity?[37]

Clearly, at the Nuremberg Trials individual responsibility was used as the basis for accomplishing both. And in his response to the first trial, Sartre argued that individuals can be held totally responsible for the immediate past and immediate future because they are absolutely free in their actions, as I have explained above.[38] Only insistence on total responsibility and complete accountability can save future generations from the brutality of our age. But in light of his existential analysis—particularly his analysis of thrownness and historicality—Heidegger could not agree with Sartre's claims about total responsibility and absolute freedom, even with the prospect that his own contribution to the debate would be perceived as a wretched attempt to escape blame. Perhaps he was trying to escape blame, given the fact that his own denazification hearings at the University of Freiburg were going on at that time. This aspect of the matter should not be ignored, but examining it here would distract from the discussion of the main issue on the table at the Nuremberg Trials. As Habermas describes it, Heidegger's attitude to his own past after 1945, that is, his "unwavering practice" of denying, repressing, glossing over, and falsifying, was symptomatic of a whole generation of Germans well into the sixties. Habermas appropriately pleads that we must (1) inform ourselves about what they concealed and (2) critically reexamine "*every* tradition that served to make us blind to the Nazi regime," especially a philosophical one like Heidegger's.[39] Some of my own teachers, both in Austria and Germany, confessed in private shame about their involvement, but with their public silence and evasiveness they instilled in us, who were their students in the fifties and sixties, a pervasive suspicion that made it nearly impossible to learn any lesson from their experiences.[40]

Sartre's belief that his understanding of individual responsibility was supported by Heidegger's phenomenological analysis was a misunderstanding inspired, perhaps, by the Cartesian and neo-Kantian overtones of phenomenology that Heidegger had come to see, by the time of his contribution to the French debate, as an obstacle in his efforts to deal with the vexing metamorphosis of the scheme of things and the dynamic temporality of the truth of Being. In light of Heidegger's existential analysis, one could easily be tempted to agree with Sartre and insist that, without any reservations, we can hold people individually responsible for the crimes listed in Article 6 of the Charter of the Nuremberg Trials, because everything we do is a matter of personal choice. Since in each case the range of possibilities and options to choose from seems to be infinite, in principle no one could have an excuse for taking a particular course of action.

But in his existential analysis Heidegger had already demonstrated that this understanding of the human condition is a pernicious Cartesian abstraction that conceals our mortality and seduces us to take things too simplistically. Ordinary individuals are not like the calculating God of Leibniz, strictly single-minded, with a clear line of discrete possible worlds to choose from. Instead, in a fierce struggle over their heritage with the community in which they live, individuals have to establish in each case what is actually possible for them and what their options are. Unlike the clean-cut decisions of God, their choices are messy, fateful, and part of the destiny of their community, not only because they always have yet to figure out what their options are but also because they cannot exclude the possibility that the decision for a certain course of action might sooner or later lead to disaster and thereby demonstrate the inadequacy of the inherited setup of things for dealing with changing conditions. For Heidegger, whatever option individuals decide on has been "inherited and yet chosen," and whatever course of action they take remains dreadfully tentative. No matter how we turn it, then, the only form of freedom within our power is that of "finite freedom." Consequently, Heidegger could unequivocally agree with Article 6 of the Nuremberg Charter about individual responsibility, but would have to disagree with Sartre's claims about unlimited choice and complete responsibility.[41]

The crimes at issue in the Nuremberg Trials, especially the crimes against humanity, make it difficult for all of us not to dismiss as offensive the insistence on the limits of freedom and individual responsibility in Heidegger's contribution to the philosophical debate inaugurated by Sartre in the fall of 1945, at the beginning of the trials. It looks as if Heidegger was trying to find excuses for those who committed the crimes and pleading for sympathy with all who felt that they had no other option but to go along or who did not have the strength for voicing their protest against the Nazi regime. As Habermas observes, it seems that Heidegger revised his existential analysis such that all determinations of human existence turn out to be functions of a process that takes place in a "domain removed from all empirical (and ultimately all argumentative) grasp," somewhere "*behind* or *above* real history," in the "idealistically deified history" of metaphysics.[42] Human beings turn out to be Platonic puppets, after all, who cannot be held individually responsible for their decisions.

But it seems to me that in this case Habermas's observation is quite mistaken. As Heidegger originally argued in the existential analysis, we cannot, in principle, discuss what individuals actually decide in any particular case, but we can meaningfully ask what determines the options they have whenever they are faced with a decision.[43] Only in a trial and the judicial investigation of the facts of each case can we find out, I believe, to what extent we can and must hold individuals responsible for the decisions they made. What Habermas describes as "the *individualistic* heritage of existential philosophy" is characteristic of Sartre's existentialism, but it is ostensibly at odds with Heidegger's original analysis. For Heidegger insisted that individuals exist necessarily with others, and for the sake of others, and that they develop what options they have not in isolation, but in the concerted efforts of a community and the struggles of a people with its heritage.[44] Consequently, Heidegger's insistence on such bondage, against Sartre's "individualistic" account, does not amount to a revision of his original analysis, and it does not seem to be the late result of a conversion to the *Volk*-philosophy of the Nazi movement in the 1930s, as Habermas suggests.[45]

If one ignores what is at issue in the philosophical debate about the Nuremberg Trials, then, of course, Heidegger's insistence could also be seen as a ploy against the "individual responsibility" in Article 6 of the Nuremberg Charter, that is, as an attempt to dissolve individual guilt in the murky sea of collective guilt. But clearly, whereas proving guilt, that is, establishing responsibility for gross violations of "common standards" (such as those subsequently listed in the Universal Declaration of Human Rights), was the declared business of the International Military Tribunal, the philosophical debate was, as William James would say, an effort to "procure the license" for and to establish the limitations of appeals to such "common standards."[46] Thus, the philosophical debate is primarily concerned with the clarification of the roles individuals and groups play in setting them up and of the extent to which we can meaningfully expect that they accept them as binding measures for what they can do and, of course, for what they cannot do.

Naturally, what we can do and what we cannot do largely depends on the way things are. But, as Heidegger tried to demonstrate in his existential analysis, we can say what things are only within a given context of references and assignments, and there is no compelling evidence that some such context or scheme of things has been definitively fixed for all times and all places, or ever will be (except in abstract formalizations in which what gives meaning to the lives of individuals and determines what their options are is ignored or suppressed in favor of some contrived universal needs or the unacknowledged interests of a privileged group).[47] In each case, the context is rearticulated in the probing discourse of the living generation about its own actual condition. In this discourse, the living generation takes part with all its concerns, interests, needs, emotions, desires, dreams, and ideas, and it generously draws on the discourse of past generations and on what it imagines to be the topic of conversation in the future. Consequently, if we want to catch in the act what determines how things are and what options we have—Being, in Heidegger's technical terminology—in order to see what say individuals could have in this determination, then we would have to look for it in this ongoing conversation and transaction. At any given time, whatever measure there is for human behavior would have to be something that has materialized in this transaction and has been expressed in language. In other words, "the residency of Being," and the proper place to look for the scheme of things in operation, is language, broadly understood as the expression of discourse, and not the realm of things with permanently fixed connections and definitive assignments.[48]

If individual responsibility must be measured in light of the referential context of assignments that determines our form of life, then analytically understanding human discourse, that is, the transaction in which any such context gets created or transformed, and temporarily fixed, must become the prime target of our philosophical efforts concerning the "common standards" for dealing with the Nuremberg issues. The connections that we make and articulate in this process may have been voiced before but then forgotten or suppressed; they may have been presupposed but never acknowledged; or they may be utterly new and unheard of. In Heidegger's earlier account of human existence, hermeneutical analysis is restricted to the articulation and temporal interpretation of some hidden connections that are necessarily presupposed in everyday life.[49] In the analysis of the affinities and ties that govern public discourse, Heidegger gave a frightening account of the connection between the genuine care for each other and the tendency of individuals to take things easy. When things appear to be settled by the public, going with the flow seems to be the right thing to do and individuals may feel relieved of the responsibility for the choices they make.[50] During the Nazi reign, Goebbels's *Reichsministerium für Volksaufklärung und Propaganda* and Rosenberg's *Hauptamt Wissenschaft* demonstrated how easy it was for ambitious individuals and organized groups with advanced technologies to engineer the settling of things in public discourse in their interests and to impose their established truths on others. But the "Si quis dixerit atque crediderit . . . A.S." (Whosoever says or believes . . . be damned) and the persecution of heretics show that the threat and strategic use of violence for the control of discourse has a long and "noble" history.[51]

Of course, Heidegger's existential analyses of mortality and authenticity show on what grounds individuals could resist the manipulations of public discourse and engage in it responsibly, but they proved inadequate. There is little in them that encourages the creation, or reform, of institutional structures that could safeguard what Dewey describes as "back-and-forth give-and-take discussion until final decision represents a workable consensus of the ideas of all who take part."[52] Like others, Dewey finds that such structures were missing in Germany, and he argues at length that there is little hope for coping with the problems of the public without them.[53] Perhaps the firm control of public discourse by a single party, with its horrible fallout, could largely be blamed on the lack, or the decay, of such structures in Germany. Naturally, the apparatus developed by the party, including such organizations as the Gestapo, was designed to magnify the voices that served its program and to muffle, and ultimately silence, all expression of resistance against it. With its control of education, research, and the modern media, the party dictated the terms of public discourse, that is, "the management" decided what could be said and which voices of the past could be brought to life, again. In the party program, everything had, in principle, its proper place assigned, and the main purpose of discourse was to promote the program and to convince individuals of their responsibility to act on it. Discourse, as described in Heidegger's existential analysis, that is, the anguish and continuous struggle of individuals and groups over the articulation of the context that determines what things are and in light of which we judge what is good and evil, had ground to a halt. Individual responsibility had been transformed into obedience to the party and the new order of things.

By the time ordinary individuals realized what had happened, it was too late to ask questions and to keep the conversation going.[54] The catastrophe had become unavoidable because not enough people had worried about who had a say in setting the terms for dealing with matters of public interest, and too few had cared to express in public what they or others (dead or alive) had to say about the good life that, perhaps, would have made a difference.

In public discourse, broadly understood, we continuously recreate the context in light of which we both design in each case our research program and decide in each case our course of action. The articulation of such a context, says Heidegger, is a function of the care for "the light in which a seeing, as *theoria*, can first live and move," and it is also a deed that "surpasses all *praxis*."[55] Much of what necessarily belongs to such a context goes without saying. As I have indicated above, for Heidegger the prime business of hermeneutical and existential analysis was to make explicit what remained hidden and to express what remained unsaid in what had been said in public discourse.[56] Turning or no turning, in his contribution to the French debate he still insists that being thoughtful and philosophical means to bring "the unspoken word of Being" into public discourse, that is, to open up for public inspection and scrutiny what has not been recognized and acknowledged but is necessarily presupposed in what has already been spelled out of the context that governs our handling of human affairs. Heidegger admits that this is a very modest contribution to the struggle for "common standards" of conduct that could save future generations from the inhumanity of our age, and it very much looks as if nothing at all could be accomplished by it.[57] But we could see in it a *crucial* contribution, I believe, if we come to realize that turning public conversation to such hidden common assumptions is a necessary first step for an open discussion of the secret beliefs that may have led to much of the carnage of our time, and for a radical reorientation of our dealing with the human condition. In short, it could be an excellent way for constantly bringing us to our senses and putting us on guard.[58]

But clearly, during the Nazi reign, the greater majority of individuals, and particularly those who had made it their professional business to be thoughtful, had failed miserably and share much of the blame for untold suffering with those who claimed to have merely carried out the programs for establishing and maintaining the new order. As I have shown above, in "Plato's Doctrine of Truth" Heidegger had tried to challenge a most basic hidden assumption in our tradition and in the Nazi outlook on human affairs by exposing its totalitarian and terrorist character. And I have also shown that the Nazi establishment perceived it as a challenge. But there are two things, on Heidegger's part, that explain why his challenge was not effective at the time and, in Habermas's words, kept people "blind to the Nazi regime," namely, Heidegger's sympathies with and public support for the Nazi movement in general and his philosophical style. Perhaps the observations about Germans reported by Dewey are overblown and could be made about the great mass of people anywhere, namely, that in intellectual matters they have no "use for discussion and conversation. They depend upon *ipse dixits*, upon finality of utterance, upon telling and being told."[59] It seems to me that with his style Heidegger was catering to this tendency. Even his early existential analysis largely consists of long lines of definitive "statements." True, with his statements Heidegger wanted to initiate discussions, but what he stated in each case appeared to be settled and invited no further inquiry.[60] It is, perhaps, primarily this lapidary style that explains why Heidegger's efforts to open the discussion largely failed during the Nazi reign, and why his analyses are widely treated today as "doctrines."

But even more important for understanding why Heidegger did not succeed in his efforts to open the discussion of the Nazi outlook on things and their approach to human affairs, and for appreciating his contribution to the French debate of the Nuremberg issues, is his brief response to the third and last question raised by his challenge of Plato's doctrine of truth and the view of the human condition entailed in it: Without recourse to a fixed scheme of things and the ready-made order of things, how is it possible to avoid the bankruptcy of "anything goes"?[61]

Given Heidegger's own analysis of the human condition, there seems to be nothing that could independently and from outside, as it were, guide, direct, and regulate the formation of the outlook on human affairs in public discourse. What we experience in the world around us, what we establish in scientific research, and what we bring about through human action are all inspired by an endlessly changing outlook on things and human affairs formed in public discourse. What guides the conversation, if anything, are such images of the good life as the Platonic one. These images, for better or worse, affect not only what we see, think, and expect to accomplish, but also what we try to do to enhance and to replace them in our efforts to develop strictly neutral scientific or multicultural postmodern images. No matter how we try, we cannot get away from them, and we have to struggle with them whenever our inherited outlook on human affairs threatens to turn into a nightmare. At such moments, the proper and thoughtful thing to do seems to be to ask what is wrong with our inherited outlook, rather than what to substitute for it. Seeing whether some hidden assumptions in our heritage might have inspired crimes against humanity is a more promising strategy for dealing with the Nuremberg issues than adventurous journeys into the unknown. In other words, incessantly reopening for public inspection and scrutiny the context that determines what we experience and expect (our inherited scheme of things) ought to be the prime concern of every philosopher and thoughtful person.[62] Philosophers would then have to be *rigorous* in their insistence on such reviewing, *meticulous* in their spelling out of hidden assumptions, and *modest* about what can be said and achieved in public discourse.[63]

Many of us who escaped extermination will be sadly disappointed and, possibly, angry about such an apparently meager philosophical contribution to the debate of the Nuremberg issues.[64] We wish, perhaps innocently, that our ability to think has something to do with our ability to tell right from wrong, such that "we must be able to 'demand' its exercise from every sane person, no matter how erudite or ignorant, intelligent or stupid, he may happen to be."[65] In our efforts to fight "the outbreak of crimes against humanity," we want to be able to appeal to some common standards that are not constantly questioned and that do not have to be endlessly renegotiated and perpetually defended. But "doctrines," declarations, and mere appeals to what is good in us won't do, says Heidegger. We have to get clear about our place in the scheme of things and the role of individuals in the play of forces that determine what really happens today. What we need most, however, is a sense for the proportions and consequences of the technological approach to everything. It is not at all clear whether the horrors at issue in the Nuremberg Trials are the dawning of a new age or merely the beginning of the end of a development that began with decisions made three hundred years ago.[66] Efforts to understand individual responsibility in abstraction and apart from this wider context are doomed to failure. Sartre was right in arguing that we must come to terms with the human condition without recourse to a fixed and readily available order of things, but he was simplistic with his insistence that the decisions of individuals are completely responsible for events in the immediate past, the present, and the immediate future of the living generation.

Heidegger's contribution to the French debate, thus, shows an acute sense for the importance of the central issue on the table at the Nuremberg Trials and for what needs to be said about it, but only in general. In his contribution, he refocuses and sharpens what was already his main concern in his earlier analysis of the human condition, namely, the development of an adequate and comprehensive understanding of the responsibility of individuals for what they do and for the way they live and die. It also shows that much of what he subsequently published, some of it written during the Nazi reign, was devoted to this single issue.

The problem remains that although Heidegger shows that we have a hand in, and are responsible for, the setup, he does not examine what was wrong with having a hand in the particular setup at issue at the Nuremberg Trials, namely, the Nazi regime. Something concrete is missing in his analysis, just as it was in his initial involvement. The problem is that Heidegger can be numbered among those professional philosophers who, as Dewey observed, tend "to approach their subject-matter through its formulation in received systems" rather than "through recourse to specific events in all their diversity and thatness."[67] They consequently fail to "develop ideas relevant to the actual crises of life, ideas influential in dealing with them and tested by the assistance they afford."[68] This distancing from the actual conditions of our being-in-the-world still seems to characterize professional philosophy, as I have observed over the years in business meetings of the American Philosophical Association. Motions pronouncing judgment on political or social matters, such as the Vietnam war or, more recently, multiculturalism and feminism, were stubbornly resisted, and hardly ever passed, on the grounds that philosophers, as philosophers, have no special expertise on and business in passing judgment and taking a stand on political and social matters. In doing so, it was usually pointed out that members of the American Philosophical Association could, of course, do so as private citizens. But isn't this the position that we now find so damning in Heidegger's professional aloofness?!

There seems to be no point in talking about individual responsibility unless we individuals can have a say in the determination of the world around us and do not merely have to slavishly adapt to what in principle has been permanently fixed or to what inevitably establishes itself without us. As time went on, Heidegger became more, not less, preoccupied with his efforts to show that in one way or another we all unavoidably participate in the organization of the world in which we live. Like a clearing in a forest, our world is established and sustained in the struggle of individuals with what encroaches on us and what we experience; it cannot establish itself without us. But notoriously, representations in art and descriptions in science suggest that there is a preestablished world. They are supposed to display in different ways how things are and what the world is like without us. So Heidegger tried to demonstrate in sufficient detail that what we get in each case is a strategic organization or setup (*Ge-stell*), that is, the promotion of a cause and opening of a struggle (*Streit*) against the resistances of things, and not the "mere" display of a preestablished order.[69] And he insisted, with Sartre as it were, that this strategic organization of things cannot be accomplished without "human doing," and against Sartre, that it does not happen "exclusively *in*" or "decisively *through*" us.[70] In what has been called Heidegger's testament, this concern very much looks like an obsession: The world is what it is not because of us, and yet it cannot be what it is without us. Helping to gain this insight is the end of philosophy.[71]

Finally, one may well ask whether what I have been developing in this paper was actually on Heidegger's mind when he wrote his "Letter on Humanism" and the essays on art and technology. I don't know, and I doubt that anyone will ever know. But if read in this way, I suggest that what he said then could still provide some help today for dealing with one of the central issues of the Nuremberg Trials, namely, individual responsibility for crimes against humanity, such as the Holocaust.

NOTES

1. In light of their legal flaws, we might want to agree with István Deák's conclusion that "the lesson of the Nuremberg trials is that there should be no other trials following the model of the Nuremberg trials" (p. 52), but still agree with Telford Taylor that the first trial was a success because it adopted some important legal principles, particularly the concept of crimes against humanity. See István Deák, "Misjudgment at Nuremberg," in *The New York Review of Books*, 40 (October 7, 1993), pp. 46–52.
2. See "Charter of the International Military Tribunal at Nuremberg," in Robert K. Woetzel, *The Nuremberg Trials in International Law* (New York: Frederick A. Praeger, 1962), Appendix, p. 274f.
3. See Robert K. Woetzel's report, "The Nuremberg Trial and Subsequent Developments in International Law," ibid., pp. 218–244.
4. It was proposed that an International Bill of Rights be included in the Charter, but that was postponed on the grounds that further study was required. Such a bill, the Universal Declaration of Human Rights, was finally adopted on December 10, 1948, by the General Assembly of the United Nations at the Palais de Chaillot, Paris. See Egon Schwelb, *Human Rights and the International Community: The Roots and Growth of the Universal Declaration of Human Rights, 1948–*

1963 (Chicago: Quadrangle Books, 1964), p. 34. That it was considered inherent in the Charter is indicated in its preamble: "We, the peoples of the United Nations. . . . To reaffirm faith in the fundamental rights, in the dignity and worth of the human person, . . . have resolved to combine our efforts to accomplish these aims." See "Charter of the United Nations," in *Webster's New Twentieth Century Dictionary of the English Language: Unabridged*, Supplements, 2nd ed. (New York: Simon and Schuster, 1979), p. 145.

5. "Charter of the United Nations," ibid.
6. See Annie Cohen-Solal, *Sartre: A Life*, translated by Anna Cancogni and edited by Norman MacAfee (New York: Pantheon Books, 1987), p. 252.
7. See Jean-Paul Sartre, "Existentialism Is a Humanism," translated by Walter Kaufmann, in *Existentialism from Dostoevsky to Sartre*, edited by Walter Kaufmann (New York: Meridian Books, 1957), 293f.
8. Jean-Paul Sartre, "Existentialism Is a Humanism," 290f.
9. See Hitler's claim that "only the German people has made moral law the governing principle of action," in *Hitler's Secret Conversations 1941–1944* [Bormann-Vermerke], edited by [Martin Bormann], translated by Norman Cameron and R. H. Stevens (New York: Farrar, Straus and Young, 1953), p. 6, and Himmler's notorious remarks in his speech in Posen, on October 4, 1943, in which he praised the virtues and the moral decency of SS men, in *Trials of the Major War Criminals before the International Military Tribunal*, Vol. 29, edited by S. Paul A. Joosten (Nuremberg: International Military Tribunal, 1948), pp. 145f, and 149–165.
10. See Hugo Ott, "Der Fall Hermann Staudinger," in *Martin Heidegger: Unterwegs zu seiner Biographie* (Frankfurt: Campus Verlag, 1988), pp. 201–213: "If the Staudinger case viz. 'Operation Sternheim' would have been known then, Heidegger's chances for rehabilitation would have been nil. For this inhuman act ["dieses menschliche Versagen"] . . . would definitely have branded him—for all time!" p. 211.
11. See Hugo Ott, *Martin Heidegger*, p. 309.
12. See p. 190, above.
13. See Hugo Ott, "Die Verspottung der Philosophie—oder: Was ist Humanismus?" *Martin Heidegger*, pp. 268–278; see also Heidegger's "Anmerkung" in the first edition of *Platons Lehre von der Wahrheit: Mit einem Brief über den "Humanismus"* (Bern: Francke Verlag, 1947).
14. See Martin Heidegger, "Plato's Doctrine of Truth," translated by John Barlow, in *Philosophy in the Twentieth Century*, Vol. 2, edited by William Barrett and Henry D. Aiken (New York: Random House, 1962), p. 269f. For the German original, see Martin Heidegger, *Platons Lehre von der Wahrheit: Mit einem Brief über den "Humanismus,"* 2nd ed. (Bern: Francke Verlag, 1954), pp. 49–52.
15. See Martin Heidegger, "German Students: November 3, 1933," in *The Heidegger Controversy: A Critical Reader*, edited by Richard Wolin (New York: Columbia University Press, 1991), p. 47: "The Führer alone *is* the present and future German reality and its law. Learn to know ever more deeply: from now on every single thing demands decision and every action responsibility. Heil Hitler!" For the German text, see *Martin Heidegger und das "Dritte Reich": Ein Kompendium*, edited by Bernd Martin (Darmstadt: Wissenschaftliche Buchgesellschaft, 1989), p. 177: "Der Führer selbst und allein *ist* die heutige und künftige deutsche Wirklichkeit und ihr Gesetz. Lernet immer tiefer zu wissen: Von nun an fordert jedwedes Ding Entscheidung und alles Tun Verantwortung. Heil Hitler!" With

this plea Heidegger tried to mobilize student support for the plebiscite of November 12 on Hitler's withdrawal from the League of Nations. Responsibility, i.e., the duty to conform with the true order of things, was understood as cooperation with the Nazi regime.

16. See Plato, *Laws vii*, 803c.
17. For Heidegger's formal concept of Being, see Martin Heidegger, *Being and Time*, translated by John Macquarrie and Edward Robinson (New York: Harper & Row, 1962), ¶2, p. 25f, and Martin Heidegger, *Kant and the Problem of Metaphysics*, translated by James S. Churchill (Bloomington: Indiana University Press, 1962), ¶40, p. 230.
18. For Heidegger's definition of the Being of environmental things as "context of assignments" (p. 121), see *Being and Time*, ¶15, pp. 95–102.
19. For the decisive quote from Wilhelm Brachmann's article, "Antike und Gegenwart: Ein Beitrag zum Problem des gegenwärtigen Humanismus in Deutschland und Italien," in *Nationalsozialistische Monatshefte*, Heft 140 (November 1941), pp. 926–932, see Hugo Ott, *Martin Heidegger*, p. 270.
20. See Heidegger's review of Friedrich Wilhelm Foerster's *Autorität und Freiheit*, extensively quoted in Hugo Ott, *Martin Heidegger*, p. 63f. The review appeared in 1910, in the May issue of the conservative Catholic journal *Der Akademiker*. Within the context of his Catholic belief in the divine order of things, which he still accepted without questioning it at that time, Heidegger used the phrase with the approving enthusiasm of a Christian fundamentalist.
21. See p. 191, above.
22. In his response, Heidegger listed three such questions in Beaufret's phrasing. See Martin Heidegger, "Letter on Humanism," translated by Frank A. Capuzzi in collaboration with J. Glenn Gray, in Martin Heidegger, *Basic Writings*, edited by David Farrell Krell (New York: Harper & Row, 1977): (1) "Comment redonner un sens au mot 'Humanisme'?" (p. 195); (2) "Is not that effort entirely essential which you express in the sentence 'Ce que je cherche à faire, depuis longtemps déjà, c'est préciser le rapport de l'ontologie avec une éthique possible'?" (p. 231); and (3) "Comment sauver l'élément d'aventure que comport toute recherche sans faire de la philosophie une simple aventurière?" (p. 240).
23. See Martin Heidegger, *Being and Time*, ¶41, pp. 235–241, esp. p. 238; see also ¶13, pp. 86–90, and ¶69, (b), pp. 408–415.
24. See Martin Heidegger, "Letter on Humanism": First question, pp. 195–231; second question, pp. 231–240; and third question, pp. 240–242.
25. Heidegger's point that the process of disclosure depends on our active involvement, and not on the mere fact that we are around, is lost in both translations available in English. See the German text in Martin Heidegger, "Über den Humanismus: Brief an Jean Beaufret, Paris," in *Platons Lehre von der Wahrheit: Mit einem Brief über den "Humanismus,"* 2nd ed. (Bern: Francke Verlag, 1954), p. 94: "'Humanismus' bedeutet jetzt, falls wir uns entschließen das Wort festzuhalten: das Wesen des Menschen ist für die Wahrheit des Seins wesentlich, so zwar, daß es demzufolge gerade nicht auf den Menschen, lediglich als solchen, ankommt." Compare with my restatement of Heidegger's point, above, Edgar Lohner's translation, "'Humanism' means now, should we decide to retain the word: the essence of man is essential for the truth of Being, and apart from this truth of Being man himself does not matter," in *Philosophy in the Twentieth Century*, Vol. 2, edited by William Barrett and Henry D. Aiken (New York: Random House, 1962), p. 290; and Frank A. Capuzzi's version, "'Humanism'

now means, in case we decide to retain the word, that the essence of man is essential for the truth of Being, specifically in such a way that the word does not pertain to man simply as such," in *Basic Writings*, p. 224.

26. See Martin Heidegger, "Letter on Humanism," p. 217.
27. Ibid., p. 232.
28. Ibid., p. 236.
29. See Martin Heidegger, "Brief über den 'Humanismus'," p. 112.
30. See Martin Heidegger, "Letter on Humanism," p. 237. The translation was made "by Frank A. Capuzzi in collaboration with J. Glenn Gray," ibid., p. 193, note. David Farrell Krell has edited it "with reference to the helpful French bilingual edition," but without paying much attention to the German original, so it seems.
31. Heidegger's remarks have become equally nonsensical in Edgar Lohner's translation in *Philosophy in the Twentieth Century*, Vol. 2, p. 298: "With grace, evil appears in the clearing of Being."
32. See Martin Heidegger, "Brief über den 'Humanismus,'" p. 114: "Sein erst gewährt dem Heilen Aufgang in Huld and Andrang zu Unheil dem Grimm."
33. See "Charter of the United Nations," *Webster's New Twentieth Century Dictionary of the English Language*.
34. See Martin Heidegger, "Letter on Humanism," p. 238f.
35. See p. 194, above.
36. For Heidegger's idea of an empirically grounded, scientific philosophy, see *Being and Time*, p. 490, note x.
37. For *Durchleuchtungskraft*, the power to make transparent, as justification for constructive theoretical accounts of experience and their interpretations, see Martin Heidegger, *Kant and the Problem of Metaphysics*, pp. 207 and 241.
38. See p. 190, above.
39. See Jürgen Habermas, "Work and Weltanschauung: The Heidegger Controversy from a German Perspective" (written for the German edition of Victor Farías's book, *Heidegger und der Nationalsozialismus*), translated by John McCumber, in *Critical Inquiry*, 15 (Winter 1989), pp. 435–436.
40. See George Leaman, *Heidegger im Kontext: Gesamtüberblick zum NS-Engagement der Universitätsphilosophen* (Hamburg: Argument-Verlag, 1993). An early English version is available from UMI Dissertation Information Service, Ann Arbor: *Contextual Misreadings: The US Reception of Heidegger's Political Thought* (1991 dissertation, University of Massachusetts). It is depressing to see how many of the philosophers teaching at German universities in the early sixties had managed to conceal their involvement in the Nazi movement (at my alma mater, the University of Bonn: Jakob Barion, Heinrich Lützeler, Gottfried Martin, Erich Rothacker, Vinzenz Rüfner, and Johannes Thyssen). For Heidegger's private confession, see his letters of March 7 and April 8, 1950, in Martin Heidegger/Karl Jaspers, *Briefwechsel: 1920–1963*, edited by Walter Biemel and Hans Saner (Frankfurt: Vittorio Klostermann, 1990), pp. 196f and 200ff.
41. See Martin Heidegger, *Being and Time*, ¶74, "The Basic Constitution of Historicality," pp. 434–439, esp. p. 435f.
42. See Jürgen Habermas, "Work and Weltanschauung," p. 441f.
43. See Martin Heidegger, *Being and Time*, p. 434: "In the existential analysis we cannot, in principle, discuss what Dasein *factically* resolves in any particular case. . . . Nevertheless, we must ask whence, *in general*, Dasein can draw those possibilities upon which it factically projects itself."

44. Ibid., p. 436: "But if fateful Dasein . . . exists essentially in Being-with Others ['is' essentially for the sake of Others, p. 160], its historizing is a co-historizing and is determinative for it as *destiny*. This is how we designate the historizing of the community, of a people. . . . Dasein's fateful destiny in and with its 'generation' goes to make up the full authentic historizing of Dasein." This is a good reason for social and political involvement, *any* such involvement, and, as Karl Löwith reports, Heidegger, naturally, acknowledges it as the basis for his political engagement in the Nazi movement. See Karl Löwith, "My Last Meeting with Heidegger in Rome, 1936," translated by Richard Wolin, in *The Heidegger Controversy: A Critical Reader*, edited by Richard Wolin (Cambridge: MIT Press, 1993), p. 142.
45. See Jürgen Habermas, "Work and Weltanschauung," p. 442: "The pathos of bondage and letting-be, . . . the thesis that 'language is the house of Being in which man ek-sists by dwelling, in that he belongs to the truth of Being, guarding it'—all this is only the later result of the deliverance of philosophical thinking over to a 'World-destiny' that, between 1930 and 1945, prescribed various twists and turns to a philosopher who was quite ready to go along."
46. See William James, "The Types of Philosophic Thinking," in *A Pluralistic Universe*, edited by Frederick H. Burkhardt et al. (Cambridge: Harvard University Press, 1977), p. 11f.
47. For the loss of formalization and functionalization, see Martin Heidegger, *Being and Time*, p. 121f.
48. See Martin Heidegger, "Letter on Humanism," p. 239. For the definition of language as the expression of discourse, see *Being and Time*, p. 204.
49. For the hidden connections, see Martin Heidegger, *Being and Time*, p. 59, and for their temporal interpretation, ibid., p. 38.
50. See Martin Heidegger, *Being and Time*, ¶¶ 27 and 35–38.
51. The formula was used by the Church as early as A.D. 400. See Henrici Denzinger, *Enchiridion Symbolorum Definitionum et Declarationum de Rebus Fidei et Morum*, ed. Carolus Rahner, editio 31 (Rome: Herder, 1957), p. 15.
52. John Dewey, "The One-World of Hitler's National Socialism" (1942), in *The Middle Works, 1899–1924*, Vol. 8: 1915, edited by Jo Ann Boydston (Carbondale: Southern Illinois University Press, 1979), p. 443.
53. Ibid. For Dewey's in-depth analysis, see *The Public and Its Problems* (1926), in *The Later Works: 1925–1953*, Vol. 2: 1925–1927, edited by Jo Ann Boydston (Carbondale: Southern Illinois University Press, 1984), pp. 235–372.
54. For an excellent description of this development, see Milton Mayer, *They Thought They Were Free: The Germans 1933–45* (Chicago: The University of Chicago Press, 1955), Chap. 13, "But Then It Was Too Late," pp. 166–173. A detailed analysis of the process by which an organization becomes an instrument to obliterate individual responsibility can be found in Zygmunt Bauman, *Modernity and the Holocaust* (Ithaca: Cornell University Press, 1991), Chap. 6, "The Ethics of Obedience (Reading Milgram)," pp. 151–168.
55. See Martin Heidegger, "Letter on Humanism," p. 239.
56. See note 49. In the opening section of *Being and Time*, p. 23f, Heidegger insists with Kant that "the covert judgments of common reason" should become and remain the precise and exclusive target of the "analytic—'the business of philosophers.'"
57. Martin Heidegger, "Letter on Humanism," p. 239f.
58. Recall Heidegger's remarks about the importance (*Würde*) of merely reflective

philosophical thinking as being on guard. The "recollection [*Andenken*] of Being," he says, is a response to the challenge [*Anspruch*] of the experienced need for "the preservation of Being's truth" ("Letter on Humanism," pp. 236, 221). If we could but avoid being stupefied by Heidegger's shepherd metaphor, perhaps we could agree that in the face of our generation's crimes against humanity, there is no saving grace at all in merely "recollective" thinking and remembering, unless it is the expression of care for openness about such hidden assumptions in our understanding of the scheme of things.

59. See John Dewey, "The One-World of Hitler's National Socialism," p. 443.
60. Jaspers, for instance, deplores this style more than anything else in Heidegger's writings. See Karl Jaspers, *Notizen zu Heidegger*, edited by Hans Saner (Munich: R. Piper, 1978), passim, especially: "Heidegger denkt polemisch, aber nicht diskutierend,—denkt beschwörend, nicht eigentlich begründend,—sagt aus, vollzieht nicht Gedankenoperationen" (p. 77).
61. See p. 196, above.
62. Martin Heidegger, "Letter on Humanism," p. 241: "To bring to language ever and again this advent of Being which remains, and in its remaining waits for man, is the sole matter of thinking."
63. Ibid.
64. For an expression of disappointment, see Paul Celan, "Todtnauberg," in *Gesammelte Werke*, Bd. 2 (Frankfurt: Suhrkamp, 1986), p. 255f; and for bitterness and anger over the complete absence of easily recognizable signs of care for those who were exterminated in the death camps, together with the lack of assurance that questioning the scheme of things is not itself diabolical, see Emmanuel Levinas, "As if Consenting to Horror," translated by Paula Wissing, in *Critical Inquiry*, 15 (1989), pp. 485–488.
65. See Hannah Arendt, *The Life of the Mind* (London: Secker and Warburg, 1978), Vol. 1, p. 13.
66. See Heidegger's letter of March 3, 1947, to Elisabeth Blochmann, in *Martin Heidegger/Elisabeth Blochmann: Briefwechsel 1918–1969*, edited by Joachim W. Storck (Marbach: Marbacher Schriften, 1989), p. 92.
67. See John Dewey, "The Need for a Recovery of Philosophy," in *The Middle Works, 1899–1924*, Vol. 10: 1916–1917, edited by Jo Ann Boydston (Carbondale: Southern Illinois University Press, 1980), pp. 4 and 39.
68. Ibid., p. 43. See also my remarks on p. 195, above.
69. For display as setup (*Ge-stell*) and onslaught (*Anstiftung des Streites der Wahrheit*) in art, see Martin Heidegger, "The Origin of the Work of Art," in *Poetry, Language, Thought*, translated by Albert Hofstadter (New York: Harper & Row, 1971), pp. 64 and 76; for such display in science and technology, see "The Question Concerning Technology," in *The Question Concerning Technology and Other Essays*, translated by William Lovitt (New York: Harper Colophon Books, 1977), pp. 19–21. See also Hans Seigfried, "Art and the Origin of Truth," in *Man and World*, 11 (1978), 45–58.
70. See Martin Heidegger, *The Question Concerning Technology and Other Essays*, p. 24. See also Hans Seigfried, "Autonomy and Quantum Physics: Nietzsche, Heidegger, and Heisenberg," in *Philosophy of Science*, 57 (1990), 619–620.
71. See "Only a God Can Save Us: Der Spiegel's Interview with Martin Heidegger" [1966], translated by Maria P. Alter and John D. Caputo, in *Philosophy Today*, 20 (1976), p. 278.

13

Heidegger, Planetary Technics, and the Holocaust

ALAN MILCHMAN AND ALAN ROSENBERG

Of the many facets of Martin Heidegger's complex relationship to National Socialism, perhaps the most disturbing is his almost total silence with respect to the Holocaust. In the more than thirty years between the destruction of the *Hitler-Staat* and his own death in 1976, Heidegger refused to "think Auschwitz," to confront the monstrous product of Nazism.

Heidegger's silence is all the more unsettling for those of us who are convinced that the Holocaust marks a caesura in the history of the West, an event that is decisive for the future of our civilization. In contrast to the other cases of mass murder and genocide which litter the history of our own and other civilizations, the Holocaust stands out as a transformative event because it forged an integral link between mass extermination and technology, because it established as a social reality the industrialization of death. At Auschwitz, the fruits of modern science and technology were exclusively devoted to the systematic production of corpses! In the face of this union of technology and extermination, and Heidegger's inability or unwillingness to confront it, a number of thinkers for whom the Holocaust is a transformative event, and for whom Heidegger's thinking has constituted a source of intellectual sustenance, have reacted with shock and dismay.

For Jacques Derrida, Heidegger's silence concerning the Holocaust is "as monstrous as that about which he remained silent."[1] For Philippe Lacoue-Labarthe, that silence constitutes an "irreparable wrong [*faute*]" and is "strictly unpardonable."[2] As Lacoue-labarthe was to subsequently explain, what made Heidegger's silence so objectionable was the very centrality of the Holocaust to the history of the West:

> In the apocalypse at Auschwitz, it is no more or less than the essence of the West that is revealed—and that has not ceased since that time to reveal itself. And it was the thought guiding this event that Heidegger failed to recognize.[3]

In response to those who have disingenuously asserted that this very silence is a mark of Heidegger's decency and dignity in the face of incomprehensible events,[4] Jean-François Lyotard has argued that Heidegger's "is a mute silence that lets nothing be heard. A leaden silence."[5] George Steiner, surveying the record of Heidegger's Rectorate, his active support for the *Hitler-Staat* (however limited in duration it may have been), and that deafening silence that spans thirty years, has concluded that "the disabling fact is Heidegger's silence after 1945. This appalling abstention is contemporaneous with some of his most far-reaching work in reference to the nature of planetary-ecological crises. . . . But the thinker of Being found nothing to say of the Holocaust and the death-camps."[6] Finally, Richard Bernstein has asserted:

> What is still most scandalous and incomprehensible is not what [Heidegger] did and said in 1933–34, but his refusal after 1945 to confront *directly* and *unambiguously* the full horror of the *Shoah* and the barbaric crimes of the Nazis. How can we explain why Heidegger—who claimed that what is most thought-provoking about our epoch is the refusal to think—failed himself to think through the most shocking events of the twentieth century that "call forth" thinking?[7]

The reactions of Derrida, Lacoue-Labarthe, Lyotard, Steiner, and Bernstein appear to us to reflect the conviction that on the basis of his thinking, Heidegger might have, could have, and even should have, confronted the Holocaust, and "thought Auschwitz." Indeed, such a conclusion is not unreasonable. What originally attracted Heidegger to National Socialism, as he pointed out in a number of places,[8] was his belief that it constituted a response to the domination of modern technology, or planetary technics, to the spread of nihilism which triumphs with technology. According to Heidegger, his growing disenchantment with National Socialism after 1934 had its basis in his conviction that it (or at any rate the form it took in the *Hitler-Staat* and NSDAP) was itself one more manifestation of the reign of planetary technics, one more expression of nihilism. For Lacoue-Labarthe, "if it is true that the age is that of the accomplishment of nihilism, then it is at Auschwitz that that accomplishment took place in the purest formless form."[9] Given the depth and scope of his critique of nihilism, and given his acknowledgment of the link between nihilism and Nazism, it is difficult not to be shocked by Heidegger's silence in the face of the Holocaust, by his failure to provide us with a meditation on the hell that was Auschwitz.[10]

In fact, Heidegger did break his public silence about the Holocaust on one occasion, in December 1949, in the course of his Bremen lectures, *Einblick in das, was ist.* Twice, once in the lecture "Das Ge-Stell" ("The Enframing") and once in the lecture "Die Gefahr" ("The Danger"), Heidegger explicitly spoke of the Holocaust and its victims.[11] The reference in "Das Ge-Stell" was removed when the lecture was subsequently printed as *Die Frage nach der Technik* (*The Question Concerning Technology*) in 1954. The other lecture, "Die Gefahr," has never been published in any form. The portions of these lectures in question were first made public by Wolfgang Schirmacher, in his *Technik und Gelassenheit.*

In "Das Ge-Stell", Heidegger says:

> Agriculture is now a motorized food industry: in its essence it is the same thing as the manufacture of corpses in gas chambers and extermination camps, the same thing as blockades and the reduction of an area to hunger, the same as the manufacture of hydrogen bombs.[12]

The first thing that strikes us about this statement is what Jürgen Habermas has described as "abstraction by essentialization": "Under the leveling gaze of the philosopher of Being even the extermination of the Jews seems merely an equivalent to many others."[13] The gas chambers are situated on the same plane as motorized agriculture. By abstracting from their fundamental differences, Heidegger asserts that the two are essentially the same, the same with respect to their *Wesen.*[14] Even if motorized agriculture ultimately "produces" death, and not food, through its exhaustion of the soil, the pesticides that poison the rivers and seas, the climatic changes (e.g., the process of desiccation) that are set in motion, and so on, the death—however massive—that *indirectly* results is not simply reducible to the conscious and deliberate extermination of millions of humans that occurred in the death-camps. Even if motorized agriculture and the death-camps ultimately proceed from the same manner of disclosing entities, that which characterizes planetary technics, what Heidegger terms *das Ge-Stell* (enframing), the *identity* between the two that Heidegger seeks to establish is profoundly mistaken. We agree with Lyotard here:

> It is not necessary to be a humanist to reject the identity, or even the analogy, between the factories for neutrons and peas and those for gassing and cremation. One only needs to think.[15]

No less shocking and unacceptable than Heidegger's reduction of motorized agriculture to gas chambers is his equation of the fate of the Jews in the death-camps and the fate of the Germans faced with the privations brought on by the Berlin Blockade. However brutal the policy of Stalinist Russia in deliberately seeking to starve Berlin, it is a mistake simply to put an equal sign between that cruel event and the systematic, technological extermination of millions in the death-camps. The different scale of the two events, the fact that the policy of blockade—despicable though it is—obeys a certain military-imperialist logic, while the Holocaust escapes just such a logic, and the fact that death in the one case (the blockade) is the means to an end, while in the other it is the end itself, pursued with all the means available to a techno-scientific civilization, prohibits the equation that Heidegger seeks to establish here.[16]

Yet it is also necessary to recognize the fact that by situating the Holocaust on the same plane as motorized agriculture and blockades, Heidegger is not merely pursuing an exculpatory strategy with respect to the extermination of the Jews. Without in any way denying this facet of the Heideggerian statement in "Das Ge-Stell," we also recognize that in including the death camps and gas chambers in his statement, Heidegger explicitly accorded the Holocaust an *historial* status, acknowledged its *Geschichtliche* character. Like those other manifestations of the reign of planetary technics, motorized agriculture, and hydrogen bombs, Auschwitz here receives its recognition as an expression of enframing.[17]

To our "post-Holocaust mind," what is most striking about this statement is Heidegger's offensive equation of motorized agriculture and the gas chambers, his equation of the fate of Jews and Germans during and after the war. But imagine the surprise of Heidegger's auditors in that Bremen hall in 1949, when they heard Germany's greatest *Denker,* once a partisan of the "National Revolution," who had been denied the right to teach by the victorious allies, utter those words: *Gaskammern* (gas chambers) and *Vernichtungslagern* (extermination camps); putting the fate of the Jews on the same historial plane as that of Germans enduring the Berlin blockade or the devastation of war.

In his other explicit reference to the Holocaust and its victims, in "Die Gefahr," Heidegger tells us:

> Hundreds of thousands die *en masse.* Do they die? They perish. They become items of the standing reserve available for the manufacture of corpses [*Bestandes der Fabrikation von Leichen*]. Do they die? Hardly noticed they are liquidated in extermination camps. . . . Dying, however, means bearing death in its essence. To be capable of dying means to be capable of bearing this death. But we are able to do so only when the essence of death has an affinity to our esssence.[18]

This distinction between dying, the capacity to bear death in its essence, which is the hallmark of mortals (*Sterblichen*), and perishing, which denies humans their mortality, is fundamental to the later Heidegger's vision of the fourfold (*das Geviert*), the play of earth, sky, mortals, and gods, and the danger (*die Gefahr*) which threatens it in the form of *das Ge-Stell.*

When Heidegger asks, clearly referring to the victims of the extermination camps, "Do they die? They perish," one is immediately struck by the similarity of Heidegger's formulation to those of Hannah Arendt and Primo Levi. Heidegger's vision of masses of humans robbed of their possibility of mortality by the smooth, technological functioning of the factories of death is also found in the descriptions of Arendt and Levi.[19] For Arendt:

> The concentration camps, by making death anonymous . . . robbed death of its meaning as the end of a fulfilled life. In a sense they took away the individual's own death, proving that henceforth nothing belonged to him and he belonged to no one. His death merely set a seal on the fact that he had never really existed.[20]

Levi's description of the victims stems from his own grim experience of the camps:

> Their life is short, but their number is endless; they, the *Muselmänner*, the drowned, form the back-bone of the camp, an anonymous mass . . . of non-men who march and labor in silence, the divine spark dead within them, already too empty really to suffer. One hesitates to call them living; one hesitates to call their death death.[21]

Heidegger's acknowledgment that the victim of the extermination camps is even denied a death, which in virtually identical terms is confirmed by Arendt and Levi, ignores what Emil L. Fackenheim has termed "the spectrum of resistance during the Holocaust."[22] Yet it is crucial to recognize that, for Heidegger, what denied the victims their death in the camps was not any defect of their "race," any biological feature, nor even their specific culture or values, but the juggernaut of planetary technics, of *das Ge-Stell*, which reduced large numbers of them to "standing reserve" (*Bestand*).

Heidegger did not go beyond these two brief references to the Holocaust in his public statements, and the fact that even these two references were never published by him only makes his silence concerning the Holocaust that much more deafening.

Nonetheless, we believe that it is possible to read Heidegger against Heidegger, and thus to demonstrate a dialectical link between Heidegger's thinking and the Holocaust. Following Derrida, we need "to read Heidegger the way he did not read himself."[23] In his powerful reinterpretation of the young Heidegger's hermeneutic phenomenology, John van Buren has argued that in approaching Heidegger's thinking we should be prepared to strike out on new, and hitherto untraveled, paths. Such an approach is not merely warranted by the need to grapple with what Heidegger termed "the topic for thinking," but was actually enjoined by the thinker himself: "In spite of his own lapses, the last thing that he wanted was to have the *mens autoris*, i.e., his own self-interpretation, determining the reader's appropriation of his texts and confrontation with *die Sache selbst*, the matter itself."[24]

Despite the paucity of explicit statements, we believe that there is a nearness (*Nähre*) of Heidegger's thinking and the Holocaust. This nearness can be established by the very method which Heidegger himself utilized in his confrontations (*Auseinandersetzungen*) with the great figures in the Western metaphysical tradition, such as Kant and Nietzsche. In his *Kantbuch*, Heidegger spells out the method of interpretation that guides him in his confrontations:

> Certainly, in order to wring [*abzuringen*] from what the words say, what it is they want to say, every interpretation [*Interpretation*] must neccessarily use violence. Such violence, however, cannot be roving arbitrariness. The power of an idea which shines forth must drive and guide the laying-out [*Auslegung*]. Only in the power of this idea can an interpretation risk what is always audacious, namely, entrusting itself to the concealed inner passion of a work in order to be able, through this, to place itself within the unsaid and force it into speech. That is one way, however, by which the guiding idea, in its power to illuminate, comes to light.[25]

Within this Heideggerian approach to a text, what seems relevant to us, in arguing for the nearness of Heidegger's thinking to the Holocaust, is precisely the need to bring what is unsaid into speech. Even if one questions the essentialism of this Heideggerian approach, its conviction that there is an interpretation that actually "gets the text right," a sure interpretative guide is provided by the need to bring out what is unstated, which provides the prospect of opening up a text, of questioning old and established interpretations become dogma, and providing the new metaphors—to use a Rortian trope—that may open up hitherto unimagined possibilities.

In utilizing this approach to grasp the nearness of Heidegger's thinking to the Holocaust, we intend first to show how Heidegger's *Denken* can illuminate the centrality of the Holocaust to the history of the West. Several constitutive features of the triumph of planetary technics, which were delineated by Heidegger in his later writings, made possible the unleashing of the destructive forces embodied in the Holocaust. We will then show how the Holocaust can illuminate the significance of basic elements of the later Heidegger's understanding of the reign of *das Ge-Stell*. We believe that on the basis of the experience of the Holocaust, it is possible to "unpack" the meaning of Heidegger's often enigmatic reflections on the history of Being.

We do not believe that Heidegger's thinking can "explain" the Holocaust, provide an account of its unfolding or its causality. Heidegger's concerns are historial, not historical, ontological, not ontic. Yet it is precisely on the basis of Heidegger's *Seinsgeschichte* that it may be possible to illuminate certain facets of the Holocaust that could elude the historian.

For Heidegger, the roots of *das Ge-Stell*, as the essence of modern technology, are to be found in the tradition of Western metaphysics. The Cartesian conception of humans as the "masters and possessors of nature" is a fertile source for the unfolding of planetary technics, the culminating point of which is embodied in Nietzsche's *Wille zur Macht*, which constitutes for Heidegger the completion of Western metaphysics. This absolutization of the subject, which recognizes no limit whatsoever to the human will, has its expression in Cartesian and Nietzschean metaphysics, and is the fundament from which could emerge a project such as the one embodied in the *Hitler-Staat*. One component of the project of Nazism was the attempt to control and reshape not merely external nature but the whole of human life itself. This latter manifested itself in the effort to utilize science and technology to create an Aryan (sic) racial elite, and to exterminate those races (beginning with the Jews) which were seen as congenitally diseased and tainted. This vast operation of social engineering, conceived as a massive hygienic undertaking, which sought to recreate man, is one outcome of the techno-scientific will to world mastery. However important it may be to elucidate the social, economic, and political genesis of Nazism in order to understand that phenomenon, its metaphysical bases in the conception of power that underlies planetary technics must also not be overlooked.

While Descartes and Nietzsche provided the bases for the metaphysics of the subject, and of the will-to-will, which Heidegger, in the late 1930s and 1940s, saw as the ground of planetary technics, in the 1950s he made a compelling case for the inclusion of Leibniz as a key figure in that tradition. In both his 1955/56 lecture course at the University of Freiburg, on "The Principle of Reason," and in his shorter 1956 address of the same title, Heidegger argued that Leibniz had codified the principle of reason—that nothing *is* without reason—as the veritable basis for the disclosing of entities:

> Modern technology pushes toward the greatest possible perfection. Perfection is based on the thoroughgoing calculability of objects. The calculability of objects presupposes the unqualified validity of the *principium rationis*. It is in this way that the authority characteristic of the principle of reason determines the essence of the modern, technological age.[26]

For Heidegger, so omnipotent and pervasive is the principle of reason that it "determines all cognition and behavior."[27] Moreover, the principle of reason, first codified by Leibniz in the seventeenth century, is only now revealing its sheer power and awesome imperialistic tendencies:

> The thinking of Leibniz supports and molds the chief tendency of . . . the metaphysics of the modern age. Therefore, for us the name of Leibniz does not stand as a tag for a bygone system of philosophy. The name names the presence of a thinking whose strength has not yet been experienced,

> a presence that still awaits to encounter us. Only through looking back on what Leibniz thought can we characterize the present age—an age one calls the atomic age—as an age pervasively bepowered by the power of the *principium reddendae rationis sufficientis*.[28]

This principle of sufficient reason, the basis of calculative thinking, in its totalizing, and imperialistic, form, can be seen as the metaphysical underpinning which made the Holocaust possible. Modern science and technology, applied to the task of genocide; the bureaucratic organization of the factories of death; and the transportation system which supplied them with their "raw material"; indeed, the very fact that there could be something called "the Jewish problem," requiring a scientific and bureaucratic solution, the "Final Solution," are all ways in which reality can show up for us when it is governed by the principle of reason. Standing reserve is, for Heidegger, the way in which beings are disclosed under the sway of the *principium rationis*.

The Heideggerian understanding of *Machenschaft* (machination), of *das Ge-Stell*, of *Bestand* (standing reserve), illuminates the industrialization of death symbolized by Auschwitz. We believe that the gas chambers constituted a decisive moment in the process of unfettered techno-scientific manipulation of reality that Heidegger elucidated, in his reflections on *Machenschaft*, in the *Beiträge zur Philosophie*, composed in 1936–38 and only published in 1989. With respect to their victims, as opposed to their operation, these same gas chambers represented a crucial point in the process by which human beings were reduced to the status of raw material, of standing reserve, to be disposed of by other humans, like so many waste products to be turned into ashes. In his history of Being, did Heidegger ever envisage the possibility of such an outcome, of humans becoming not merely objects but raw material or standing reserve? In his "Overcoming Metaphysics," notes written between 1936 and 1946, Heidegger—writing in the midst of the World War—spoke of humans as "raw material" (*Rohstoff*).[29] Several years later, in "The Question Concerning Technology," Heidegger entertained the prospect that humans were in danger of being reduced to *Bestand*[30]: "As soon as what is unconcealed no longer concerns man even as object, but does so, rather, exclusively as standing-reserve . . . then he comes to the very brink of a precipitous fall; that is, he comes to the point where he himself will have to be taken as standing-reserve."[31] In his contemporaneous lecture on "Science and Reflection," this grim prospect was conceived thusly:

> The subject-object relation thus reaches, for the first time, its pure "relational," i.e., ordering, character in which both the subject and the object are sucked up as standing-reserves. That does not mean that the subject-object relation vanishes, but rather the opposite: it now attains to its most extreme dominance, which is predetermined from out of Enframing. It becomes a standing-reserve to be commanded and set in order.[32]

Heidegger's account of the danger, of the reduction of humans to raw material or standing reserve, which is one leitmotiv of his later thinking, is—as Hans-Georg Gadamer said of the conclusions reached by the young Heidegger in his early Marburg days—"A genuine Heidegger-statement, full of ambiguity."[33] In this instance, the ambiguity lies in whether we take the reduction of humans to raw material or *Bestand* as already completed, as the citations from "Overcoming Metaphysics" or "Science and Reflection" strongly imply, or as a tendency, far advanced, but not yet complete, a conclusion to which a reading of "The Question Concerning Technology" seems to lead. Our own reading of Heidegger, as well as our view of the horrendous experience of humankind in the death-world of Auschwitz, inclines us to the view that there is a space for human action (*Handeln*) to find a way out of the danger, which we conceive as an awesome threat. We believe that the smokestacks of Auschwitz are one of the most gruesome expressions of precisely that danger to which Heidegger pointed.[34] The Auschwitz-apocalypse expresses this danger both in the action of the bureaucrats who organized and administered the Extermination and in the victims who succumbed to it.

The Heideggerian understanding of the absence of meditative, or reflective, thinking as a hallmark of the reign of planetary technics illuminates the role of the human type necessary to the actual implementation of the Holocaust, the desk killer.[35] It was these desk killers, typified by Adolf Eichmann, who made possible the smooth and efficient operation of the complex technological network that culminated in the operation of the gas chambers. The bureaucrats whose task it was to organize and manage the industrial production of death were less the product of ideological fanaticism than of the ambient thoughtlessness. For Heidegger "[t]houghtlessness is an uncanny visitor who comes and goes everywhere in today's world,"[36] and thus the total absence of a capacity for radical questioning is a pre-eminent feature of the "essential distress" (*Not*) created by *Machenschaft* and enframing. The desk killer is an exemplar of just such thoughtlessness, of the absence of any capacity to question the orders he or she so assiduously executes. Where such thoughtlessness reigns, even the very language which humans speak is transformed, and the moral responsibility of the official ceases to be factor in his or her behavior. When murder becomes a hygienic act, when the disposal of corpses becomes an act of sanitation, the new "language rules" make it possible for the bureaucrat to be smoothly transformed into the desk killer.

The fate of the desk killer's victims, those consumed by the operation of the gas chambers, is revealed in all its starkness by Heidegger's reflections on what it means to be a mortal (*Sterblicher*) and the conditions under which that mortality is denied and humans perish but do not die. We have already pointed to this aspect of Heidegger's thinking, but we are now able to tie it more directly to the phenomenon of the *Muselmänner* in the death camps.

As Fackenheim has pointed out: "The most characteristic success of the Holocaust world . . . is another new man: the *Muselmann* who is already dead while still alive."[37] This human type, virtually incapable of the range of human emotions, of thought and responsibility, was one of the most frightening products of the death camps. For Fackenheim, the *Muselmann* exemplifies the objective of Nazism: "The Nazi state had no higher aim than to murder souls while bodies were still alive."[38] Heidegger's thinking permits us to see that the *Muselmann* is not so much dead while alive, or a human type whose soul is dead, but rather a person denied his very mortality, her possibility of confronting an authentic death. Heidegger's insights make it possible to understand that the *Muselmann* is denied the possibility of facing his finitude, of facing up to her freedom toward death, a dimension of the *Muselmann* that is overlooked by conventional historical and psychological accounts. However, the existence of the *Muselmann* should not obscure the fact that all the victims were not reduced to this state. Fackenheim's "spectrum of resistance" reveals the existence of large numbers of victims who escaped the fate of the *Muselmänner*, who resisted, and were thus able to die and not perish. Moreover, the process by which mortals were turned into *Muselmänner* was an exceedingly complex one.[39] That notwithstanding, Heidegger's reflections on dying and perishing provide an important insight into a particularly disturbing aspect of the Holocaust.

While facets of Heidegger's thinking can provide insight into the experience of the Extermination, make it possible for *us* to think Auschwitz, the Holocaust can also help us to penetrate the opaqueness of the later Heidegger's thinking. Heidegger's "narrative," as it emerges in his Bremen lectures (published as "The Question Concerning Technology," "The Thing," and "The Turning"), and related texts such as "Building Dwelling Thinking" and *Identity and Difference*, concerns the fourfold (*das Geviert*) of earth, sky, mortals, and gods, whose interplay and oneness constitutes a world. This primordial realm is challenged by enframing and the reign of planetary technics, from which arises the danger. The shattering of the fourfold, the reduction of all beings, including humans, to *Bestand*, raises the specter that humans will cease to be mortals. World no longer worlds, and the *Unwelt* spawned by nihilism looms on the horizon. Yet Heidegger's narrative does not end here. At this point, Heidegger turns to Hölderlin and recalls the poet's words:

> But where danger is, grows
> the saving power also. . . .

The experience of *das Ge-Stell* can lead to *das Er-eignis*, the event of appropriation, in which man and Being are delivered over to each other:

> What we experience in enframing as the constellation of Being and man through the modern world of technology is a prelude [*Vorspiel*] to what is called the event of appropriation.[40]

How can we penetrate the veil of obscurity that surrounds Heidegger's narrative? How can we unpack the meaning of Heidegger's language, replete with gods and mortals, danger and saving? We believe that the experience of the Holocaust, that transformative event, can illuminate the meaning of Heidegger's narrative and make his tale pellucid.

The Holocaust can provide insight into the meaning of the danger that threatens the West. We are not suggesting that the Holocaust constitutes that danger, but rather that it is a *sign* of that danger. For Heidegger the danger was that, as a result of the reduction of nature and humans to standing reserve, the oneness of the fourfold would be definitively shattered and modern man would cease to be a mortal and would henceforth perish but not die. For Heidegger, such a condition would be marked not simply by the forgetting of Being, but—far worse—by a forgetting of the forgetting of Being; the essential distress of modernity would be immeasurably heightened by the inability of humans to any longer "feel" that distress. In place of a world, humankind would inhabit an un-world (*Unwelt*). While Heidegger is eloquent concerning the danger in his later writings, the fashion in which man's factical existence would be actually transformed by the growing specter of an un-world, the stages by which such an *Unwelt* would emerge, as the danger loomed, was never clearly spelled out.

Hubert Dreyfus, basing himself on Heidegger's own insistence that what threatened man, the "real" danger, was less the atomic bomb than the technological understanding of Being that tendentially reduced all beings to standing reserve, has concluded that the un-world that Heidegger saw emerging might be a "perfectly ordered society dedicated to the welfare of all."[41] This view, that the *Unwelt* might be a smoothly functioning, consumerist society, though one in which man no longer felt distress and no longer manifested a concern for Being, a society in which there would seem to be no place for Auschwitz and its death-world, seems questionable to us.

If Heidegger was determined to show that what threatens man was not the atomic bomb but the reign of *das Ge-Stell*, it was not to deny the threat posed by the bomb, but rather to make clear that the bomb was the culmination of a process that began with the technological understanding of Being. As Heidegger asserts in "The Thing": "Man stares at what the explosion of the atom bomb could bring with it. He does not see that the atom bomb and its explosion are the mere final emission of what has long since taken place, has already happened."[42] Heidegger does not deny the threat posed by the bomb, or the train of destruction that would characterize such an un-world, so much as insist on its source, and identify what he sees as its *Grund.*

Moreover, what is implied in Dreyfus's position is that the smoothly functioning society and the death-world are mutually exclusive, that the man-made mass death symbolized by Auschwitz cannot be factored into the un-world. But why is the extermination of those designated as the Other, those who are the embodiment of alterity, incompatible with this image of a "perfectly ordered society"? It seems to us that the horror of the death-world can all too easily be routinized and normalized in an *Unwelt,* where humans have been turned into standing reserve.

Finally, the image of the un-world as a site where "everyone might simply become healthy and happy," even as they forget their forgetting of Being,[43] overlooks Heidegger's insistence, in his "Overcoming Metaphysics," that: "The 'world wars' and their character of 'totality' are already a consequence of the abandonment of Being."[44] It is precisely this character of the *Unwelt* as a site of misery and devastation which seems to stamp Heidegger's thinking. Thus, in his Heraclitus lecture course of 1943, Heidegger raises the question of the "progress" to which humankind can look forward under the reign of planetary technics: "Forward? Where to, please? To the shattered cities on the Rhine and the Ruhr?"[45] This imagery of broken cities and people seems to us to better accord with Heidegger's vision of the un-world than that of a consumer society.

Thus, we believe that Auschwitz constitutes a grim sign of what it would mean for the oneness of *das Geviert* to be shattered, for the dwelling (*Wohnung*) of mortals to be destroyed, and of just how close that threat is. At Auschwitz the Heideggerian imagery became real: Behind its barbed wire we can see, in all its horror, what in Heideggerian terms might constitute the end of the world. The Holocaust thereby provides an indication of what an *Unwelt* would look like. The linkage of the Holocaust to the image of the un-world makes it possible to bring out what is *latent* in the Heideggerian text.

Just as the Holocaust may enable us to better grasp what Heidegger means when he speaks of the danger and the *Unwelt,* so too might it provide insight into the saving (*das Rettende*), which, for Heidegger, appears where the danger is. It most certainly is not our intention to claim that the Holocaust in any way is the saving; we can imagine no more obscene a formulation. The experience of the Holocaust, however, may provide insight into the prospects for such a saving.

Heidegger's vision of the saving often appears to exclude human action, to be conceived in terms of "Only a god can save us," to recall the title of Heidegger's *Spiegel* interview. Certainly the later Heidegger, with whom we are here concerned, had abandoned the Nietzschean voluntarism based on a heroic concept of "resoluteness" that characterized his thinking in 1933. For the later Heidegger, the saving, no less than the danger, is a *Geschick* of

Being,[46] and not the outcome of human will. However, the concept of *Geschick* must be distinguished from that of *Schicksal* (fate). As Bernstein puts it: "Destining is never a fate that compels."[47] If Heidegger tries to show that a *Geschick* of Being comprises what he means by freedom, he nonetheless understands it as a sending of Being. If *Geschick* is a mittence of Being, Heidegger has only limited space to maneuver if he is to avoid an hypostasization of Being. While Heidegger insists that the *Geschick* of Being does not determine an unalterable course *within* the epoch that Being sends, it is not always clear what role humans play in the generation of the epoch in which they find themselves, or in the abrupt irruption of a new one. At this point a profound ambiguity shapes the Heideggerian discourse. On the one hand, if the saving is a *Geschick* of Being, then it nonetheless seems to proceed through the action (*Handeln*) of mortals. As Edith Wyschogrod puts it: "Being needs the coming to presence of man, who is the safekeeper of Being. Thus any change in the destining of Being requires man's cooperation."[48] On the other hand, Heidegger has also suggested that Being creates man to manifest itself, thereby transferring all agency from a being (mortals) to Being. Thus, in his 1935 lecture course, *An Introduction to Metaphysics*, Heidegger said that "The *Da-sein* of historical man means: to be posited as the breach into which the preponderant power of Being [*Seins*] bursts in its appearing, in order that this breach should shatter against Being."[49]

If we follow this latter path with Heidegger, then the saving would appear to have little to do with the *Handeln* of mortals. If we follow the former path, then it is the nature of this "cooperation," or rather Heidegger's understanding of action, that must concern us if we are to address the question of the saving and the possible insight into it that is provided by the Holocaust. Heidegger makes a distinction between *Handeln* (action) and *Tun* (doing or making). The latter is integrally linked to *Technik* and its mode of disclosing entities. As such it is part of the danger and not the saving. As Heidegger asserts in "The Question Concerning Technology": "Human activity [*menschliches Tun*] can never directly counter this danger."[50] *Handeln*, however, includes thinking or reflection (*Besinnung*), and this latter is a crucial factor in the saving. Heidegger insists that thinking is itself action, and that the readiness for the saving—without which it cannot take place—occurs through thinking and poetry. In 1966, in the *Spiegel* interview, Heidegger forged a link, albeit not a causal one, between thinking and the saving:

> It is not a matter of simply waiting until something occurs to human beings after three hundred years have gone by; it is about thinking ahead, without prophetic claims, into the coming time from the standpoint of the fundamental characteristics of the present age, which have hardly been thought through. Thinking is not inactivity, but is itself the action that has a dialogue with the world's destiny. . . . I do not think the situation

> of human beings in the world of planetary technology is an inextricable and inescapable disastrous fate; rather I think that the task of thinking is precisely to help . . . human beings to attain an adequate relationship to the essence of technology. . . .[51]

Such a thinking that can prepare for the saving involves a radical questioning of every facet of reality and its *Weltanschauungen*, including philosophy and science. That at least is one way to understand the meaning of the statement with which Heidegger concludes "The Question Concerning Technology": "For questioning is the piety of thinking."[52]

The Heideggerian concepts of thinking and questioning seem to us to provide too little in the way of agency. We agree with Richard Bernstein that what is needed to face the challenge of planetary technics is a concept of praxis or *phronesis*, precisely those concepts which Heidegger rejected as early as the 1920s, concepts taken up and elaborated by his students, Hannah Arendt and Hans-Georg Gadamer.[53] Nonetheless, despite our reservations concerning Heidegger's rejection of a concept of praxis, we can still share his insistence on the centrality of thinking and questioning. Yet, for thinking and questioning to even arise, there must already be a limit to the process by which human beings are turned into standing reserve. In "The Question Concerning Technology," Heidegger alludes to just such a limit: "Precisely because man is challenged more originally than are the energies of nature, i.e., into the process of ordering, he never is transformed into mere standing-reserve."[54] A limit short of the complete transformation of humans into standing reserve would itself be, in Heideggerian terms, a *Geschick* of Being, one which perforce involved human action. Such a *Geschick* of Being would, we suggest, manifest itself in a Refusal; a refusal to become standing reserve and to perish and not die.

Can the experience of the Holocaust shed any light on the possibility of such a refusal, of a limit to the transformation of humans into *Bestand*? The experience of the death-camps may provide an answer to the question of whether or not anyone can resist the process of being turned into a *Muselmann*, of being reduced to standing reserve.

Confronted by the reign of planetary technics, in which all the fruits of modern science and technology were devoted to the industrial production of death, what is astonishing is not that humans could be turned into *Muselmänner* but that anyone could escape that seemingly inexorable fate. Astonishing though it is, the triumph of nihilism, exemplified by Nazism and its death-camps, did not succeed in reducing all of its victims to *Muselmänner* before exterminating them. As Emil Fackenheim has pointed out:

> The Holocaust may paralyze *thought*, even *after* the event. Astoundingly, it did not *wholly* succeed in paralyzing the *existence singled out by it*—the

> victims—*during* the event itself, i.e. while the Holocaust world held undisputed sway. . . . *The Nazi logic was irresistible, yet was being resisted*: this is the enormous fact that must be grasped. And thought, if it grasps but a single instance of such resistance, and of but the most prosaic sort, has no choice but to be radically, permanently astonished.[55]

The acts of resistance undertaken by the inmates of the death-camps were for the most part not violent, although camp revolts did occur. The *act* of resistance, however, cannot be limited to violence:

> Oppression as violent as that under which we lived automatically provoked resistance. Our entire existence in the camp was marked by it. When the employees of "Canada" detoured items destined for Germany to the benefit of their fellow internees, it was resistance. When labourers at the spinning mills dared to slacken their working pace, it was resistance. . . . When clandestinely, we passed letters from one camp to another, it was resistance. When we endeavored, and sometimes with success, to reunite two members of the same family—for example, by substituting one internee for another in a gang of stretcher bearers—it was resistance.[56]

This capacity for resistance, which marks a limit to the possibility of transforming humans into standing reserve, was not extinguished even where the reign of planetary technics and nihilism had reached their zenith.

Another facet of such a Refusal which found expression even in the death-camps was the capacity to face death and not to perish, which constitutes the very hallmark of being mortal for Heidegger. Here the voice of a survivor, Pelagia Lewinska, is exemplary:

> I felt under orders to live. . . . And if I did die in Auschwitz, it would be as a human being, I would hold onto my dignity. I was not going to become the contemptible, disgusting brute my enemy wished me to be. . . . And a terrible struggle began which went on day and night.[57]

For Heidegger, the saving is linked to our continued existence as mortals and, therefore, we would add, to the prospects for refusal to become standing reserve. The Holocaust can illuminate the possibilities for the saving to appear where the danger is, because even within the factories of death themselves it was still possible for a human to be mortal and for the Refusal to find expression.

The Holocaust can provide a sign of the saving, not only through the horrendous experience of its victims yesterday but also through its impact on us today. We, who are living through the actuality of the reign of planetary technics, and therefore under the shadow of new technicized genocides, can be goaded into thinking and questioning by the Holocaust and the lessons we draw from it. And it is precisely on the basis of such thinking and on the insight (*Einblick*) the Holocaust may provide that the readiness for the saving may arise. Otto Pöggeler's *Martin Heidegger's Path of Thinking*, which was based on frequent and ongoing discussion with his subject, provides us with an understanding of what is at stake:

> The "insight" does not bind man ultimately to that which is valid today as real. If this insight discerns that which is as the danger, then it becomes the "lightning flashing in" [*Einblitz*] which draws man into the precipitous holding sway of unconcealment, which brings man before the breaking open of the structural fitting-together of unconcealment, of world as the fourfold of earth and sky, gods and mortals.[58]

Such insight, which for Heidegger is itself a *Geschick* of Being, proceeds from thinking understood as disruption that leads to questioning. Thinking provoked by the disruption of what is taken for granted can spark a radical questioning of that which is. The Holocaust, an expression of *das Ge-Stell*, even while it interrupts its facade of normalcy can also disrupt our accepted patterns of thinking. The Holocaust should make the taken-for-granted world appear strange and uncanny, thereby generating a compelling need to question what we "normally" do not question: the techno-scientific world which shapes our experience. In Heideggerian terms, such a disruption and the thinking it compels can prepare us to receive a new *Geschick* of Being. In that way, the Holocaust may yet be an antechamber to the Heideggerian *Einblitz*.

How should we think Auschwitz, what lessons should we draw from the experience of the Holocaust, in order to have this insight? The dominant trend in contemporary philosophy and social theory has viewed Nazism largely as a violent reaction to modernity, an atavistic reversion to the barbarism of the distant past, born of Germany's peculiar *Sonderweg*, purportedly so different from the path to technological civilization taken in the West. On this reading, the Holocaust is seen as an historical aberration, the product of a society that repudiated modernity, and not as one possible expression of the triumph of planetary technics. Such a reading, in our view, precludes the insight that the experience of Auschwitz makes possible: that modernity, with its basis in planetary technics, contains as one of its possibilities the industrial production of death, the technological extermination of masses of humans; that such an outcome, far from constituting a repudiation of modernity, is one possibility inherent in it.[59] The thinking that recognizes in the Holocaust an event born not of a deviation from the trajectory of our civilization, but rather the actualization of a potential contained within it, can perhaps spark the Heideggerian *Einblick*.

That such an insight did not explicitly arise from the thinking of Martin Heidegger is a part of the tragedy of the man who would be one of the West's great *Denkers*. His failing in this respect is monumental, his responsibility enormous. And that not because of his actions as Rector of Freiburg University, odious though they were, but rather precisely because the nearness of his thinking to the Holocaust could have—in the three decades after the destruction of the Third Reich—given rise to the insight, and altered the very terms in which we envisage the relationship of the Holocaust to our Western, now global, civilization.

NOTES

1. Jacques Derrida, "On Reading Heidegger: An Outline of Remarks to the Essex Colloquium", in *Research in Phenomenology*, XVII (1987), p. 173.
2. Philippe Lacoue-Labarthe, *La poésie comme expérience* (Paris: Christian Bourgois Éditeur, 1986), pp. 167–168.
3. Philippe Lacoue-Labarthe, "Neither an Accident nor a Mistake", in *Critical Inquiry*, 15, 2 (Winter 1989), p. 484.
4. See François Fédier, *Heidegger: anatomie d'un scandale* (Paris: éditions Robert Laffont, 1988), pp. 240–241.
5. Jean-François Lyotard, *Heidegger and "the jews"* (Minneapolis: University of Minnesota Press, 1990), p. 52.
6. George Steiner, "Heidegger, Again," in *Salmagundi*, 82–83 (Spring-Summer 1989), pp. 48–49.
7. Richard Bernstein, "Heidegger's Silence?: *Ethos* and Technology," in Richard Bernstein, *The New Constellation: The Ethical-Political Horizons of Modernity/Postmodernity* (Cambridge: The MIT Press, 1992), p. 80.
8. See in particular "The Rectorate 1933/34: Facts and Thoughts," and the "Spiegel Interview with Martin Heidegger," in Günther Neske and Emil Kettering, *Martin Heidegger and National Socialism: Questions and Answers* (New York: Paragon House, 1990).
9. Philippe Lacoue-Labarthe, *Heidegger, Art and Politics* (Oxford: Basil Blackwell, 1990), p. 37.
10. One factor in Heidegger's silence concerning the Holocaust may have been that to have confronted it would have also involved him in a confrontation with his own political engagement on behalf of Nazism. Such a confrontation would have entailed an acknowledgment of the fact that his support for the *Hitler-Staat*, however shortlived and qualified, implicated him in the crimes of the regime. In the event, Heidegger's silence concerning the Holocaust is of a piece with his carefully crafted version of a brief and only peripheral involvement with Nazism. For an analysis of Heidegger's thinking, and its relationship to Nazism, see Alan Milchman and Alan Rosenberg, "Resoluteness and Ambiguity: Martin Heidegger's Ontological Politics, 1933–35," in *The Philosophical Forum*, XXV, 1 (Fall 1993), pp. 72–93.
11. These two statements have been the occasion for extensive commentary in the critical literature. See in particular: Karsten Harries, "Introduction" to Neske and Kettering, *Martin Heidegger and National Socialism*; Wolfgang Schirmacher, *Technik und Gelassenheit: Zeitkritik nach Heidegger* (Freiburg/Munich: Verlag Karl Alber, 1983), pp. 25–28; Michael Zimmerman, *Heidegger's Confrontation with Modernity: Technology, Politics, Art* (Bloomington and Indianapolis: Indiana University

Press, 1990), p. 43; Richard Wolin, *The Politics of Being: The Political Thought of Martin Heidegger* (New York: Columbia University Press, 1991) pp. 168–169; Thomas Sheehan, "Heidegger and the Nazis," in *The New York Review of Books*, June 16, 1988; Richard Bernstein, "Heidegger's Silence?" pp. 130–131; and Philippe Lacoue-Labarthe, *Heidegger, Art and Politics*, pp. 34–37.

12. Neske and Kettering, *Martin Heidegger and National Socialism*, p. xxx. The German original can be found in Schirmacher, *Technik und Gelassenheit*, p. 25.
13. Jürgen Habermas, "Work and Weltanschauung: The Heidegger Controversy from a German Perspective," in Jürgen Habermas, *The New Conservatism: Cultural Criticism and the Historians' Debate* (Cambridge: The MIT Press, 1989), p. 163.
14. See John D. Caputo, "Heidegger's Scandal: Thinking and the Essence of the Victim," in Tom Rockmore and Joseph Margolis (eds.), *The Heidegger Case: On Philosophy and Politics* (Philadelphia: Temple University Press, 1992), pp. 268–269.
15. Lyotard, *Heidegger and "the jews"*, p. 88.
16. Heidegger also equates the fate of the Jews and the Germans (in this case, the German inhabitants of the eastern lands, East Prussia, Silesia, etc.) in postwar correspondence with his old student, Herbert Marcuse. In his letter of January 20, 1948, Heidegger says that the treatment of the Jews by the Nazis, and that of the Germans in the eastern lands driven out by the Russians, was the same. Quite apart from the difference in the scale of the butchery (which in no way mitigates the slaughter wrought by the Russians), what separates the two events is the techno-scientific basis of the Holocaust, the existence of death-camps and gas chambers, which was not replicated in the uprooting of the German population in the East. That, most of all, renders Heidegger's position so reprehensible. For Heidegger's letter, see Richard Wolin, ed., *The Heidegger Controversy: A Critical Reader* (New York: Columbia University Press, 1991), pp. 162–163.
17. The acknowledgment that the Holocaust can be understood as an expression of *das Ge-Stell*, perhaps even as its apotheosis, is rare in the critical literature. Besides the argument put forth in the present essay, this view is present in Lacoue-Labarthe's writings on Heidegger, as well as in Bernstein's essay on "Heidegger's Silence?" Bernstein, commenting on Lacoue-Labarthe, puts it this way: "Ironically, Lacoue-Labarthe fails to appreciate how close he is to Heidegger when he claims 'In the Auschwitz apocalypse, it was nothing less than the West, in its essence, that revealed itself.' For even though Heidegger does not say this, nevertheless this is entailed by his analysis of the destining of *Gestell*. For *Gestell* itself is a consequence of the metaphysical humanism that has been the essence of the West. When we focus our attention on the *essence* of technology then Heidegger would agree that 'in the Auschwitz apocalypse, it is nothing less than the West, *in its essence*, that revealed itself.'" See Bernstein, "Heidegger's Silence?" p. 89.
18. Neske and Kettering, *Martin Heidegger and National Socialism*, p. xxix. The German original is in Schirmacher, *Technik und Gelassenheit*, p. 25.
19. Thomas Sheehan has read this same statement not as a lament for the horror of a denial of death to the victims of the extermination camps, but rather as an example of Heidegger's inhuman detachment from the evil of the Holocaust, a vision that is "damning beyond commentary." See Thomas Sheehan, "Heidegger and the Nazis," in *The New York Review of Books*, June 16, 1988, pp. 41–42. If we may extrapolate, it is as if, having been slaughtered by the Nazis, the victims were now to be denied the dignity of death by Heidegger, the thinker. Such a reading seems to us to miss the significance of perishing and not dying

for Heidegger: It is not a reflection on the one who perishes but on the nihilistic *Unwelt* (un-world), in which humans no longer face death, in which they cease to be mortals.

20. Hannah Arendt, *The Origins of Totalitarianism* (Cleveland: Meridian Books, 1958), p. 452.
21. Primo Levi, *Survival in Auschwitz* (New York: Orion Press, 1959), p. 82.
22. See Emil L. Fackenheim, *To Mend the World: Foundations of Post-Holocaust Thought* (New York: Schocken Books, 1989), pp. 201, 225.
23. Jacques Derrida, "Heidegger's Silence," in Neske and Kettering, *Martin Heidegger and National Socialism*, p. 148.
24. Edward J. van Buren, "The Young Heidegger: The Rumor of a Hidden King (1919–1926)," in *Philosophy Today*, 32, 2 (Summer 1989), p. 106.
25. Martin Heidegger, *Kant and the Problem of Metaphysics* (Bloomington: Indiana University Press, 1990), p. 138.
26. Martin Heidegger, *The Principle of Reason* (Bloomington and Indianapolis: Indiana University Press, 1991), p. 121.
27. Ibid.
28. Ibid., p. 33.
29. Martin Heidegger, "Overcoming Metaphysics," in Richard Wolin, ed., *The Heidegger Controversy: A Critical Reader* (New York: Columbia University Press, 1993), pp. 84 and 86. For the German original, see Heidegger, "Überwindung der Metaphysik," in Heidegger, *Vorträge und Aufsätze* (Pfullingen: Verlag Günther Neske, 1985), pp. 88 and 91.
30. For the purposes of the present essay, we are emphasizing the continuity in Heidegger's meditation on *Technik* in the period from the *Beiträge* to "The Question Concerning Technology." Nonetheless, it is also important to acknowledge the significant conceptual shifts in the Heideggerian *Denkweg*, precisely in this period when the thinker responds to the danger presented by the triumph, and globalization, of planetary technics. In the *Beiträge* (1936–38), Heidegger's concept of *Machenshaft* conveys the reduction of entities to objects to be mastered, administered, and controlled by subjects; in "Overcoming Metaphysics" (1940s), Heidegger focuses on the reduction of entities to "raw materials" (*Rohstoff*); in "The Question Concerning Technology" and contemporaneous writings of the late 1940s and early 1950s, Heidegger argues that entities have become *Bestand*, as the outcome of a process where the disclosure of beings is a "setting upon" (*Bestellen*), under the reign of *das Ge-stell*. The path traversed has been aptly grasped by Otto Pöggeler: "The standing reserve are no longer objects; rather, the objects which still maintain a certain vis-à-vis toward man in his capacity for presentation vanish into objectlessness when they become standing reserve." See Otto Pöggeler, *Martin Heidegger's Path of Thinking* (Atlantic Highlands, NJ: Humanities Press International, Inc., 1987), p. 197, translation modified.
31. Martin Heidegger, "The Question Concerning Technology," in Martin Heidegger, *The Question Concerning Technology and Other Essays* (New York: Harper Colophon Books, 1977), pp. 26–27.
32. Martin Heidegger, "Science and Reflection," in Heidegger, *The Question Concerning Technology*, p. 173.
33. Hans-Georg Gadamer, "Martin Heidegger and Marburg Theology (1964)," in Gadamer, *Philosophical Hermeneutics* (Berkeley: University of California Press, 1977), p. 198.

34. However, it was not only in the death-camps that humans were turned into *Bestand.* It seems to us that the totalitarian project of Nazism sought not merely to reduce those designated as "life unworthy of life," the *Untermenschen,* to standing reserve, but in a somewhat different fashion the whole of the German population as well. The mass of Germans were to be treated as raw materials, to be disposed of by the state in its imperialistic wars, expected to perish for the fatherland on its farflung battlefields.
35. For an analysis of the desk killer, see Alan Milchman and Alan Rosenberg, "Hannah Arendt and the Etiology of the Desk Killer: The Holocaust as Portent," in the *History of European Ideas,* 14, 2 (1992), pp. 213–226.
36. Martin Heidegger, *Discourse on Thinking: A Translation of Gelassenheit* (New York: Harper & Row, Publishers, 1966), p. 45.
37. Fackenheim, *To Mend the World,* p. 215.
38. Ibid., p. 100.
39. Both Barrington Moore Jr., in his *Injustice: The Social Bases of Obedience and Revolt,* and Anthony Giddens, in his *The Constitution of Society: Outline of the Theory of Structuration,* provide important theoretical reflections on the formation of the *Muselmann.*
40. Martin Heidegger, *Identity and Difference* (New York: Harper & Row, Publishers, 1969), pp. 36–37.
41. Hubert L. Dreyfus, "Heidegger on the Connection between Nihilism, Art, Technology, and Politics," in Charles B. Guignon, ed., *The Cambridge Companion to Heidegger,* (Cambridge: Cambridge University Press, 1993), p. 306.
42. Martin Heidegger, "The Thing," in *Poetry, Language, Thought* (New York: Harper Colophon Books, 1971), p. 166.
43. Dreyfus, "Heidegger on the Connection between Nihilism, Art, Technology, and Politics," p. 314.
44. Martin Heidegger, "Overcoming Metaphysics," in Wolin, *The Heidegger Controversy,* p. 84.
45. Martin Heidegger, *Heraklit: 1. Der Anfang des abendländischen Denkens; 2. Heraklits Lehre vom Logos, Gesamtausgabe,* Vol. 55 (Frankfurt am Main: Vittorio Klostermann, 1987), p. 78.
46. We will follow Reginald Lilly, who, in his translation of Heidegger's *Der Satz vom Grund* (*The Principle of Reason*), in which the concept of *Geschick* plays an important role, has chosen not to translate this term. The Heideggerian *Geschick* is fraught with ambiguity. On the one hand, it means "destiny," which even if it is distinguished from "fate" (*Schicksal*) nonetheless has strong theological overtones and seems to exclude human action; it can be translated as a "sending" or "mittence," but that raises the question of a possible hegemony of Being, as the sender, in which human action again disappears. For an account of the difficulty of translating *Geschick,* see the "Translators Introduction" to Martin Heidegger, *The Principle of Reason* (Bloomington and Indianapolis: Indiana University Press, 1991), pp. xiv–xv. For us, there is no way around the ambiguity that surrounds the Heideggerian *Geschick.* At times, it can mean that humans can react against the epoch that Being sends, though they have no part in shaping the contours of that self-same epoch; at other times, the *Geschick* of Being is itself not an unalterable course, and human action has a role in shaping it.
47. Bernstein, "Heidegger's Silence?" p. 40.
48. Edith Wyshogrod, *Spirit in Ashes: Hegel, Heidegger, and Man-Made Mass Death* (New Haven: Yale University Press, 1985), pp. 183–184.

49. Martin Heidegger, *An Introduction to Metaphysics* (New Haven: Yale University Press, 1959), p. 163, translation modified.
50. Heidegger, "The Question Concerning Technology," p. 33.
51. Neske and Kettering, *Martin Heidegger and National Socialism*, pp. 60–61.
52. Heidegger, "The Question Concerning Technology," p. 35. This is the way in which the young Heidegger pursued radical questioning in his early Freiburg, and first Marburg, lecture courses (1919–26). However, it should be noted that Heidegger himself explicated his comment on questioning as the piety of thinking to emphasize the "submissive" or "obedient" meaning of piety, in the ancient sense; even while he insisted that what is entailed by thinking "is to listen to the grant, not to ask questions." See Martin Heidegger, "The Nature of Language," in Heidegger, *On the Way to Language* (San Francisco: Harper & Row, Publishers, 1982), pp. 72 and 75. Our own earlier comments on interpretation, and the treatment of text, provide the basis for understanding the choice that we are here making.
53. Richard Bernstein has examined *phronesis* and praxis, their absence in the later Heidegger, and their centrality for Gadamer, in "Heidegger on Humanism" and "From Hermeneutics to *Praxis*." See Richard Bernstein, *Philosophical Profiles* (Philadelphia: University of Pennsylvania Press, 1986).
54. Heidegger, "The Question Concerning Technology," p. 18.
55. Fackenheim, *To Mend the World*, p. 201.
56. Olga Lengyel, *Five Chimneys: The Story of Auschwitz* (Chicago: Ziff-Davis, 1947), p. 154.
57. Pelagia Lewinska, *Twenty Months at Auschwitz* (New York: Lyle Stuart, 1968), p. 150.
58. Otto Pöggeler, *Martin Heidegger's Path of Thinking*, p. 200.
59. Such a view of modernity and its relationship to the Holocaust is found, for example, in the writings of Hannah Arendt; the first generation of Frankfurt School thinkers, such as Max Horkheimer and Theodor W. Adorno; Zygmunt Bauman; and such French postmodernists as Michel Foucault, Jacques Derrida, Jean-Luc Nancy, Philippe Lacoue-Labarthe, and Jean-François Lyotard. For a more detailed analysis of the connection between modernity and the Holocaust, see Alan Milchman and Alan Rosenberg, "The Unlearned Lessons of the Holocaust," in *Modern Judaism*, 13, 2 (1993), pp. 177–190.

14

"In Its Essence the Same Thing"

ELISABETH DE FONTENAY[1]

> The attempts to build up a European elite with a program of intra-European understanding based on the common European experience of the concentration camps have foundered. . . .
>
> —Hannah Arendt[2]

I

Let us examine this phrase which Heidegger uttered in Bremen in 1949: "Agriculture is now a mechanized food industry, the same thing in its essence as the production of corpses in the the gas chambers and the extermination camps, the same thing as blockades and the reduction of countries to famine, the same thing as the manufacture of hydrogen bombs." It is drawn from a lecture on technology which remains unpublished, cited for the first time in French by Philippe Lacoue-Labarthe.[3] I also cited it in "Fribourg-Prague-Paris,"[4] because it seemed to both confirm and invalidate the hypothesis that Heidegger misses the very point he is trying to make. This sentence is remarkable in that one of its clauses is a hapax, for it seems that Heidegger only once broke his silence about the extermination. "This sentence is . . . absolutely correct. But . . . scandalous and lamentably inadequate,"[5] writes Lacoue-Labarthe in a text which, as far as I know, is one of the few to confront the enigma of Heidegger's silence. It is precisely because of this exactitude and this inadequacy that Heidegger's thinking of technology and the historical reality of the death-camps must continue to be questioned together.

Heidegger's statement may, at first glance, appear as a provocation: The practice of the gas chambers deserves no more attention than other practices of modernity, which, from the perspective of their "essence," are analogous to it. The enumeration of signs of the age of technology which are at once heterogeneous and equivalent serves to drown the greatest crime recorded by history and by memory in the fatal banality of the techno-industrial process. Thus, it suggests that the combine-harvester pulled by the tractor treats the countryside and the traditional mode of life in the same way that Zyklon B treats unwanted peoples, as the strategy of famine treats civilian populations, and as the militaro-industrial techno-politics of the cold war treats the inhabitants of the planet. Thus, despite the euphemism of *Sonderbehandlung*, which the Nazis used until 1942, the "treatment" inflicted on the human beings exterminated in the gas chambers was nothing special. For Heidegger, the specificity which some attribute to it stems from an historical, humanistic, axiological approach, itself compromised by this metaphysics of representation involved in the disposition of all beings.

II

Should we not read this fragment more attentively, setting aside the nervous haste of indictments and apologies, and agreeing to follow a path of thought modelled on the *Holzwege*, the paths that lead nowhere of the woodcutters, rather than on those traced by the gas vans of the forest of Chelmno?[6] Anyone who overcomes their aversion and decides to walk for a while in Heidegger's path discovers that such a phrase illuminates, at the same time that it conceals, the disappropriating Event which names this, our epoch of Being. This speech of 1949 follows on the meditation "Overcoming Metaphysics,"[7] which took shape from 1936 to 1946 and even up until 1951, and in which the thinking of his *Nietzsche* on the will to will and its nihilism is still being painfully worked through.

Each section of this text raises harrowing questions in its reader. In what year was such and such a page written, in what month; what does this or that indication really mean; can one indeed read a difference in tone or intensity between what may have been written before and after 1945? The great motifs of the Heideggerian "turning point" are struck one by one in this rhapsody of the new world, in this dissonant and desolate suite for that which is no longer a world and no longer has an "essence."

First we hear the theme, Jüngerian in origin, of the *rational animal*, become the "working being," deployed as "laboring animal" and as "raw material," and left to the "giddy whirl of its products, so that it may tear itself to pieces and annihilate itself in empty nothingness."[8] To this theme is added that of technology as consummate and planetary metaphysics, whose fatality is opposed to the destiny of Being, and which calculates and organizes all things in all domains: science, culture, politics, values. . . . This will to will is characterized by its aimlessness, it "absolutely denies every goal and only admits goals as means."[9] It is "the anarchy of catastrophes and invents . . . the talk about mission."[10] In Fragments XXVI appear motifs of the Führer and of the overman, pathetically driven by absolute calculation and by the goal of securing an aimless action.

In "Overcoming Metaphysics" there are historical references to the "great facts of history which have marked this century," transparent allusions to Nazism, and a lament for the devastation of the earth which, without wishing either to provoke or to assimilate, I would compare to this text by Horkheimer: "Once it was the endeavor of art, literature and philosophy to express the meaning of things and of life, to be the voice of all that is dumb, to endow nature with an organ for making known her sufferings, or we ought to say, to call reality by its rightful name. Today nature's tongue is taken away. Once it was thought that each utterance, word or cry or gesture had an intrinsic meaning; today it is merely an occurrence."[11]

III

The sequence of 1949 must thus be understood within such a progression, even if one might legitimately question an experience of thinking which dismisses historical experience. Despite the ruse of denial—conscious or not—there is here an act of recognition which testifies to a certain audacity. Words are spoken which are significant, since they come from a man who was once a member of the Nazi party: death-camp, gas chamber. Heidegger denies, no doubt, but he does not use euphemisms. And the mention, in 1949, of such realities, by the names which designate their function, is worthy of note. For in this period, and even later, it was concentration camps and crematoria which named the culmination of the Nazi crime. "An effort is needed to recall as much," writes Pierre Vidal-Naquet, "but in the years following the war, the symbol of the world of the concentration camps was not Auschwitz but Buchenwald. . . . in 1962, the number of books published on Buchenwald clearly exceeded the number devoted to the great Silesian slaughterhouse."[12] Similarly, people spoke for a long time of "crematoria," the *Krematorium* designating the death camp as a whole. The Nazis practiced euphemism by synecdoche, and the survivors adopted their mode of reference, also sanctioning the inappropriate term "holocaust," as though the destruction by fire of the corpses were more horrifying than the destruction by gas of the living. Paradoxically, it is revisionism which, by antiphrasis, has, so to speak, popularized knowledge of the Nazi extermination process, and thus made us so sensitive to this moment in Heidegger. In any event, the philosopher goes straight to the fact, avowing his knowledge and attempting to compass it. Granted, he denies its singularity, but he nevertheless invests it with historial status, suggesting that the very destiny of Being is at stake in this process. In view of the dead, one may find this derisory, and deplore the fact that this reference, very particular in style, is the only one. But one cannot, at least if one has read Heidegger, say that it lacks "grandeur." The gas chambers have, in some sense, irrupted into his train of thought, even if they have not directed it.

IV

What is in question, then, is the "manufacture of corpses." The extermination does not, Heidegger suggests, consist in causing or allowing the death of populations by means of execution, torture, forced labor, hunger or typhus, but in *working* toward their elimination as though the production of raw materials depended on it. The exterminators, neither soldiers nor policemen nor ruffians, were conscientious workers who, in difficult work conditions, took the burden on themselves and made productivity their only concern. The use of the gas chambers is thus not a case of murder, and barely resembles an execution: No blood is shed. "What meaning has the concept of murder," asks Hannah Arendt, "when we are confronted with the mass production of corpses?"[13] Moreover, the neighboring populations and even the victims themselves were not supposed to suspect the nature of the process. Again, Hannah Arendt writes: "That one wanted to eliminate all personal motives and passions during the executions and thus keep the cruelties to a minimum is revealed by the fact that a group of doctors and engineers entrusted with handling the gas installations were making constant improvements that were not only designed to raise the productive capacity of the corpse factories but also to accelerate and ease the agony of death."[14]

Yet this massive production is always already an overproduction, requiring destruction, and as such it appears demented: Heidegger had to make the detour through his *Nietzsche*, in other words, through the discovery that the apparently irrationalist vitalism of the will to power found its truth in the Cartesian ideal of total mobilization in the service of the dispositive, to reach his 1949 evocation of the Nazi machine and its special actions as the completion of technologism, rather than some base impulse of a *Sturm und Drang* gone mad. Thus the production-destruction of corpses serves no purpose, at least in its genocidal phase, which is, "in essence," more nihilistic than its euthanasiac phase. It is auto-referential and in no way furthers either military objectives or those of a wartime economy—unless one regards as utilitarian the theory that the perspective of total mobilization demands the elimination of unmobilizable women, children, and the elderly, and, of course, able-bodied men who, as survivors, might try to avenge their people.

What is involved is rather a Stakhanovist wasting of raw materials and work force. It was denounced by Hans Frank in 1941, in a speech which is cited by Hannah Arendt: "His numerous complaints as Governor General of Poland testify to a total lack of understanding of the deliberately anti-utilitarian tendencies of Nazi policy. He cannot understand why the subjected peoples are not exploited but exterminated." In the same vein, "Rosenberg, in the eyes of Hitler, was racially unreliable because he meant to establish satellite states in the conquered eastern territories and did not understand that Hitler's population policy aimed at depopulating these territories."[15] One can thus follow Heidegger and Arendt in suggesting that Nazism represents the implacable, endless finality of the *Gestell*:[16] an a-teleology which even enables us to differentiate this practice of extermination from the phenomena of slavery, colonialism, and concentration camps to which it has habitually been compared. The Wannsee conference planned and inaugurated a process of annihilation which should be defined as a laboratory, in which, irrespective of utility, all possibilities were experimented with, and whose sole applied research consisted in the quantitative and qualitative improvement of the relation of *quo modo* to *quantum*.

To the extent that the administrative massacres by means of gas manifest the inordinate power of the pure will to will, "the uniformity of calculation transformable into planning . . . (which) has aimlessness as its aim,"[17] the economic interpretation becomes redundant. For technology, in its completed, metaphysical form and phase is in no sense technological, and industry in no sense industrial. Heidegger said in Zurich in 1951 that "The atom bomb exploded already in the Cartesian cogito."[18] In Bremen, he might have claimed that the gas chambers were already functioning in the cogito: an untenable foreshortening. Yet no contemporary philosopher should shrink from this question, since the assurances of the humanist and subjectivist tradition are not immune to this radical questioning, which bears less on their capacity to resist than on the types of hegemony which they have nurtured within their protective body. Our civilization is not prefaced by any testament," writes Char, cited by Arendt.[19]

If Heidegger only once broke his silence, and did so to note the historial status of the gas chambers, he did not say *nothing* about the thing itself, despite the terseness of this passing reference. When Kogon, Langbein, and Rückerl evoke the "gigantic and meticulous, bureaucratic and technocratic exercise of barbarism,"[20] when Gérard Granel speaks of "infinite production,"[21] when Raul Hilberg analyzes the order of transport route no. 587,[22] when Franz Suchomel, *Untersharführer* at Treblinka, exclaims of the rival camp: "Auschwitz was a factory!"[23] and when Adorno reflects on the "administrative murder of millions,"[24] they are saying the same thing, even if they are saying it differently.

V

Now, does the thinking which reveals the historicity of the extermination not also mask its historical singularity, and politically exonerate protagonists somewhat rapidly declared "pre-determined"? "The gas chambers . . . if only because of their enormous capacity, could not be intended for individual cases but only for people in general"[25] wrote Hannah Arendt in 1951. She would confirm and develop this thought in 1963: "Only the choice of the victims, not the nature of the crime, could be derived from the long history of Jew-hatred and anti-semitism."[26] Though she seems to forget page 678 of *Mein Kampf*, which explicitly links Jews and gas, Arendt leads us toward a clearer representation, by proposing something of the order of an articulation of two strands. One is the analysis of the origins of antisemitism in Christianity, in German thought and art, and indeed elsewhere: a task which does not require the Heideggerian thinking of planetarization. The other is a meditation on technology which would draw extensively on the thinking of the *Gestell* and which would exclusively concern the planning of an extermination, by gas, of various categories of people excluded from humanity. Anyone who, in working toward a representation of the unrepresentable, neglects one of these two strands will fall short of the most difficult questioning. Of a question which might be formulated thus: How did the juncture of atheist antisemitism and Christian anti-Judaism with an errant and implacable techno-scientific logic come about?

Here we touch on the limits of the approach suggested by Heidegger: One might say that, armed with the will not to know which durably equipped so many Germans, he is unable to cross the line and to ask why the Nazis planned and, despite their bureaucratic quarrels, to some extent realized, this final or definitive solution, which consisted in the annihilation of eleven million Jews. Why did the calculating machination single out this population? Jews, or perhaps Judaism, are Heidegger's shibboleth, as they were, rather consistently, that of Kant, Hegel, Feuerbach, and Marx. Not that one cannot graft racism onto a systematic technology of depopulation related to the *Gestell*—moreover, in "Overcoming Metaphysics" there is talk of the "room to live,"[27] of an axiology calculating who is and who is not worthwhile, and deciding who does not have the right to share the earth with the evaluators. But, in the end, we must still ask why the final solution was reserved for certain people? Treblinka, in which only Jews were gassed, retains its impenetrable singularity, even though Franz Suchomel complained of the primitive character of its installations.[28] This aporia brings the recognition of a deficiency: Since Heidegger views America as the reign of the culmination of technological errance and devastation, he is unable to differentiate—and this difference should nevertheless be able to be thought—Nazism from "Americanism."

We must therefore return again to the sentence, and to the analogy which it sustains. Initially, it is the comparison of extermination by gas with mechanized agriculture which is most profoundly shocking. Yet this is in fact a relationship which gives rise to thought, and which can even be said to forge a path along which Heidegger never ventured any further. He could have made a more precise reference to the agro-alimentary industry, evoking its experiments, the concentrational treatment often inflicted on animals, the constant fact of extermination. Adorno and Horkheimer adopt this approach, which they consider conclusive, in their reflexion on the dialectic of *Aufklärung*.[29] And Marguerite Yourcenar does not hesitate to link the cattle wagons and those "cattle cars in which animals die without food or water en route to the slaughterhouse."[30] As for Heidegger, if he is spectacularly silent about Judaism, and Jewishness, he has a lot to say about animality, though only to differentiate it from *Dasein*, as texts from all periods of his work testify.[31] He only fleetingly evokes the production of living beings and the genetic, manipulations next to which, he says, the hydrogen bomb seems insignificant.[32] But, in the end, he seems no more concerned for the fate of animals than for that of the Jews.

One should thus not precipitously conclude that Heidegger banalizes the extermination by gas in treating it as the equivalent of mechanized agriculture. On the contrary, his intention is to reveal the terrifying secret of an apparently inoffensive and even positive food industry. He relates the most hidden emergence of nihilism to a referent—the gas chamber—which is its most obscene manifestation.

VI

On a third reading of the "sentence," what suddenly resists and stands out, to the point that it disrupts the historical meditation, is the mention of the historical and classical practice of blockades, which, unlike machines, gas, and bombs, does not seem to stem from metaphysico-technological enframing. One need not invoke Descartes to account for this doubtless immemorial strategy! Since "blockade" is in the plural, it is possible that Heidegger also had the siege of Leningrad in mind, but when we recall his solemn recommendation to his students—albeit some years later—to visit an exhibition devoted to German prisoners of war in Russia,[33] it seems very likely that he was thinking of the Soviet blockade of Berlin. The functioning of the profound analogy, the secret identity set in motion by the *Gestell*, stumbles over two points. First, it must be reiterated, because this economico-military measure, which consists in turning civilian populations into hostages, has always existed and thus cannot be portrayed as a feature of planetary nihilism. In addition, and more curiously, if the point is to recall the blockade of Berlin, Heidegger is simply taking up, under cover of meditative thought, the old refrain of reciprocity in horror, to which former Nazis and their friends continually return: What one side did, the other did in turn. Dresden equals Auschwitz. Or, to be sure of avoiding accusations, Berlin equals Auschwitz equals Leningrad. There was really no need for Heidegger to mention the gas chambers if it was only to evoke, along with the historicity which must be thought, this history which had already been the subject of a great deal of thought. Thus, in the segment on blockades, the phrase harbors, beneath its meditation on the technicist Occident, the feeble and cunning equation of Soviet, Nazi, and American exactions.

Can we accept that there is no need to think in itself an extermination which was, overwhelmingly, that of the Jews; that the meditation must "transcend" the seemingly unique character of the "final solution," in the light of, from the perspective of, a more originary questioning which deconstructs the metaphysical tradition of subjectivity? To propose this kind of questioning is not to forget, but to work toward shaping a notion of singularity and a notion of humanity which is not weakened by instrumentalized pathos. What seems unacceptable, on the other hand, is to relate the use of gas chambers to that of blockades or of a single blockade. In this segment of the sequence, Heidegger convokes extreme horror only to restrict, minimize, relativize it. The only response should be to ask whether it is still the philosopher who is speaking. Again, it would be inappropriate. When the distinction between the theoretical and the ideological collapses, reveals its futility, as is the case with Heidegger, for Heidegger, the difference between ordinary Nazism and the philosophy of this epoch of Being in which we are becomes infinitesimal.

Yet again, it is America and not Nazi Germany which most perfectly embodies the will to will and the management (*être agi*) of total manipulation. Thus the text that is without doubt the most scabrous among those which have been cited against Heidegger would seem to be this fragment from a lecture on Hölderlin, given in 1942, after the United States entered the war. I will cite the first French translation of it, by Marc Froment-Meurice: "We know today that the Anglo-Saxon world of Americanism is determined to destroy Europe, and this means the fatherland and this means the principle of the West. The principle is indestructible. America's entry into this planetary war is not an entry into history, but already the last American act of American a-historicity and self-destruction. This act is, in effect, the abandonment of the principle and the choice of the anarchic. The hidden spirit of the Western principle will not even deign to look with scorn upon this anarchic process of self-destruction, but will await its star with the calm serenity which marks all that flows from the principle. . . . Could something of the like ever happen unless the historical humanity stemming from the principle had first, thanks to the pain of sacrifice, grown ripe for the principle as for its own good."[34] Even if, in terms of historicity, one can regard "Americanism" as the completed form of a nihilism which has even forgotten its European origin, it remains true that, historically speaking, the United States became at that time the potential liberator and savior of the whole of that wretched humanity condemned to extermination, slavery, and oppression, and that Heidegger did not see this, did not want it to be so.[35] Moreover, the Nazis had no doubts as to the importance of the event since, in the very month in which the Americans entered the war, they held the Wannsee conference during which the planning and organization of the "final solution" was completed.

Deconstruction has forged paths so disorienting that the urgent need to bring an end to the ontic practices of National Socialism could not appear to Heidegger without his suspecting that it remained caught up in the subjectivist-humanist closure of representation. In the same way—and this is the internal critique which must be brought to his sentence of 1949—Heidegger did not allow the extermination to enter into his thinking of Being because he continued to ignore the encounter of planetary technology with this German destiny, whose motif nevertheless also haunts his work.

Translated by Madeleine Dobie

NOTES

1. This essay originally appeared in *Le Messager européen*, 2 (1988), pp. 159–177.
2. Hannah Arendt, *The Origins of Totalitarianism* (New York: Harcourt, Brace and World, 1952), Vol. 3, pp. 139–140.
3. Philippe Lacoue-Labarthe, *Heidegger, Art, and Politics* (Oxford: Basil Blackwell, 1990), p. 34. His source is Wolfgang Schirmacher, *Technik und Gelassenheit* (Freiburg/Munich: Verlag Karl Alber, 1984).
4. Elisabeth de Fontenay, "Fribourg-Prague-Paris," *Le Messager européen*, 1 (1987), note 90, p. 121.
5. Lacoue-Labarthe, *Heidegger*, p. 34.
6. Translators note: "Paths that lead nowhere" translates "Chemins qui ne mènent nulle part," the title of the French translation of *Holzwege*.
7. Martin Heidegger, *The End of Philosophy* (New York: Harper & Row, 1973).
8. Ibid., pp. 86–87 and 104.
9. Ibid., p. 101.
10. Ibid., p. 102.
11. Max Horkheimer, *Eclipse of Reason* (New York: Continuum Books, 1974), p. 101.
12. Pierre Vidal-Naquet, *Assassins of Memory* (New York: Columbia University Press, 1992), p. 175, note 92.
13. Hannah Arendt, *The Origins of Totalitarianism*, Vol. 3, p. 139.

14. Ibid., p. 152, note 159.
15. Ibid., p. 102, note 44.
16. *Gestell*: the enframing of nature by technology. See Martin Heidegger, "The Question Concerning Technology," in David Farrell Krell (ed.), *Martin Heidegger: Basic Writings* (New York: Harper & Row, 1977), p. 301.
17. "Overcoming Metaphysics," in *The End of Philosophy*, pp. 102 and 106.
18. Cited by Dominique Janicaud, in *Magazine littéraire*, No. 235, p. 49.
19. Hannah Arendt, *La Crise de la Culture* (Paris: Gallimard, 1972), p. 11.
20. E. Kogon, H. Langbein, A. Rückerl, *Les Chambres à gaz, secret d'état* (Paris: Seuil, 1987), p. 261.
21. Gérard Granel, *De l'Université* (Paris: TER, 1982), p. 142.
22. Claude Lanzmann, *Shoah* (New York: Pantheon Books, 1985), pp. 138–141.
23. Ibid., p. 62.
24. Theodor W. Adorno, *Negative Dialectics* (New York: Continuum, 1992), p. 362.
25. Arendt, *The Origins of Totalitarianism*, Vol. 3, p. 146.
26. Hannah Arendt, *Eichmann in Jerusalem* (New York: Penguin, 1977), p. 269.
27. Heidegger, "Overcoming Metaphysics," p. 107.
28. Lanzmann, *Shoah*, p. 62.
29. T. W. Adorno and Max Horkheimer, *Dialectic of the Enlightenment* (New York: Continuum, 1982).
30. Marguerite Yourcenar, *That Mighty Sculptor, Time* (New York: Farrar, Straus and Giroux, 1992), p. 150.
31. For example, the lectures of 1929–30, *Die Grundbegriffe der Metaphysik, Gesamtausgabe*, Vol. 29/30 (Frankfurt/M. Vittorio Klostermann, 1983; "Letter on Humanism," in *Martin Heidegger: Basic Writings*, p. 204ff; "Building, Dwelling, Thinking," in *Martin Heidegger: Basic Writings*, p. 328; *Introduction à la métaphysique* (Paris: Gallimard, 1967), p. 56; *What Is Called Thinking* (New York: Harper Colophon books, 1968), pp. 61–62. Also see Michel Haar, *The Song of the Earth* (Bloomington: Indiana University Press, 1993), pp. 25–33; Jacques Derrida, *Of Spirit* (Chicago: The University of Chicago Press, 1989), pp. 11–13 and 47–57; Jacques Derrida, *Psyché* (Paris: Galilée, 1987), pp. 415–451; and Didier Franck, "L'étre et le vivant," in *Philosophie*, 16.
32. Heidegger, "Overcoming Metaphysics," p. 106.
33. Martin Heidegger, *Qu'appelle-t-on penser?* (Paris: PUF, 1959), p. 240.
34. Martin Heidegger, *Le Temps de la réflexion*, VII (Paris; Gallimard, 1987), p. 105. Also see Martin Heidegger, *Concepts fondamentaux* (Paris: Gallimard, 1985), pp. 111 and 120.
35. What was known? What did he know? In January 1939, Hitler had warned the Jews and the world: "A world war waged against Germany would incur the extermination of the Jewish race in Europe." He would reiterate his "prophecy" twice in 1941. Five times in 1942.

15

The Death of God at Auschwitz?

MICHAEL E. ZIMMERMAN

Reading Heidegger's reflections of the 1930s on Hölderlin's poetry, I am often struck by the discrepancy between his lofty abstractions and the brutal reality of National Socialism.[1] How could he have possibly imagined, even in the early stages of Hitler's regime, that there existed some inner relation between Hölderlin's "holy wildness" and National Socialism? Why, long after the end of World War II, did he continue to harbor such an ambiguous attitude toward National Socialism? Why did he express a reluctance, bordering on defiance, to condemn the Holocaust, or to grapple seriously with the historical and cultural antisemitic issues (not merely the metaphysical ones) that were obviously so central to National Socialism? More broadly, how are we—given such self-damning silence—to evaluate his extraordinary yet idiosyncratic reading of Western history as the unpredictale "play" of being? May we not question the historical judgment of a man who engaged in what Hugo Ott has described as extravagant "self-mythification" regarding his own place in the scheme of Western history? There are no easy answer to these questions.

Heidegger continued to interpret Germany's history in the light of the tragic categories of Nietzsche and Hölderlin even after—and perhaps even *especially* after—Germany's destruction in World War II. In 1945, for example Heidegger argued that the war had arisen because of the technological frenzy provoked by the "death of God." This "death," he assured his reader, had nothing to do with "ordinary atheism," but resulted instead from the fact that "the world of the Christian God has lost its effective force in history. (Cf. my 1943 lecture on Nietzsche's word 'God is dead.') If things had been different, would the First World War have been possible? And even more, had things been different, would the Second World War have become possible?"[2] In Heidegger's reading of the period from 1933 to 1945, the Germans, blinded by the death of God, had made a valiant effort to prepare for a new advent of the Divine, but were led astray when the technological Will to Power perverted the National Socialist "revolution."

In *La fiction du politique*, Lacoue-Labarthe uses Hölderlin's conception of tragedy to provide an alternative to Heidegger's interpretation of what happened to Germany from 1933 to 1945. Lacoue-Labarthe maintains that Auschwitz represents what Hölderlin called a caesura, a radical break in history that occurs when God and humanity become radically separated. "In fact," we are told, "God died at Auschwitz, in any case the God of the Greco-Christian West."[3] For Hölderlin, such a caesura, such a radical withdrawing of God, is a basic law of the tragic character of finite existence.[4] The postwar Heidegger erred by not applying his recurring theme of the death of God to Auschwitz, because—if Lacoue-Labarthe is right—this constitutes what he himself surely had in mind by the radical withdrawal of being and the sacred in technological modernity. Lacoue-Labarthe maintains that in the tragic caesura God reveals Itself as an abyss, a total absence which signals either the possibility for a new beginning or else the end of all historical possibilities. Heidegger, however, believed that the real caesura had *already occurred* in the death of the biblical God and the Christian-Platonic table of values, which Hölderlin and Nietzsche had surmised in the nineteenth century. From Heidegger's viewpoint, subsequent events, including world wars and death-camps, were not themselves the caesura of which Hölderlin spoke, but instead were *symptoms of it.* For Lacoue-Labarthe, by way of contrast, there did occur at Auschwitz a radical break between God and humanity, a caesura, from which the West has not recovered.

In the 1930s, Heidegger believed that Hitler represented the leader who was divinely inspired to lead Germany and the West *out* of the ontological desert, which has resulted from the tragic caesura, and *into* a new historical beginning, which would restore meaning and ontological "weight" to history, human existence, and entities. Emphasizing the role played by the ancient Greeks in Western history, Heidegger either ignored the role played by the Jews in that history or maintained that Judaisms's offshoot, Christianity, impeded Germany's attempt at radical ontological renewal. Presumably influenced by Nietzsche's critique of Jewish-Christian "slave morality," including its concern for the weak and oppressed, Heidegger adopted the Nazi attitude that only ruthlessness, martial courage, and hardness could save Germany in its hour of need. Renouncing the moral constraints imposed by a decadent "Christendom," he continued to support the Nazis long after the first concentration camps sprang up around Freiburg in 1933, and long after his own Jewish students had been forced out of their academic posts. To be sure, he could not have predicted in the 1930s that the Nazis would resort to a "final solution" for the "problem" posed by European Jewry, but his fascination with the Greek tradition and his desperate longing for the "complete transformation of German *Dasein*," prevented him from acknowledging the extent to which antisemitism was *not* an incidental dimension of Nazi Germany. Even with the advantage of hindsight, Heidegger was either unwilling or unable to concede that the attempted extermination of the Jews manifested a dark and unreconciled dimension of Germany in particular and the West in general.

In his postwar writings, Heidegger did suggest that the historical reality of Nazi Germany (if not its "inner truth and greatness") manifested a kind of *hubris*, an attempt by mortals to raise themselves to the level of the Divine. But Heidegger did not link this *hubris* with Nazi antisemitism; instead, he regarded National Socialism, considered at least in its crude reality, as being akin to liberal capitalism and communism. In his view, these three modern ideologies are metaphysically "the same" insofar as they are manifestations of anthropocentric humanism, the self-assertion of mortal Western "man" against being. According to Lacoue-Labarthe, Nazi Germans did in fact exhibit *hubris* in attempting to constitute their own mythic origin, by "creating" themselves as a national, all-embracing work of art (*Gesamtkunstwerk*). In this attempt, they defied their own finitude and sought an underived and unmediated existence that is impossible for mortals. Once again calling on Hölderlin, Lacoue-Labarthe refers to a second law of tragedy: namely, that the hero, faced with the absence of God, must finally submit to his own finitude and mortality. The hero's *hubris* invites a cleansing punishment. Heidegger agreed that such submission is vital to the possibility of an authentic *Volksgeist*.

Lacoue-Labarthe argues, however, that Heidegger offered only a partial or confused interpretation of Germany's "tragic" situation. Though finally admitting that the historical reality of National Socialism was an episode in the technological will to will that grips anthropocentric modern humankind, Heidegger never conceded that either *true* National Socialism, or *authentic* German *Geist*, or *he himself* considered as spokesman for being, could have been guilty of *hubris*. Heidegger's assessment of German behavior has, not surprisingly, provoked consternation even on the part of those sympathetic to his thinking. If Germany had been guilty of ontological *hubris*, so Heidegger suggested, Germany would have suffered a cleansing punishment. One might think that such punishment was meted out by the victorious allies, who not only obliterated the German army but also carried out militarily pointless bombing raids against countless German cities toward the end of the war. Refusing to blame Germany or himself for what occurred between 1933 and 1945, however, Heidegger viewed the destruction suffered by his country not as ontological catharsis, but instead as ontical castigation imposed by the French, English, Americans, and Soviets, people so seized by technological nihilism that they were incapable of recognizing the importance of what National Socialism had tried to achieve. In July 1945 after Germany had been crushed by the victorious Allies, Heidegger wrote: "Now everyone thinks of the decline. We Germans cannot go under, however, because we have not at all yet arisen and must only persevere through the night."[5]

In Lacoue-Labarthe's eyes, Nazi Germans did engage in hubristic acts, but the people who really suffered as a consequence of German *hubris* were, finally, not so much the Germans but the Jews, whom Heidegger conveniently left out of any formulation of the tragic "equation." In almost a literal sense, according to Lacoue-Labarthe, the Jews were the tragic "purgation" or "cleansing" (catharsis) of Germany and the West. Had postwar Heidegger been more courageous, we are told, he not only would have connected Auschwitz explicitly with German *hubris*, but would have also regarded the Holocaust itself—not the gradual withdrawal of the biblical God prior to Germany's attempted "new beginning" in 1933—as a real caesura in Western history.

Questioning Lacoue-Labarthe's use of Hölderlin's theory of tragedy to interpret the meaning of Auschwitz, Jean-François Lyotard argues that Auschwitz cannot have represented a tragic caesura, because nothing has really changed since World War II: The West has not been released from the technological impulse.[6] In this respect, Lyotard agrees with Heidegger's assessment that World War II changed nothing. Moreover, Lyotard asks, if the Germans were guilty of *hubris*, why did the *Jews* die in the extermination camps? If the Germans were playing the role of the hubristic hero, why were *they* not the ones forced to acknowledge their finitude and accept the tragic law of destruction and death?

Lyotard offers a different interpretation of the meaning of Auschwitz, an interpretation informed more by theology than by tragedy. He argues that the Jews died in Auschwitz and other concentration camps because the Greco-Roman West has long resented them as reminders of the impotence of those great projects (commercial, legal, scientific, technological, military, cultural) whose aim is to deny human dependence on the nameless Divine.[7] The Jews, who experienced the trauma of being uprooted and made hostage to the unnamable Divinity, represent the memory of the unconquerable *obstacle* to the Western quest to make everything representable, present, and thus controllable. As bearers of the memory of human finitude and dependence, Lyotard argues, the Jews had to be excluded. In destroying the Jews, then, German National Socialist believed that they were saving the West. The extermination of the Jews, the most extreme attempt to erase this unwanted memory, was carried out in secret so that the very memory of the obliteration of memory would also be forgotten.

In a powerful essay, "Through That Glass Darkly," George Steiner has made a similar point. The *Shoah* and pogroms, we are told, represent

> a desperate endeavor by Christianity and by its pagan-parodistic off-shoots such as Nazism, to silence once and for all the curse of the ideal inherent in the Mosaic covenant with God, in the more-than-humaneness of Isaiah, in the teaching of Jesus the Jew. Eradicate the Jew and you will have eradicated from within the Christian west an unendurable remembrance of moral and social failure. There is, in consequence, an awful symmetry in the fact that by instituting and allowing the world of the death-camps, European gentile civilization has striven to make it unbearable for Jews *to remember*. For it is in Judaism that there has been the obsessive, maddening remembrance which Christianity worked furiously to stifle inside itself.[8]

According to Lyotard, World War II was a massive *distraction*, designed to conceal what was really going on, namely, the attempted obliteration of those who act as a thorn in the side of the Christian West by reminding it of its perpetual bad conscience.[9] According to Lyotard, the Western technological impulse to make everything "present" for use and thus to gain total control over it results from Western man's attempt to free himself from the stern biblical God's injunction to be perfectly obedient to Divine Law. Lyotard contrasts this theological interpretation of Western history with Heidegger's claim that the technological impulse is a manifestation of Western humankind's insurrection against being. Yet this insurrection itself cannot be explained in terms of human decision; instead, the arrogant, world-conquering human subject itself arose in connection with the self-concealment of being, which defines the history of foundationalist-productionist metaphysics.

Even if Auschwitz cannot be conceived in terms of the artistic laws of tragedy, however, Lyotard still agrees up to a point with a view that can be attributed to Heidegger, namely, that Auschwitz exemplifies the dreadful "art work" typical of the union of art and politics in the technological era. While an authentic work of art—such as a Greek temple—founded a world by letting entities present themselves appropriately and distinctly, the perverse technological work of art—such as a hydroelectric station—differentiates nothing, but rather reveals things indiscriminately as sources of power. Both temple and power station are instances of *techne*; both reveal entities, but the former constitutes a world, while the latter contributes to an unworld.[10] About a decade after the end of the war, Heidegger commented on "the monstrousness that speaks out of the two titles, 'The Rhine,' as dammed up into the *power* works, and 'the Rhine' as uttered out of the *art work*, in Hölderlin's hymn by that name."[11]

Lyotard rejects Heidegger's view that the Nazi crematoria were metaphysically equivalent to hydroelectric dams. Such a view ignores that the crematoria were for the efficient production of corpses, while dams were for efficient production of electricity. Gliding over such merely "ontical" distinctions is justified, in Heidegger's opinion, because both crematoria and dams are manifestations of the same Western impulse toward total technological domination. In some respects, Heidegger, then, would agree with Lacoue-Labarthe that Auschwitz reveals the "essence" of the West, because at Auschwitz Western humanism's drive toward total domination achieved its apogee: Humans disposed of other humans like industrial waste, burning them in crematoria built according to the latest technology. But Lyotard is right in saying that Heidegger went astray in maintaining that death-camps, H-bombs, and mechanized agriculture are metaphysically equivalent, for such an assertion ignores the crucial role played in National Socialism by violent antisemitism, which reached its grim conclusion in Auschwitz. By equating crematoria with dams, by saying that they are both manifestations of the Western will to will, Heidegger refused to entertain the possibility that there was both a theological dimension and a specifically *German* dimension to the decisions that led to the crematoria. Moreover, in equating German war deaths at the hands of Russian soldiers with the deaths of Jews at the hands of Nazi functionaries, Heidegger failed to see that while both events were slaughters, the German soldiers died as combatants, but the Jews died as innocent victims of state-organized antisemitic violence.

Heidegger's insensitivity to this issue may be less surprising when we consider how seldom in his writings he commented on the concrete aspects of human personality and social interaction. Even his political speeches about the need for a new workers' society are remarkably devoid of practical insight and specific recommendations. Edith Wyschogrod has argued that Heidegger could speak of crematoria and hydroelectric dams in the same breath because of his focus on the history of *productionist* metaphysics. His concern with the transformation of *things*—how they are produced, analyzed, and used—in Western history led him to neglect the transformation of *social institutions and practices.* "The priorities established remain nothing short of astounding. For Heidegger, such facts as the damming of the Rhine are important data attesting devastation, but the unnumbered dead of the two world wars and the creation of death and slave labor camps as institutional forms are never so much as mentioned in his major essays."[12]

Heidegger's equation of death-camps and powerplants confirms, in Lyotard's eyes, the hypothesis that Heidegger was like other Germans in wanting to forget the historical significance of the Jews. Yet Lyotard allows that Heidegger, by claiming that Western humanity had forgotten the originating event and thus ended in technological nihilism, may have appropriated the role of the Jewish prophet for his own ontological purposes: Just as Jewish prophets reminded their people to remember the unnamable Origin, so too Heidegger reminded his people to remember the nameless Origin. The crucial difference here, of course, is the difference between Jerusalem and Athens—the difference between captivation by the Divine and enthrallment to being. According to Lyotard, Heidegger's scandalous postwar silence about the Holocaust revealed his refusal to deconstruct his most basic assumption: that the history of the West is identical with the history of being initiated by the Greeks. The history of the Jews, however, testifies that there is yet *another* dimension to that history: faithfulness to the Divine Law.

Lyotard's critique of Heidegger is reminiscent of Emmanuel Levinas's famous charge that Heidegger went astray, despite his brilliance, by elevating being above the moral law, ontology over ethics. To some extent, Heidegger was following his predecessors Hegel and Nietzsche in claiming that the world-historical individual is "beyond good and evil." By portraying ethical matters as secondary considerations, which arise within and which are limited to a particular historical world, however, Heidegger ran the risk of justifying whatever ethical form of life happened to emerge in a world "founded" by a new work of art. The demented "world" of National Socialism reveals what may be "justified" when ontologico-aesthetic considerations are allowed to triumph over liberal-democratic norms and over the "decadent" Jewish-Christian religious beliefs from which those secular norms were in part derived.

In his "Letter on Humanism" (1946), Heidegger defended his views on ethics and, indirectly, his self-understanding regarding his role in National Socialism. He explained that he did not intend to develop a systematic ethics, since he regarded ethics as a branch of metaphysics.[13] Modern ethical systems were concerned with "values," which he regarded as positions posited by the human subject (collectively or individually) in order to enhance the will to power. The idea of "ethics," then, was part and parcel of the nihilistic modern age. Instead of ethics, what Western humanity needed was a new *ethos*, a new way of dwelling on the earth that would establish proper limits for human behavior. Such an *ethos* could come only as a gift; it could never be founded by merely human actions. For Heidegger, Hölderlin's poetry held open the possibility of the arrival of a gift that would restore meaning and order to a technologically powerful but nihilistic world. Heidegger, then, did acknowledge the importance of establishing limits and law for human conduct. To this extent, his view can be said to agree with that of Lyotard. He also believed, however, unlike Lyotard, that the "law" (not the Law) governing a world is historical, not eternal. In his Schelling lectures (1936), Heidegger forcefully articulated Schelling's view that "evil" arose from human self-assertion over against the Divine Law. If Heidegger had a theology, it would be close to the one developed by Schelling. But, for Heidegger if not for Schelling, this "law" to which humans are called upon to submit was bound up not with the Eternal Divine but with historically limited goods—manifestations of "holy wildness."

Heidegger's thought, including his critique of modernity, can be understood in part as his agonized response to a widely shared concern about the "disenchantment" of the world in technological modernity. By disclosing the cosmos as little more than matter in motion, modernity has not only encouraged an unprecedented assault against nature, but also invited modern societies to treat their own populations as the most important "raw material." Today, especially in view of institutionalized social and ecological violence, not least in the former Soviet bloc, even many leftist thinkers concede that Enlightenment modernity's metaphysical and political principles must be revised and possibly even transformed if emancipatory ideals are ever fully to be realized. Heidegger maintained, however, that modernity's very idea of "freedom" was misguided. The modern subject understands freedom as unbinding its animalistic cravings for security and for material consumption. Enslaved by such cravings, the "clever animal" (Nietzsche) totally mobilizes society and turns the planet into a titanic foundry.

By way of contrast to modern humanists, Heidegger defined freedom as the ontologically disclosive capacity granted solely to human existence. To be free means to "let things be," that is, to let them manifest themselves in ways that accord with their own possibilities. Genuine freedom and authenticity, then, involve submitting to the ontological power at work through human existence. There would seem to be clear parallels between this idea of authenticity and the Christian idea that salvation means submitting to the will of God. In supporting Hitler, however, Heidegger maintained that the widespread hunger for a new meaning-restoring "mythology" could not be fed by the biblical religions, whose God had vanished from the world. Instead, Heidegger sang the praises of Hölderlin's "coming god," the Dionysian, who would restore ontological weight to things rendered one-dimensional by technological modernity's constricted understanding of being.

Heidegger's meditations on Hölderlin reveal ties to early German romanticism, which longed for an artistic, poetic, or mythic "reason" to temper the abstract rationality of modern science and commerce. That elements of such romanticism can be discerned not only in Heidegger's work, but also in the writings of Nazi ideologues, has led some to conclude that Germany's reactionary and irrational movements were the "culmination" of romanticism. Manfred Frank has replied, however, that early German romantics often had broadly democratic political attitudes that were simply incompatible with the authoritarian irrationalism and racism of later *völkish* movements, including National Socialism.[14] Furthermore, as Kathleen Wright has pointed out, Heidegger's commentaries on Hölderlin ignore that romantic poet's passionate interest in the French Revolution's democratic ideals, which were anathema to Heidegger and other "conservative revolutionaries."[15] Insofar as they establish significant differences between early German romanticism and National Socialism, Frank and Wright may be read as attempting to remove the shroud of suspicion that surrounds today's continuing longing for a new self-understanding, one that would restore a sense of connectedness among humans, on the one hand, and between humankind and nature, on the other. Even though acknowledging the importance of that longing, however, Frank and Wright warn that those who criticize modernity's totalizing control-impulse, and simultaneously call for a meaning-restoring mythology, should not only keep in mind the laudable emancipatory goals of modernity but should also heed the political lessons taught by, and ponder the self-delusion involved in, Heidegger's support for National Socialism, Europe's last great mythic revolt against modernity.

The self-deluding and self-mythifying Heidegger believed that he had been destined to proclaim the saving vision of his hero, Hölderlin, and that he himself was thus the world-historical figure who would transform the fate of the West. Consider Heidegger's astonishing account, presented in 1942, of the "destiny" linking him with Hölderlin: "Perhaps Hölderlin, the poet, must become the determining destiny [*Geschick*] of confrontation for one who thinks [Heidegger], whose grandfather, according to the records, was born in a manger [*in ovili*] (in the sheep-fold of a farmer), which lay in the upper Donautal near the edge of a stream under the cliff. The hidden history of saying knows no accidents. All is destiny [*Schickung*]."[16] The grandson of the man born in a manger in Hölderlin's beloved Swabian countryside knew that he was destined to change the course of history! Even as Germany was being destroyed in 1944, Heidegger did not hesitate to say, "In truth, however, my works belong not to my person, but instead they serve the German future and belong to it. Their safe-keeping should demand a corresponding carefulness."[17] Heidegger's postwar utterances never deviated from the conviction, described by Ott as showing "monstrous *hubris*," that his vision of history remained the key to the past and future of the West.[18] Given Heidegger's apparent *hubris* and his refusal, even at the urging of his old friends Karl Jaspers and Rudolf Bultmann, to acknowledge some measure of guilt for the role he played in promoting Germany's catastrophe, we may readily see why his critics have been so suspicious both of his understanding of Western history and of the interpretation of modern technology he derived from it.[19]

Many contemporary critics, including a number of French theorists influenced by Heidegger, join him in maintaining that the French Revolution's "terror," the Soviet Gulag, Nazi extermination camps, and American economic imperialism are all metaphysically "the same," that is, symptoms of modernity's totalizing rationality, which justifies its horrendous means by appealing to the noble end of "perfecting" humankind and society. Though rightly criticizing this dark side of modernity, these critics not only ignore modernity's positive achievements but also view modernity in terms of a "leveling gaze" (Jürgen Habermas) that ignores significant political and historical differences between liberal capitalism, Soviet communism, and German National Socialism. Moreover, Heidegger and his contemporary theoretical followers ignore the extent to which Enlightenment modernity contains within itself at least some of the political and ethical principles necessary not only for criticizing its own excesses, for example, Soviet totalitarianism, but also for opposing the racist authoritarianism embodied in National Socialism.

As I noted earlier, by the early 1940s, Heidegger apparently concluded that such voluntarism was a manifestation of the metaphysical will to power at work in all of technological modernity, including the historical reality of National Socialism. In his idea of *Gelassenheit*, the later Heidegger presumably abandoned the voluntarism and subjectivism that led him to believe that existential resoluteness and hardness were needed to help initiate the new beginning proposed by Hitler. Though not wishing to underestimate the importance of Heidegger's apparent renunciation of the subjectivism that he associated with his early support for Nazism, I also refuse to overestimate the political significance of this philosophical shift. After the war, he portrayed democratic ideas as tolerable only until a new god arrived to save the West from the nihilism represented by those allegedly bankrupt ideals. Further, though conceding that I myself might well have failed to display any particular moral courage in the face of National Socialism, and though admitting that I have no authority on the basis of which to make a moral assessment of Heidegger's behavior, I am unwilling to concede that such assessments are inappropriate on the part of various communities attempting to come to terms with Heidegger's actions, and perhaps especially on the part of contemporary philosophers, who may once again be faced with the prospect of succumbing to the temptation of supporting (even if only by failing to protest) morally unacceptable solutions to difficult political circumstances.

Heidegger himself, by refusing to speak of the horrors to which National Socialism led, by refusing to acknowledge any moral responsibility for having helped to consolidate Nazi power at a crucial historical juncture, and by refusing to renounce unequivocally his support for Nazism, invited a skeptical response to his notion that genuine freedom involves submitting to the call of being. For Jews and Christians, such submission is appropriate not in respect to impersonal "being," but only in respect to the personal biblical God, who commands people to love their neighbors as themselves. Submitting oneself to being, so Jews and Christians would argue, amounts to surrendering to merely temporal-historical forces, whose hubristic and violent record is all too clear. For those who retain a commitment to modernity's emancipatory ideals, moreover, the idea of submitting to "the call of being" is all too consistent with anti-democratic, reactionary movements led by elites who—supposedly "inspired" by mysterious revelations—seek to save the world by remythologizing it.

Despite progressive suspicions of today's widespread longing for spiritual and ontological renewal, such longing is an understandable response to a secularized world that has often failed to elicit adequate respect not only for human life but for the rest of life on earth. National Socialism triumphed in part because liberals and leftists alike either ignored, or else dismissed as "irrational" and "reactionary," the crucial issues of purpose and meaning, themes which the Nazis were happy to appropriate. Fearing the potentially suicidal consequences of technological modernity's treatment of nature, many people are once again seeking a new mythology, often in the guise of a "new ecological paradigm," that would disclose once more the sacred dimensions of all life. Theodore Roszak has recently stated that "what Auschwitz was to its human inmates—an expertly rationalized, efficiently organized killing ground—our urban-industrial system is fast becoming for the biosphere at large, and for ourselves as an inseparable part of that environment."[20] Though politically perceptive new paradigmers such as Rozsak affirm cultural pluralism and democratic practices, even Roszak does not seem to recognize the extent to which the Nazi "religion of nature" sharply contrasted the allegedly decadent, life-hating, anti-naturalistic, urban-oriented Jews with the vital, life-affirming, naturalistic, nature-inspired Aryans.[21] As Edward Pois has pointed out, National Socialism proved so appealing to many Germans because it promised them relief from the stringent ethical demands imposed by the transcendent Divine on an imperfect humanity, and because it offered a radically immanent nature mythology that promised a more "natural" way of life with close ties to local culture, traditions, and land—if only the Germans would live according to "nature's laws."[22]

Just as there are parallels between the attempted Nazi annihilation of the Jews and other genocidal projects in human history, so too there are parallels between the Holocaust and today's destruction of thousands of species. But there are differences as well, differences that may help Western humankind better to understand its own destructive and self-destructive impulses. Arguably, the Jews remind Western humanity not only of the limitations of all historical projects, but also of the difficulties involved in living as historical people with profound obligations to a transcendent, extra-historical domain. Today, some radical ecologists attempt to blame the ongoing destruction of the biosphere on a patriarchal culture that has been deeply influenced by the idea of a wholly transcendent biblical God who lacks any relationship to Creation. Arguing that the biblical God displaced the goddesses of an earlier age, ecofeminists often maintain that Western patriarchal religions emphasized cultural binaries, such as divine male mind vs. created female body, eternity vs. finitude, culture vs. nature, which eventually justified modern "man's" attempts to dominate nature. Countless wars have been fought, pogroms carried out, and natural wonders decimated by patriarchal egos who proclaimed the "greater glory of God," but who were in fact motivated by desire to deny their own mortality and finitude. By projecting mortality upon an enemy to be slain, upon a land to be conquered, or upon a woman (or some other "inferior") to be dominated, the patriarchal ego reassured itself about its own survival.[23] To the extent that patriarchal biblical religions are otherworldly in orientation, and to the extent that they invite domineering attitudes toward non-believers and nature, those religions are problematic. An acceptable alternative, however, is not to be found in a wholly immanent, nature-worshipping religion that regards all talk of the transcendent dimension as a sign of life-hating, patriarchal decadence.

In the racist naturalism favored by so many Nazi ideologues, and which he himself rejected, Heidegger recognized this problematic "immanentism." Hence, he criticized modernity's death-denying ego-subject not because this subject was the culmination of the patriarchal craving for transcendence, but instead because the modern subject had become a death-denying, power-craving animal that *denied* any transcendent domain and installed itself as the ground for all meaning, purpose, and value. For Heidegger, modernity went astray not because it renounced the transcendence spoken of by biblical theology, but instead because it was blind to the truly transcendent: being as such. Maintaining that being absolutely transcends entities, Heidegger held that Western metaphysicians and theologians went astray by equating being with the highest entity (God, Platonic forms, will to power). Neo-Hegelians claim that evolutionary trends in human history are manifestations of the Divine coming to self-awareness in Creation, but Heidegger could not take seriously the possibility that anthropocentric humanism, instead of being the final stage in the degenerative history of Western metaphysics, might be a temporary stage in the evolution of a postmodern awareness that deconstructs dualism and re-establishes a relation with the transcendent.[24] But what is meant by the "transcendent" in this connection is not what Heidegger meant by that term. Rather than take seriously alternative conceptions of transcendence, he tended to lump them into the same metaphysical heap.

In his concept of the fourfold of earth and sky, gods and mortals, Heidegger sought to reconcile transcendence and immanence, but this attempt met with only limited success. There are other attempts to achieve such a reconciliation. For example, a number of contemporary theologians, including some feminists, propose that an evolving awareness might move beyond the polarity of absolute transcendence and complete immanence, a polarity that has had such tragic consequences for human history. Presumably, a more evolved awareness would recognize that humankind participates simultaneously in the transcendent and the immanent, in the eternal and the historical, in the spiritual and the incarnate. Such awareness would be consistent with the theological doctrine of "panentheism." As opposed to pantheism, which identifies the spatio-temporal domain with the Divine, panentheism asserts that the Divine includes the spatio-temporal domain but is not identical with it. If there is an "evolution" of consciousness, perhaps it involves a growing sense that all life is incarnate spirit. Awareness of participating in the eternal might make it possible for the ego to affirm its mortal, incarnate status and also to surrender some of its control obsession, which is manifest in binary oppositions between mind and body, male and female, "man" and nature. These days, versions of this evolutionary-developmental view of human history, especially as informed by contemporary developments in cosmology, are finding favor among those who promote a new ecological paradigm and a post-patriarchal sense of the Divine.[25]

Hostile both to traditional biblical religions as well as to progressive, evolutionary, neo-Hegelian appropriations of them, however, Heidegger invented his own "private religion," according to which the gods name the meaning-giving powers that appear in the historical dawn initiated by the "destiny of being." He believed that only these new gods, constituted by a new disclosure of transcendent being, could "save us" from the nihilism of technological modernity. Neither Heidegger's gods nor the biblical God forestalled the horrors of the twentieth century, including Auschwitz. Yet the widespread sense that the sacred has vanished from the world does not mean that this baleful condition is permanent; the sacred sensibility may return, though there is no guarantee that this might occur before humankind has managed to engineer its own destruction and that of many other terrestrial forms of life. No one can say whether the Divine will manifest itself again, though I for one hope that the next manifestation would emphasize the *interpenetration* of the immanent and transcendent in a way that undermines old dualisms and fears. Those who hope for major spiritual changes, however, need to pay special attention to Heidegger's political experience, which shows that even the most intellectually gifted can be tempted to heal their own existential agony by surrendering to charismatic leaders who promise salvation, but deliver death and destruction.

NOTES

1. An earlier version of this essay appeared as part of Chapter Eight of my book, *Heidegger's Confrontation with Modernity: Technology, Politics, Art* (Bloomington and London: Indiana University Press, 1990). See also my essays "Ontological Aestheticism: Heidegger, Jünger, and National Socialism," in Tom Rockmore and Joseph Margolis (eds.), *The Heidegger Case: On Philosophy and Politics*

(Philadelphia: Temple University Press, 1992); "The Thorn in Heidegger's Side: The Question of National Socialism," *The Philosophical Forum*, XX (Summer 1989), pp. 326–365; "The Search for a Heideggerian Ethics," in *Ethics and Responsibility in the Phenomenological Tradition* (Pittsburgh: The Simon Silverman Phenomenology Center of Duquesne University, 1992). The recent secondary literature on Heidegger's politics is vast, but see John D. Caputo, *Demythologizing Heidegger* (Bloomington and London: Indiana University Press, 1994); Hans Sluga, *Heidegger's Crisis: Philosophy and Politics in Nazi Germany* (Cambridge and London: Harvard University Press, 1993); Tom Rockmore, *On Heidegger's Nazism and Philosophy* (Berkeley and Los Angeles: University of California Press, 1992); Richard Wolin, *The Politics of Being* (New York: Columbia University Press, 1990); Frank Schalow, "A Question Concerning Heidegger's involvement in National Socialism," *Journal of the British Society for Phenomenology*, 24, 2 (May 1993), pp. 121–139; Thomas J. Sheehan, "Heidegger and the Nazis," *The New York Review of Books*, XXXV, 10 (June 16, 1988), 38–47.

2. Martin Heidegger, *Das Rektorat 1933/34. Tatsachen und Gedanken*, ed. Hermann Heidegger (Frankfurt am Main: Vittorio Klostermann, 1983), p. 25; "The Rectorate 1933/34. Facts and Thoughts," trans. Karsten Harries, *The Review of Metaphysics*, 38, 3 (March 1985), p. 485.
3. Philippe Lacoue-Labarthe, *La fiction du politique* (Paris: Christian Bourgeois, 1987), p. 62; see *Heidegger, Art and Politics: The Fiction of the Political*, trans. Chris Turner (Cambridge, MA: Basil Blackwell, 1990), p. 37. See also Lacoue-Labarthe, *L'imitation des Modernes* (Paris: Galilée, 1986).
4. Lacoue-Labarthe, *La fiction du politique*, pp. 64ff; *Heidegger, Art and Politics*, pp. 41–46.
5. Cited by Hugo Ott, *Martin Heidegger; Unterwegs zu seiner Biographie* (Frankfurt and New York: Campus Verlag, 1988), p. 157.
6. Jean-François Lyotard, *Heidegger et "les juifs"* (Paris: Galilée, 1988); Lyotard, *Heidegger and "the jews,"* trans. Andreas Michel and Mark Roberts (Minneapolis: University of Minnesota Press, 1990).
7. Lyotard, *Heidegger et "les juifs,"* p. 45ff; *Heidegger and "the Jews,"* p. 22.
8. George Steiner, "Through that Glass Darkly," *Salmagundi*, No. 93 (Winter 1992), p. 45.
9. Lyotard, *Heidegger et "les juifs,"* p. 55; *Heidegger and "the Jews,"* p. 28.
10. I am grateful to Hubert Dreyfus for this comparison.
11. Martin Heidegger, "Die Frage nach der Technik," *Vorträge und Aufsätze*, Vol. I (Pfullingen: Günther Neske, 1967), p. 15; "The Question Concerning Technology," in *The Question Concerning Technology*, trans. William Lovitt (New York: Harper & Row, 1977), p. 16.
12. Edith Wyschogrod, *Spirit in Ashes: Hegel, Heidegger, and Man-Made Mass Death* (New Haven: Yale University Press, 1985), p. 188.
13. Charles M. Sherover has written several interesting essays in which he attempts to develop an existential ethics based on Heidegger's thought. For example, see "Founding an Existential Ethic," *Human Studies*, 4 (1981), pp. 223–236. See also Frank Schalow, *The Renewal of the Heidegger-Kant Dialogue: Action, Thought, and Responsibility* (Albany: SUNY Press, 1992), and Charles Scott, "Heidegger and the Question of Ethics," *Research in Phenomenology*, XVIII (1988), 23–40.
14. Manfred Frank, *Der kommende Gott: Vorlesungen über die Neue Mythologie* (Frankfurt am Main: Suhrkamp, 1982).
15. Kathleen Wright, "Heidegger's Hölderlin and the Mo(u)rning of History,"

forthcoming in a special issue of *Philosophy Today* in honor of the 150th anniversary of the death of Hölderlin.

16. Cited in Ott, *Martin Heidegger*, p. 20. Heidegger originally made this statement in his 1942 lecture course, *Hölderlins Hymne "Der Ister,"* but the statement was not included in the version published in Volume 53 of his *Gesamtausgabe*.
17. Ott, *Martin Heidegger*, p. 157.
18. Ibid., p. 159.
19. On Heidegger's postwar relation to Jaspers and Bultmann, see Ott, *Martin Heidegger*.
20. Theodore Roszak, *The Voice of the Earth* (New York: Simon and Schuster, 1992), p. 73.
21. On the political dangers posed by the search for a new paradigm, see my book, *Contesting Earth's Future: Radical Ecology and Postmodernity* (Berkeley and Los Angeles: University of California Press, 1994).
22. Edward A. Pois, *National Socialism and the Religion of Nature* (London and Sydney: Croom Helm, 1986). This book is highly recommended.
23. See Katherine Keller, *From a Broken Web: Separation, Sexism, and Self* (Boston: Beacon Press, 1986).
24. See Ken Wilber, *Up from Eden: A Transpersonal View of Human Evolution* (Boston: Shambhala, 1981).
25. See my essay "Quantum Theory, Intrinsic Value, and Non-Dualism," *Environmental Ethics*, X (Spring 1988), pp. 3–30.

Contributors

RAINER ALISCH is currently engaged in research in Austria. He has published "Heidegger's Rektoratsrede im Kontext," in W. F. Haug (ed.), *Deutsche Philosophen 1933* (Berlin/Hamburg: Argument-Verlag, 1989), and "Heidegger, Technologie und Faschismus," in W. Blumberger and D. Nemeth (eds.), *Der Technologische Imperativ: Philosophische Orte der Technologischen Formation. Heinz Hülsmann zum 75. Geburtstag* (Munich/Vienna: Profil-Verlag, 1992).

HENRI CRÉTELLA is a professor at the lycée Michelet in Montauban, France. Among his recent publications are "La théologie de Heidegger," in *Heidegger Studies*, 6 (1990), "Le Chemin et les tournants," in *Heidegger Studies*, 8 (1992), and "Staurologie," in *Heidegger Studies*, 9 (1993).

ELISABETH DE FONTENAY teaches at the Université de Paris 1 (Sorbonne). Her publications include *Les Figures juives de Marx* (Paris: Galilée, 1973), *Diderot ou le matérialisme enchanté* (Paris: Grasset, 1981), and "Fribourg - Prague - Paris. Comme l'Etre, la détresse se dit de multiple manières," in *Le Messager Européen*, 1 (1987).

BEREL LANG is professor of philosophy and humanistic studies and chair of the Department of Philosophy at the State University of New York at Albany. He edited *Writing and the Holocaust* (New York: Holmes & Meier, 1988). Among his recent publications are *Act and Idea in the Nazi Genocide* (Chicago: The University of Chicago Press, 1990), "The History of Evil and the Future of the Holocaust," in Peter Hayes (ed.), *Lessons and Legacies: The Meaning of the Holocaust in a Changing World* (Evanston: Northwestern University Press, 1991), and "The Representation of Limits," in Saul Friedlander (ed.), *Probing the Limits of Representation: Nazism and the "Final Solution"* (Cambridge: Harvard University Press, 1992).

GEORGE LEAMAN is acting director of the Philosophy Documentation Center and adjunct assistant professor of philosophy at Bowling Green State University. Among his publications are "Kant-Studien im Dritten Reich" co-author with Gerd Simon in *Kant-Studien* 85 (1994) 443–69, "Deutsche Philosophen und das 'Amt Rosenberg,'" in Ilse Korotin (ed.), *Philosophie und Nationalsozialismus* (Vienna: Picus Verlag, 1994), *Heidegger im Kontext: Gesamtüberblick zum NS-Engagement der Universitätsphilosophen* (Hamburg: Argument-Verlag, 1993).

ROBERT JOHN SHEFFLER MANNING is assistant professor of philosophy at Quincy College. He has published "Thinking the Other without Violence: Levinas' Relation to Feminism," in *The Journal of Speculative Philosophy*, 5, 2 (1991), and *Interpreting Otherwise than Heidegger: Emmanuel Levinas's Ethics as First Philosophy* (Pittsburgh: Duquesne University Press, 1993).

JOSEPH MARGOLIS is professor of philosophy at Temple University. His most recent major work is a trilogy, *The Persistence of Reality*, whose parts are: *Pragmatism without Foundations: Reconciling Realism and Relativism*; *Science without Unity: Reconciling the Human and Natural Sciences*; and *Texts without Referents: Reconciling Science and Narrative*.

With Tom Rockmore, he has edited Victor Farías, *Heidegger and Nazism* (Philadelphia: Temple University Press, 1989), and *The Heidegger Case: On Philosophy and Politics* (Philadelphia: Temple University Press, 1992).

ALAN MILCHMAN teaches in the Department of Political Science at Queens College, CUNY. He is completing a book (with Alan Rosenberg), *Experiments in Thinking the Holocaust: Auschwitz, Modernity, and Philosophy*, and is finishing a manuscript on Ernst Bloch and Georg Lukács. Among his publications are "Max Weber on Capitalism, Socialism and Democracy," in *Socialism and Democracy*, 7 (Fall/Winter 1988), 'Paul de Man, Deconstruction and Nazism," in *German Politics and Society*, Issue 20 (Summer 1990), and (with Alan Rosenberg) "Resoluteness and Ambiguity: Martin Heidegger's Ontological Politics, 1933–35," in *The Philosophical Forum*, XXV, 1 (Fall 1993).

OTTO PÖGGELER is professor of philosophy and director of the Hegel Archives at the University of Bochum, Germany. Among his publications are *Martin Heidegger's Path of Thinking* (Atlantic Highlands, NJ: Humanities Press International, Inc., 1987), *Philosophie und Politik bei Heidegger* (Freiburg/Munich: Verlag Karl Alber, 1974), *Heidegger und die hermeneutische Philosophie* (Freiburg/Munich: Verlag Karl Alber, 1983), *Spur des Worts: Zur Lyrik Paul Celans* (Freiburg/Munich: Verlag Karl Alber, 1986), and *Neue Wege mit Heidegger* (Freiburg/Munich: Verlag Karl Alber, 1992).

TOM ROCKMORE is professor of philosophy at Duquesne University. Among his recent publications are *Irrationalism: Lukács and the Marxist View of Reason* (Philadelphia: Temple University Press, 1992), *On Heidegger's Nazism and Philosophy* (Berkeley: University of California Press, 1992), and *Heidegger and French Philosophy* (London and New York: Routledge, 1995). He has edited (with Joseph Margolis) *Antifoundationalism Old and New* (Philadelphia: Temple University Press, 1992).

ALAN ROSENBERG is an assistant professor in the department of philosophy at Queens College, CUNY. He is the co-editor of *Echoes from the Holocaust: Philosophical Reflections on a Dark Time* (Philadelphia: Temple University Press; 1988), and *Healing Their Wounds: Psychotherapy with Holocaust Survivors and Their Families* (New York: Praeger, 1989). Among his recent publications are "Hannah Arendt and the Etiology of the Desk Killer: The Holocaust as Portent," in *History of European Ideas*, 14, 2 (1992), "The Unlearned Lessons of the Holocaust," in *Modern Judaism*, 13 (1993), and "The Philosophical Stakes of the Heidegger Wars, Part I: Methodologies for the Reading of Heidegger," in *The Journal of Value Inquiry*, 27 (1993), all with Alan Milchman. He is also the special editor (with Paul Marcus) of an issue of *The Psychoanalytic Review* devoted to Bruno Bettelheim, 81, 3 (Fall 1994).

HANS SEIGFRIED is a professor of philosophy at Loyola University (Chicago). Among his recent publications are "Against Naturalizing Preconceptual Experience," in *Philosophy and Phenomenological Research*, 48 (March 1988), "Transcendental Experiments," in G. Funke and T. M. Seebohm (eds.), *Proceedings of the Sixth International Kant Congress* (Washington, DC: University Press of America, 1989), "Transcendental Experiments (II): Kant and Heidegger," in J. J. Kockelmans (ed.), *Hermeneutic Phenomenology: Lectures and Essays* (Washington, DC: University Press of America, 1988), "Zur Ambivalenz des Fortschritts bei Nietzsche und Heidegger: Wissenschaft und Technik als Vermittler," in *Allgemeine Zeitschrift für Philosophie*, 16 (1991), and "Dewey's Critique of Kant's Copernican Revolution Revisited," in *Kant-Studien*, 83. Jahrg. (1993).

WILLIAM VAUGHAN completed a dissertation on Heidegger at the University of Illinois at Urbana-Champaign and is teaching in the department of philosophy at Ohio Northern University.

JAMES R. WATSON is a professor at Loyola University (New Orleans). His most recent publications include "Auschwitz and the Limits of Transcendence," in *Philosophy and Social Criticism*, 18,2 (1992), "Easy Becoming Uneasy Images," in Hugh J. Silverman (ed.), *Questioning Foundations* (New York: Routledge, 1993), and *Between Auschwitz and Tradition: Postmodern Reflections on the Task of Thinking* (Amsterdam-Atlanta, GA: Rodopi, 1994).

WILHELM S. WURZER is associate professor of philosophy at Duquesne University. He is the author of *Nietzsche and Spinoza* and *Filming and Judgment: Between Heidegger and Adorno* (Atlantic Highlands, NJ: Humanities Press International, 1990).

MICHAEL E. ZIMMERMAN is professor of philosophy at Tulane University and clinical professor of psychiatry at Louisiana State University Medical School. Among his publications are *Eclipse of the Self: The Development of Heidegger's Concept of Authenticity* (Athens-London: Ohio University Press, 1986), "The Thorn in Heidegger's Side: The Question of National Socialism," in *The Philosophical Forum*, XX, 4 (Summer 1989), and *Heidegger's Confrontation with Modernity: Technology, Politics, Art* (Bloomington and Indianapolis: Indiana University Press, 1990).

Index